ASP.NET Core 3 and React

Hands-On full stack web development using ASP.NET Core, React, and TypeScript 3

Carl Rippon

BIRMINGHAM - MUMBAI

ASP.NET Core 3 and React

Commissioning Editor: Pavan Ramchandani
Acquisition Editor: Reshma Raman
Content Development Editor: Divya Vijayan
Senior Editor: Mohammed Yusuf Imaratwale
Technical Editor: Jane Dsouza
Copy Editor: Safis Editing
Project Coordinator: Manthan Patel
Proofreader: Safis Editing
Indexer: Rekha Nair
Production Designer: Jyoti Chauhan

First published: December 2019

Production reference: 1261219

Published by Packt Publishing Ltd.
Livery Place
35 Livery Street
Birmingham
B3 2PB, UK.

ISBN 978-1-78995-022-9

www.packt.com

I'd like to thank Sarah, Ellie-Jayne, and Lily-Rose for all the encouragement and support they've given me while writing this book. A special thanks to everyone in the Packt editorial team for their hard work and great feedback, especially Arun Nadar, Divya Vijayan, and Jane D'souza.

- Carl Rippon

Packt.com

Subscribe to our online digital library for full access to over 7,000 books and videos, as well as industry leading tools to help you plan your personal development and advance your career. For more information, please visit our website.

Why subscribe?

- Spend less time learning and more time coding with practical eBooks and Videos from over 4,000 industry professionals

- Improve your learning with Skill Plans built especially for you

- Get a free eBook or video every month

- Fully searchable for easy access to vital information

- Copy and paste, print, and bookmark content

Did you know that Packt offers eBook versions of every book published, with PDF and ePub files available? You can upgrade to the eBook version at www.packt.com and as a print book customer, you are entitled to a discount on the eBook copy. Get in touch with us at customercare@packtpub.com for more details.

At www.packt.com, you can also read a collection of free technical articles, sign up for a range of free newsletters, and receive exclusive discounts and offers on Packt books and eBooks.

Contributors

About the author

Carl Rippon has been involved in the software industry for over 20 years, developing a complex line of business applications across various sectors. He has spent the last 8 years building single-page applications using a wide range of JavaScript technologies, including Angular, ReactJS, and TypeScript. Carl has written over 100 blog posts on various technologies.

About the reviewers

Carlo Wahlstedt is a Jesus Follower, family man, and technologist. The latter leading to a diverse interest in anything technology can affect. Name a technology and Carlo as tried it, has it on his list to try, or is going to add what you mention to his list. He loves macOS and tolerates Windows but loves the platform Microsoft provides. At work, he currently enjoys all things web, being involved in software architecture, containers, kubernetes, and all things automation. He is also a remote worker, an assistant high school boys basketball coach, and non-profit board member.

Ed Spencer is a web focused contract software developer based in the Midlands in the UK. He has over 15 years of delivering high performance, business critical applications for a long list of well known brands.

Originally starting out as a database developer and on the Microsoft stack, he has transitioned into a full stack developer well versed in numerous technologies, ranging from .NET Core and Node.js on the server, to React and Angular on the client. Ed is also adept at performance tuning web applications.

He has been blogging for 10 years at `https://edspencer.me.uk`, which is his way of giving something back to the web development community.

Outside of development, Ed enjoys reading, exploring new places, and catching up with friends.

Packt is searching for authors like you

If you're interested in becoming an author for Packt, please visit `authors.packtpub.com` and apply today. We have worked with thousands of developers and tech professionals, just like you, to help them share their insight with the global tech community. You can make a general application, apply for a specific hot topic that we are recruiting an author for, or submit your own idea.

Table of Contents

Preface

ASP.NET Core is an open source and cross-platform web application framework built by Microsoft. It follows on from the hugely popular ASP.NET version 4, with significant architectural changes making it much leaner and much more modular. ASP.NET Core is a great choice for building highly performant backends that interact with databases such as SQL Server that are hosted in the cloud, such as in Microsoft's cloud platform, Azure.

React was built by Facebook in order to improve the scalability of their code base, and was eventually open sourced in 2013. React is now a massively popular library for building component-based frontends and works fantastically well with many backend technologies, including ASP.NET Core.

This book will teach you how you can use both these technologies to create secure and performant **single-page applications (SPAs)** on top of SQL Server databases hosted in Microsoft Azure.

Who this book is for

This book is primarily aimed at developers with an understanding of C# and a basic knowledge of JavaScript and who are interested in building SPAs with ASP.NET Core and React.

What this book covers

Chapter 1, *Understanding the ASP.NET Core React Template*, covers the standard SPA template that ASP.NET Core offers for React apps. It covers the programmatic entry points for both the frontend and backend and how they work together in the Visual Studio solution.

Chapter 2, *Creating Decoupled React and ASP.NET Core Apps*, explains how a more up-to-date ASP.NET Core and React solution can be created. This chapter includes the use of TypeScript, which is hugely beneficial when creating large-scale frontends.

Chapter 3, *Getting Started with React and TypeScript*, covers the fundamentals of React, such as JSX, props, state, and events. The chapter also covers how to create strongly typed components with TypeScript.

Chapter 4, *Routing with React Router*, introduces a library that enables apps with multiple pages to be efficiently created. It covers how to declare all the routes in an app and how these map to React components, including routes with parameters.

Chapter 5, *Working with Forms*, covers how to build forms efficiently in React. Generic form and field components are built step by step, which includes validation and submission. These components are then used to rapidly build forms in an app.

Chapter 6, *Managing State with Redux*, steps through how this popular library can help manage state across an app. A strongly typed Redux store is built along with actions and reducers with the help of TypeScript.

Chapter 7, *Interacting with the Database with Dapper*, introduces a library that enables us to interact with SQL Server databases in a performant manner. Both reading and writing to a database are covered, including mapping SQL parameters and results with C# classes.

Chapter 8, *Creating REST API Endpoints*, covers how to create a REST API that interacts with a data repository. Along the way, dependency injection, model binding, and model validation are also covered.

Chapter 9, *Creating a Real-Time API with SignalR*, starts by covering how these APIs differ from REST APIs. The chapter then covers how a React frontend can connect to a SignalR API and automatically receive updates on areas of the database without making an HTTP request.

Chapter 10, *Improving Performance and Scalability*, covers several ways of improving the performance and scalability of the backend, including reducing database round trips, making APIs asynchronous, and data caching. Along the way, several tools are used to measure the impact of the improvements.

Chapter 11, *Securing the Backend*, leverages ASP.NET identity along with JSON web tokens in order to add authentication to an ASP.NET Core backend. This chapter also covers the protection of REST API endpoints through the use of standard and custom authorization policies.

Chapter 12, *Interacting with RESTful APIs*, covers how a React frontend can talk to an ASP.NET Core backend using the JavaScript `fetch` function. This chapter also covers how a React frontend can gain access to protected REST API endpoints with a JSON web token.

Chapter 13, *Adding Automated Tests*, covers how to create a unit test and integration tests on the ASP.NET Core backend using xUnit. This chapter also covers how to create tests on pure JavaScript functions, as well as React components, using Jest.

`Chapter 14`, *Configuring and Deploying to Azure*, introduces Azure and then steps through deploying both the backend and frontend to separate Azure app services. This chapter also covers the deployment of a SQL Server database to SQL Azure.

`Chapter 15`, *Implementing CI and CD with Azure DevOps*, introduces Azure DevOps, before stepping through the creation of a build pipeline that automatically triggers when code is pushed to a source code repository. This chapter then examines setting up a release pipeline that deploys the artifacts from the build into Azure.

To get the most out of this book

You need to know the fundamentals of C#, including the following:

- How to create variables and reference them, including arrays and objects
- How to create classes and use them
- How to create conditional statements with the `if` and `else` keywords

You need to know the basics of JavaScript, including the following:

- How to create variables and reference them, including arrays and objects
- How to create functions and call them
- How to create conditional statements with the `if` and `else` keywords

You need to know the basics of HTML, including the following:

- Basic HTML tags, such as `div`, `ul`, `p`, `a`, `h1`, and `h2`, and how to compose them together to create a web page
- How to reference a CSS class to style an HTML element

You need to have an understanding of basic CSS, including the following:

- How to size elements and include margins and padding
- How to position elements
- How to color elements

An understanding of basic SQL is helpful, but not essential.

You will need the following technologies installed on your computer:

- **Google Chrome**: This can be installed at `https://www.google.com/chrome/`.
- **Visual Studio 2019**: This can be download and installed from `https://visualstudio.microsoft.com/vs/`.
- **.NET Core 3**: This can be downloaded and installed from `https://dotnet.microsoft.com/download/dotnet-core`.
- **Visual Studio Code**: This can be downloaded and installed from `https://code.visualstudio.com/`.
- **Node.js and npm**: This can be download and installed from `https://nodejs.org/`. If you already have these installed, make sure that Node.js is at least version 8.2 and that npm is at least version 5.2.
- **SQL Server 2017 Express Edition**: This can be downloaded and installed from `https://www.microsoft.com/en-gb/sql-server/sql-server-editions-express`.
- **SQL Server Management Studio**: This can be downloaded and installed from `https://docs.microsoft.com/en-us/sql/ssms/download-sql-server-management-studio-ssms?view=sql-server-2017`.

Download the example code files

You can download the example code files for this book from your account at `www.packt.com`. If you purchased this book elsewhere, you can visit `www.packtpub.com/support` and register to have the files emailed directly to you.

You can download the code files by following these steps:

1. Log in or register at `www.packt.com`.
2. Select the **Support** tab.
3. Click on **Code Downloads**.
4. Enter the name of the book in the **Search** box and follow the onscreen instructions.

Once the file is downloaded, please make sure that you unzip or extract the folder using the latest version of:

- WinRAR/7-Zip for Windows
- Zipeg/iZip/UnRarX for Mac
- 7-Zip/PeaZip for Linux

The code bundle for the book is also hosted on GitHub at `https://github.com/PacktPublishing/ASP.NET-Core-3-and-React-17`. In case there's an update to the code, it will be updated on the existing GitHub repository.

We also have other code bundles from our rich catalog of books and videos available at `https://github.com/PacktPublishing/`. Check them out!

Download the color images

We also provide a PDF file that has color images of the screenshots/diagrams used in this book. You can download it here: `https://static.packt-cdn.com/downloads/9781789950229_ColorImages.pdf`.

Code in Action

Visit the following link to check out videos of the code being run:

`http://bit.ly/2sZjjlp`

Conventions used

There are a number of text conventions used throughout this book.

`CodeInText`: Indicates code words in text, database table names, folder names, filenames, file extensions, pathnames, dummy URLs, user input, and Twitter handles. Here is an example: "Let's create a file called `.eslintrc.json` in the `frontend` folder with the following code."

A block of code is set as follows:

```
{
  "extends": "react-app"
}
```

When we wish to draw your attention to a particular part of a code block, the relevant lines or items are set in bold:

```
const App: React.FC = () => {
  const unused = 'something';
  return (
    ...
  );
};
```

Any command-line input or output is written as follows:

```
> cd frontend
> npm start
```

Bold: Indicates a new term, an important word, or words that you see on screen. For example, words in menus or dialog boxes appear in the text like this. Here is an example: "Click on the **Install** button to install the extension and then the **Reload** button to complete the installation."

 Warnings or important notes appear like this.

 Tips and tricks appear like this.

Get in touch

Feedback from our readers is always welcome.

General feedback: If you have questions about any aspect of this book, mention the book title in the subject of your message and email us at customercare@packtpub.com.

Errata: Although we have taken every care to ensure the accuracy of our content, mistakes do happen. If you have found a mistake in this book, we would be grateful if you would report this to us. Please visit www.packtpub.com/support/errata, selecting your book, clicking on the Errata Submission Form link, and entering the details.

Piracy: If you come across any illegal copies of our works in any form on the internet, we would be grateful if you would provide us with the location address or website name. Please contact us at copyright@packt.com with a link to the material.

If you are interested in becoming an author: If there is a topic that you have expertise in, and you are interested in either writing or contributing to a book, please visit authors.packtpub.com.

Reviews

Please leave a review. Once you have read and used this book, why not leave a review on the site that you purchased it from? Potential readers can then see and use your unbiased opinion to make purchase decisions, we at Packt can understand what you think about our products, and our authors can see your feedback on their book. Thank you!

For more information about Packt, please visit `packt.com`.

Section 1: Getting Started

This section provides a high-level introduction to ASP.NET Core and React and how to create projects that enable them to work well together. We will create the project for the app that we'll build throughout this book, which will allow users to submit questions and other users to submit answers to them—a Q&A app.

This section comprises the following chapters:

- Chapter 1, *Understanding the ASP.NET Core React Template*
- Chapter 2, *Creating Decoupled React and ASP.NET Core Apps*

1
Understanding the ASP.NET Core React Template

React was Facebook's answer to helping more people work on the Facebook code base and deliver features quicker. React worked so well for Facebook that they eventually open sourced it (https://github.com/facebook/react). Today, React is a mature library for building component-based frontends (client-side code that runs in the browser); it is extremely popular and has a massive community and ecosystem. At the time of writing, React is downloaded over 5.8 million times per day, which has more than doubled in the last year.

ASP.NET Core was first released in 2016 and is now a mature open source and cross-platform web application framework. It's an excellent choice for building backends (application code that runs on the server) that interact with databases such as SQL Server. It also works well in cloud platforms such as Microsoft Azure.

In this first chapter, we'll start by learning about the **single-page application (SPA)** architecture. Then, we'll create an ASP.NET Core and React app using the standard template in Visual Studio. We will use this to review and understand the critical parts of a React and ASP.NET Core app. We'll learn where the entry points of both the ASP.NET Core and React apps are and how they integrate with each other. We'll also learn how Visual Studio runs both the frontend and backend together in development mode, as well as how it packages them up, ready for production. By the end of this chapter, we'll have gained fundamental knowledge so that we can start building an app that uses both of these awesome technologies, and that we'll gradually build throughout this book.

In this chapter, we'll cover the following topics:

- SPA architecture
- Understanding the backend
- Understanding the frontend

Technical requirements

We'll use the following tools in this chapter:

- **Visual Studio 2019**: This can be downloaded and installed from `https://visualstudio.microsoft.com/vs/`. Make sure that the following features are selected in the installer:
  - ASP.NET and web development
  - Azure development
  - Node.js development

- **.NET Core 3.0**: This can be downloaded and installed from `https://dotnet.microsoft.com/download/dotnet-core`.
- **Node.js and npm**: These can be downloaded from `https://nodejs.org/`.

All the code snippets in this chapter can be found online at `https://github.com/PacktPublishing/ASP.NET-Core-3-and-React-17`. In order to restore code from this chapter, the source code repository should be downloaded and the project in the `Chapter01` folder should be opened in Visual Studio.

Check out the following video to see the code in action:

`http://bit.ly/2ZpsqaZ`

SPA architecture

An SPA is a web app that loads a single HTML page that is dynamically updated by JavaScript as the user interacts with the app. Imagine a simple sign-up form where a user can enter a name and an email address. Once the user fills out and submits the form, a whole page refresh doesn't occur. Instead, some JavaScript in the browser handles the form submission with an HTTP POST request and then updates the page with the result of the request. Refer to the following diagram:

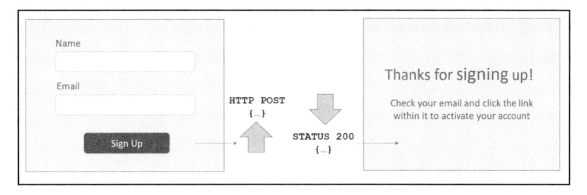

So, after the first HTTP request that returns the single HTML page, subsequent HTTP requests are only for data and not HTML markup. All the pages are rendered in the client's browser by JavaScript.

So, how are different pages with different URL paths handled? For example, if I enter https://qanda/questions/32139 in the browser's address bar, how does it go to the correct page in the app? Well, the browser's history API lets us change the browser's URL and handle changes in JavaScript. This process is often referred to as routing and, in Chapter 4, *Routing with React Router*, we'll learn how we can build apps with different pages.

The SPA architecture is what we are going to use throughout this book. We'll use React to render our frontend and ASP.NET Core for the backend API.

Now that we have a basic understanding of the SPA architecture, we'll take a closer look at a SPA-templated app that Visual Studio can create for us.

Understanding the backend

In this section, we are going to start by creating an ASP.NET Core and React app using the standard template in Visual Studio. This template is perfect for us to review and understand basic backend components in an ASP.NET Core SPA.

Creating an ASP.NET Core and React templated app

Let's open Visual Studio and carry out the following steps to create our templated app:

1. In the start-up dialog, choose **Create a new project**:

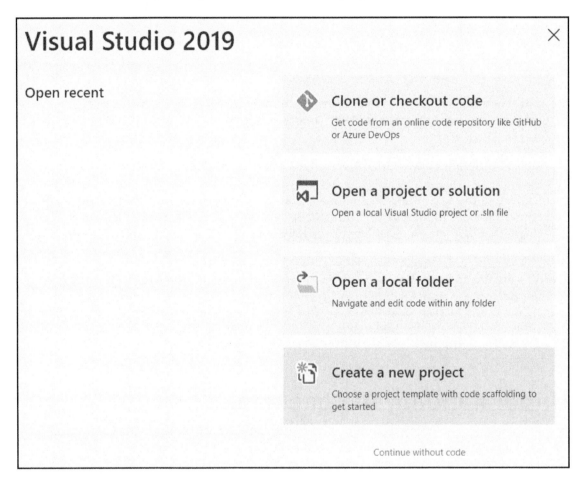

2. Next, choose **ASP.NET Core Web Application** in the wizard that opens and click the **Next** button:

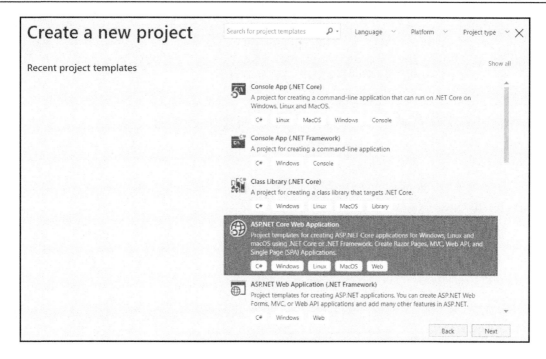

3. Give the project a name of your choice and choose an appropriate location to save the project to. Click the **Create** button to create the project:

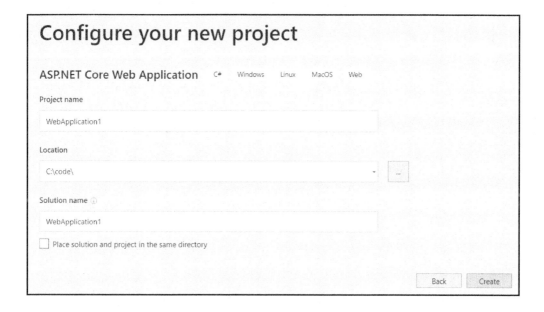

4. Another dialog will appear that allows us to specify the version of ASP.NET Core we want to use, as well as the specific type of project we want to create. Select **ASP.NET Core 3.0** as the version and **React.js** in the dialog, and then click the **Create** button, which will create the project:

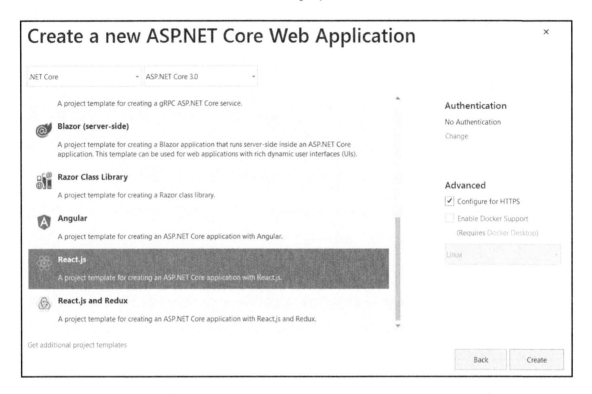

 If ASP.NET Core 3.0 isn't listed, make sure the latest version of Visual Studio is installed. This can be done by choosing the **Check for Updates** option on the **Help** menu.

5. Now that the project has been created, let's press *F5* to run the app. After a minute or so, the app will appear in a browser:

WebApplication1   Home   Counter   Fetch data

Hello, world!

Welcome to your new single-page application, built with:

- ASP.NET Core and C# for cross-platform server-side code
- React for client-side code
- Bootstrap for layout and styling

To help you get started, we have also set up:

- **Client-side navigation**. For example, click *Counter* then *Back* to return here.
- **Development server integration**. In development mode, the development server from create-react-app runs in the background automatically, so your client-side resources are dynamically built on demand and the page refreshes when you modify any file.
- **Efficient production builds**. In production mode, development-time features are disabled, and your dotnet publish configuration produces minified, efficiently bundled JavaScript files.

The ClientApp subdirectory is a standard React application based on the create-react-app template. If you open a command prompt in that directory, you can run npm commands such as npm test or npm install.

We'll find out later in the chapter why the app took so long to run the first time. Great—we've created the ASP.NET Core React SPA. Now, let's inspect the backend code.

Understanding the backend entry point

An ASP.NET Core app is a console app that creates a web server. The entry point for the app is a method called Main in a class called Program, which can be found in the Program.cs file in the root of the project:

```
public class Program
{
    public static void Main(string[] args)
    {
        CreateWebHostBuilder(args).Build().Run();
    }

    public static IWebHostBuilder CreateWebHostBuilder(string[] args)
    =>
        WebHost.CreateDefaultBuilder(args)
            .UseStartup<Startup>();
}
```

This method creates a web host using `WebHost.CreateDefaultBuilder`, which configures items such as the following:

- The location of the root of the web content
- Where the settings are for items such as the database connection string
- The logging level and where the logs are output

We can override the default builder using fluent APIs, which start with `Use`. For example, to adjust the root of the web content, we can add the highlighted line in the following snippet:

```
public static IWebHostBuilder CreateWebHostBuilder(string[] args) =>
        WebHost.CreateDefaultBuilder(args)
            .UseContentRoot("some-path")
            .UseStartup<Startup>();
```

The last thing that is specified in the builder is the `Startup` class, which we'll look at in the following section.

Understanding the Startup class

The `Startup` class is found in `Startup.cs` and configures the services that the app uses, as well as the request/response pipeline.

The ConfigureServices method

Services are configured using a method called `ConfigureServices`. It is this method we will use to register items such as the following:

- Our authentication user model and password policy
- Our authorization policies
- Whether we want to use MVC to handle requests
- Whether we want to enable CORS
- Our own classes that need to be available in dependency injection

Services are added by calling methods on the `services` parameter and, generally, start with `Add`. Notice the call to the `AddSpaStaticFiles` method in the following code snippet:

```
public void ConfigureServices(IServiceCollection services)
{0
```

```
services.AddControllersWithViews();

services.AddSpaStaticFiles(configuration =>
{
    configuration.RootPath = "ClientApp/build";
});
}
```

This is a key part of how the React app is integrated into ASP.NET Core in production because this specifies the location of the React app.

 It is important to understand that the ASP.NET Core app runs on the server, with the React app running on the client in the browser. The ASP.NET Core app simply serves the files in the `ClientApp/Build` folder without any interpretation or manipulation.

The `ClientApp/Build` files are only used in production mode, though. Next, we'll find out how the React app is integrated into ASP.NET Core in development mode next.

The Configure method

When a request comes into ASP.NET Core, it goes through what is called the **request/response pipeline**, where some middleware code is executed. This pipeline is configured using a method called `Configure`. It is this method we will use to define exactly which middleware is executed and in what order. Middleware code is invoked by methods that generally start with `Use` in the `app` parameter. So, we would typically specify middleware such as authentication early in the `Configure` method, and MVC middleware toward the end. The pipeline that the template created is as follows:

```
public void Configure(IApplicationBuilder app, IWebHostEnvironment env)
{
    ...
    app.UseStaticFiles();
    app.UseSpaStaticFiles();
    app.UseRouting();
    app.UseEndpoints( ... );

    app.UseSpa(spa =>
    {
        spa.Options.SourcePath = "ClientApp";

        if (env.IsDevelopment())
        {
            spa.UseReactDevelopmentServer(npmScript: "start");
        }
```

```
    });
  }
```

Notice that a method called `UseSpaStaticFiles` is called in the pipeline, just before the routing and endpoints are set up. This allows the host to serve the React app, as well as the web API.

Also, notice that a `UseSpa` method is called after the endpoint middleware. This is the middleware that will handle requests to the React app, which will simply serve the single page in the React app. It is placed after `UseEndpoints` so that requests to the web API take precedence over requests to the React app.

The `UseSpa` method has a parameter that is actually a function that executes when the app is first run. This function contains a branch of logic that calls `spa.UseReactDevelopmentServer(npmScript: "start")` if you're in development mode. This tells ASP.NET Core to use a development server by running `npm start`. We'll delve into the `npm start` command later in this chapter. So, in development mode, the React app will be run on a development server rather than ASP.NET Core serving the files from `ClientApp/Build`. We'll learn more about this development server later in this chapter.

Custom middleware

We can create our own middleware using a class such as the following one. This middleware logs information about every single request that is handled by the ASP.NET Core app:

```
public class CustomLogger
{
    private readonly RequestDelegate _next;

    public CustomLogger(RequestDelegate next)
    {
        _next = next ?? throw new ArgumentNullException(nameof(next));
    }

    public async Task Invoke(HttpContext httpContext)
    {
        if (httpContext == null) throw new
        ArgumentNullException(nameof(httpContext));

        // TODO - log the request

        await _next(httpContext);
```

```
                    // TODO - log the response
        }
    }
```

This class contains a method called Invoke, which is the code that is executed in the request/response pipeline. The next method to call in the pipeline is passed into the class and held in the _next variable, which we need to invoke at the appropriate point in our Invoke method. The preceding example is a skeleton class for a custom logger. We would log the request details at the start of the Invoke method and log the response details after the _next delegate has been executed, which will be when the rest of the pipeline has been executed.

The following diagram is a visualization of the request/response pipeline and shows how each piece of middleware in the pipeline is invoked:

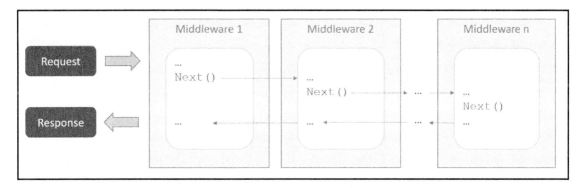

We make our middleware available as an extension method on the IApplicationBuilder interface in a new source file:

```
public static class MiddlewareExtensions
{
    public static IApplicationBuilder UseCustomLogger(this
    IApplicationBuilder app)
    {
        return app.UseMiddleware<CustomLogger>();
    }
}
```

The UseMiddleware method in IApplicationBuilder is used to register the middleware class. The middleware will now be available in an instance of IApplicationBuilder in a method called UseCustomLogger.

So, the middleware can be added to the pipeline in the `Configure` method in the `Startup` class, as follows:

```
public void Configure(IApplicationBuilder app, IWebHostEnvironment env)
{
    app.UseCustomLogger();

    if (env.IsDevelopment())
    {
        app.UseDeveloperExceptionPage();
    }
    else
    {
        app.UseExceptionHandler("/Error");
        app.UseHsts();
    }

    app.UseHttpsRedirection();
    app.UseStaticFiles();
    app.UseSpaStaticFiles();

    app.UseMvc(...);

    app.UseSpa(...);
}
```

In the previous example, the custom logger is invoked at the start of the pipeline so that the request is logged before it is handled by any other middleware. The response that is logged in our middleware will have been handled by all the other middleware as well.

So, the `Startup` class allows us to configure how all requests are generally handled. How can we specify exactly what happens when requests are made to a specific resource in a web API? Let's find out.

Understanding controllers

Web API resources are implemented using **controllers**. Let's have a look at the controller the template project created by opening `WeatherForecastController.cs`. This contains a class called `WeatherForecastController` that inherits from `ControllerBase` with a `Route` annotation:

```
[ApiController]
[Route("[controller]")]
public class WeatherForecastController : ControllerBase
{
```

```
    . . .
}
```

The annotation specifies the web API resource URL that the controller handles. The `[controller]` object is a placeholder for the controller name, minus the word `Controller`. This controller will handle requests to `weatherforecast`.

The method called `Get` in the class is called an **action method**. Action methods handle specific requests to the resource for a specific HTTP method and subpath. We decorate the method with an attribute to specify the HTTP method and subpath the method handles. In our example, we are handling an HTTP `GET` request to the root path (`weatherforecast`) on the resource:

```
[HttpGet]
public IEnumerable<WeatherForecast> Get()
{
    . . .
}
```

Let's have a closer look at the web API at runtime by carrying out the following steps:

1. Run the app in Visual Studio by pressing *F5*.
2. When the app has opened in our browser, press *F12* to open the browser developer tools and select the **Network** panel.
3. Select the **Fetch data** option on the top navigation bar. An HTTP `GET` request to `weatherforecast` will be shown:

4. An HTTP response with a `200` status code is returned with JSON content:

WebApplication				Home Counter Fetch data

Weather forecast

This component demonstrates fetching data from the server.

Date	Temp. (C)	Temp. (F)	Summary
2019-07-28T09:53:01.1336185+01:00	42	107	Freezing
2019-07-29T09:53:01.1336185+01:00	-1	31	Cool
2019-07-30T09:53:01.1336185+01:00	42	107	Hot
2019-07-31T09:53:01.1336185+01:00	31	87	Sweltering
2019-08-01T09:53:01.1336185+01:00	36	96	Warm

If we look back at the `Get` action method, we are returning an object of the `IEnumerable<WeatherForecast>` type. The MVC middleware automatically converts this object into JSON and puts it in the response body with a `200` status code for us.

So, that was a quick look at the backend that the template scaffolded for us. In the next section, we'll walk through the React frontend.

Understanding the frontend

It's time to turn our attention to the React frontend. In this section, we'll discover where the single HTML page is that hosts the React app. We'll also understand why it took over a minute to run the app for the first time.

Understanding the frontend entry point

We have a good clue as to where the entry point is from our examination of the `Startup` class in the ASP.NET Core backend. In the `Configure` method, the SPA middleware is set up with the source path as `ClientApp`:

```
app.UseSpa(spa =>
{
    spa.Options.SourcePath = "ClientApp";

    if (env.IsDevelopment())
    {
        spa.UseReactDevelopmentServer(npmScript: "start");
    }
});
```

If we look in the `ClientApp` folder, we'll see a file called `package.json`. This is a file that is often used in React apps and contains information about the project, its npm dependencies, and the scripts that can be run to perform tasks.

 npm is a popular package manager for JavaScript. The dependencies in `package.json` reference packages in the npm registry.

If we open the `package.json` file, we will see react listed as a dependency:

```
"dependencies": {
    "react": "^16.0.0",
    "react-scripts": "^3.0.1",
    ...
},
```

So, we are definitely in the right place! The `react-scripts` dependency gives us a big clue as to how exactly React was scaffolded. `react-scripts` is a set of scripts from the popular **Create React App (CRA)** tool that was built by the developers at Facebook. This tool has done a huge amount of configuration for us, including a development server, bundling, linting, and unit testing. We'll learn more about CRA in the next chapter.

The root HTML page for an app scaffolded by CRA is `index.html`, which can be found in the `public` folder in the `ClientApp` folder. It is this page that hosts the React app. The root JavaScript file that is executed for an app scaffolded by CRA is `index.js`, which is in the `ClientApp` folder. We'll examine both the `index.html` and `index.js` files later in this chapter.

Running in development mode

In the following steps, we'll examine the ASP.NET Core project file to see what happens when the app runs in development mode:

1. We can open the project file by right-clicking on the web application project in **Solution Explorer** and selecting the **Edit Project File** option:

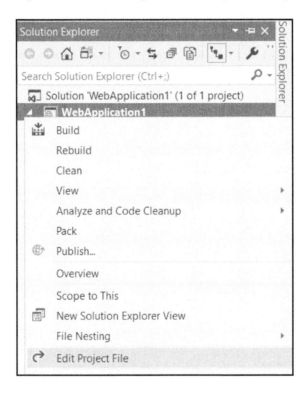

This is an XML file that contains information about the Visual Studio project.

2. Let's look at the `Target` element, which has a `Name` attribute of `DebugEnsureNodeEnv`:

```
<Target Name="DebugEnsureNodeEnv" BeforeTargets="Build" Condition="
'$(Configuration)' == 'Debug' And !Exists('$(SpaRoot)node_modules')
">
  <!-- Ensure Node.js is installed -->
  <Exec Command="node --version" ContinueOnError="true">
    <Output TaskParameter="ExitCode" PropertyName="ErrorCode" />
  </Exec>
  <Error Condition="'$(ErrorCode)' != '0'" Text="Node.js is
```

```
required to
    build and run this project. To continue, please install Node.js
from
    https://nodejs.org/, and then restart your command prompt or
IDE."
    />
  <Message Importance="high" Text="Restoring dependencies using
'npm'.
    This may take several minutes..." />
  <Exec WorkingDirectory="$(SpaRoot)" Command="npm install" />
</Target>
```

This executes tasks when the `ClientApp/node-modules` folder doesn't exist and the Visual Studio project is run in debug mode, which is the mode that's used when we press *F5*.

3. The first task that is run in the `Target` element is the execution of the following command via an `Exec` task:

    > **node --version**

This command returns the version of Node that is installed. This may seem like an odd thing to do, but its purpose is to determine whether node is installed. If node is not installed, the command will error and be caught by the `Error` task, which informs the user that Node needs to the installed and where to install it from.

4. The next task in the `Target` element uses a `Message` command, which outputs `Restoring dependencies using 'npm'. This may take several minutes...` to the **Output** window. We'll see this message when running the project for the first time:

```
Output
Show output from: Build                                                          ⟳  ⟰ ⟱  ⤭ ⅋⤸
1>------ Build started: Project: WebApplication1, Configuration: Debug Any CPU ------
1>WebApplication1 -> C:\code\WebApplication1\WebApplication1\bin\Debug\netcoreapp2.2\WebApplication1.dll
1>WebApplication1 -> C:\code\WebApplication1\WebApplication1\bin\Debug\netcoreapp2.2\WebApplication1.Views.dll
1>v10.13.0
1>Restoring dependencies using 'npm'. This may take several minutes...
```

5. The final task that is carried out when the project is run in debug mode is another `Exec` task that executes the following npm command:

    > **npm install**

This command downloads all the packages that are listed as dependencies in `package.json` into a folder called `node_modules`:

We can see this in **Solution Explorer** if the `Show All Files` option is on. Notice that there are a lot more folders in `node_modules` than dependencies listed in `package.json`. This is because the dependencies will have dependencies. So, the packages in `node_modules` are all the dependencies in the dependency tree.

At the start of this section, we asked ourselves the question: Why did it take such a long time for the project to run the app for the first time? The answer is that this last task takes a while because there are a lot of dependencies to download and install. On subsequent runs, `node_modules` will have been created, so these sets of tasks won't get invoked.

Earlier in this chapter, we learned that ASP.NET Core invokes an `npm start` command when the app is in development mode. If we look at the `scripts` section in `package.json`, we'll see the definition of this command:

```
"scripts": {
  "start": "rimraf ./build && react-scripts start",
  ...
}
```

This command deletes a folder called `build` and runs a **Webpack** development server.

 Webpack is a tool that transforms, bundles, and packages up files for use in a browser. Webpack also has a development server. The CRA tool has configured Webpack for us so that all the transformation and the bundling configuration are already set up for us.

Why would we want to use the Webpack development server when we already have our ASP.NET Core backend running in IIS Express? The answer is a shortened feedback loop which will increase our productivity. Later, we'll see that we can make a change to a React app running in the Webpack development server and that those changes are automatically loaded. There is no stopping and restarting the application, and so there's a really quick feedback loop and great productivity.

Publishing process

The publishing process is the process of building artifacts to run an application in a production environment.

Let's carry on and inspect the XML ASP.NET Core project file and look at the `Target` element, which has the following `Name` attribute: `PublishRunWebPack`. The following code executes a set of tasks when the Visual Studio project is published:

```
<Target Name="PublishRunWebpack" AfterTargets="ComputeFilesToPublish">
  <!-- As part of publishing, ensure the JS resources are freshly built
  in production mode -->
  <Exec WorkingDirectory="$(SpaRoot)" Command="npm install" />
  <Exec WorkingDirectory="$(SpaRoot)" Command="npm run build" />

  <!-- Include the newly-built files in the publish output -->
  <ItemGroup>
    <DistFiles Include="$(SpaRoot)build\**" />
    <ResolvedFileToPublish Include="@(DistFiles->'%(FullPath)')"
    Exclude="@(ResolvedFileToPublish)">
      <RelativePath>%(DistFiles.Identity)</RelativePath>
      <CopyToPublishDirectory>PreserveNewest</CopyToPublishDirectory>
    </ResolvedFileToPublish>
  </ItemGroup>
</Target>
```

The first task that is run is the execution of the `npm install` command via an `Exec` task. This will ensure that all the dependencies are downloaded and installed. Obviously, if we've already run our project in debug mode, then the dependencies should already be in place.

The next task is an `Exec` task that runs the following `npm` command:

```
> npm run build
```

This task will run an `npm` script called `build`. If we look in the `package.json` file again, we'll see this script in the `scripts` section:

```
"scripts": {
  "start": "rimraf ./build && react-scripts start",
  "build": "react-scripts build",
  "test": "cross-env CI=true react-scripts test --env=jsdom",
  "eject": "react-scripts eject",
  "lint": "eslint ./src/"
}
```

This references the `create-react-app` scripts, which bundle the React app ready for production, optimizing it for great performance, and outputting the content into a folder called `build`.

The next set of tasks defined in the `ItemGroup` element take their content from the `build` folder and place it in the publish location, along with the rest of the content to publish.

Let's give this a try and publish our app:

1. In **Solution Explorer**, right-click on the project and select the **Publish...** option.
2. Choose **Folder** as the target and enter a folder to output the content to.
3. Click the **Publish** drop-down menu and then choose the **Publish immediately** option to start the publishing process:

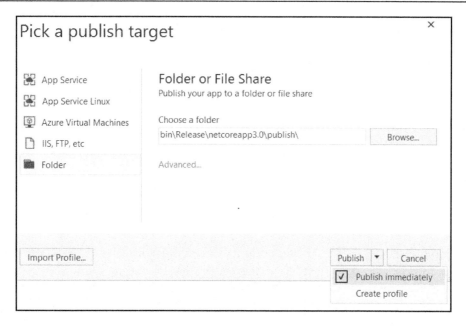

After a while, we'll see the content appear in the folder we specified, including a
ClientApp folder. If we look in this ClientApp folder, we'll see a build folder containing
the React app, ready to be run in a production environment. Notice that the build folder
contains index.html, which is the single page that will host the React app in production.

It is important to note that publishing from a developer's machine is not
ideal. Instead, it is good practice to carry out this process on a build
server to make sure that built applications are consistent, and code
committed to the repository goes into the build. We'll cover this in
Chapter 15, *Implementing CI and CD in Azure DevOps*.

Understanding the frontend dependencies

Earlier, we learned that frontend dependencies are defined in package.json. Why not just
list all the dependencies as script tags in index.html? Why do we need the extra
complexity of npm package management in our project? The answer is that a long list of
dependencies is hard to manage. If we used script tags, we'd need to make sure these are
ordered correctly. We'd also be responsible for downloading the packages, placing them
locally in our project, and keeping them up to date. We have a huge list of dependencies in
our scaffolded project already, without starting work on any functionality in our app. For
these reasons, managing dependencies with npm has become an industry standard.

Let's open `package.json` again and look at the `dependencies` section:

```
"dependencies": {
  "bootstrap": "^4.1.3",
  "jquery": "3.4.1",
  "merge": "^1.2.1",
  "oidc-client": "^1.9.0",
  "react": "^16.0.0",
  "react-dom": "^16.0.0",
  "react-router-bootstrap": "^0.24.4",
  "react-router-dom": "^4.2.2",
  "react-scripts": "^3.0.1",
  "reactstrap": "^6.3.0",
  "rimraf": "^2.6.2"
},
```

We've already observed the `react` dependency, but what is the `react-dom` dependency? Well, React doesn't just target the web; it also targets native mobile apps. This means that `react` is the core React library that is used for both web and mobile, and `react-dom` is the library that's specified for targeting the web.

The `react-router-dom` package is the npm package for **React Router** and helps us to manage the different pages in our app in the React frontend without a round-trip to the server. We'll learn more about React Router in `Chapter 4`, *Routing with React Router*. The `react-router-bootstrap` package allows Bootstrap to work nicely with React Router.

We can see that this React app has a dependency for **Bootstrap 4.1** with the `bootstrap` npm package. So, Bootstrap CSS classes and components can be referenced to build the frontend in our project. The `reactstrap` package is an additional package that allows us to consume Bootstrap nicely in React apps. Bootstrap 4.1 has a dependency on jQuery, which is the reason for the `jquery` package dependency.

The `merge` package contains a function that merges objects together and `oidc-client` is a package for interacting with **OpenID Connect (OIDC)** and OAuth2. We'll make use of the `oidc-client` package in `Chapter 11`, *Securing the Backend*.

The final dependency that we haven't covered yet is `rimraf`. This simply allows files to be deleted, regardless of the host operating system. We can see that this is referenced in the start script:

```
"scripts": {
  "start": "rimraf ./build && react-scripts start",
  ...
}
```

Earlier in this chapter, we learned that this script is invoked when our app is running in development mode. So, `rimraf ./build` deletes the build folder and its contents before the development server starts.

If we look further down, we'll see a section called `devDependencies`. These are dependencies that are only used during development and not in production:

```
"devDependencies": {
  "ajv": "^6.9.1",
  "babel-eslint": "^10.0.1",
  "cross-env": "^5.2.0",
  "eslint": "^5.12.0",
  "eslint-config-react-app": "^4.0.1",
  "eslint-plugin-flowtype": "^2.0.0",
  "eslint-plugin-import": "^2.14.0",
  "eslint-plugin-jsx-a11y": "^6.2.1",
  "eslint-plugin-react": "^7.11.1"
},
```

The following is a brief description of these dependencies:

- `ajv` allows us to validate JSON files.
- `cross-env` allows us to set environment variables, regardless of the host operating system. If you look at the `test` script in the `scripts` section of the `package.json` file, it uses `cross-env` to set a `CI` environment variable.
- The remaining dependencies are all designed to enable linting with **ESLint**. The linting process checks for problematic patterns in code according to a set of rules. We'll learn more about ESLint in `Chapter 3`, *Getting Started with React and TypeScript*.

Let's move on and learn how the single page is served and how the React app is injected into it.

Understanding how the single page is served

We know that the single page that hosts the React app is `index.html`, so let's examine this file. This file is found in the `public` folder in the `ClientApp` folder. The React app will be injected into the `div` tag that has an `id` of `root`:

```
<div id="root"></div>
```

Let's run our app again in Visual Studio to confirm that this is the case by pressing *F5*. If we open the developer tools in the browser page that opens and inspect the DOM in the **Elements** panel, we'll see this `div` with the React content inside it:

Notice the `script` tag at the bottom of the `body` tag. This contains all the JavaScript code for our React app, including the React library itself. However, this `script` tag doesn't exist in the source `index.html` file, so how did it get there in the served page? Webpack added it after bundling all the JavaScript together into `bundle.js`. If we look in the `ClientApp` folder and subfolders, the `static` folder doesn't exist. The `bundle.js` file doesn't exist either. What's going on? These are virtual files that are created by the Webpack development server. Remember that, when we run the app with Visual Studio debugger, the Webpack development server serves `index.html`. So, `bundle.js` is a virtual file that the Webpack development server creates.

Now, what happens in production mode when the Webpack development server isn't running? Let's have a closer look at the app we published earlier in this chapter. Let's look in the `index.html` file in the `Build` folder in the `ClientApp` folder. The `script` tag at the bottom of the `body` tag will look something like the following:

```
<script src="/static/js/main.eebeebd5.js"></script>
```

The highlighted part of the filename will vary each time the app is published. The filename is unique for each build in order to break browser caching. If we look for this JavaScript file in our project, we'll find that it does exist. So, in production mode, the web server will serve this physical JavaScript file.

If we open this JavaScript file, it contains all the JavaScript for our app. The JavaScript is minified so that the file can be downloaded to the browser nice and quick.

 Minification is the process of removing unnecessary characters in files without affecting how it is processed by the browser. This includes code comments and formatting, unused code, using shorter variable and function names, and so on.

However, the file isn't small and contains a lot of JavaScript. What's going on here? Well, the file contains not only our JavaScript app code but also the code from all the dependencies, including React itself.

Understanding how components fit together

Now it's time to start looking at the React app code and how components are implemented. Remember that the root JavaScript file is `index.js` in the `ClientApp` folder. Let's open this file and look closely at the following block of code:

```
const rootElement = document.getElementById('root');

ReactDOM.render(
<BrowserRouter basename={baseUrl}>
  <App />
</BrowserRouter>,
rootElement);
```

The first statement selects the `div` tag we discovered earlier, which has the `root` ID and stores it in a variable called `rootElement`.

The next statement extends over multiple lines and calls the `render` function from the React DOM library. It is this function that injects the React app content into the root `div` tag. The `rootElement` variable, which contains a reference to the root `div` tag, is passed into this function as the second parameter.

The first parameter that is passed into the `render` function is more interesting. In fact, it doesn't even look like legal JavaScript! This is, in fact, **JSX**, which we'll learn about in detail in `Chapter 3`, *Getting Started with React and TypeScript*.

JSX is transformed into regular JavaScript by Webpack using a tool called **Babel**. This is one of many tasks that CRA configured for us when our app was scaffolded.

So, the first parameter passes in the root React component called `BrowserRouter`, which comes from the React Router library. We'll learn more about this component in `Chapter 4`, *Routing with React Router*.

Nested inside the `BrowserRouter` component is a component called `App`. If we look at the top of the `index.js` file, we can see that the `App` component is imported from a file called `App.js`:

```
import App from './App';
```

`import` statement is used to import items that are exported by another JavaScript module. The module is specified by its file location, with the `js` extension omitted.

The `import` statements that import items from npm packages don't need the path to be specified because CRA has configured a `resolver` in Webpack to automatically look in the `node_modules` folder during the bundling process.

So, the `App` component is contained in the `App.js` file. Let's have a look at this file. A class called `App` is defined in this file:

```
export default class App extends Component {
  static displayName = App.name;

  render () {
    return (
      <Layout>
        <Route exact path='/' component={Home} />
        <Route path='/counter' component={Counter} />
```

```
        <Route path='/fetch-data' component={FetchData} />
      </Layout>
    );
  }
}
```

Notice the `export` and `default` keywords before the `class` keyword.

 The `export` keyword is used to export an item from a JavaScript module. The `default` keyword defines the export as the default export, which means it can be imported without curly braces. So, a default export can be imported as `import App from './App'` rather than `import {App} from './App'`.

A method called `render` defines the output of the component. This method returns JSX, which, in this case, references a `Layout` component in our app code and a `Route` component from React Router.

So, we are starting to understand how React components can be composed together to form a UI.

Let's now start to go through the React development experience by making a simple change:

1. Run the app in Visual Studio by pressing *F5* if it's not already running.
2. Open up the `Home.js` file, which can be found at `ClientApp\src\components`. This contains the component that renders the home page.
3. With the app still running, in the `render` method, change the `h1` tag in the JSX to render a different string:

```
render () {
  return (
    <div>
      <h1>Hello, React!</h1>
      <p>Welcome to your new single-page application, built with:
      </p>
      ...
    </div>
  );
}
```

4. Save the file and look at the running app:

Hello, React!

Welcome to your new single-page application, built with:

- ASP.NET Core and C# for cross-platform server-side code
- React for client-side code
- Bootstrap for layout and styling

The app is automatically updated with our change. The Webpack development server automatically updated the running app with the change when the file was saved. The experience of seeing our changes implemented almost immediately gives us a really productive experience when developing our React frontend.

Understanding how components access the backend web API

The final topic in this chapter is how the React frontend consumes the backend web API. If the app isn't running, then run it by pressing *F5* in Visual Studio. If we click on the **Fetch data** option in the top navigation bar in the app that opens in the browser, we'll see a page showing weather forecasts:

WebApplication   Home   Counter   Fetch data

Weather forecast

This component demonstrates fetching data from the server.

Date	Temp. (C)	Temp. (F)	Summary
2019-07-28T09:53:01.1336185+01:00	42	107	Freezing
2019-07-29T09:53:01.1336185+01:00	-1	31	Cool
2019-07-30T09:53:01.1336185+01:00	42	107	Hot
2019-07-31T09:53:01.1336185+01:00	31	87	Sweltering
2019-08-01T09:53:01.1336185+01:00	36	96	Warm

If we cast our minds back to earlier in this chapter, in the *Understanding controllers* section, we looked at the ASP.NET Core controller that surfaced a web API that exposed this data at weatherforecast. So, this is a great place to have a quick look at how a React app can call an ASP.NET Core web API.

The component that renders this page is in FetchData.js. Let's open this file and look at the constructor class:

```
constructor (props) {
  super(props);
  this.state = { forecasts: [], loading: true };
}
```

 The constructor in a JavaScript class is a special method that automatically gets invoked when a class instance is created. So, it's a great place to initialize class-level variables.

The constructor initializes some component state which contains the weather forecast data and a flag to indicate whether the data is being fetched. We'll learn more about component state in Chapter 3, *Getting Started with React and TypeScript*.

Let's have a look at the componentDidMount method:

```
componentDidMount() {
  this.populateWeatherData();
}
```

This method gets invoked by React when the component is inserted into the tree and is the perfect place to load data. This method calls a populateWeatherData method, so, let's have a look at that:

```
async populateWeatherData() {
  const response = await fetch('weatherforecast');
  const data = await response.json();
  this.setState({ forecasts: data, loading: false });
}
```

Notice the async keyword before the populateWeatherData function name. Notice also the await keywords within the function.

An `await` keyword is used to wait for an asynchronous function to complete. A function must be declared as asynchronous in order to use the `await` keyword within. This is done by placing an `async` keyword in front of the function name. This is very much like `async` and `await` in .NET.

We can see that a function called `fetch` is used within this method.

The `fetch` function is a native JavaScript function for interacting with web APIs. The `fetch` function supersedes `XMLHttpRequest` and works a lot nicer with JSON-based web APIs.

The parameter that's passed into the `fetch` function is the path to the web API resource: `weatherforecast`. A relative path can be used because the React app and web API are in the same origin.

Once the weather forecast data has been fetched from the web API and the response has been parsed, the data is placed in the component's state.

Hang on a minute, though—the native `fetch` function isn't implemented in **Internet Explorer (IE)**. Does that mean our app won't work in IE? Well, the `fetch` function isn't available in IE, but CRA has set up a polyfill for this so that it works perfectly fine.

A **polyfill** is a piece of code that implements a feature we expect the browser to provide natively. Polyfills allow us to develop against features that aren't supported in all browsers yet.

Let's now turn our attention to the `render` method:

```
render () {
  let contents = this.state.loading
    ? <p><em>Loading...</em></p>
    : FetchData.renderForecastsTable(this.state.forecasts);

  return (
    <div>
      <h1 id="tabelLabel">Weather forecast</h1>
      <p>This component demonstrates fetching data from the server.</p>
      {contents}
    </div>
  );
}
```

The code may contain concepts you aren't familiar with, so don't worry if this doesn't make sense to you at this point. I promise that it will make sense as we progress through this book!

We already know that the render method in a React component returns JSX, and we can see that JSX is returned in this render method as well. Notice the {contents} reference in the JSX, which injects the contents JavaScript variable into the markup below the p tag at the bottom of the div tag. The contents variable is set in the first statement in the render method and is set so that **Loading...** is displayed while the web API request is taking place along with the result of FetchData.renderForecastsTable when the request has finished, which we'll have a quick look at now:

```
static renderForecastsTable (forecasts) {
    return (
      <table className='table table-striped' aria-labelledby="tabelLabel">
        <thead>
          <tr>
            <th>Date</th>
            <th>Temp. (C)</th>
            <th>Temp. (F)</th>
            <th>Summary</th>
          </tr>
        </thead>
        <tbody>
          {forecasts.map(forecast =>
            <tr key={forecast.dateFormatted}>
              <td>{forecast.dateFormatted}</td>
              <td>{forecast.temperatureC}</td>
              <td>{forecast.temperatureF}</td>
              <td>{forecast.summary}</td>
            </tr>
          )}
        </tbody>
      </table>
    );
}
```

This function returns JSX, which contains an HTML table with the data from the forecasts data array injected into it. The map method on the forecasts array is used to iterate through the items in the array and render tr tags in the HTML table containing the data.

The `map` method is a native JavaScript method that is available in an array. It takes in a function parameter that is called for each array element. The return values of the function calls then make up a new array. The `map` method is commonly used in JSX when iteration is needed.

Notice that we have applied a `key` attribute to each `tr` tag. What is this for? This isn't a standard attribute on an HTML table row, is it?

 The `key` attribute helps React detect when an element changes, or is added or removed. So, it's not a standard HTML table row attribute. Where we output content in a loop, it is good practice to apply this attribute and set it to a unique value within the loop so that React can distinguish it from the other elements. Omitting keys can also lead to performance problems on large datasets as React will unnecessarily re-render the table when it doesn't need to.

Again, this is a lot to take in at this point, so don't worry if there are bits you don't fully understand. This will all have become second nature by the end of this book.

Summary

In this chapter, we started off by learning that all pages in an SPA are rendered in JavaScript with the help of a framework such as React, along with requests for data handled by a backend API with the help of a framework such as ASP.NET Core. We now understand that a class called `Startup` configures services that are used in the ASP.NET Core backend, as well as the request/response pipeline. Requests to specific backend API resources are handled by controller classes.

We also saw how CRA was leveraged by the ASP.NET Core React template to create the React app. This tool did a huge amount of setup and configuration for us, including a development server, bundling, linting, and even key polyfills for IE. We learned that the React app lives in the `ClientApp` folder in an ASP.NET Core React templated project, with a file called `index.html` being the single page. A file called `package.json` defines key project information for the React app, including its dependencies and the tasks that are used to run and build the React app.

This chapter has given us a great overview of all the basic parts of an ASP.NET Core React app and how they work together. We'll explore many of the topics we've covered in this chapter in greater depth throughout this book.

With the knowledge from this chapter, we are now ready to start creating the app we are going to build through this book, which we'll start to do in the next chapter.

Questions

Have a go at the following questions to test the knowledge that you have acquired in this chapter:

1. What is the entry point method in an ASP.NET Core app?
2. What is the single HTML page filename in an ASP.NET Core React app that's created by a template? What folder is this located in?
3. What file are React app dependencies defined in?
4. What npm command will run the React app in the Webpack development server?
5. What npm command builds the React app so that it's ready for production?
6. What is the method name in a React component class that renders the component?
7. Have a look at the following code snippet, which configures the request/response pipeline in an ASP.NET Core app:

```
public void Configure(IApplicationBuilder app, IHostingEnvironment
env)
{
  app.UseAuthentication();
  app.UseHttpsRedirection();
  app.UseMvc();
}
```

8. Which is invoked first in the request/response pipeline—authentication or the MVC controllers?
9. Does the class that configures the services and request/response pipeline need to be called Startup? Can we give it a different name?
10. What browsers are supported by a React app created by CRA?

Further reading

The following are some useful links so that you can learn more about the topics that were covered in this chapter:

- ASP.NET Core startup: `https://docs.microsoft.com/en-us/aspnet/core/fundamentals/startup`
- ASP.NET Core web API controllers: `https://docs.microsoft.com/en-us/aspnet/core/web-api`
- Create React app: `https://facebook.github.io/create-react-app/`
- WebPack development server: `https://webpack.js.org/configuration/dev-server/`
- npm: `https://docs.npmjs.com/`
- JSX: `https://reactjs.org/docs/introducing-jsx.html`
- JavaScript module import: `https://developer.mozilla.org/en-US/docs/Web/JavaScript/Reference/Statements/import`
- JavaScript module export: `https://developer.mozilla.org/en-US/docs/Web/JavaScript/Reference/Statements/export`
- JavaScript fetch: `https://developer.mozilla.org/en-US/docs/Web/API/Fetch_API`
- JavaScript array map: `https://developer.mozilla.org/en-US/docs/Web/JavaScript/Reference/Global_Objects/Array/map`
- React lists and keys: `https://reactjs.org/docs/lists-and-keys.html`

2
Creating Decoupled React and ASP.NET Core Apps

Throughout this book, we are going to develop a question and answer app; we will refer to it as the Q&A app. Users will be able to submit a question and other users will be able to submit answers. They will also be able to search for previous questions and view the answers that were given for them. In this chapter, we are going to start building this app by creating the ASP.NET Core and React projects.

In the previous chapter, we learned how to create an ASP.NET Core and React app using the template in Visual Studio. However, we'll create our app in a slightly different manner in this chapter and understand the reasoning behind this decision.

Our React app will use TypeScript 3, so we'll learn about the benefits of TypeScript and how to create a React and TypeScript app.

We'll cover the following topics in this chapter:

- Creating an ASP.NET Core Web API project
- Creating a React and TypeScript app
- Adding linting to React and TypeScript
- Adding automatic code formatting to React and TypeScript

Technical requirements

We'll use the following tools in this chapter:

- **Visual Studio 2019**: We'll use this to edit our ASP.NET Core code. This can be downloaded from `https://visualstudio.microsoft.com/vs/`.
- **.NET Core 3.0**: This can be downloaded from `https://dotnet.microsoft.com/download/dotnet-core`.
- **Visual Studio Code**: We'll use this to edit our React code. This can be downloaded from `https://code.visualstudio.com/`.
- **Node.js and npm**: These can be downloaded from `https://nodejs.org/`. If you already have these installed, make sure that Node.js is at least version 8.2 and that npm is at least version 5.2.

All the code snippets in this chapter can be found online at `https://github.com/PacktPublishing/ASP.NET-Core-3-and-React-17`. In order to restore code from a chapter, the source code repository can be downloaded and the relevant folder opened in the relevant editor. If the code is frontend code, then `npm install` can be entered in the Terminal to restore the dependencies.

Check out the following video to see the code in action:

`http://bit.ly/2SqFUSr`

Creating an ASP.NET Core Web API project

We are going to create the ASP.NET Core and React projects separately in this chapter. In `Chapter 1`, *Understanding the ASP.NET Core React Template,* we discovered that old versions of React and create-react-app were used. Creating the React project separately allows us to use a more recent version of React and create-react-app. Creating the React project separately also allows us to use TypeScript with React, which will help us be more productive as the code base grows.

Let's open Visual Studio and carry out the following steps to create our ASP.NET Core backend:

1. In the startup dialog, select **Create a new project**:

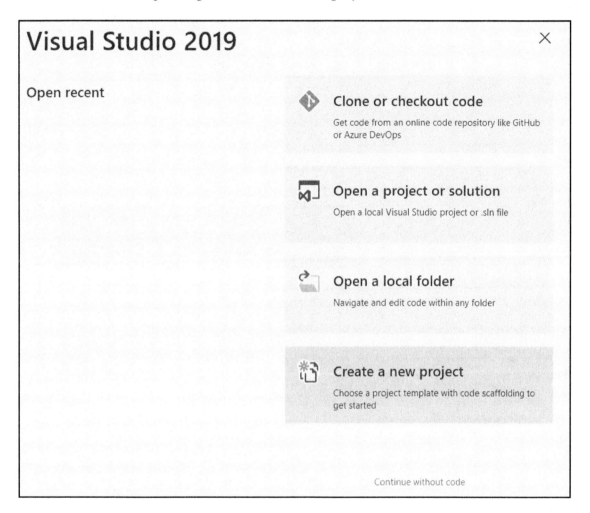

2. Choose **ASP.NET Core Web Application** in the wizard that opens and click the **Next** button:

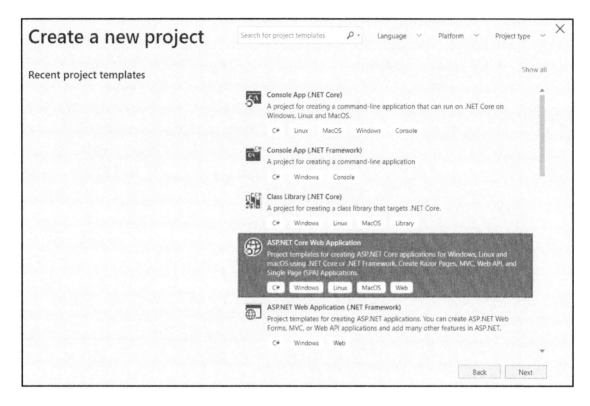

3. Create a folder called `backend` in an appropriate location.

4. Name the project QandA and choose the backend folder location to save the project. Tick **Place solution and project in the same directory** and click the **Create** button to create the project:

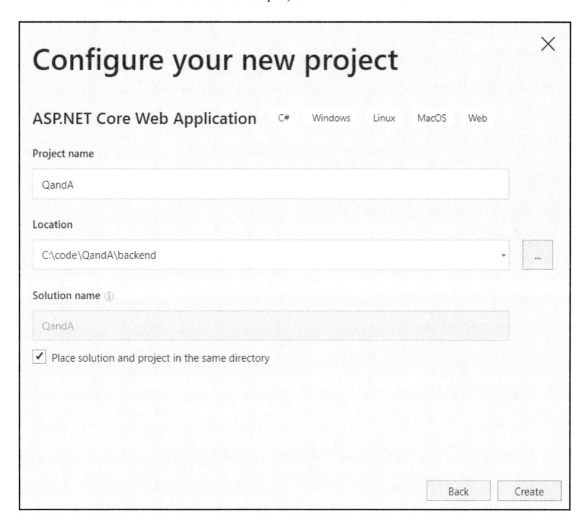

5. Now, another dialog will appear that will allow us to specify the version of ASP.NET Core we want to use, as well as the specific type of project we want to create. Select **ASP.NET Core 3.0** as the version and **API** in the dialog and click the **Create** button, which will create the project:

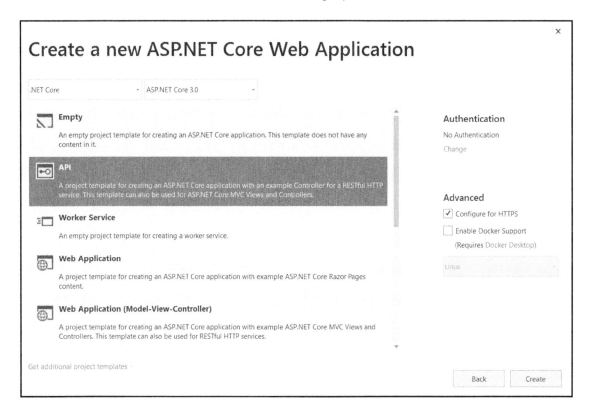

6. After the project is created, open `Startup.cs` and move the `app.UseHttpsRedirection()` line of code so that it is not used while in development:

```
public void Configure(IApplicationBuilder app, IWebHostEnvironment
env)
{
  if (env.IsDevelopment())
  {
    app.UseDeveloperExceptionPage();
  }
  else
  {
    app.UseHttpsRedirection();
```

```
    }
    app.UseRouting();

    ...
}
```

We have made this change because, in development mode, our frontend will use the HTTP protocol. By default, the Firefox browser doesn't allow network requests for an app that has a different protocol to the backend. Due to this, we want the frontend and backend to use the HTTP protocol in development mode.

That's the only change we are going to make to our backend in this chapter. In the next section, we'll create the React frontend project.

Creating a React and TypeScript app

In Chapter 1, *Understanding the ASP.NET Core React Template*, we discovered that **create-react-app (CRA)** was leveraged by the Visual Studio template to create the React app. We also learned that CRA did a lot of valuable setup and configuration for us. We are going to leverage CRA in this section to create our React app.

We are also going to leverage some additional tools for building our React app and look at the benefits that each one brings, starting with TypeScript.

Understanding the benefits of TypeScript

TypeScript adds an optional static typing layer on top of JavaScript that we can use during our development. Static types allow us to catch certain problems earlier in the development process. For example, if we make a mistake when referencing a variable, TypeScript will spot this immediately after we've mistyped the variable, as shown in the following screenshot:

```
function sayHello (firstName: string, lastName: string) {
                                              Cannot find name 'surname'. ts(2304)
  return "Hello " + firstName + " " + surname;
                                              any
};
```

Another example is that, if we forget to pass a required attribute when referencing a React component, TypeScript informs us of the mistake straight away:

```
                Property 'userName' is missing in type '{}' but required in
                type 'IProps'. ts(2741)
class App
  public      • Header.tsx(4, 3): 'userName' is declared here.
    retur  (alias) const Header: React.FunctionComponent<IProps>
      <di  import Header
        <Header />
      </div>
    );
  }
}
```

This means we get a build-time error rather than a runtime error.

This also helps tools such as Visual Studio Code provide accurate IntelliSense; robust refactoring features, such as renaming a class; and great code navigation.

As we start building our frontend, we'll quickly experience the types of benefits that make us more productive.

Creating the app with CRA

Let's create the React and TypeScript app with CRA by carrying out the following steps:

1. Open Visual Studio Code in the `QandA` folder we created earlier. Note that we shouldn't be inside the `backend` folder.
2. Open the Terminal in Visual Studio Code, which can be found in the **View** menu or by pressing *Ctrl + '*. Execute the following command in the Terminal:

   ```
   > npx create-react-app frontend --typescript
   ```

   The `npx` tool is part of npm that temporarily installs the `create-react-app` npm package and uses it to create our project.

   The `--typescript` option will create our React project with TypeScript.

3. If we look in the `src` folder, we'll see that the `App` component has a `tsx` extension. This means that this is a TypeScript component.

4. Let's verify whether the app runs okay by executing the following commands in the Terminal:

```
> cd frontend
> npm start
```

5. The app will appear in our browser after a few seconds:

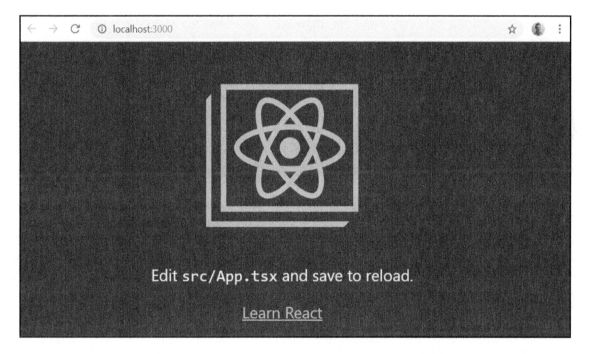

6. Press *Ctrl + C* to stop the running app and *Y* when asked to terminate the job.

So, why are we using Visual Studio Code to develop our React app and not Visual Studio? Well, the overall experience is a little better and faster when developing frontend code with Visual Studio Code.

So, we now have a React and TypeScript app using the latest version of CRA. In the next section, we are going to add more automated checks to our code by introducing **linting** into our project.

Adding linting to React and TypeScript

Linting is a series of checks that are used to identify code that is potentially problematic. A linter is a tool that performs linting, and it can be run in our code editor as well as the **continuous integration (CI)** process. So, linting helps us write consistent and high-quality code as it is being written.

ESLint is the most popular linter in the React community and has already been installed into our project for us by CRA. So, we will be using ESLint as our linting tool for our app.

 TSLint has been a popular alternative to ESLint for linting TypeScript code but is now deprecated. More information can be found at `https://medium.com/palantir/tslint-in-2019-1a144c2317a9`.

In the following subsections, we will learn how to configure ESLints rules, as well as configuring Visual Studio Code to highlight violations.

Configuring Visual Studio Code to lint TypeScript code

CRA has already installed ESLint and configured it for us.

 Note that ESLint doesn't appear in our `package.json` file. Instead, it is part of the CRA package. This can be confirmed by opening the `package.json` file in `node_modules\react-scripts`.

We need to tell Visual Studio Code to lint TypeScript code. Let's carry out the following steps to do this:

1. First, let's reopen Visual Studio Code in the `frontend` folder. This is required for an extension that we are going to install in a later step.
2. Create a new folder called `.vscode`.
3. Create a new file in the `.vscode` folder called `settings.json`. This file is the Visual Studio Code settings file for this project.
4. Let's add the following content into the `settings.json` file:

```
{
  "eslint.validate": [
    "javascript",
```

```
      "javascriptreact",
      { "language": "typescript", "autoFix": true },
      { "language": "typescriptreact", "autoFix": true }
   ]
}
```

These settings tell Visual Studio Code to validate TypeScript code, as well as JavaScript code, with ESLint.

5. Now, we can go to the **Extensions** area in Visual Studio Code (*Ctrl + Shift + X*) and type `eslint` into the search box in the top-left corner. The extension we are looking for is called **ESLint** and is published by **Dirk Baeumer**:

6. Click on the **Install** button to install the extension.

Now, Visual Studio Code will be using ESLint to validate our code.

Configuring linting rules

Now that Visual Studio Code is linting our code, let's carry out the following steps to understand how we can configure the rules that ESLint executes:

1. Let's create a file called `.eslintrc.json` in the `frontend` folder with the following code:

```
{
  "extends": "react-app"
}
```

This file defines the rules that ESLint executes. We have just told it to execute all the rules that are configured in CRA.

2. Let's check that Visual Studio Code is linting our code by adding the following highlighted line to `App.tsx`, just before the `return` statement:

```
const App: React.FC = () => {
  const unused = 'something';
  return (
    ...
  );
};
```

We'll see that ESLint immediately flags this line as being unused:

```
App.tsx   ✕
1   import R  const unused: "something"
2   import 1  'unused' is declared but its value is never read. ts(6133)
3   import '
4            'unused' is assigned a value but never used. eslint(@typescript-eslint/no-unused-vars)
5   const Ap  Quick Fix...   Peek Problem
6     const unused = 'something';
7     return (
```

That's great—this means our code is being linted.

3. Now, let's add a rule that CRA hasn't been configured to apply. In the `.eslintrc.json` file, let's add the following highlighted lines:

```
{
  "extends": "react-app",
  "rules": {
    "no-debugger":"warn"
  }
}
```

We have told ESLint to warn us about the use of `debugger` statements.

 The list of available ESLint rules is at `https://eslint.org/docs/rules/`.

4. Let's add a `debugger` statement below our unused variable in `App.tsx` like so:

```
const App: React.FC = () => {
  const unused = 'something';
  debugger;
  return (
```

```
    . . .
  );
};
```

We will immediately see that ESLint flags this up:

```
App.tsx    ✕
1    import React from 'react';
2    import logo from './logo.svg';
3    import './App.css';
4
5    co  Unexpected 'debugger' statement. eslint(no-debugger)
6        Quick Fix...   Peek Problem
7        debugger;
```

5. Now that we understand how to configure the rules that are run by ESLint, let's remove the unused line of code and `debugger` statement from `App.tsx`. Let's also remove the `no-debugger` rule from the `.eslintrc.json` file.

Now, we have linting configured in our project. In the next section, we'll look at how we can autoformat the code.

Adding automatic code formatting to React and TypeScript

Enforcing a consistent code style improves the readability of the code base, but it can be a pain, even if ESLint reminds us to do this. Wouldn't it be great if those semicolons we forgot to add to the end of our statements were just automatically added for us? Well, that is what automatic code formatting tools can do for us, and **Prettier** is one of these great tools.

Adding Prettier

We are going to add Prettier to our project by following these steps in Visual Studio Code:

1. Make sure you are in the `frontend` directory and execute the following command to install Prettier:

   ```
   > npm install prettier --save-dev
   ```

2. Now, we want Prettier to take responsibility for the style rules of ESLint. Let's install some npm packages that will do this:

   ```
   > npm install eslint-config-prettier eslint-plugin-prettier --save-dev
   ```

   `eslint-config-prettier` disables ESLint rules that conflict with Prettier. Here, `eslint-plugin-prettier` is an ESLint rule that formats code using Prettier.

3. Now, let's tell ESLint to let Prettier take care of the code formatting by adding the following highlighted changes to `.eslintrc.json`:

   ```
   {
     "extends": ["react-app","prettier"],
     "plugins": ["prettier"],
     "rules": {
       "prettier/prettier": "error"
     }
   }
   ```

4. Now, let's specify the formatting rules we want in a `.prettierrc` file in the `frontend` folder. So, let's create this file with the following content:

   ```
   {
     "printWidth": 80,
     "singleQuote": true,
     "semi": true,
     "tabWidth": 2,
     "trailingComma": "all"
   }
   ```

   These rules will result in lines over 80 characters long being sensibly wrapped, double quotes being automatically converted into single quotes, semicolons being automatically added to the end of statements, indentations automatically being set to two spaces, and trailing commas being automatically added wherever possible to items such as arrays on multiple lines.

5. Now, we can go to the **Extensions** area in Visual Studio Code (*Ctrl + Shift + X*) and type `prettier` into the search box in the top-left corner. The extension we are looking for is called **Prettier – Code formatter** and is published by **Esben Petersen**:

6. Click on the **Install** button to install the extension.

7. We can get Prettier to format our code when a file is saved in Visual Studio Code by adding the following highlighted line to the `settings.json` file in the `.vscode` folder:

```
{
  "eslint.validate": [
  "javascript",
  "javascriptreact",
  { "language": "typescript", "autoFix": true },
  { "language": "typescriptreact", "autoFix": true }
  ],
  "editor.formatOnSave": true
}
```

So, that's Prettier set up. Whenever we save a file in Visual Studio Code, it will be automatically formatted.

Summary

In this chapter, we have created our projects for the Q&A app that we are going to build throughout this book. We created the backend using the API ASP.NET Core template and the frontend using Create React App. We included TypeScript so that our frontend code is strongly typed, which will help us catch problems earlier and will help Visual Studio Code provide a better development experience.

We added linting to our frontend code to drive quality and consistency into our code base. ESLint is our linter and its rules are configured in a file called .eslintrc.json. We also added Prettier to our frontend code, which automatically formats our code. This is really helpful in code reviews. We configured the formatting rules in a .prettierrc file and used eslint-config-prettier to stop ESLint conflicting with Prettier.

So, we now have two separate projects for the frontend and backend, unlike what we have with the SPA template. This makes sense, mainly because we'll be using Visual Studio to develop the backend and Visual Studio Code to develop the frontend. So, there isn't any need to start both the frontend and backend together from within Visual Studio.

In the next chapter, we are going to start to build the frontend in React and TypeScript.

Questions

Have a go at the following questions to test what you have learned in this chapter:

1. What class does an API controller need to inherit from in order for invalid models to automatically return HTTP status code 400?
2. What option from create-react-app did we use to create a React with TypeScript project?
3. What ESLint rule could we use to help prevent console.log statements being added to our code?
4. What setting in .prettierrc could we set to use single quotes in our code?
5. What file can we use to tell Visual Studio Code to validate TypeScript code using ESLint and to automatically format code using Prettier?

Further reading

The following are some useful links for learning more about the topics that were covered in this chapter:

- ASP.NET Core API controllers: https://docs.microsoft.com/en-us/aspnet/core/web-api
- npx: https://www.npmjs.com/package/npx
- Create React app: https://facebook.github.io/create-react-app/
- ESLint: https://eslint.org/
- Prettier: https://prettier.io/

2
Section 2: Building a Frontend with React and TypeScript

In this section, we will build the frontend of our Q&A app using React and TypeScript, which will interact with the RESTful API we built in the previous section.

This section comprises the following chapters:

- Chapter 3, *Getting Started with React and TypeScript*
- Chapter 4, *Routing with React Router*
- Chapter 5, *Working with Forms*
- Chapter 6, *Managing State with Redux*

Getting Started with React and TypeScript

3

In this chapter, we are going to pick up where we left off and start coding the frontend of the Q&A app.

We'll be focusing on building the home page of the app and implementing all the components that make up the page. We'll start by gaining a good understanding of how to create function-based components with JSX. We'll understand the different approaches we can take in order to style our app and use one of these methods. Then, we'll learn how we can implement properties on components in order to make them configurable. Finally, we'll learn about what component state is and how it can help us implement an interactive component, along with how to handle events in React.

By the end of this chapter, we'll have an understanding of when components are rerendered and how we can optimize this process.

We'll cover the following topics in this chapter:

- Understanding JSX
- Creating function-based components
- Styling components
- Implementing component props
- Implementing component state
- Handling events
- Rendering optimization

Technical requirements

We'll use the following tools in this chapter:

- **Visual Studio Code**: We'll use this to edit our React code. This can be downloaded and installed from `https://code.visualstudio.com/`.
- **Node.js and npm**: These can be downloaded from `https://nodejs.org/`. If you already have these installed, make sure that Node.js is at least version 8.2 and that npm is at least version 5.2
- **Babel REPL**: We'll use this online tool briefly to explore JSX. This can be found at `https://babeljs.io/repl`.
- **Zondicons**: We'll use one of these icons in our app. The icon we'll be using can be downloaded from `https://www.zondicons.com/`.
- **Q&A**: We'll start with the Q&A frontend project we finished in Chapter 2, *Creating Decoupled React and ASP.NET Core Apps*. This is available on GitHub at `https://github.com/PacktPublishing/ASP.NET-Core-3-and-React-17`.

All the code snippets in this chapter can be found online at `https://github.com/PacktPublishing/ASP.NET-Core-3-and-React-17`. In order to restore code from a chapter, the source code repository can be downloaded and the relevant folder can be opened in the relevant editor. If the code is frontend code, then you can use `npm install` in the Terminal to restore the dependencies.

Check out the following video to see the code in action:

`http://bit.ly/34VCk5r`

Understanding JSX

In this section, we're going to understand JSX, which we briefly touched on in Chapter 1, *Understanding the ASP.NET Core React Template*. We already know that JSX isn't a valid JavaScript and that we need a preprocessor step to convert it into JavaScript. We are going to use the Babel REPL to play with JSX to get an understanding of how it maps to JavaScript by carrying out the following steps:

1. Open a browser, go to `https://babeljs.io/repl`, and enter the following JSX in the left-hand pane:

   ```
   <span>Q and A</span>
   ```

The following appears in the right-hand pane, which is what our JSX has compiled down to:

```
React.createElement(
  "span",
  null,
  "Q and A"
);
```

2. We can see that it compiles down to a call to `React.createElement`, which has three parameters:
   - The element type, which can be an HTML tag name (such as `span`), a React component type, or a React fragment type
   - An object containing the properties to be applied to the element
   - The children of the element

3. Let's expand our example by putting a `header` tag around our `span`:

```
<header><span>Q and A</span></header>
```

4. This compiles down to two calls with `React.createElement`, with `span` being passed in as a child to the `header` element that's created:

```
React.createElement(
  "header",
  null,
  React.createElement(
    "span",
    null,
    "Q and A"
  )
);
```

5. Let's change the `span` tag to an anchor tag and add an `href` attribute:

```
<header><a href="/">Q and A</a></header>
```

6. In the compiled JavaScript, we can see that the nested `React.createElement` call has changed to have `"a"` passed in as the element type, along with a properties object containing the `href` as the second parameter:

```
React.createElement(
  "header",
  null,
  React.createElement(
    "a",
```

```
      { href: "/" },
      "Q and A"
    )
  );
```

7. This is starting to make sense, but, so far, our JSX only contains HTML. Let's start to mix in some JavaScript. We'll do this by declaring and initializing a variable and referencing it inside the anchor tag:

```
var appName = "Q and A";
<header><a href="/">{appName}</a></header>
```

We can see that this compiles to the following with the JavaScript code:

```
var appName = "Q and A";
React.createElement(
  "header",
  null,
  React.createElement(
    "a",
    { href: "/" },
    appName
  )
);
```

So, the `appName` variable is declared in the first statement, exactly how we defined it, and is passed in as the children parameter in the nested `React.createElement` call.

8. The key point to note here is that we can inject JavaScript into HTML in JSX by using curly braces. To further illustrate this point, let's add the word app to the end of the appName:

```
const appName = "Q and A";
<header><a href="/">{appName + " app"}</a></header>
```

This compiles down to the following:

```
var appName = "Q and A";
React.createElement(
  "header",
  null,
  React.createElement(
    "a",
    { href: "/" },
    appName + " app"
  )
);
```

So, JSX can be thought of as HTML with JavaScript mixed in using curly braces. This makes it incredibly powerful since regular JavaScript can be used to conditionally render elements, as well as render elements in a loop.

Now that we have an understanding of JSX, we are going to start creating the components for the home page in our app.

Creating function-based components

In this section, we are going to start by creating a component for the header of our app, which will contain our app name and the ability to search for questions. Then, we'll implement some components so that we can start to build the home page of the app, along with some mock data.

Creating a Header component

If the frontend project isn't open in Visual Studio Code, open it. We are about to create our first function-based component.

Creating our first component

We can create a basic Header component and reference it within our App component by carrying out the following steps:

1. Create a new file called Header.tsx in the src folder.
2. Import React into the file with the following import statement:

```
import React from 'react';
```

3. Our component is just going to render the word `header` initially. So, enter the following as our initial `Header` component:

```
export const Header = () => <div>header</div>;
```

Congratulations! We have implemented our first function-based React component!

The preceding component is actually an arrow function that is set to the `Header` variable.

 An arrow function is an alternative function syntax that was introduced in ES6. The arrow function syntax is a little shorter than the original syntax and it also preserves the lexical scope of `this`. The function parameters are defined in parentheses and the code that the function executes follows a =>, which is often referred to as a *fat arrow*.

Notice that there are no curly braces or a `return` keyword. Instead, we just define the JSX that the function should return directly after the fat arrow. This is called an **implicit return**. We use the `const` keyword to declare and initialize the `Header` variable.

 The `const` keyword can be used to declare and initialize a variable where its reference won't change later in the program. Alternatively, the `let` keyword can be used to declare a variable whose reference can change later in the program.

4. The `export` keyword allows the component to be used in other files. So, let's use this in our `App` component by importing it into `App.tsx`:

```
import { Header } from './Header';
```

5. Now, we can reference the `Header` component in the `App` component's `render` method. Let's replace the `header` tag that CRA created for us with our `Header` component. Let's remove the redundant `logo` import as well:

```
import React from 'react';
import './App.css';
import { Header } from './Header';

const App: React:FC = () => {
  return (
    <div className="App">
      <Header />
```

```
        </div>
    );
};

export default App;
```

6. In the Visual Studio Code Terminal, enter `npm start` to run the app. We'll see that the word **header** appears at the top of the page, centered like so:

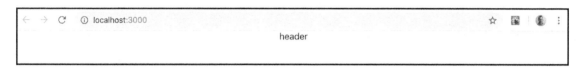

Congratulations again – we have just consumed our first React component!

So, the arrow function syntax is a really nice way of implementing function-based components. The implicit return feature that arrow functions have reduces the number of characters we need to type. We'll use arrow functions with implicit returns heavily throughout this book.

Adding elements to the Header component

We're going to work on the `Header` component a little more so that it eventually looks as follows:

So, the `Header` component will contain the app name, which will be **Q & A**, a search input, and a **Sign In** link.

With the app still running, carry out the following steps to modify the `Header` component:

1. Add the app name inside an anchor tag inside the `div` tag by replacing the word `header`, which was previously used inside the `div`:

```
export const Header = () => (
  <div>
    <a href="./">Q & A</a>
  </div>
);
```

Notice that the implicit return statement containing the JSX is now in parentheses.

 When an implicit return statement is over multiple lines, parentheses are required. When an implicit return is on just a single line, we can get away without the parentheses.

Prettier automatically adds parentheses in an implicit return if they are needed, so we don't need to worry about remembering this rule.

2. Add an `input` to allow the user to perform a search:

```
<div>
  <a href="./">Q & A</a>
  <input type="text" placeholder="Search..." />
</div>
```

3. Add a link to allow users to sign in:

```
<div>
  <a href="./">Q & A</a>
  <input type="text" placeholder="Search..." />
  <a href="./signin"><span>Sign In</span></a>
</div>
```

4. The **Sign In** link needs a user icon next to it. We're going to use the `user.svg` icon from Zondicons. So, if you haven't downloaded these icons, do so and place `user.svg` in our project's `src` folder.

5. We are going to create a component to host this icon, so create a file called `Icons.tsx` and enter the following content into it:

```
import React from 'react';
import user from './user.svg';

export const UserIcon = () =>
  <img src={user} alt="User" width="12px" />;
```

Here, we have created a component called `UserIcon` that renders an `img` tag, with the `src` attribute set to the `svg` file we imported from `user.svg`.

6. Let's go back to `Header.tsx` and import the icon component we just created:

```
import { UserIcon } from './Icons';
```

7. Now, we can place an instance of the `UserIcon` component in the `Header` component inside the `button`, before the `span`:

```
export const Header = () => (
  <div>
    <a href="./">Q & A</a>
    <input type="text" placeholder="Search..." />
    <a href="./signin">
      <UserIcon />
      <span>Sign In</span>
    </a>
  </div>
);
```

8. Let's look at the running app:

Our header doesn't look great, but we can see the elements in the `Header` component we just created. We'll tidy our `Header` component up later in this chapter, that is, when we learn how to style components.

Creating a HomePage component

Let's create another component to get more familiar with the process. This time, we'll create a component for the home page by carrying out the following steps:

1. Create a file called `HomePage.tsx` with the following content:

```
import React from 'react';

export const HomePage = () => (
  <div>
    <div>
      <h2>Unanswered Questions</h2>
      <button>Ask a question</button>
    </div>
  </div>
);
```

Our home page simply consists of a title containing the text, **Unanswered Questions**, and a button to submit a question.

2. Open `App.tsx` and import our `HomePage` component:

```
import { HomePage } from './HomePage';
```

3. Now, we can add an instance of `HomePage` under the `Header` component in the `render` method:

```
<div className="App">
  <Header />
  <HomePage />
</div>
```

4. If we look at the running app, we'll see the title and button under the content of the `Header` component.

We are going to leave this component for now and come back and style it, as well as add a list of unanswered questions, later in this chapter.

Creating mock data

We desperately need some data so that we can develop our frontend. In this section, we'll create some mock data in our frontend that will expose a function to get data. We will use this when we plug our real ASP.NET Core backend in. Follow these steps:

1. Create a new file in the `src` folder called `QuestionsData.ts` with the following interface:

```
export interface QuestionData {
  questionId: number;
  title: string;
  content: string;
  userName: string;
  created: Date;
}
```

Before moving on, let's understand the code we have just entered because we have just written some TypeScript.

An **interface** is a contract that defines a type with a collection of property and method definitions without any implementation. Interfaces don't exist in JavaScript, so they are purely used by the TypeScript compiler to enforce the contract by type checking. We create an interface with the `interface` keyword, followed by its name, followed by the bits that make up the interface in curly braces.

So, our interface is called `QuestionData` and it defines the structure of the questions we expect to be working with. We have exported the interface so that it can be used throughout our app where we interact with question data.

Also, notice what appears to be a type after the property names in the interface. These are called **type annotations** and are a TypeScript feature that doesn't exist in JavaScript.

Type annotations let us declare variables, properties, and function parameters with specific types. This allows the TypeScript compiler to check that the code adheres to these types. In short, type annotations allow TypeScript to catch bugs where our code is using the wrong type much earlier than we would if we were writing our code in JavaScript.

2. Let's create another interface for the structure of the answers we expect:

```
export interface AnswerData {
   answerId: number;
   content: string;
   userName: string;
   created: Date;
}
```

3. Now, we can adjust the `QuestionData` interface so that it includes an array of answers:

```
export interface QuestionData {
   questionId: number;
   title: string;
   content: string;
   userName: string;
   created: Date;
   answers: AnswerData[];
}
```

Notice the square brackets in the type annotation for the `answers` property.

Square brackets after a type denote an array of the type.

4. Let's create some mock questions below the interfaces:

```
const questions: QuestionData[] = [
  {
    questionId: 1,
    title: 'Why should I learn TypeScript?',
    content:
      'TypeScript seems to be getting popular so I wondered whether
      it is worth my time learning it? What benefits does it give
      over JavaScript?',
    userName: 'Bob',
    created: new Date(),
    answers: [
      {
        answerId: 1,
        content: 'To catch problems earlier speeding up your
        developments',
        userName: 'Jane',
        created: new Date(),
      },
      {
        answerId: 2,
        content:
          'So, that you can use the JavaScript features of
tomorrow,
            today',
        userName: 'Fred',
        created: new Date(),
      },
    ],
  },
  {
    questionId: 2,
    title: 'Which state management tool should I use?',
    content:
      'There seem to be a fair few state management tools around
for
      React - React, Unstated, ... Which one should I use?',
    userName: 'Bob',
    created: new Date(),
```

```
        answers: [],
      },
  ];
```

Notice that we typed our `questions` variable with an array of the `QuestionData` interface we have just created. If we miss a property out or misspell it, the TypeScript compiler will complain.

5. Let's create a function that returns unanswered questions:

```
export const getUnansweredQuestions = (): QuestionData[] => {
  return questions.filter(q => q.answers.length === 0);
};
```

This function returns the question array items we have just created that have no answers by making use of the `array.filter` method.

 The `array.filter` method in an array executes the function that was passed into it for each array item and creates a new array with all the elements that return truthy from the function. A truthy value is any value other than `false`, 0, `""`, `null`, `undefined`, or NaN.

Notice that we defined the return type, `QuestionData[]`, for the function after the function parameters.

We are going to use this function in `HomePage` a little later in this chapter when we learn about component properties. However, before this, we are going to learn how we can style our app.

Styling components

In this section, we're going to make our app look a lot better by adding some styling. Eventually, we're going to use a popular library called **Emotion** in order to style our app. However, before we do this, we need to understand how we would style an app in a more traditional way, as well as the benefits of using Emotion.

Styling using CSS class references

We could style our app in the traditional way by defining CSS classes in a CSS file and referencing these within our components. In fact, this is what CRA did with the `App` component. We have removed a lot of the content in `App.tsx`, but if we look at the JSX, we'll see a reference to a CSS class called `App`:

```
<div className="App">
  <Header />
  <HomePage />
</div>
```

We'll also see a file called `App.css`, which has been imported into `App.tsx`:

```
import './App.css';
```

If we look in `App.css`, we'll see the `App` CSS class, along with lots of others that are now redundant because we've replaced a lot of the content in the `App` component:

```
.App {
  text-align: center;
}
```

Why is a `className` attribute used to reference CSS classes? Shouldn't we use the `class` attribute? Well, we already know that JSX compiles down to JavaScript, and since `class` is a keyword in JavaScript, React uses a `className` attribute instead.

 The React team is currently working on allowing `class` attributes to be used instead of `className`. See `https://github.com/facebook/react/issues/13525` for more information.

This is a traditional approach to styling that we could use and it is great if our team has developers who only work in the CSS layer in our app with other developers implementing the React components. However, there are downsides to the traditional approach.

Understanding the benefits of CSS in JS

CSS is global in nature. So, if we use a CSS class name called `container` within a `Header` component, it would collide with another CSS class called `container` in a different CSS file if a page references both CSS files:

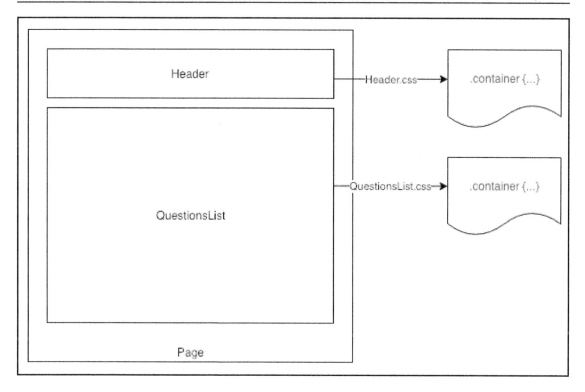

As the app grows and new team members join the development team, the risk of CSS changes impacting areas of the app we don't expect increases. We reduce this risk by being careful when naming and structuring our CSS by using something such as BEM.

Reusability in CSS is also a challenge. CSS custom properties give us the ability to use variables, but they are global variables and are not supported in IE. CSS preprocessors such as SCSS can, of course, help us with this.

Ideally, we want to easily scope styles to a component. It would also be nice if local styles were defined in the component code, so that we can see and understand the structure, logic, and styling for a component without having to navigate through different files. This is exactly what CSS in JS libraries do, and **Emotion** is a popular CSS in the JS library. The syntax for defining the styling properties is exactly the same as defining properties in CSS, which is nice if we already know CSS well. We can even nest CSS properties in a similar manner to how we can do this in SCSS.

Later in this chapter, we'll see that Emotion will generate real CSS classes for the elements on the page to reference so that we still get the performance gain of CSS. Emotion just helps us scope the styles to specific components.

Installing Emotion

With our frontend project open in Visual Studio Code, let's install Emotion into our project by carrying out the following steps:

1. Open the Terminal, make sure you are in the `frontend` folder, and execute the following command:

    ```
    > npm install @emotion/core @emotion/styled
    ```

2. There is a nice Visual Studio Code extension that will provide CSS syntax highlighting and IntelliSense for Emotion. Open the **Extensions** area (*Ctrl + Shift + X*) and type `styled components` in the search box at the top-left. The extension we are looking for is called **vscode-styled-components** and was published by **Julien Poissonnier**:

 This extension was primarily developed for the Styled Components CSS in the JS library. CSS highlighting and IntelliSense works for Emotion as well, though.

3. Click on the **Install** button to install the extension and then the **Reload** button to complete the installation.

That's Emotion installed within our project and set up nicely in Visual Studio Code.

Styling the document body

We are going to use the traditional approach to style the document's body. Follow these steps to do so:

1. We already have CSS in place for the `body` tag in the `index.css` file. Let's remove everything apart from the `margin` and add a `background color`:

   ```
   body {
     margin: 0;
     background-color: #f7f8fa;
   }
   ```

2. Let's also remove the redundant `code` CSS class in `index.css`.

3. Let's remove the `App.css` file from our project and the references from within the `App.tsx` file. Now, it should contain the following content:

   ```
   import React, { Component } from 'react';
   import { Header } from './Header';
   import { HomePage } from './HomePage';

   const App: React.FC = () => {
     return (
       <div>
         <Header />
         <HomePage />
       </div>
     );
   };

   export default App;
   ```

That's tidied up the `index.css` and `App.tsx` files nicely.

Styling components using Emotion

Now, we are ready to start implementing styles in our components. We'll style the `App`, `Header`, and `HomePage` components we created earlier.

Styling the App component

Let's start with the `App` component by carrying out the following steps:

1. In `App.tsx`, let's start by importing some functions from the Emotion library:

```
/** @jsx jsx */
import { css, jsx } from '@emotion/core';
```

The `css` function is what we'll use to style an HTML element. The `jsx` function is used to transform the component into JavaScript by Babel. The comment above the import statement tells Babel to use this `jsx` function to transform JSX into JavaScript.

 It is important to include the `/** @jsx jsx */` comment; otherwise, the transpilation process will error out.

2. Let's use the `css` function to style the component's `div` container:

```
const App: React.FC = () => {
  return (
    <div
      css={css`
        font-family: 'Segoe UI', 'Helvetica Neue', sans-serif;
        font-size: 16px;
        color: #5c5a5a;
      `}
    >
      <Header />
      <HomePage />
    </div>
  );
};
```

So, we put the styles in a `css` attribute on an HTML element in what is called a **tagged template literal**.

A **template literal** is a string enclosed by backticks (` `` `) that can span multiple lines and can include a JavaScript expression in curly braces, prefixed with a dollar sign (`${expression}`). Template literals are great when we need to merge static text with variables.

A **tagged template literal** is a template string that is executed through a function that is specified immediately before the template literal string. The function is executed on the template literal before the string is rendered in the browser.

So, Emotion's `css` function is being used in a tagged template literal to render the styles defined in backticks (` `` `) on the HTML element.

3. We actually want to specify the font family, size, and color in various components in our app. To do this, we are going to extract these values into variables in a separate file. Let's create a file called `Styles.ts` that contains the following variables:

```
export const gray1 = '#383737';
export const gray2 = '#5c5a5a';
export const gray3 = '#857c81';
export const gray4 = '#b9b9b9';
export const gray5 = '#e3e2e2';
export const gray6 = '#f7f8fa';

export const primary1 = '#681c41';
export const primary2 = '#824c67';

export const accent1 = '#dbb365';
export const accent2 = '#efd197';

export const fontFamily = "'Segoe UI', 'Helvetica Neue', sans-serif";
export const fontSize = '16px';
```

Here, we have defined six shades of gray, two shades of the primary color for our app, two shades of an accent color, as well as the font family we'll use with the standard font size.

4. Let's import the variables we need into `App.tsx`:

```
import { fontFamily, fontSize, gray2 } from './Styles';
```

5. Now, we can use these variables inside the CSS template literal using interpolation:

```
<div
  css={css`
    font-family: ${fontFamily};
    font-size: ${fontSize};
    color: ${gray2};
  `}
>
  <Header />
  <HomePage />
</div>
```

Congratulations – we have just styled our first component with Emotion!

6. Let's run the app (if it's not already running) by executing `npm start` in the Terminal.

7. Let's inspect the DOM in the browser page by pressing *F12*:

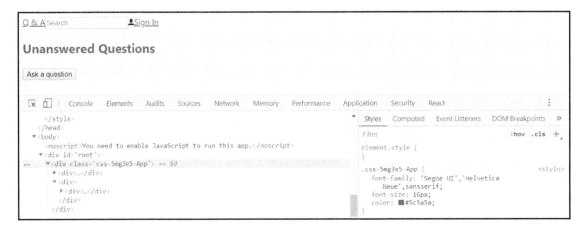

We can see that the `div` we styled has a random-looking CSS class name that references the CSS properties we defined. These CSS classes reference the styles we defined in our styled-components. So, the styles aren't inline styles on the elements as we might have thought. Instead, the styles are held in unique CSS classes. If we look in the HTML header, we'll see the CSS class defined in a `style` tag:

```
▼ <style data-emotion="css">
    .css-5mg3e5-App{font-family:'Segoe UI','Helvetica Neue',sansserif;font-size:16px;color:#5c5a5a;}
  </style>
 </head>
 ▶ <body>...</body>
</html>
```

So, during the app's build process, Emotion has transformed the styles into a real CSS class.

Styling the Header component

We can style the Header component by carrying out the following steps:

1. Import the Emotion functions and some of the style variables we set up previously into `Header.tsx`:

   ```
   /** @jsx jsx */
   import { css, jsx } from '@emotion/core';
   import { fontFamily, fontSize, gray1, gray2, gray5 } from './Styles';
   ```

2. Remove the `React` import statement. We don't need it anymore since we aren't importing anything from React and the `@jsx` comment is now telling Babel how to transpile the JSX.

3. Now, we can define the following style on the `div` container element:

   ```
   <div
     css={css`
       position: fixed;
       box-sizing: border-box;
       top: 0;
       width: 100%;
       display: flex;
       align-items: center;
       justify-content: space-between;
       padding: 10px 20px;
       background-color: #fff;
       border-bottom: 1px solid ${gray5};
       box-shadow: 0 3px 7px 0 rgba(110, 112, 114, 0.21);
     `}
   >
     ...
   </div>
   ```

We are fixing this element to the top of the page by taking the whole width of the page up. We're also using a Flexbox layout, which will layout the app name, search box, and **Sign In** link nicely. We are also using background color and a nice box shadow to make the header pop out a bit.

4. Still in `Header.tsx`, we are going to move on to implementing styles on the anchor tag:

```
<a
  href="./"
  css={css`
    font-size: 24px;
    font-weight: bold;
    color: ${gray1};
    text-decoration: none;
  `}
>
  Q & A
</a>
```

Here, we are making the app name fairly big, bold, and dark gray, and also removing the underline.

5. Let's move on and style the search box:

```
<input
  type="text"
  placeholder="Search..."
  css={css`
    box-sizing: border-box;
    font-family: ${fontFamily};
    font-size: ${fontSize};
    padding: 8px 10px;
    border: 1px solid ${gray5};
    border-radius: 3px;
    color: ${gray2};
    background-color: white;
    width: 200px;
    height: 30px;
    :focus {
      outline-color: ${gray5};
    }
  `}
/>
```

Here, we are using the standard font family and size and giving the search box a light gray rounded border. Notice the nested pseudo-class definitions for defining the outline color when the search box has focus. This is very much like how we can structure the CSS in SCSS.

6. The last change we'll make in the `Header.tsx` file is being done to style the **Sign In** link:

```
<a
  href="./signin"
  css={css`
    font-family: ${fontFamily};
    font-size: ${fontSize};
    padding: 5px 10px;
    background-color: transparent;
    color: ${gray2};
    text-decoration: none;
    cursor: pointer;
    span {
      margin-left: 10px;
    }
    :focus {
      outline-color: ${gray5};
    }
  `}
>
  <UserIcon />
  <span>Sign In</span>
</a>
```

7. Next up is styling the `UserIcon` component in the `Icons.tsx` file. Let's import the Emotion functions and remove the React import:

```
/** @jsx jsx */
import { css, jsx } from '@emotion/core';
import user from './user.svg';
```

8. Now, we can define the styles on the `ImgIcon` component on the `img` tag:

```
<img
  src={user}
  alt="User"
  css={css`
    width: 12px;
    opacity: 0.6;
  `}
/>
```

We've moved the width from the attribute on the `img` tag into its CSS style. Now, the icon is a nice size and appears to be a little lighter in color.

9. If we look at the running app, we'll see that our app header is looking much nicer now:

We are getting the hang of Emotion now. The remaining component to style is `HomePage` – we'll look at that next.

Styling the HomePage component

It's time to style the `HomePage` component. Follow these steps to do so:

1. As usual, we start by importing the functions from Emotion and removing the React import from `HomePage.tsx`:

```
/** @jsx jsx */
import { css, jsx } from '@emotion/core';
```

2. Let's style the container element in the `HomePage` component by placing the page content in the center of the screen:

```
export const HomePage = () => (
  <div
    css={css`
      margin: 50px auto 20px auto;
      padding: 30px 20px;
      max-width: 600px;
    `}
  >
    <div>
      <h2>Unanswered Questions</h2>
      <button>Ask a question</button>
    </div>
  </div>
);
```

3. Next, we will style the `div` that wraps the page title and **Ask a question** button:

```
<div
  css={css`
    margin: 50px auto 20px auto;
    padding: 30px 20px;
    max-width: 600px;
  `}
>
  <div
    css={css`
      display: flex;
      align-items: center;
      justify-content: space-between;
    `}
  >
    <h2>Unanswered Questions</h2>
    <button>Ask a question</button>
  </div>
</div>
```

4. Now, let's style the page title:

```
<h2
  css={css`
    font-size: 15px;
    font-weight: bold;
    margin: 10px 0px 5px;
    text-align: center;
    text-transform: uppercase;
  `}
>
  Unanswered Questions
</h2>
```

This reduces the size of the page title and makes it uppercase, which will make the page's content stand out more when we implement this.

5. Finally, we have the **Ask a question** button, which is the primary button on the page. Eventually, we are going to have primary buttons on several pages, so let's create a reusable `PrimaryButton` styled component in the `Styles.ts` file. First, we need to import the styled function from Emotion:

```
import styled from '@emotion/styled';
```

6. Now, we can create the primary button styled component:

```
export const PrimaryButton = styled.button`
  background-color: ${primary2};
  border-color: ${primary2};
  border-style: solid;
  border-radius: 5px;
  font-family: ${fontFamily};
  font-size: ${fontSize};
  padding: 5px 10px;
  color: white;
  cursor: pointer;
  :hover {
    background-color: ${primary1};
  }
  :focus {
    outline-color: ${primary2};
  }
  :disabled {
    opacity: 0.5;
    cursor: not-allowed;
  }
`;
```

Here, we've created a styled component in Emotion by using a tagged template literal. The function before the backticks (` `) references a function within Emotion's `styled` function and is the HTML element tag name we want to render.

So, this styled component creates a flat, slightly rounded button with our chosen primary color.

7. Let's import this into the `HomePage.tsx` file:

```
import { PrimaryButton } from './Styles';
```

8. Now, we can replace the `button` tag in the `HomePage` JSX with our `PrimaryButton` styled component:

```
export const HomePage = () => (
  <div ... >
  <div ... >
  <h2 ... >
  Unanswered Questions
  </h2>
  <PrimaryButton>Ask a question</PrimaryButton>
  </div>
```

```
      </div>
    );
```

9. If we look at the running app, we'll see that it's looking much nicer:

There is still work to do in terms of the home page's implementation, such as rendering the list of unanswered questions. We need to learn about props in order to do this, which we'll do in the next section.

Implementing component props

Components can have *props* to allow consumers to pass parameters into them, just like we pass parameters into a JavaScript function.

The word **props** is short for properties.

In this section, we'll learn all about how to implement strongly-typed props, including optional and default props. Then, we'll implement the rest of the home page to assist in our learning.

Creating HomePage child components

We are going to implement some child components that the HomePage component will use. We will pass the unanswered questions data to the child components via props.

Creating the QuestionList component

Let's go through the following steps to implement the QuestionList component:

1. Let's create a file called QuestionList.tsx and add the following import statements:

```
import { FC } from 'react';
/** @jsx jsx */
import { css, jsx } from '@emotion/core';
import { gray5, accent2 } from './Styles';
import { QuestionData } from './QuestionsData';
```

Notice that we have imported FC from React.

 A **Functional Component (FC)** is a generic TypeScript type we can use to pass strongly-typed props to a function-based component. The syntax is FC<Props>, where Props is the interface for the props.

2. Now, let's define the interface for the component props underneath the import statements:

```
interface Props {
  data: QuestionData[];
}
```

We have called the props interface Props and it contains a single property to hold an array of questions.

3. Let's start by implementing the QuestionList component:

```
export const QuestionList: FC<Props> = props => null;
```

We have defined props that can be passed into the component of the Props type. This means we can pass a data prop into QuestionList when we reference it in JSX.

4. At the moment, we aren't rendering anything in the QuestionList component. We are going to render the questions in an unordered list:

```
export const QuestionList: FC<Props> = props => (
  <ul
    css={css`
      list-style: none;
      margin: 10px 0 0 0;
```

```
      padding: 0px 20px;
      background-color: #fff;
      border-bottom-left-radius: 4px;
      border-bottom-right-radius: 4px;
      border-top: 3px solid ${accent2};
      box-shadow: 0 3px 5px 0 rgba(0, 0, 0, 0.16);
    `}
  >
  </ul>
);
```

So, the unordered list will appear without the bullet points and with a rounded border. The top border will be slightly thicker and in the accent color. We've added a box shadow to make the list pop out a bit.

5. Now, let's start to create the list items:

```
export const QuestionList: FC<Props> = props => (
  <ul ...
  >
    <li
      css={css`
        border-top: 1px solid ${gray5};
        :first-of-type {
          border-top: none;
        }
      `}
    >
    </li>
  </ul>
);
```

So, the list items will have a light gray line between them.

6. Now, we can inject the data into the list:

```
export const QuestionList: FC<Props> = props => (
  <ul ...
  >
    {props.data.map(question => (
      <li
        key={question.questionId}
        css={{...}}
      >
      </li>
    ))}
  </ul>
);
```

Note that we're referencing the `data` prop and calling a `map` function nested inside the `List` component. `map` iterates through the items in the array, calling the function passed to it for each item. So, we iterate through the questions that are passed into `QuestionList` and render a `li` HTML element for each array item.

Notice the `key` prop we pass into the `li` element.

The `key` prop helps React detect when the element changes or is added or removed. Where we output content in a loop, in React, it is good practice to apply this prop and set it to a unique value within the loop so that React can distinguish it from the other elements during the rendering process. If we don't provide a key prop, React will unnecessarily rerender this element, which makes the rendering process slower.

7. Our `QuestionList` component will work perfectly fine, but we are going to make one small change that will arguably make the implementation a little more succinct. The change is to destructure the props into a data variable in the function parameter:

```
export const QuestionList: FC<Props> = ({ data }) => (
  <ul ... >
    {data.map(question => (
      <li ... >
      </li>
    ))}
  </ul>
);
```

Destructuring is a special syntax that allows us to unpack objects or arrays into variables.

Notice that we directly reference the data variable in the JSX and not through the `props` variable, like we did in the previous example. This is a nice pattern to use, particularly when there are more props.

Before we can complete the `QuestionList` component, we are going to create its child component, `Question`, which we'll do next.

Creating the Question component

Follow these steps to implement the `Question` component:

1. Create a file called `Question.tsx` that contains the following import statements:

```
import { FC } from 'react';
/** @jsx jsx */
import { css, jsx } from '@emotion/core';
import { QuestionData } from './QuestionsData';
import { gray3 } from './Styles';
```

2. Let's create the props for the `Question` component, which will simply contain a prop for the question data:

```
interface Props {
  data: QuestionData;
}
```

3. Now, we can create the component:

```
export const Question: FC<Props> = ({ data }) => (
  <div
    css={css`
      padding: 10px 0px;
    `}
  >
    <div
      css={css`
        padding: 10px 0px;
        font-size: 19px;
      `}
    >
      {data.title}
    </div>
    <div
      css={css`
        font-size: 12px;
        font-style: italic;
        color: ${gray3};
      `}
    >
      {`Asked by ${data.userName} on
        ${data.created.toLocaleDateString()}
${data.created.toLocaleTimeString()}`}
    </div>
  </div>
);
```

So, we are rendering the question title, who asked the question, and when it was asked.

Notice that we use the `toLocaleDateString` and `toLocaleTimeString` functions on the `data.created Date` object to output when the question was asked, formatted in the browser's locale.

That completes our `Question` component nicely.

Wiring up the components

Now, we can wire up the components we have just created using the props so that we get the unanswered questions rendered on the home page. Follow these steps to do so:

1. Let's go back to `QuestionList.tsx` and import the `Question` component we just created:

   ```
   import { Question } from './Question';
   ```

2. Now, we can place an instance of the `Question` component in the `QuestionList` JSX nested within `ListItem`:

   ```
   {data.map(question => (
     <li ... >
       <Question data={question} />
     </li>
   ))}
   ```

3. Moving on to the `HomePage` component in `HomePage.tsx`, let's import the `QuestionList` component. Let's also import the `getUnansweredQuestions` function we created earlier, which returns some mock questions:

   ```
   import { QuestionList } from './QuestionList';
   import { getUnansweredQuestions } from './QuestionsData';
   ```

4. Now, we can place an instance of `QuestionList` in the `HomePage` component JSX inside the outermost `div` tag:

   ```
   <div css={ ... } >
     <div css={ ... } >
       <h2 css={ ... } >
         Unanswered Questions
       </h2>
       <PrimaryButton>Ask a question</PrimaryButton>
   ```

```
    </div>
    <QuestionList data={getUnansweredQuestions()} />
</div>
```

Notice that we pass the array of questions into the `data` prop by calling the `getUnansweredQuestions` function we created and imported earlier in this chapter.

5. If we look at the running app now, we'll see one unanswered question nicely rendered:

Our home page is looking nice now. We are going to finish this section on props by understanding optional and default props, which can make our components more flexible for consumers.

Optional and default props

A prop can be optional so that the consumer doesn't necessarily have to pass it into a component. For example, we could have an optional prop in the `Question` component that allows a consumer to change whether the content of the question is rendered or not. We'll do this now:

1. First, let's import the `gray2` color from our global styles into `Question.tsx`:

```
import { gray2, gray3 } from './Styles';
```

2. We need to add the content into the `Question` component, so add the following code beneath the question title in the JSX:

```
export const Question: FC<Props> = ({ data }) => (
  <div ... >
```

```
<div ... >
  {data.title}
</div>
<div
  css={css`
    padding-bottom: 10px;
    font-size: 15px;
    color: ${gray2};
  `}
>
  {data.content.length > 50
    ? `${data.content.substring(0, 50)}...`
    : data.content}
</div>
<div ... >
  {`Asked by ${data.userName} on
    ${data.created.toLocaleDateString()}
${data.created.toLocaleTimeString()}`}
</div>
</div>
);
```

Here, we have used a JavaScript ternary operator to truncate the content if it is longer than 50 characters.

 A JavaScript ternary is a short way of implementing a conditional statement that results in one of two branches of logic being executed. The statement has three operands. The first operand is a condition, the second is what is returned if the condition is `true`, and the third is what is returned if the condition is `false`. The ternary operator is a popular way of implementing conditional logic in JSX.

3. Create an additional property in the `Props` interface in `Question.tsx` regarding whether the question's content is shown:

```
interface Props {
  data: QuestionData;
  showContent: boolean;
}
```

4. Let's destructure the `showContent` prop in the `Question` component parameter:

```
export const Question: FC<Props> = ({ data, showContent }) =>
```

5. Let's change where we render the question content to the following:

```
<div ... >
  {data.title}
</div>
{showContent && (
  <div ... >
    {data.content.length > 50
      ? `${data.content.substring(0, 50)}...`
      : data.content}
  </div>
)}
<div ...>
  {`Asked by ${data.userName} on
    ${data.created.toLocaleDateString()}
${data.created.toLocaleTimeString()}`}
</div>
```

We have just changed the component to only render the question content if the showContent prop is true using the short-circuit operator, &&.

The short-circuit operator (&&) is another way of expressing conditional logic. It has two operands, with the first being the condition and the second being the logic to execute if the condition evaluates to true. It is often used in JSX to conditionally render an element if the condition is true.

6. If we go back to QuestionList.tsx, we'll see a TypeScript compilation error:

```
(alias) const Question: FunctionComponent<Props>
import Question

Property 'showContent' is missing in type '{ data:
QuestionData; }' but required in type 'Props'. ts(2741)

Question.tsx(9, 3): 'showContent' is declared here.

Quick Fix...   Peek Problem
    <Question data={question} />
```

This is because showContent is a required prop in the Question component and we haven't passed it in. It can be a pain to always have to update consuming components when a prop is added. Couldn't showContent just default to false if we don't pass it in? Well, this is exactly what we are going to do next.

7. Let's start by making the `showContent` prop optional by adding a question mark after the name of the prop:

```
interface Props {
  data: QuestionData;
  showContent?: boolean;
}
```

Optional properties are actually a TypeScript feature. Function parameters can also be made optional by putting a question mark at the end of the parameter name before the type annotation, for example, `(duration?: number)`.

Now, the compilation error in `QuestionList.tsx` has gone away and the app will render the unanswered questions without their content.

What if we wanted to show the question content by default and allow consumers to suppress this if required? We'll do just this using two different approaches to default props.

8. We can set a special object literal called `defaultProps` on the component to define the default values:

```
export const Question: FC<Props> = ({ data, showContent }) => (
  ...
);
Question.defaultProps = {
  showContent: true,
};
```

If we look at the running app, we'll see the question content being rendered as we expect:

9. There is another way of setting default props that's arguably neater. Let's remove the `defaultProps` object literal and specify the default after the destructured component's `showContent` parameter:

```
export const Question: FC<Props> = ({ data, showContent = true })
=> ( ... )
```

This arguably makes the code more readable because the default is right next to its parameter and our eyes don't need to scan right down to the bottom of the function to see that there is a default value for a parameter.

> Destructuring is an ES6 feature and is commonly used in React apps. For more information on destructuring, see `https://developer.mozilla.org/en-US/docs/Web/JavaScript/Reference/Operators/Destructuring_assignment`.

So, our home page is looking good visually, as well as in terms of code structure. There are a couple of components in `HomePage.tsx` that can be extracted so that we can reuse them as we develop the rest of the app. We'll do this next.

Children prop

The `children` prop is a magical prop that all React components automatically have. It can be used to render child nodes. It's magical because it's automatically there, without us having to do anything, as well as being extremely powerful. In the following steps, we'll use the `children` prop when creating `Page` and `PageTitle` components:

1. First, let's create a file called `PageTitle.tsx` with the following content:

```
import styled from '@emotion/styled';

export const PageTitle = styled.h2`
  font-size: 15px;
  font-weight: bold;
  margin: 10px 0px 5px;
  text-align: center;
  text-transform: uppercase;
`;
```

2. Let's create a file called `Page.tsx` with the following content:

```
import { FC } from 'react';
/** @jsx jsx */
import { css, jsx } from '@emotion/core';
```

```
import { PageTitle } from './PageTitle';

interface Props {
  title?: string;
}
export const Page: FC<Props> = ({ title }) => (
  <div
    css={css`
      margin: 50px auto 20px auto;
      padding: 30px 20px;
      max-width: 600px;
    `}
  >
  {title && <PageTitle>{title}</PageTitle>}
  </div>
);
```

Here, the component takes in an optional `title` prop and renders this inside the `PageTitle` component. The page component horizontally centers its content in a 600px space.

3. Now, it's time to use the `children` prop. First, let's destructure it in the component parameters:

```
export const Page: FC<Props> = ({ title, children })
```

Notice that we didn't need to define `children` in our `Props` interface. This is because it's already been made available via the `FC` type.

4. Now, we can reference the `children` prop after the title in the JSX:

```
export const Page: FC<Props> = ({ title, children }) => (
  <div ...>
    {title && <PageTitle>{title}</PageTitle>}
    {children}
  </div>
);
```

In the consuming component, the content nested within the `Page` component will be rendered where we have just placed the `children` prop.

5. Let's move back to `HomePage.tsx` now and import the `Page` and `PageTitle` components:

```
import { Page } from './Page';
import { PageTitle } from './PageTitle';
```

6. Let's use the `Page` and `PageTitle` components in the `HomePage` component:

```
export const HomePage = () => (
  <Page>
    <div
      css={{css`
        display: flex;
        align-items: center;
        justify-content: space-between;
      `}
    >
      <PageTitle>Unanswered Questions</PageTitle>
      <PrimaryButton>Ask a question</PrimaryButton>
    </div>
    <QuestionList data={getUnansweredQuestions()} />
  </Page>
);
```

Notice that we aren't taking advantage of the `title` prop in the `Page` component in `HomePage`. This is because this page needs to have the **Ask a question** button to the right of the title, so we are rendering this within `HomePage`. However, other pages that we implement will take advantage of the `title` prop we have implemented.

So, the `children` prop allows a consumer to render custom content within the component. This gives the component flexibility and makes it highly reusable, as we'll discover as we use the `Page` component throughout our app. Something you may not know, however, is that the `children` prop is actually a function prop. We'll learn about function props in the next section.

Function props

Props can consist of primitive types such as the `boolean showContent` prop we implemented in the `Question` component. Props can also be objects and arrays as we have experienced in the `Question` and `QuestionList` components. This in itself is powerful. However, props can also be functions, which allows us to implement components that are extremely flexible.

Using the following steps, we are going to implement a function prop on the `QuestionList` component that allows the consumer to render the question as an alternative to `QuestionList` rendering it:

1. In `QuestionList.tsx`, add a `renderItem` function prop to the `Props` interface, as follows:

   ```
   interface Props {
     data: QuestionData[];
     renderItem?: (item: QuestionData) => JSX.Element;
   }
   ```

   So, the `renderItem` prop is a function that takes in a parameter containing the question and returns a JSX element. Notice that we have made this an optional prop so that our app will continue to run just as it was before.

2. Let's destructure the function parameters into a `renderItem` variable:

   ```
   export const QuestionList: FC<Props> = ({ data, renderItem }) => (
   ... )
   ```

3. Now, we can call the `renderItem` function prop in the JSX if it has been passed and, if not, render the `Question` component:

   ```
   {data.map(question => (
     <li ... >
       {renderItem ? renderItem(question) : <Question data={question} />}
     </li>
   ))}
   ```

   Notice that we use `renderItem` in the ternary condition, even though it isn't a boolean.

    Conditions in `if` statements and ternaries will execute the second operand if the condition evaluates to **truthy**, and the third operand if the condition evaluates to **falsy**. `true` is only one of many truthy values. In fact, `false`, `0`, `""`, `null`, `undefined`, and `NaN` are falsy values and everything else is truthy.

   So, `renderItem` will be truthy and will execute if it has been passed as a prop.

4. Our app will render the unanswered questions, just like it did before, by rendering the `Question` component. Let's try our `renderItem` prop out by opening `HomePage.tsx` and adding the `Question` interface to the import statement from `Data`:

```
import { getUnansweredQuestions, QuestionData } from
'./QuestionsData';
```

5. Next, let's create a function to render the question just above the `HomePage` component:

```
const renderQuestion = (question: QuestionData) =>
  <div>{question.title}</div>;
```

6. Now, we can pass this function into the `renderItem` prop on `QuestionList` in the `HomePage` JSX:

```
<QuestionList
  data={getUnansweredQuestions()}
  renderItem={renderQuestion}
/>
```

If we look at the running app, we'll see this in effect:

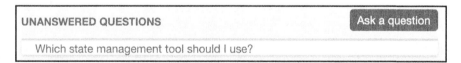

 The pattern of implementing a function prop to allow consumers to render an internal piece of the component is often referred to as a **render prop**. It makes the component extremely flexible and useable in many different scenarios.

7. This doesn't look quite a good as it did previously, so we won't pass the `renderItem` prop. Let's have `QuestionList` take back control of rendering the questions:

```
<QuestionList data={getUnansweredQuestions()} />
```

8. To complete this section, let's remove the `renderQuestion` function from `HomePage.tsx`, as well as the imported `QuestionData` interface, now that we aren't using them anymore.

We can already see that function props are extremely powerful. We'll use these again when we cover handling events later in this chapter. Before we look at events, we are going to cover another fundamental part of a component, which is state.

Implementing component state

Components can use what is called **state** to have the component rerender when a variable in the component changes. This is crucial for implementing interactive components. For example, when filling out a form, if there is a problem with a field value, we can use state to render information about that problem. State can also be used to implement behavior when external things interact with a component, such as a web API. We are going to do this in this section after changing the getUnansweredQuestions function in order to simulate a web API call.

Changing getUnansweredQuestions so that it's asynchronous

The getUnansweredQuestions function doesn't simulate a web API call very well because it isn't asynchronous. In this section, we'll change this. Follow these steps to do so:

1. Open QuestionsData.ts and create an asynchronous wait function that we can use in our getUnansweredQuestions function:

```
const wait = (ms: number): Promise<void> => {
 return new Promise(resolve => setTimeout(resolve, ms));
};
```

This function will wait asynchronously for the number of milliseconds we pass into it. The function uses the native JavaScript setTimeout function internally, so that it returns after the specified number of milliseconds.

Notice the function returns a Promise object.

 A promise is a JavaScript object that represents the eventual completion (or failure) of an asynchronous operation and its resulting value. The Promise type in TypeScript is like the Task type in .NET.

Notice the `<void>` after the `Promise` type in the return type annotation. Angle brackets after a TypeScript type indicate that this is a generic type.

Generic types are a mechanism for allowing the consumer's own type to be used in the internal implementation of the generic type. The angle brackets allow the consumer type to be passed in as a parameter. Generics in TypeScript is very much like generics in .NET.

We are passing a `void` type into the generic `Promise` type. But what is the `void` type?

The `void` type is another TypeScript-specific type that is used to represent a non-returning function. So, `void` in TypeScript is like `void` in .NET.

2. Now, we can use the `wait` function in our `getUnansweredQuestions` function to wait half a second:

```
export const getUnansweredQuestions = async ():
Promise<QuestionData[]> => {
  await wait(500);
  return questions.filter(q => q.answers.length === 0);
};
```

Notice the `await` keyword before the call to the `wait` function and the `async` keyword before the function signature.

`async` and `await` are two JavaScript keywords we can use to make asynchronous code read almost identically to synchronous code. `await` stops the next line from executing until the asynchronous statement has completed, while `async` simply indicates that the function contains asynchronous statements. So, these keywords are very much like `async` and `await` in .NET.

We return a `Promise<QuestionData[]>` rather than `QuestionData[]` because the function doesn't return the questions straight away. Instead, it returns the questions eventually.

3. So, the `getUnansweredQuestions` function is now asynchronous. If we open `HomePage.tsx`, which is where this function is consumed, we'll see a compilation error:

```
<Page>
  <div
    css={css`
      display: flex;
      align-item  (JSX attribute) Props.data: QuestionData[]
      justify-co
      `}           Type 'Promise<QuestionData[]>' is missing the following properties from type 'QuestionData[]': length,
    >             pop, push, concat, and 28 more. ts(2740)
    <PageTitle>U  QuestionList.tsx(9, 3): The expected type comes from property 'data' which is declared here on type
    <PrimaryButt  'IntrinsicAttributes & Props & { children?: ReactNode; }'
  </div>         Quick Fix... Peek Problem
  <QuestionList data={getUnansweredQuestions()} />
</Page>
```

This is because the return type of the function has changed and no longer matches what we defined in the `QuestionList` props interface.

4. For now, let's comment the instance of `QuestionList` out so that our app compiles:

```
{/* <QuestionList data={getUnansweredQuestions()} /> */}
```

Lines of code can be commented out in Visual Studio Code by highlighting the lines and pressing *CTRL+/* (forward slash).

Eventually, we're going to change `HomePage` so that we store the questions in the local state and then use this value in the local state to pass to `QuestionList`. To do this, we need to invoke `getUnansweredQuestions` when the component is first rendered and set the value that's returned to state. We'll do this in the next section.

Using useEffect to execute logic

So, how do we execute logic when a function-based component is rendered? Well, we can use a `useEffect` hook in React, which is what we are going to do in the following steps:

1. Let's add an import statement to import the `useEffect` function from React into `HomePage.tsx`:

```
import { useEffect } from 'react';
```

2. We need to change `HomePage` so that it has an explicit return statement since we want to write some JavaScript logic in the component, as well as return JSX:

```
export const HomePage = () => {
  return (
    <Page>
      . . .
    </Page>
  );
};
```

3. Now, we can call the `useEffect` hook before we return the JSX:

```
export const HomePage = () => {
  useEffect(() => {
  console.log('first rendered');
  }, []);
   return (
     . . .
   );
};
```

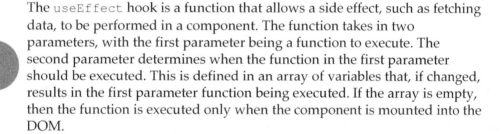

The `useEffect` hook is a function that allows a side effect, such as fetching data, to be performed in a component. The function takes in two parameters, with the first parameter being a function to execute. The second parameter determines when the function in the first parameter should be executed. This is defined in an array of variables that, if changed, results in the first parameter function being executed. If the array is empty, then the function is executed only when the component is mounted into the DOM.

So, we output **first rendered** into the console when the `HomePage` component is first rendered.

4. In the running app, let's open the browser developer tools and inspect the console:

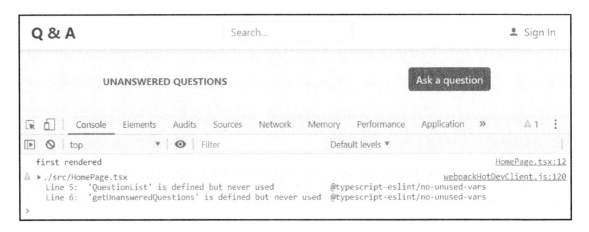

So, our code is executed when the component is first rendered, which is great.

Note that we shouldn't worry about the ESLint warnings about the unused `QuestionList` component and `getUnansweredQuestions` variable because these will be used when we uncomment the reference to the `QuestionList` component.

Using useState to implement component state

The time has come to implement state in the `HomePage` component so that we can store any unanswered questions. But how do we do this in function-based components? Well, the answer is to use another React hook called `useState`. Follow the steps listed in `HomePage.tsx` to do this:

1. Add the `useState` hook to the React import and the `QuestionData` interface to the `QuestionsData` import:

```
import { useEffect, useState } from 'react';
...
import {
  getUnansweredQuestions,
  QuestionData
} from './QuestionsData';
```

2. We'll use this hook just above the `useEffect` statement in the `HomePage` component to declare the state variable:

```
const [questions, setQuestions]
  = useState<QuestionData[] | null>(null);

useEffect(() => {
  console.log('first rendered');
}, []);
```

The `useState` function returns an array containing the state variable in the first element and a function to set the state in the second element. The initial value of the state variable is passed into the function as a parameter. The TypeScript type for the state variable can be passed to the function as a generic type parameter.

Notice that we have destructured the array that's returned from `useState` into a state variable called `questions`, which is initially `null`, and a function to set the state called `setQuestions`.

We can destructure arrays to unpack their contents, just like we did previously with objects.

Notice that we have also used a union type for the type of the `questions` state variable.

A **union type** is a way of specifying that a type can be one of multiple types. The different types in the union are separated by a pipe character (|).

So, the type of the `questions` state variable is an array of `QuestionData` or `null`.

3. Let's add a second piece of state called `questionsLoading` to indicate whether the questions are being fetched:

```
const [questions, setQuestions] = useState<QuestionData[] |
null>(null);
const [questionsLoading, setQuestionsLoading] = useState(true);
```

We have initialized this state to `true` because the questions are being fetched immediately in the first rendering cycle. Notice that we haven't passed a type in the generic parameter. This is because, in this case, TypeScript can cleverly infer that this is a `boolean` state from the default value, `true`, that we passed into the `useState` parameter.

4. Now, we need to set these pieces of state when we fetch the unanswered questions. First, we need to call the `getUnansweredQuestions` function asynchronously in the `useEffect` hook. Let's add this and remove the `console.log` statement:

```
useEffect(() => {
  const questions = await getUnansweredQuestions();
});
```

We immediately get a compilation error:

```
                         [ts] 'await' expression is only allowed within an async function.
useEffect(() => {            [1308]
  const questions = await getUnansweredQuestions();
});
```

5. This error has occurred because the `useEffect` function callback isn't flagged as `async`. So, let's try to make it `async`:

```
useEffect(async () => {
  const questions = await getUnansweredQuestions();
});
```

Unfortunately, we get another error:

```
            [ts]
            Argument of type '() => Promise<void>' is not assignable to paramet
            er of type 'EffectCallback'.
              Type 'Promise<void>' is not assignable to type 'void | (() => voi
            d)'.
                Type 'Promise<void>' is not assignable to type '() => void'.
                  Type 'Promise<void>' provides no match for the signature '():
            void'. [2345]

            function(): Promise<void>
useEffect(async () => {
  const questions = await getUnansweredQuestions();
});
```

Unfortunately, we can't specify an asynchronous callback in the useEffect parameter.

6. Instead, we can create a function that calls getUnansweredQuestions asynchronously and call this function within the useEffect callback function:

```
useEffect(() => {
  const doGetUnansweredQuestions = async () => {
    const unansweredQuestions = await getUnansweredQuestions();
  };
  doGetUnansweredQuestions();
});
```

7. Now, we need to set the questions and questionsLoading states when we have retrieved the data:

```
useEffect(() => {
  const doGetUnansweredQuestions = async () => {
    const unansweredQuestions = await getUnansweredQuestions();
    setQuestions(unansweredQuestions);
    setQuestionsLoading(false);
  };
  doGetUnansweredQuestions();
}, []);
```

8. In the HomePage JSX, we can uncomment the QuestionList reference and pass in our question state:

```
<Page>
  <div ... >
    ...
  </div>
  <QuestionList data={questions || []} />
</Page>
```

Notice that we have passed in questions || [] to the data prop.

 || is a logical OR operator and returns the operand before if it is truthy; otherwise, it returns the operand after.

So, if the `questions` state is `null` (a `falsy` value), then an empty array is passed into the `data` prop. Note that an alternative approach would have been to initialize the `questions` state to an empty array, rather than `null`. If we look at the running app, we'll see that the questions are being rendered nicely again.

9. We haven't made use of the `questionsLoading` state yet. So, let's change the `HomePage` JSX to the following:

```
<Page>
  <div ... >
    ...
  </div>
  {questionsLoading ? (
    <div
      css={css`
        font-size: 16px;
        font-style: italic;
      `}
    >
      Loading...
    </div>
  ) : (
    <QuestionList data={questions || []} />
  )}
</Page>
```

Here, we are rendering a **Loading...** message while the questions are being fetched. Our home page will render nicely again in the running app and we should see a **Loading...** message while the questions are being fetched.

10. Before we move on, let's take some time to start to understand when components are rerendered. Still in `HomePage.tsx`, let's add the following statement before the `return` statement:

```
useEffect(() => {
  ...
}, []);

console.log('rendered');
return ...
```

Every time the `HomePage` component is rendered, we'll see a rendered message in the console:

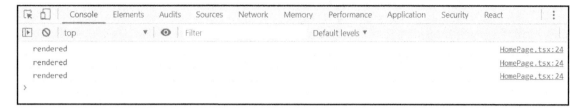

So, the component is rerendered twice after the initial render. What is causing this rerender to occur? React components are rerendered whenever their states change. In the `HomePage` component, the state changes twice in the initial render in the `useEffect` hook when the `questions` and `questionsLoading` states are set. This results in the `HomePage` component being rendered three times when the home page is loaded.

11. Let's remove the `console.log` statement before continuing.

So, we are starting to understand how we can use state to control what is rendered when external things such as users or a web API interact with components. A key point that we need to take away is that when we change state in a component, React will automatically rerender the component.

The `HomePage` component is what is called a **container** component, with `QuestionList` and `Question` being **presentational** components. Container components are responsible for how things work, fetching any data from a web API, and managing state. Presentational components are responsible for how things look. Presentational components receive data via their props and also have property event handlers so that their containers can manage user interactions.

Structuring a React app into a container and presentational components often allows presentation components to be used in different scenarios. Later in this book, we'll see that we can easily reuse `QuestionList` on other pages in our app.

In the next section, we are going to learn how to implement logic when users interact with components using events.

Handling events

JavaScript events are invoked when a user interacts with a web app. For example, when a user clicks a button, a `click` event will be raised from that button. We can implement a JavaScript function to execute some logic when the event is raised. This function is often referred to as an **event listener**.

 In JavaScript, event listeners are attached to an element using its `addEventListener` method and removed using its `removeEventListener` method.

React allows us to declaratively attach events in JSX using function props, without the need to use `addEventListener` and `removeEventListener`. In this section, we are going to implement a couple of event listeners in React.

Handling a button click event

In this section, we are going to implement an event listener on the **Ask a question** button in the `HomePage` component. Follow these steps to do so:

1. Open `HomePage.tsx` and add a `click` event listener to the `PrimaryButton` instance in the JSX:

```
<PrimaryButton onClick={handleAskQuestionClick}>
  Ask a question
</PrimaryButton>
```

 Event listeners in JSX can be attached using a function prop that is named with `on` before the native JavaScript event name in camel case. So, a native `click` event can be attached using an `onClick` function prop. React will automatically remove the event listener for us before the element is destroyed.

2. Let's implement the `handleAskQuestionClick` function, just above the `return` statement in the `HomePage` component:

```
const handleAskQuestionClick = () => {
  console.log('TODO - move to the AskPage');
};

return ...
```

3. If we click on the **Ask a question** button in the running app, we'll see the following message in the console:

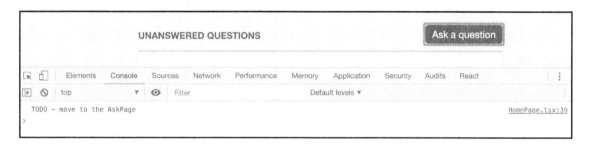

So, handling events in React is super easy! In Chapter 4, *Routing with React Router*, we'll finish off the implementation of the handleAskQuestionClick function and navigate to the page where a question can be asked.

Handling an input change event

In this section, we are going to handle the change event on the input element and interact with the event parameter in the event listener. Follow these steps to do so:

1. Open Header.tsx and add a change event listener to the input element in the JSX:

```
<input
  type="text"
  placeholder="Search..."
  onChange={handleSearchInputChange}
  css={ ... }
/>
```

2. Let's change the Header component so that it has an explicit return statement and implement the handleSearchInputChange function just above it:

```
export const Header = () => {
  const handleSearchInputChange = (e:
ChangeEvent<HTMLInputElement>)
    => {
    console.log(e.currentTarget.value);
  };
  return ( ... );
};
```

Notice the type of annotation for the event parameter. This ensures the interactions with the event parameter are strongly-typed.

 To find a list of all the available events, along with their corresponding types, take a look in the `index.d.ts` file, which can be found in the `node_modules/@types/react` folder.

3. We need to import the `ChangeEvent` type from React for the app to compile:

```
import { ChangeEvent } from 'react';
```

4. If we type something into the search box in the running app, we'll see each change in the console:

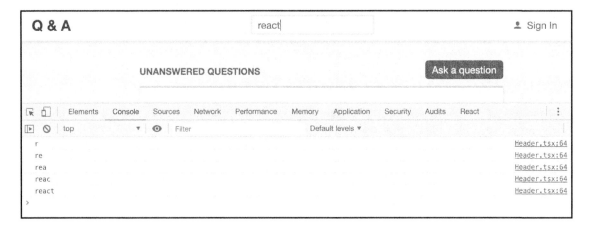

In this section, we've learned that we can implement strongly-typed event listeners, which will help us avoid making mistakes when using the event parameter. We'll finish off the implementation of the search input in `Chapter 5`, *Working with Forms*.

Before we finish this chapter, we are going to deepen our understanding of when components are rendered and how we can optimize this.

Rendering optimization

Earlier in this chapter, we saw that a React component is rerendered when its state changes. A component is also rerendered when its props change. It is important to understand that child components are rerendered when their parent component re-renders. So, changing some state could be an expensive change if there are lots of components that contain lots of elements that get rerendered as a result.

In this section, we are going to force one of the components we have implemented to be rendered multiple times unnecessarily. Then, we'll optimize it. Follow these steps to do so:

1. In `QuestionList.tsx`, change the `QuestionList` component so that it has an explicit `return` statement and add a statement to output that the component is rendering in the console:

   ```
   export const QuestionList: FC<Props> = ({ data, renderItem }) => {
     console.log('Rendering QuestionList', data, renderItem);
     return (
       ...
     );
   };
   ```

2. If we refresh the running app, we'll see that this component is only rendered once, which is great.

3. Let's implement some state and change it in its parent component, that is, `HomePage`. We are going to implement a counter that increments when the **Ask a question** button is clicked. Let's start in `HomePage.tsx` by implementing the state for the counter:

   ```
   const [questions, setQuestions] = useState<QuestionData[] |
   null>(null);
   const [questionsLoading, setQuestionsLoading] = useState(true);
   const [count, setCount] = useState(0);
   ```

4. Now, we can increment the state when the **Ask a question** button is clicked:

   ```
   const handleAskQuestionClick = () => {
     setCount(count + 1);
     console.log('TODO - move to the AskPage');
   };
   ```

5. Let's go to the running app and click the **Ask a question** button. Here, we can see that the `QuestionList` component has been rerendered:

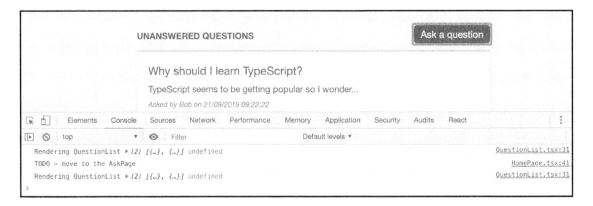

6. So, the `QuestionList` component is being rerendered unnecessarily. How can we prevent these unnecessary rerenders? Well, the answer is to use a React function called `memo`. Let's give this a try by importing it into `QuestionList.tsx`:

```
import { FC, memo } from 'react';
```

7. Now, we need to wrap the `QuestionList` component with the `memo` function:

```
export const QuestionList: FC<Props> = memo(({ data, renderItem })
=> {
  console.log('Rendering QuestionList', data, renderItem);
  return (
    ...
  );
});
```

8. In the running app, click the **Ask a question** button a few times. We will see that the `QuestionList` component is not being rendered now:

The memo function ensures that the component that's passed into it only rerenders when its props change.

So, given how simple this is, shouldn't we just wrap all our function components with memo? No! There is a performance cost when memo determines whether a component has changed. If the component doesn't actually do any unnecessary rendering, using memo would result in the component being slower. So, memo should be used with care and considered only if a component has some of the following traits:

- The component returns the same output for a given set of props
- The component renders often
- The component outputs lots of elements

Before we finish this chapter, we are going to undo the changes we have made because we don't need the counter when the **Ask a question** button is clicked and, therefore, don't need to optimize QuestionList. Follow these steps in order to revert the changes we made in this section:

1. In QuestionList.tsx, remove memo from the import statement and from being wrapped around the QuestionList component.
2. In QuestionList.tsx, remove the console.log statement that informed us that the component was rendering.
3. In HomePage.tsx, remove the count state declaration statement and the call to setCount in the handleAskQuestionClick function so that it looks like this:

```
const handleAskQuestionClick = () => {
  console.log('TODO - move to the AskPage');
};
```

That completes our cleanup.

Summary

In this chapter, we learned that JSX compiles JavaScript nested calls into createElement functions in React, which allows us to mix HTML and JavaScript. We learned that we can create a React component using functions with strongly-typed props passed in as parameters. Now, we know that a prop can be a function, which is how events are handled.

The component state is used to implement behavior when users or other external things interact with it. Due to this, we understand that a component and its children are rerendered when the state is changed and that the memo function can be used to prevent components from rendering unnecessarily.

We also learned that components can be styled using traditional CSS approaches, such as by using Emotion, which helps us scope styles to specific components and arguably helps with component readability.

In the next chapter, we are going to add more pages to our app and learn how to implement routing, which is managed on the client.

Questions

Try to answer the following questions to test your knowledge of this chapter:

1. Does a component rerender when its props change?
2. Does a component rerender when its parents props changes?
3. How can we ensure a component rerenders only when its props change?
4. What function prop would we use to add a `keydown` event listener?
5. A component has the following props interface:

   ```
   interface Props {
     name: string;
     active: boolean;
   }
   ```

   How can we destructure the props parameter and default `active` to `true`?

6. Let's say we have a state called `dateOfBirth`. How can we type this so that it's a `Date`?
7. How could we use the `useEffect` hook to call a synchronous function called `getItems` when a piece of state called `category` changes while passing `category` to `getItems`?

Further reading

The following are some useful links so that you can learn more about the topics that were covered in this chapter:

- **React getting started:** https://reactjs.org/docs/getting-started.html.
- **TypeScript:** https://www.typescriptlang.org/.
- **Arrow functions:** https://developer.mozilla.org/en-US/docs/Web/JavaScript/Reference/Functions/Arrow_functions.
- **const:** https://developer.mozilla.org/en-US/docs/Web/JavaScript/Reference/Statements/const.
- **Emotion:** https://emotion.sh/docs/introduction.
- **Components and Props:** https://reactjs.org/docs/components-and-props.html.
- **JavaScript array map:** https://developer.mozilla.org/en-US/docs/Web/JavaScript/Reference/Global_Objects/Array/map.
- **React lists and keys:** https://reactjs.org/docs/lists-and-keys.html.
- **JavaScript ternary:** https://developer.mozilla.org/en-US/docs/Web/JavaScript/Reference/Operators/Conditional_Operator.
- **useState hook:** https://reactjs.org/docs/hooks-state.html.
- **useEffect hook:** https://reactjs.org/docs/hooks-effect.html.
- **memo:** https://reactjs.org/docs/react-api.html#reactmemo.

4
Routing with React Router

So far, our Q&A app only contains a single page and the time has come to add more pages to the app. React Router is a great library that helps us manage navigating between different pages, so we are going to bring it into our project in this chapter.

In this chapter, we will declaratively define the routes that are available in our app and handle pages that aren't found. We'll implement a page that displays the details of a question, along with its answers, where we will learn how to implement route parameters. We'll begin by implementing the question search feature, where we will learn how to handle query parameters. We will also start to implement the page for asking a question and optimize this so that its JavaScript is loaded on demand rather than when the app loads.

We'll cover the following topics in this chapter:

- Installing React Router with types
- Declaring routes
- Handling routes not found
- Implementing links
- Using route parameters
- Using query parameters
- Lazy loading routes

Technical requirements

We'll use the following tools in this chapter:

- **Visual Studio Code**: We'll use this to edit our React code. This can be downloaded from `https://code.visualstudio.com/`.
- **Node.js and npm**: These can be downloaded from `https://nodejs.org/`. If you already have these installed, make sure that Node.js is at least version 8.2 and that npm is at least version 5.2.
- **Q&A**: We'll start with the Q&A frontend project we finished in `Chapter 3`, *Getting Started with React and TypeScript*. This is available on GitHub at `https://github.com/PacktPublishing/ASP.NET-Core-3-and-React-17`.

All the code snippets in this chapter can be found online at `https://github.com/PacktPublishing/ASP.NET-Core-3-and-React-17`. In order to restore code from a chapter, the source code repository can be downloaded and the relevant folder opened in the relevant editor. If the code is frontend code, then `npm install` can be entered in the Terminal to restore the dependencies.

Check out the following video to see the code in action:

`http://bit.ly/34XoKyz`

Installing React Router with types

In this section, we are going to install React Router with the corresponding TypeScript types by carrying out the following steps:

1. Make sure the frontend project is open in Visual Studio Code and enter the following command to install React Router in the Terminal:

   ```
   > npm install react-router-dom
   ```

2. Install the TypeScript types for React Router using the following command:

   ```
   > npm install @types/react-router-dom --save-dev
   ```

That's it—nice and simple! We'll start to declare the routes in our app in the next section.

Declaring routes

We declare the pages in our app using the `BrowserRouter` and `Route` components. `BrowserRouter` is the top-level component that looks for `Route` components beneath it to determine all the different page paths.

We are going to start this section by creating blank pages that we'll eventually implement throughout this book. Then, we'll declare these pages in our app using `BrowserRouter` and `Route`.

Creating some blank pages

Let's create blank pages for signing in, asking a question, viewing search results, and viewing a question with its answers by carrying out the following steps:

1. Create a file called `SignInPage.tsx` with the following content:

    ```
    import React from 'react';
    import { Page } from './Page';

    export const SignInPage = () => <Page title="Sign In" />;
    ```

    Here, we have used the `Page` component we created in the previous chapter to create an empty page that has the title **Sign In**. We are going to use a similar approach for the other pages we need to create.

2. Create a file called `AskPage.tsx` with the following content:

    ```
    import React from 'react';
    import { Page } from './Page';

    export const AskPage = () => <Page title="Ask a question" />;
    ```

3. Create a file called `SearchPage.tsx` with the following content:

    ```
    import React from 'react';
    import { Page } from './Page';

    export const SearchPage = () => <Page title="Search Results" />;
    ```

4. Create a file called `QuestionPage.tsx` with the following content:

```
import React from 'react';
import { Page } from './Page';

export const QuestionPage = () => <Page>Question Page</Page>;
```

The title on the question page is going to be styled differently, which is why we are not using the `title` prop on the `Page` component. We have simply added some text on the page for the time being so that we can distinguish this page from the other pages.

So, that's our pages created. Now, it's time to define all the routes to these pages.

Creating a component containing routes

We are going to define all of the routes to the pages we created by carrying out the following steps:

1. Open `App.tsx` and add the following import statements:

```
import { BrowserRouter, Route } from 'react-router-dom';
import { AskPage } from './AskPage';
import { SearchPage } from './SearchPage';
import { SignInPage } from './SignInPage';
```

2. In the `App` component's JSX, add `BrowserRouter` as the outermost element:

```
<BrowserRouter>
  <div css={ ... } >
    <Header />
    <HomePage />
  </div>
</BrowserRouter>
```

The `BrowserRouter` component will look for `Route` components nested within it and render the component defined if the route matches the location in the browser.

3. Let's define some `Route` components in the JSX by replacing the previous reference to `HomePage`:

```
<BrowserRouter>
  <div css={ ... } >
    <Header />
    <Route path="/" component={HomePage} />
    <Route path="/search" component={SearchPage} />
    <Route path="/ask" component={AskPage} />
    <Route path="/signin" component={SignInPage} />
  </div>
</BrowserRouter>
```

4. Run the app by entering the `npm start` command in the Visual Studio Code Terminal. We'll see that the home page renders just like it did before, which is great.

5. Now, enter `/search` at the end of the browser location path:

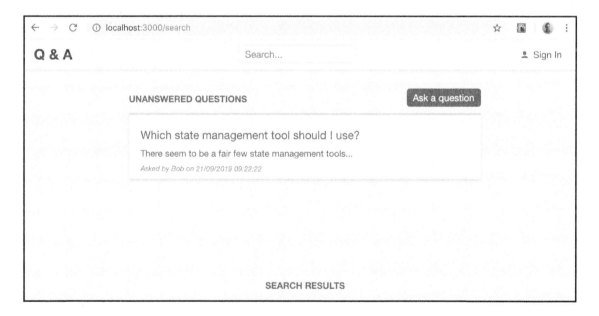

Here, we can see that the `HomePage` component has rendered, as well as the `SearchPage` component. Why has this happened? Well, `BrowserRouter` has matched the browser location path to `/`, as well as `/search` rendering both the `HomePage` and `SearchPage` components.

 By default, `BrowserRouter` does the partial matching to the browser location path and will match and render all the `Route` components it can find.

6. So, how do we resolve this problem? Well, we can tell the `Route` component that renders the `HomePage` component to do an exact match on the location in the browser:

```
<Route exact path="/" component={HomePage} />
```

Here, we use the `exact` Boolean attribute on the `Route` component to only render the specified component when there is an exact match on the path.

 Unlike other attributes, you don't need to specify the value of a Boolean attribute on an HTML element. Its presence on an element automatically means the value is `true` and its absence means the value is `false`.

7. If we look at the running app, we'll see that the search results page renders as we expect:

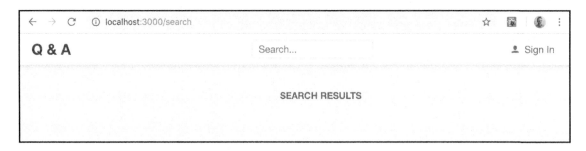

Feel free to visit the other pages as well – they will render fine now.

Redirecting a route

We'd like a /home path to render the HomePage component, as well as the / path. Let's carry out the following steps to implement this by redirecting /home to /:

1. In App.tsx, let's import the Redirect and Switch components from React Router:

   ```
   import { BrowserRouter, Route, Redirect, Switch } from 'react-router-dom';
   ```

2. Now, let's use the Redirect component to redirect the /home path to /:

   ```
   <Redirect from="/home" to="/" />
   <Route exact path="/" component={HomePage} />
   ```

3. The Redirect component needs to be nested inside a Switch component, along with the Route components, in order for it to function correctly. So, let's do this:

   ```
   <Switch>
     <Redirect from="/home" to="/" />
     <Route exact path="/" component={HomePage} />
     <Route path="/search" component={SearchPage} />
     <Route path="/ask" component={AskPage} />
     <Route path="/signin" component={SignInPage} />
   </Switch>
   ```

    The Switch component renders just the first Route or Redirect component that matches the browser location path and doesn't render any other matching routes.

4. In the running app, put the /home location path in the browser. We'll see that it successfully redirects to / and renders the home page as we wanted. The other paths will function just as they did before as well.

So, that's our basic routing configured nicely. What happens if the user enters a path in the browser that doesn't exist in our app? We'll find out in the next section.

Handling routes not found

In this section, we'll handle paths that aren't handled by any of the Route components. By following these steps, we'll start by understanding what happens if we put an unhandled path in the browser:

1. Enter a path that isn't handled in the browser and see what happens:

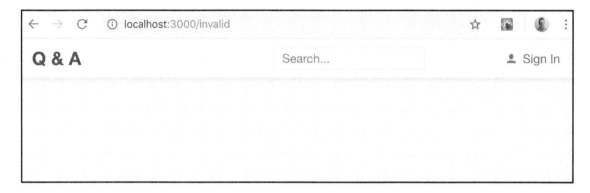

So, nothing is rendered beneath the header when we browse to a path that isn't handled by a Route component. This makes sense if we think about it.

2. We'd like to improve the user experience of routes not found and inform the user that this is the case. Let's add the following highlighted route inside the Switch component:

```
<Switch>
  <Redirect from="/home" to="/" />
  <Route exact path="/" component={HomePage} />
  <Route path="/search" component={SearchPage} />
  <Route path="/ask" component={AskPage} />
  <Route path="/signin" component={SignInPage} />
  <Route component={NotFoundPage} />
</Switch>
```

In order to understand how this works, let's think about what the Switch component does again – it renders the first Route or Redirect component that matches the browser location. If we enter an invalid path, we already know that the existing Route components won't catch it. So, the Route component at the bottom of the Switch component with no path will catch an invalid path.

Note that it is important that we place the no- found route as the last route in the `Switch` component. If we place it above any other route, that route will never be rendered because the not-found route will always result in a match and the `Switch` component only renders the first match.

3. The `NotFoundPage` hasn't been implemented yet, so let's create a file called `NotFoundPage.tsx` with the following content:

```
import React from 'react';
import { Page } from './Page';

export const NotFoundPage = () => <Page title="Page Not Found" />;
```

4. Back in `App.tsx`, let's import the `NotFoundPage` component:

```
import { NotFoundPage } from './NotFoundPage';
```

5. Now, if we enter an `/invalid` path in the browser, we'll see that our `NotFoundPage` component has been rendered:

So, once we understand how the `Switch` component works, implementing a not-found page is very easy. We simply use a `Route` component with no path as the last element inside a `Switch` component.

At the moment, we are navigating to different pages in our app by manually changing the location in the browser. In the next section, we'll learn how to implement links to perform navigation within the app itself.

Implementing links

In this section, we are going to use the `Link` component from React Router to declaratively perform navigation when clicking the app name in the app header. Then, we'll move on to programmatically performing navigation when clicking the **Ask a question** button to go to the ask page.

Using the Link component

At the moment, when we click on **Q and A** in the top-left corner of the app, it is doing an HTTP request that returns the whole React app, which, in turn, renders the home page. We are going to change this by making use of the React Routers `Link` component so that navigation happens in the browser without an HTTP request. We are also going to make use of the `Link` component for the link to the sign-in page as well. We'll learn how to achieve this by following these steps:

1. In `Header.tsx`, import the `Link` component from React Router:

   ```
   import { Link } from 'react-router-dom';
   ```

2. Let's change the anchor tag around the `Q` and `A` text to a `Link` element. The `href` attribute also needs to change to a `to` attribute:

   ```
   <Link
     to="/"
     css={ ... }
   >
     Q & A
   </Link>
   ```

3. Let's also change the sign-in link to the following:

   ```
   <Link
     to="/signin"
     css={ ... }
   >
     <UserIcon />
     <span>Sign In</span>
   </Link>
   ```

4. If we go to the running app and click the **Sign In** link, we'll see the sign-in page rendered. Now, click on **Q and A** in the app header. We will be taken back to the home page, just like we wanted.

5. Do *step 4* again but this time with the browser developer tools open and look at the **Network** tab. We'll find that, when clicking on the **Sign In** and **Q and A** links, no network requests are made.

So, the `Link` component is a great way of declaratively providing client-side navigation options in JSX. The task we performed in the last step confirms that all the navigation happens in the browser without any server requests, which is great for performance.

Navigating programmatically

Sometimes, it is necessary to do navigation programmatically. Follow these steps to programmatically navigate to the ask page when the **Ask a question** button is clicked:

1. Import `RouteComponentProps` from React Router into `HomePage.tsx`:

   ```
   import { RouteComponentProps } from 'react-router-dom';
   ```

   This will give us access to a `history` object, which can be used to programmatically navigate.

    The `history` object in React Router keeps track of the locations that have been visited in the app and contains quite a few different properties and methods. The `push` method pushes a new entry into the history stack and performs navigation to the location that's passed in as a parameter.

2. We are going to use `RouteComponentProps` as the props type for `HomePage`, so let's import the `FC` generic type from React:

   ```
   import { useEffect, useState, FC } from 'react';
   ```

3. Now, we can specify `RouteComponentProps` as the props type for `HomePage` and also destructure the `history` prop:

   ```
   export const HomePage:FC<RouteComponentProps> = ({ history }) => {
   ... }
   ```

4. In `handleAskQuestionClick`, we can replace the `console.log` statement with the navigation now:

   ```
   const handleAskQuestionClick = () => {
     history.push('/ask');
   };
   ```

5. In the running app, if we give this a try and click the **Ask a question** button, it will successfully navigate to the ask page.

So, we can declaratively navigate by using the `Link` component and programmatically navigate using the `history` object in React Router. In the next section, we are going to use the `Link` component again to perform navigation to the question page when a question is clicked on.

Using route parameters

In this section, we are going to define a `Route` component for navigating to the question page. This will contain a variable called `questionId` at the end of the path, so we will need to use what is called a **route parameter**. We'll implement more of the question page content in this section as well.

Adding the question page route

Let's carry out the following steps to add the question page route:

1. In `App.tsx`, import the `QuestionPage` component we created earlier in this chapter:

   ```
   import { QuestionPage } from './QuestionPage';
   ```

2. In the `App` component's JSX, add a `Route` component for navigation to the question page:

   ```
   <Switch>
     <Redirect from="/home" to="/" />
     <Route exact path="/" component={HomePage} />
     <Route path="/search" component={SearchPage} />
     <Route path="/ask" component={AskPage} />
     <Route path="/signin" component={SignInPage} />
     <Route path="/questions/:questionId" component={QuestionPage} />
     <Route component={NotFoundPage} />
   </Switch>
   ```

Note that the path we entered contains `questionId` at the end.

Route parameters are defined in the path with a colon in front of them. The value of the parameter is then available in `RouteComponentProps` in the `params` object, within a `match` object.

3. Let's go to `QuestionPage.tsx` and import `RouteComponentProps` from React Router:

```
import { RouteComponentProps } from 'react-router-dom';
```

4. Import the `FC` generic type from React as well:

```
import React, { FC } from 'react';
```

5. Specify `RouteComponentProps` as the props type for `QuestionPage` and also destructure the `match` prop:

```
interface RouteParams {
  questionId: string;
}
export const QuestionPage: FC<RouteComponentProps<RouteParams>> =
({
  match
}) => <Page>Question Page</Page>;
```

We have defined the type for the route parameters in a `RouteParams` interface and passed this into the generic parameter for `RouteComponentProps`. We have destructured the `match` property that React Router gives the component. This will give us strongly typed access to the `questionId` route parameter.

6. For now, we are going to output the `questionId` on the page as follows in the JSX:

```
<Page>Question Page {match.params.questionId}</Page>;
```

We access the `questionId` route parameter from the `params` property, which can be found in the `match` property we destructured in the last step. We'll come back and fully implement the question page in `Chapter 5`, *Working with Forms*. For now, we are going to link to this page from the `Question` component.

7. So, in `Question.tsx`, add the following import statement to import the `Link` component:

```
import { Link } from 'react-router-dom';
```

8. Now, we can wrap a `Link` around the title text in the `Question` JSX while specifying the path to navigate to:

```
<div
  css={css`
    padding: 10px 0px;
    font-size: 19px;
  `}
>
  <Link
    css={css`
      text-decoration: none;
      color: ${gray2};
    `}
    to={`questions/${data.questionId}`}
  >
    {data.title}
  </Link>
</div>
```

9. Go to the running app and try clicking on an unanswered question. It will successfully navigate to the question page, showing the correct `questionId`:

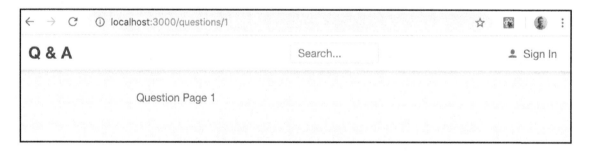

So, we implement routing parameters by defining variables in the route path with a colon in front and then picking the variable up in the `match.params` object in `RouteComponentProps`.

Implementing more of the question page

Let's carry out some more steps to implement the question page a little more:

1. In `QuestionsData.ts`, add a function that will simulate a web request to get a question:

```
export const getQuestion = async (
  questionId: number
): Promise<QuestionData | null> => {
  await wait(500);
  const results
    = questions.filter(q => q.questionId === questionId);
  return results.length === 0 ? null : results[0];
};
```

We have used the array `filter` method to get the question for the passed-in `questionId`.

2. Moving on to `QuestionPage.tsx`, let's import the function we just created, along with the question interface:

```
import { QuestionData, getQuestion } from './QuestionsData';
```

3. We are going to store the question in the state when the component is initially rendered, so let's also import some additional items from React. We're also going to remove the `React` namespace because we will be using Emotion's `jsx` function later:

```
import { FC, useState, Fragment, useEffect } from 'react';
```

4. Let's also import the `css` and `jsx` functions from Emotion and a couple of gray colors from our standard colors:

```
/** @jsx jsx */
import { css, jsx } from '@emotion/core';
import { gray3, gray6 } from './Styles';
```

5. Let's change `QuestionPage` so that it has an explicit return statement and create a state for the question:

```
export const QuestionPage: FC<RouteComponentProps<RouteParams>> =
({
  match
}) => {
  const [question, setQuestion]
```

```
      = useState<QuestionData | null>(null);

   return <Page>Question Page {match.params.questionId}</Page>;
};
```

Note that we are using a union type for the state because the state will be `null` by default while the question is being fetched and also `null` if the question isn't found.

6. We want to call the `getQuestion` function during the initial render, so let's call it inside a call to the `useEffect` hook:

```
export const QuestionPage: FC<RouteComponentProps<RouteParams>> =
({
  match
}) => {
  const [question, setQuestion] = useState<QuestionData |
null>(null);

  useEffect(() => {
    const doGetQuestion = async (questionId: number) => {
      const foundQuestion = await getQuestion(questionId);
      setQuestion(foundQuestion);
    };
    if (match.params.questionId) {
      const questionId = Number(match.params.questionId);
      doGetQuestion(questionId);
    }
  }, [match.params.questionId]);

  return ...
};
```

So, when it's first rendered, the question component will fetch the question and set it in the state that will cause a second render of the component. Note that we use the `Number` constructor to convert `match.params.questionId` from a `string` into a `number`. Also, note that the second parameter in the `useEffect` function has `match.params.questionId` in an array. This is because the function that `useEffect` runs (the first parameter) is dependent on the `match.params.questionId` value and should rerun if this value changes.

7. Let's start to implement the JSX for the `QuestionPage` component by adding a container element for the page and the question title:

```
<Page>
  <div
    css={css`
      background-color: white;
      padding: 15px 20px 20px 20px;
      border-radius: 4px;
      border: 1px solid ${gray6};
      box-shadow: 0 3px 5px 0 rgba(0, 0, 0, 0.16);
    `}
  >
    <div
      css={css`
        font-size: 19px;
        font-weight: bold;
        margin: 10px 0px 5px;
      `}
    >
      {question === null ? '' : question.title}
    </div>
  </div>
</Page>
```

We don't render the title until the `question` state has been set. The `question` state is null while the question is being fetched and it remains null if the question isn't found. Note that we use a triple equals (===) to check whether the `question` variable is `null` rather than a double equals (==).

 When using triple equals (===), we are checking for strict equality. This means both the type and the value we are comparing have to be the same. When using a double equals (==), the type isn't checked. Generally, it is good practice to use the triple equals (===) to do a strict equality check.

If we look at the running app, we will see that the question title has been rendered in a nice white card:

8. Let's implement the question content now:

```
<Page>
  <div ... >
    <div ... >
      {question === null ? '' : question.title}
    </div>
    {question !== null && (
      <Fragment>
        <p
          css={css`
            margin-top: 0px;
            background-color: white;
          `}
        >
          {question.content}
        </p>
      </Fragment>
    )}
  </div>
</Page>
```

So, we output the content if the question state has been set. Note that this is nested within a `Fragment` component—what is this for?

In React, a component can only return a single element. This rule applies to conditional rendering logic where there can be only a single parent React element being rendered. React `Fragment` allows us to work around this rule because we can nest multiple elements within it without creating a DOM node.

We can see the problem that `Fragment` solves if we try to return two elements after the short circuit operator:

```
49            {question !== null && (
50              <p
51                css={css
52                  margin-top: 0px;
53                  background-color: white;
54                }
55              >
56                {question.content}
57              </p>
58              <span>2nd element</span>
59            )}
```

```
PROBLEMS  3     OUTPUT   DEBUG CONSOLE   TERMINAL          1: node          ▼   ✚  ▥  🗑  ∧  ✕

Failed to compile.

./src/QuestionPage.tsx
  Line 59:  Parsing error: JSX expressions must have one parent element
```

9. Let's add when the question was asked and who asked it into the `Fragment`:

```
{question !== null && (
  <Fragment>
    <p ... >
      {question.content}
    </p>
    <div
      css={css`
        font-size: 12px;
        font-style: italic;
        color: ${gray3};
      `}
    >
      {`Asked by ${question.userName} on
${question.created.toLocaleDateString()}
${question.created.toLocaleTimeString()}`}
    </div>
  </Fragment>
)}
```

Now, all the details of the question will render in a nice white card in the running app on the question page:

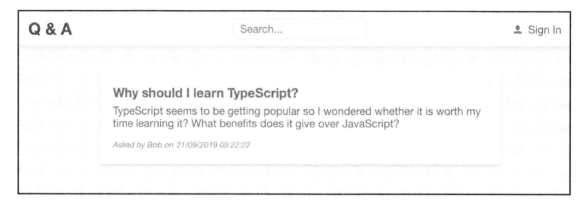

So, the question page is looking nice now. We aren't rendering any answers yet though, so let's look at that next.

Creating an AnswerList component

Follow these steps to create a component that will render a list of answers:

1. Create a new file called `AnswerList.tsx` with the following `import` statements:

```
import { FC } from 'react';
import { AnswerData } from './QuestionsData';
/** @jsx jsx */
import { css, jsx } from '@emotion/core';
import { Answer } from './Answer';
import { gray5 } from './Styles';
```

So, we are going to use an unordered list to render the answers without the bullet points. We have referenced a component, `Answer`, that we'll create later in these steps.

2. Let's define the interface so that it contains a `data` prop for the array of answers:

```
interface Props {
  data: AnswerData[];
}
```

3. Let's create the `AnswerList` component, which outputs the answers:

```
export const AnswerList: FC<Props> = ({ data }) => (
  <ul
    css={css`
      list-style: none;
      margin: 10px 0 0 0;
      padding: 0;
    `}
  >
    {data.map(answer => (
      <li
        css={css`
          border-top: 1px solid ${gray5};
        `}
        key={answer.answerId}
      >
        <Answer data={answer} />
      </li>
    ))}
  </ul>
);
```

Each answer is output in an unordered list in an `Answer` component, which we'll implement next.

4. Let's move on and implement the `Answer` component by creating a file called `Answer.tsx` with the following import statements:

```
import { FC } from 'react';
/** @jsx jsx */
import { css, jsx } from '@emotion/core';
import { AnswerData } from './QuestionsData';
import { gray3 } from './Styles';
```

5. The interface for the `Answer` component is simply going to contain the answer data:

```
interface Props {
  data: AnswerData;
}
```

6. Now, the `Answer` component will simply render the answer content, along with who answered it and when it was answered:

```
export const Answer: FC<Props> = ({ data }) => (
  <div
    css={css`
      padding: 10px 0px;
    `}
  >
    <div
      css={css`
        padding: 10px 0px;
        font-size: 13px;
      `}
    >
      {data.content}
    </div>
    <div
      css={css`
        font-size: 12px;
        font-style: italic;
        color: ${gray3};
      `}
    >
      {`Answered by ${data.userName} on
      ${data.created.toLocaleDateString()}
      ${data.created.toLocaleTimeString()}`}
    </div>
  </div>
);
```

7. Let's go back to `QuestionPage.tsx` and import `AnswerList`:

```
import { AnswerList } from './AnswerList';
```

8. Now, we can add `AnswerList` to the `Fragment` element:

```
{question !== null && (
  <Fragment>
    <p ... >
      {question.content}
    </p>
    <div ... >
      {`Asked by ${question.userName} on
    ${question.created.toLocaleDateString()}
    ${question.created.toLocaleTimeString()}`}
    </div>
    <AnswerList data={question.answers} />
```

```
        </Fragment>
    )}
```

If we look at the running app on the question page at `questions/1`, we'll see the answers nicely rendered:

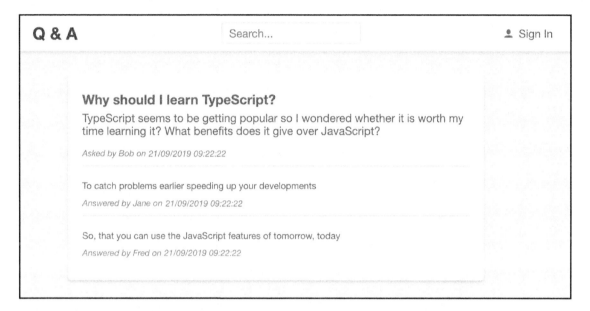

That completes the work we need to do on the question page in this chapter. However, we need to allow users to submit answers to a question, which we'll cover in `Chapter 5`, *Working with Forms*.

Next up, we'll look at how we can work with query parameters with React Router.

Using query parameters

A query parameter is part of the URL that allows additional parameters to be passed into a path. For example, `/search?criteria=typescript` has a query parameter called `criteria` with a value of `typescript`.

In this section, we are going to implement a query parameter on the search page called `criteria`, which will drive the search. We'll implement the search page along the way. Let's carry out these steps to do this:

1. We are going to start in `QuestionsData.ts` by creating a function to simulate a search via a web request:

```
export const searchQuestions = async (
  criteria: string,
): Promise<QuestionData[]> => {
  await wait(500);
  return questions.filter(
    q =>
      q.title.toLowerCase().indexOf(criteria.toLowerCase()) >=
        0 ||
      q.content.toLowerCase().indexOf(criteria.toLowerCase()) >=
        0,
  );
};
```

So, the function uses the array `filter` method and matches the criteria to any part of the question title or content.

2. Let's import this function along with the other items we need into `SearchPage.tsx`. We can also remove the `React` namespace from the existing `import` statement:

```
import { FC, useState, useEffect } from 'react';
import { RouteComponentProps } from 'react-router-dom';
import { Page } from './Page';
import { QuestionList } from './QuestionList';
import { searchQuestions, QuestionData } from './QuestionsData';
/** @jsx jsx */
import { css, jsx } from '@emotion/core';
```

3. Let's add `RouteComponentProps` as the props type for the `SearchPage` component and destructure the `location` object. We'll also change the component so that it uses an explicit return statement:

```
export const SearchPage: FC<RouteComponentProps> = ({
  location,
}) => {
  return <Page title="Search Results" />;
};
```

4. We are going to create some state to hold the matched questions in the search:

```
export const SearchPage: FC<RouteComponentProps> = ({
  location,
}) => {
  const [questions, setQuestions] = useState<QuestionData[]>([]);
  return <Page title="Search Results" />;
};
```

5. Next, we are going to get the `criteria` query parameter from the browser:

```
export const SearchPage: FC<RouteComponentProps> = ({ location })
=> {
  const [questions, setQuestions] = useState<QuestionData[]>([]);

  const searchParams = new URLSearchParams(location.search);
  const search = searchParams.get('criteria') || '';

  return <Page title="Search Results" />;
};
```

 React Router gives us access to all the query parameters in a `search` string inside the `location` object.

The `search` string from React Router for the `/search?criteria=type` path is `?criteria=type`. So, we need to parse this string in order to get the criteria value. We use the native `URLSearchParams` JavaScript function to do this.

6. We are going to invoke the search when the component first renders and when the `search` variable changes using the `useEffect` hook:

```
const searchParams = new URLSearchParams(props.location.search);
const search = searchParams.get('criteria') || '';

useEffect(() => {
  const doSearch = async (criteria: string) => {
    const foundResults = await searchQuestions(criteria);
    setQuestions(foundResults);
  };
  doSearch(search);
}, [search]);
```

7. We are going to render the search criteria under the page title:

```
<Page title="Search Results">
  {search && (
<p
css={css`
font-size: 16px;
font-style: italic;
margin-top: 0px;
`}
>
for "{search}"
</p>
)}
</Page>
```

8. The last task is to use the QuestionList component to render the questions that are returned from the search:

```
<Page title="Search Results">
  {search && (
    <p ... >
      for "{search}"
    </p>
  )}
  <QuestionList data={questions} />
</Page>
```

Our QuestionList component is now used in both the home and search pages with different data sources. The reusability of this component has been made possible because we have followed the container pattern we briefly mentioned in Chapter 3, *Getting Started with React and TypeScript*.

9. In the running app, enter /search?criteria=type in the browser. The search will be invoked and the results will be rendered as we would expect:

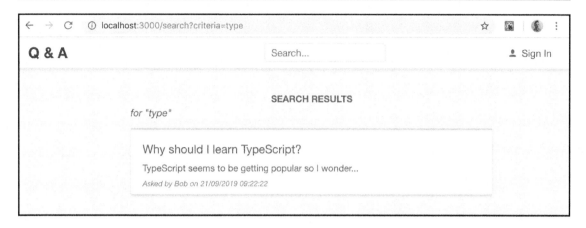

So, we need to do a bit of work beyond what React Router provides in order to handle query parameters, but this is still fairly straightforward with the help of URLSearchParams.

In Chapter 5, *Working with Forms*, we'll wire up the search box in the header to our search form.

In the next section, we'll learn how we can load components on demand.

Lazy loading routes

At the moment, all the JavaScript for our app is loaded when the app first loads. This is fine for small apps, but for large apps, this can have a negative impact on performance. There may be large pages that are rarely used in the app that we want to load the JavaScript for on demand. This process is called **lazy loading**.

We are going to lazy load the ask page in this section. It isn't a great usage of lazy loading because this is likely to be a popular page in our app, but it will help us learn how to implement this. Let's carry out the following steps:

1. First, we are going to add a default export to the AskPage component in AskPage.tsx:

```
export const AskPage = () => <Page title="Ask a question" />;
export default AskPage;
```

2. Let's open `App.tsx` and import the `lazy` function and the `Suspense` component from React:

```
import React, { lazy, Suspense } from 'react';
```

3. Now, we are going to import the `AskPage` component differently after all the other import statements:

```
const AskPage = lazy(() => import('./AskPage'));
```

We can remove the previous import statement for the `AskPage` component. It is important that this is the last import statement in the file because, otherwise, ESLint may complain that the import statements beneath it are in the body of the module.

 The `lazy` function in React lets us render a *dynamic import* as a regular component. A dynamic import returns a promise for the requested module that is resolved after it has been fetched, instantiated, and evaluated.

4. So, the `AskPage` component is being loaded on demand now but the `App` component is expecting this component to be loaded immediately. If we enter the `ask` path in the browser's address bar and press the *Enter* key, we may receive an error with a clue of how to resolve this:

← → C ⓘ localhost:3000/ask ☆

Error: A React component suspended while rendering, but no fallback UI was specified.

Add a <Suspense fallback=...> component higher in the tree to provide a loading indicator or placeholder to display.

5. As suggested by the error message, we are going to use the `Suspense` component we imported into the `App` component JSX earlier. For the `/ask` `Route`, we remove the `component` prop and nest the `Suspense` component as the `Route` child with the `AskPage` component as the child of `Suspense`:

```
<Route path="/ask">
  <Suspense
    fallback={
      <div
        css={{css`
```

```
            margin-top: 100px;
            text-align: center;
          `}
      >
        Loading...
      </div>
    }
  >
    <AskPage />
  </Suspense>
</Route>
```

The `Suspense fallback` prop allows us to render a component while the `AskPage` is loading. So, we are rendering a **Loading...** message while the `AskPage` component is being loaded.

6. Let's go to the running app on the home page and open the browser developer tools by pressing *F12*.

7. On the **Network** tab, let's clear the previous network activity by clicking the *no entry* icon. Then, if we click the **Ask a question** button, we will see confirmation that additional JavaScript has been downloaded in order to render the `AskPage` component:

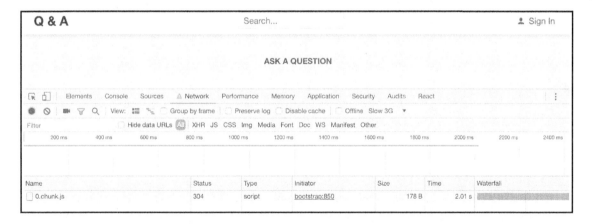

8. The `AskPage` component loads so fast that we are unlikely to see the `Loading` component being rendered. In the Chrome browser developer tools, there is an option to simulate a **Slow 3G** network in the **Network tab**:

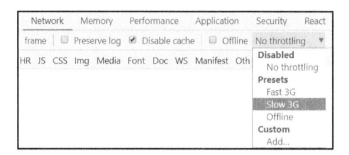

9. If we turn this on, load the app again by pressing *F5* on the home page, and click the **Ask a question** button, we will see the **Loading...** message being rendered temporarily:

In this example, the `AskPage` component is small in size, so this approach doesn't really positively impact performance. However, loading larger components on demand can really help performance, particularly on slow connections.

Summary

React Router gives us a comprehensive set of components for managing the navigation between pages in our app. We learned that the top-level component is `BrowserRouter`, which looks for `Route` components beneath it where we define what components should be rendered for certain paths. We can use the `exact` prop to instruct React Router to do a full match rather than a partial match, which it does by default.

RouteComponentProps gives us access to route parameters and query parameters via the match and location objects, respectively. We discovered that React Router doesn't parse query parameters for us, but can use the native JavaScript URLSearchParams function to do this for us. RouteComponentProps also gives us access to a history object, where we can perform navigation programmatically. The Link component allows us to link to different pages declaratively in JSX.

We learned that the React lazy function, along with its Suspense component, can be used on large components that are rarely used by users to load them on demand. This helps the performance of the startup time of our app.

In the next chapter, we are going to continue building the frontend of the Q&A app, this time focusing on implementing forms.

Questions

The following questions will cement your knowledge of what you have just learned about in this chapter:

1. We have the following routes defined:

```
<BrowserRouter>
  <Route path="/" component={HomePage} />
  <Route path="/search" component={SearchPage} />
</BrowserRouter>
```

Answer the following questions:

- What component(s) will be rendered when the / location is entered in the browser?
- What about when the /search location is entered in the browser?

2. We have the following routes defined:

```
<BrowserRouter>
  <Switch>
    <Route path="/" component={HomePage} />
    <Route path="/search" component={SearchPage} />
  </Switch>
</BrowserRouter>
```

Answer the following questions:

- What component(s) will be rendered when the / location is entered in the browser?
- What about when the /search location is entered in the browser?

3. We have the following routes defined:

```
<BrowserRouter>
  <Switch>
    <Route path="/search" component={SearchPage} />
    <Route path="/" component={HomePage} />
  </Switch>
</BrowserRouter>
```

Answer the following questions:

- What component(s) will be rendered when the / location is entered in the browser?
- What about when the /search location is entered in the browser?

4. In our Q&A app, we want a /login path to navigate to the sign-in page, as well as the /signin path. How can we implement this?

5. We have the following routes defined:

```
<BrowserRouter>
  <Switch>
    <Route path="/search" component={SearchPage} />
    <Route path="/" component={HomePage} />
    <Route component={NotFoundPage} />
  </Switch>
</BrowserRouter>
```

What component(s) will be rendered when the /signin location is entered in the browser?

6. We have the following routes defined:

```
<BrowserRouter>
  <Switch>
    <Route path="/" component={HomePage} />
    <Route path="/search" component={SearchPage} />
    <Route component={NotFoundPage} />
  </Switch>
</BrowserRouter>
```

With the preceding implementation, when a user navigates to the `/search` path or an invalid path such as `/unknown`, the `HomePage` component is rendered.

How can we change the code to render `HomePage` when only the `/` path is entered in the browser?

7. We have the following route defined:

```
<Route path="/users/:userId" component={UserPage} />
```

How can we reference the `userId` route parameter in the `UserPage` component?

Further reading

The following are some useful links for learning more about the topics that were covered in this chapter:

- React Router: `https://reacttraining.com/react-router`
- JavaScript array filter: `https://developer.mozilla.org/en-US/docs/Web/JavaScript/Reference/Global_Objects/Array/filter`
- TypeScript union types: `https://www.typescriptlang.org/docs/handbook/advanced-types.html`
- React fragments: `https://reactjs.org/docs/fragments.html`
- URLSearchParams: `https://developer.mozilla.org/en-US/docs/Web/API/URLSearchParams`
- React lazy: `https://reactjs.org/docs/code-splitting.html#reactlazy`

5
Working with Forms

Forms are an important topic because they are extremely common in the apps we build. In this chapter, we'll learn how to build forms using React-controlled components and discover that there is a fair amount of boilerplate code involved. So, we'll build generic components to help us to build several forms in our app.

Client-side validation is critical to the user experience of the forms we build, so we'll also cover this topic in a fair amount of depth. Submitting the form is also a critical consideration. We'll cover how to handle submission errors as well as success.

We'll cover the following topics in this chapter:

- Understanding controlled components
- Reducing boilerplate code with generic components
- Implementing validation
- Submitting forms

Technical requirements

We'll use the following tools in this chapter:

- **Visual Studio Code**: We'll use this to edit our React code. This can be downloaded and installed from https://code.visualstudio.com/.
- **Node.js** and **npm**: These can be downloaded from https://nodejs.org/. If you already have these installed, make sure that Node.js is at least version 8.2 and that npm is at least version 5.2.
- **Q and A**: We'll start with the Q and A frontend project we finished in Chapter 4, *Routing with React Router*. This is available on GitHub at https://github.com/PacktPublishing/ASP.NET-Core-3-and-React-17.

All of the code snippets in this chapter can be found online at `https://github.com/ PacktPublishing/ASP.NET-Core-3-and-React-17`. To restore code from a chapter, the source code repository can be downloaded and the relevant folder opened in the relevant editor. If the code is frontend code, then `npm install` can be entered in the Terminal to restore the dependencies.

Check out the following video to see the code in action:

`http://bit.ly/2PUrbNQ`

Understanding controlled components

In React, we can use what is called **controlled components** to implement a form. A controlled component has its value synchronized with the state in React. This will make more sense when we've implemented our first controlled component.

Let's open our project in Visual Studio Code and change the search box in our app header into a controlled component by carrying out the following steps:

1. Open `Header.tsx` and add the following imports:

```
import { ChangeEvent, FC, useState } from 'react';
import {
  Link,
  RouteComponentProps,
  withRouter,
} from 'react-router-dom';
```

2. Let's set the props type to `RouteComponentProps` and destructure the `history` and `location` props in the `Header` component:

```
export const Header: FC<RouteComponentProps> = ({
  history,
  location,
}) => {
  const handleSearchInputChange = (
    e: ChangeEvent<HTMLInputElement>,
  ) => { ... }
```

3. We need to wrap the component with the `withRouter` function to get these props passed into it. So, let's do this at the bottom of the file as we export this with the name `HeaderWithRouter`:

```
export const HeaderWithRouter = withRouter(Header);
```

4. In `App.tsx`, we now need to import this wrapped `Header` component:

```
import { HeaderWithRouter as Header } from './Header';
```

5. Back in `Header.tsx`, the default value for the search box is going to be the `criteria` route query parameter. So, let's get this from the destructured `location` object:

```
export const Header: FC<RouteComponentProps> = ({ history, location
}) => {
  const searchParams = new URLSearchParams(location.search);
  const criteria = searchParams.get('criteria') || '';

  const handleSearchInputChange = ...
}
```

6. Let's create some state to store the search value in, defaulting it to the `criteria` variable we have just set:

```
const searchParams = new URLSearchParams(location.search);
const criteria = searchParams.get('criteria') || '';

const [search, setSearch] = useState(criteria);
```

7. Now, let's drive the search box value from this `search` state:

```
<input
  type="text"
  placeholder="Search..."
  value={search}
  onChange={handleSearchChange}
  css={ ... }
/>
```

8. Start the app by running the `npm start` command in Visual Studio Code's Terminal.

9. Try to type something in the search box in the app header.

Nothing seems to happen; something is preventing us from entering the value.

We have just set the value to some React state, so React is now controlling the value of the search box. This is why we no longer appear to be able to type into it.

We are part-way through creating our first controlled input. However, controlled inputs aren't much use if users can't enter anything into them. So, how can we make our `input` editable again? The answer is that we need to listen to changes to the `input` value and update the state accordingly. React will then render the new value from the state.

10. We are already listening to changes with the `handleSearchInputChange` function. So, all we need to do is update the state in this function, replacing the previous `console.log` statement:

```
const handleSearchChange = (e: ChangeEvent<HTMLInputElement>) => {
  setSearch(e.currentTarget.value);
};
```

If we now go to the running app and enter something into the search box, this time, it behaves as expected.

11. We are going to wrap `input` in `form` so that we can eventually invoke the search when the user presses the *Enter* key:

```
<form>
  <input
    type="text"
    placeholder="Search..."
    onChange={handleSearchInputChange}
    value={search}
    css={ ... }
  />
</form>
```

We are going to leave the implementation there for now. We'll implement the form submission later in this chapter in the *Submitting forms* section.

React-controlled components make sense once we understand what is going on. If we were to implement a form with several controlled components, we would have to create the state and a change event listener to update the state for each field. That's quite a lot of boilerplate code to write. Can we not create an abstraction to reduce the amount of repetitive code? Yes! We'll do just this in the next section.

Reducing boilerplate code with generic components

In this section, we are going to create generic `Form` and `Field` components that will take care of the state management we implemented in the last section. This means that we won't have to implement state management for each field in the forms we are going to build. This will dramatically reduce the amount of code required to implement a form.

Creating a Form component

Let's perform the following steps to create a generic `Form` component:

1. Create a new file called `Form.tsx` with the following `import` statements:

   ```
   import { FC, useState } from 'react';
   import { PrimaryButton, gray5, gray6 } from './Styles';
   /** @jsx jsx */
   import { css, jsx } from '@emotion/core';
   ```

2. Let's define `interface` for the form field values:

   ```
   export interface Values {
     [key: string]: any;
   }
   ```

   We haven't used an interface defined in this way before. This is called an **indexable type**.

    An **indexable type** is where the index signature is defined rather than specific properties. The type in the square brackets defines the type for the keys in the object and the type after the colon defines the return type when indexed.

   In our case, the key will be the field name, and the value will be the field value. So, `Values` could be as follows:

   ```
   {
     title: "Why should I learn TypeScript?",
     content: "TypeScript seems to be getting popular so I wondered
     whether it is worth my time learning it? What benefits does it
     give over JavaScript?"
   }
   ```

3. Let's move on to define the props interface, which is going to have a single prop for the **Submit** button caption:

```
interface Props {
  submitCaption?: string;
}
```

4. Let's begin to implement the `Form` function component starting with destructuring the props:

```
export const Form: FC<Props> = ({ submitCaption, children }) =>
  null;
```

Notice that we have included the `children` prop, which we are going to use later to render content nested within the form.

5. Let's create some state for the field value, using the interface we created earlier:

```
export const Form: FC<Props> = ({ submitCaption, children }) => {
  const [values, setValues] = useState<Values>({});
  return null;
};
```

Notice that we set the initial state to an empty object literal.

6. Let's now define the JSX for the form:

```
return (
  <form noValidate={true}>
    <fieldset
      css={css`
        margin: 10px auto 0 auto;
        padding: 30px;
        width: 350px;
        background-color: ${gray6};
        border-radius: 4px;
        border: 1px solid ${gray5};
        box-shadow: 0 3px 5px 0 rgba(0, 0, 0, 0.16);
      `}
    >
      {children}
      <div
        css={css`
          margin: 30px 0px 0px 0px;
          padding: 20px 0px 0px 0px;
          border-top: 1px solid ${gray5};
        `}
      >
```

```
        <PrimaryButton type="submit">
          {submitCaption}
        </PrimaryButton>
      </div>
    </fieldset>
  </form>
);
```

So, we have created a `form` tag that has a standard HTML form validation suppressed because we are going to handle that ourselves later in this chapter.

The form contains a `fieldset` tag that will hold the form content along with a container for our Submit button, which will have a faint horizontal line at the top.

We then render any nested child components before the **Submit** button using the `children` prop.

That completes the `Form` component for the time being.

Creating a Field component

Let's perform the following steps to create a generic `Field` component:

1. Create a new file called `Field.tsx` with the following `import` statements:

```
import { FC } from 'react';
/** @jsx jsx */
import { css, jsx } from '@emotion/core';
import {
  fontFamily,
  fontSize,
  gray5,
  gray2,
  gray6,
} from './Styles';
```

2. Let's define the `Field` component `Props` interface:

```
interface Props {
  name: string;
  label?: string;
  type?: 'Text' | 'TextArea' | 'Password';
}
```

So, we have props for the `name` field, its `label`, and its `type`.

Notice the TypeScript type for the `type` prop. This is a union type of string literals and means that the `type` prop can only be `Text`, `TextArea`, or `Password`.

3. The different field types are going to have lots of CSS properties in common, so we are going to put these in a `baseCSS` variable that we'll reference when we render the field:

```
const baseCSS = css`
  box-sizing: border-box;
  font-family: ${fontFamily};
  font-size: ${fontSize};
  margin-bottom: 5px;
  padding: 8px 10px;
  border: 1px solid ${gray5};
  border-radius: 3px;
  color: ${gray2};
  background-color: white;
  width: 100%;
  :focus {
    outline-color: ${gray5};
  }
  :disabled {
    background-color: ${gray6};
  }
`;
```

4. Let's begin to define the `Field` component now with the props destructured:

```
export const Field: FC<Props> = ({
  name,
  label,
  type = 'Text',
}) => null;
```

Notice that we have defaulted the `type` prop to `Text`.

5. Let's render the `Field` container with the label inside:

```
export const Field: FC<Props> = ({
  name,
  label,
  type = 'Text',
}) => (
  <div
    css={css`
      display: flex;
      flex-direction: column;
```

```
      margin-bottom: 15px;
    `}
  >
    {label && (
      <label
        css={css`
          font-weight: bold;
        `}
        htmlFor={name}
      >
        {label}
      </label>
    )}
  </div>
);
```

Notice how we use the short-circuit syntax to only render the label if the label prop is defined.

6. Let's move on to rendering the input field:

```
<div ... >
  {label && ( ... )}
  {(type === 'Text' || type === 'Password') && (
    <input type={type.toLowerCase()} id={name} css={baseCSS} />
  )}
</div>
```

Notice how we have tied label to input using the htmlFor attribute, which will help our field to be accessible.

7. Let's also render the textarea field:

```
<div ... >
  {label && ( ... )}
  {(type === 'Text' || type === 'Password') && (
    <input type={type.toLowerCase()} id={name} css={baseCSS} />
  )}
  {type === 'TextArea' && (
    <textarea
      id={name}
      css={css`
        ${baseCSS};
        height: 100px;
      `}
    />
  )}
</div>
```

Notice how the `textarea` field composes the base CSS with the height of
`100px` with string literal interpolation.

That completes the `Field` component for the time being.

Sharing state with a React context

The state for field values lives in the `Form` component but is rendered and changed in the
`Field` component. How can the `Form` component share its state with the `Field` component
when `Form` doesn't directly reference `Field`? Well, we could use a React **context**.

Understanding a React context

A React **context** is a way to pass data through the component tree without passing it
through component props. A context is created and provided at the appropriate place in
the component tree for other components lower in the tree to consume:

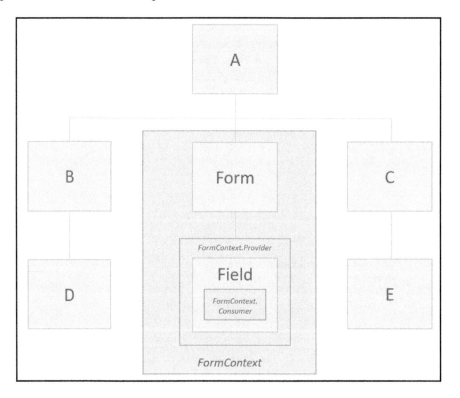

The preceding diagram shows several components in a tree. A context called `FormContext` has been created and *provided* within the `Form` component via the `Provider` component within `FormContext`. Every component beneath `FormContext.Provider` in the component tree can *consume* `FormContext` via the `Consumer` component within `FormContext`. Components A, B, C, D, E, and F cannot consume `FormContext` because they are not beneath `FormContext.Provider`.

Creating a form context

Now that we understand the React context, we are going to create a context for our generic form components. Let's carry out the following steps:

1. Let's start in `Form.tsx` by adding the `createContext` function to the React import statement:

   ```
   import { FC, useState, createContext } from 'react';
   ```

2. Next, we'll create `interface` for our context just below the `Values` interface:

   ```
   interface FormContextProps {
     values: Values;
     setValue?: (fieldName: string, value: any) => void;
   }
   ```

   So, our context will contain the form values and a function to update them.

3. Let's create the context just below this:

   ```
   export const FormContext = createContext<FormContextProps>({
     values: {},
   });
   ```

   Notice that we are required to pass in an initial value for the context, which is why we made the `setValue` function prop optional.

That completes the creation of the form context.

Creating a form context provider

Now that the form context is created, let's use its `Provider` component to give the children components of the form access to it:

```
export const Form: FC<Props> = ({ submitCaption, children }) => {
  const [values, setValues] = useState<Values>({});
```

```
    return (
      <FormContext.Provider
        value={{
          values,
          setValue: (fieldName: string, value: any) => {
            setValues({ ...values, [fieldName]: value });
          },
        }}
      >
        <form noValidate={true}>
          ...
        </form>
      </FormContext.Provider>
    );
  };
```

Notice how we create the new values object using the **spread** syntax (...).

> The **spread syntax** expands the properties in the object that is referenced after the dots. It can also be used on arrays to expand the elements in the array.

So, ...values will expand the values for each field and because we have put [fieldName]: value at the end of the object literal, it will override the previous value from the values object.

Consuming the form context

All of the components beneath the provider can access the context via a Consumer component. Let's use this within the Field component:

1. First, let's import FormContext, useContext, and ChangeEvent from React in the Field component:

```
import { FC, useContext, ChangeEvent } from 'react';
import { FormContext } from './Form';
```

2. We can then reference the context consumer in the JSX:

```
export const Field: FC<Props> = ({ name, label, type = 'Text' }) =>
(
  <FormContext.Consumer>
    {context => (
      <div
```

```
        css={css`
          display: flex;
          flex-direction: column;
          margin-bottom: 15px;
        `}
      >
        ...
      </div>
    )}
  </FormContext.Consumer>
);
);
```

3. At the moment, the `value` of the fields isn't being controlled. We now have access to the value, so let's reference this from the context:

```
{(type === 'Text' || type === 'Password') && (
  <input
    type={type.toLowerCase()}
    id={name}
    value={
      context.values[name] === undefined
        ? ''
        : context.values[name]
    }
    css={baseCSS}
  />
)}
{type === 'TextArea' && (
  <textarea
    id={name}
    value={
      context.values[name] === undefined
        ? ''
        : context.values[name]
    }
    css={css`
      ${baseCSS};
      height: 100px;
    `}
  />
)}
```

Notice that we set the `value` to an empty string if the value from `context` is `undefined`. This is so that the value is always controlled.

4. We are going to clean this up a little by destructuring the `values` property immediately from the `context` parameter:

```
<FormContext.Consumer>
  {({ values }) => (
    <div
      css={ ... }
    >
      {label && ( ... )}
      {(type === 'Text' || type === 'Password') && (
        <input
          type={type.toLowerCase()}
          id={name}
          value={values[name] === undefined ? '' : values[name]}
          css={baseCSS}
        />
      )}
      {type === 'TextArea' && (
        <textarea
          id={name}
          value={values[name] === undefined ? '' : values[name]}
          css={css`
            ${baseCSS};
            height: 100px;
          `}
        />
      )}
    </div>
  )}
</FormContext.Consumer>
```

5. We, of course, need to handle changes to the field. We are going to eventually create a change event handler to do this. First, let's get a reference to the context outside of the JSX in the `Field` component code using the `useContext` function we imported earlier:

```
export const Field: FC<Props> = ({ name, label, type = 'Text' }) =>
{
  const { setValue } = useContext(FormContext);
  return (
    ...
  );
};
```

We've destructured the `setValue` function from the context.

6. We can now add the change handler that will handle the `onChange` event and call the `setValue` function in the context:

```
const { setValue } = useContext(FormContext);
const handleChange = (
  e: ChangeEvent<HTMLInputElement> |
  ChangeEvent<HTMLTextAreaElement>
) => {
  if (setValue) {
    setValue(name, e.currentTarget.value);
  }
};
```

Notice that we have used a union type for the event parameter so that a single strongly typed handler can be used for both the `input` and `textarea`.

Notice also that we need to check that `setValue` isn't `undefined` before we call it. This is because we declared it as optional in the context interface.

7. So, we can reference this handler in the JSX now:

```
{(type === 'Text' || type === 'Password') && (
  <input
    type={type.toLowerCase()}
    id={name}
    value={values[name] === undefined ? '' : values[name]}
    onChange={handleChange}
    css={baseCSS}
  />
)}
{type === 'TextArea' && (
  <textarea
    id={name}
    value={values[name] === undefined ? '' : values[name]}
    onChange={handleChange}
    css={css`
      ${baseCSS};
      height: 100px;
    `}
  />
)}
```

That completes our `Form` and `Field` components for now. Next, we'll use them to start implementing some forms.

Implementing the ask form

It's time to implement the form to ask a question. We'll do this by taking the following steps, leveraging the `Form` and `Field` components we just created:

1. Open `AskPage.tsx` and import our `Form` and `Field` components:

   ```
   import { Form } from './Form';
   import { Field } from './Field';
   ```

2. Let's use these components to create a form:

   ```
   <Page title="Ask a Question">
     <Form submitCaption="Submit Your Question">
       <Field name="title" label="Title" />
       <Field name="content" label="Content" type="TextArea" />
     </Form>
   </Page>
   ```

   So, the form will contain fields for the question title and content and the submit button will have the caption **Submit Your Question**.

3. Let's give this a try in the running app by clicking the **Ask a question** button on the home page:

   Our form renders just as we expect.

The generic Form and Field components really made that job pretty easy. Let's try implementing another form next.

Implementing the answer form

Let's implement an answer form on the question page using the following steps:

1. Open `QuestionPage.tsx` and import our Form and Field components:

   ```
   import { Form } from './Form';
   import { Field } from './Field';
   ```

2. Let's create our form in the JSX just beneath the list of answers:

   ```
   <Fragment>
     <p ... >
       {question.content}
     </p>
     <div ... >
       {`Asked by ${question.userName} on
   ${question.created.toLocaleDateString()}
   ${question.created.toLocaleTimeString()}`}
     </div>
     <AnswerList data={question.answers} />
     <div
       css={css`
         margin-top: 20px;
       `}
     >
       <Form submitCaption="Submit Your Answer">
         <Field name="content" label="Your Answer" type="TextArea" />
       </Form>
     </div>
   </Fragment>
   ```

So, the form will contain a single field for the answer content and the submit button will have the caption **Submit Your Answer**.

3. Let's give this a try in the running app by clicking a question on the home page:

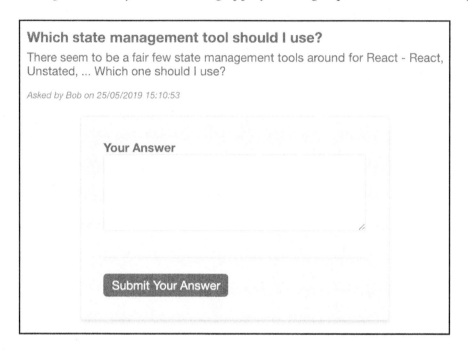

Our form renders just as we expect.

Our forms are looking good but there is no validation yet. For example, we could submit a blank answer to a question. We will enhance our forms with validation in the next section.

Implementing validation

Including validation on a form improves the user experience, by giving them immediate feedback on whether the information entered is valid. In this section, we are going to add validation rules to our generic components for ensuring a field has a value as well as ensuring a minimum number of characters have been entered. After we have enhanced our generic components, we'll implement validation in our question and answer forms.

Adding validation rules to the Form component

We are going to add validation rules to the Form component so that they can be consumed like in the following example with a validationRules prop:

```
<Form
  validationRules={{
    title: [{ validator: required }, { validator: minLength, arg:
10
    }],
    content: [{ validator: required }, { validator: minLength, arg:
    50 }],
  }}
  ...
>
  ...
</Form>
```

The validationRules prop will allow consumers to define an array of validation rules for each field in the form. A validation rule references a function that will do the necessary check on the value in the field. We will refer to these functions as *validators*.

We'll carry out the following steps to implement the validationRules prop in the Form component:

1. Let's start by creating a type for a validator just beneath FormContext in Form.tsx:

   ```
   type Validator = (value: any, args?: any) => string;
   ```

   This is a TypeScript **type alias**.

   In simple terms, a **type alias** creates a new name for a type. To define a type alias, we use the type keyword, followed by the alias name, followed by the type that we want to alias.

   When we create our validators, we can use a Validator type annotation rather than the more lengthy (fieldName: string, values: Values, args?: any) => string.

   So, a validator will be a function that takes in the field value as well as an optional additional parameter. The validator will return an error message if the check fails and an empty string if it passes.

2. Let's create our first validator now for checking that a field is populated:

```
export const required: Validator = (value: any): string =>
  value === undefined || value === null || value === ''
    ? 'This must be populated'
    : '';
```

We use a JavaScript ternary to check whether the value is populated and return the error message if it isn't.

3. Let's create another validator that checks whether the number of characters is a value is beyond a certain amount:

```
export const minLength: Validator = (
  value: any,
  length: number,
): string =>
  value && value.length < length
    ? `This must be at least ${length} characters`
    : '';
```

Notice that we use the optional parameter for the minimum number of characters.

4. Let's now add a prop to allow validation rules to be defined on the form:

```
interface Validation {
  validator: Validator;
  arg?: any;
}

interface ValidationProp {
  [key: string]: Validation | Validation[];
}

interface Props {
  submitCaption?: string;
  validationRules?: ValidationProp;
}
```

So, we can specify a single rule or an array of rules. A rule references a validator function and an optional argument to be passed into it.

5. Let's destructure the `validationRules` prop in the component function parameter:

```
export const Form: FC<Props> = ({
  submitCaption,
  children,
  validationRules
}) => { ... }
```

That's the `validationRules` prop complete.

Next, we'll track the validation error messages in preparation for rendering them on the page.

Tracking validation errors with state

We are going to track the validation error messages in the state as the user completes the form and fields become valid or invalid. Later on, we'll be able to render the error messages to the screen. We are going to store the validation errors in the `Form` component state as follows:

1. Let's start by creating `interface` for the errors in `Form.tsx` after the `Values` interface:

```
export interface Errors {
  [key: string]: string[];
}
```

This is an indexable type where an array of validation error messages is associated with a field name.

2. We are only going to render a validation error if the field has been *touched* and lost focus, so we need to track whether this is the case for each field. Let's create an interface for this:

```
export interface Touched {
  [key: string]: boolean;
}
```

3. Next, we'll add the validation errors and whether a field has been touched to the form context along with functions to set them:

```
interface FormContextProps {
  values: Values;
  setValue?: (fieldName: string, value: any) => void;
  errors: Errors;
  validate?: (fieldName: string) => void;
  touched: Touched;
  setTouched?: (fieldName: string) => void;
}

export const FormContext = createContext<IFormContext>({
  values: {},
  errors: {},
  touched: {}
});
```

4. Let's add the field validation errors and whether fields have been touched to the `Form` component state:

```
const [values, setValues] = useState<Values>({});
const [errors, setErrors] = useState<Errors>({});
const [touched, setTouched] = useState<Touched>({});
```

5. We can add the field validation errors and whether fields have been touched to the context provider:

```
<FormContext.Provider
  value={{
    values,
    setValue: (fieldName: string, value: any) => {
      setValues({ ...values, [fieldName]: value });
    },
    errors,
    validate,
    touched,
    setTouched: (fieldName: string) => {
      setTouched({ ...touched, [fieldName]: true });
    }
  }}
>
```

Notice that we use a spread expression to update the new `touched` state.

These additions to the context will allow the `Field` component to access the validation errors and whether it has been touched. We'll need access to these later when we render the validation errors.

6. For now, we'll add a skeleton `validate` function just below the state declarations:

```
const [touched, setTouched] = useState<Touched>({});

const validate = (fieldName: string): string[] => {
  return [];
};
```

We'll finish implementing this later.

The validation errors are now in the `Form` component state and in the form context for the `Field` component to access.

Invoking validation rules

We are going to execute validation rules when the field editor loses focus by carrying out the following steps:

1. In `Field.tsx`, we are already handling field changes with the `handleChange` function. Let's add a call to invoke the validation rules in this:

```
const { setValue, touched, validate } = useContext(
  FormContext,
);
const handleChange = (
  e: ChangeEvent<HTMLInputElement>
    | ChangeEvent<HTMLTextAreaElement>
) => {
  if (setValue) {
    setValue(name, e.currentTarget.value);
  }
  if (touched[name]) {
    if (validate) {
      validate(name);
    }
  }
};
```

So, we only invoke validation if the field has been touched.

2. We need to tell the `Form` component when a `Field` has been touched. Let's create a handler for the `blur` event to do this just beneath `handleChange`:

```
const { setValue, touched, setTouched, validate } = useContext(
  FormContext,
);

const handleChange = ...

const handleBlur = () => {
  if (setTouched) {
    setTouched(name);
  }
  if (validate) {
    validate(name);
  }
};
```

Notice that we also validate the field as well.

3. Let's wire this event handler up in the `Field` JSX:

```
{label && (
  <label
    css={ ... }
    htmlFor={name}
  >
    {label}
  </label>
)}
{(type === 'Text' || type === 'Password') && (
  <input
    type={type.toLowerCase()}
    id={name}
    value={
      values[name] === undefined ? '' : values[name]
    }
    onChange={handleChange}
    onBlur={handleBlur}
    css={baseCSS}
  />
)}
{type === 'TextArea' && (
  <textarea
    id={name}
    value={
      values[name] === undefined ? '' : values[name]
    }
```

```
    onChange={handleChange}
    onBlur={handleBlur}
    css={ ... }
  />
)}
```

4. Let's now go back to `Form.tsx` and finish off implementing the `validate` function. We'll start by returning an empty array if there are no rules to check:

```
const validate = (fieldName: string): string[] => {
  if (!validationRules) {
    return [];
  }
  if (!validationRules[fieldName]) {
    return [];
  }
};
```

5. The rules can either be a single `Validation` object or an array of `Validation` objects. So, let's get ourselves into a uniform situation by always working with an array of rules:

```
const validate = (fieldName: string): string[] => {
  if (!validationRules) {
    return [];
  }
  if (!validationRules[fieldName]) {
    return [];
  }
  const rules = Array.isArray(validationRules[fieldName])
    ? (validationRules[fieldName] as Validation[])
    : ([validationRules[fieldName]] as Validation[]);
};
```

Notice that we need to keep the TypeScript compiler happy by casting `validationRules[fieldName]` in each branch of the ternary to `IValidation[]` using the `as` keyword. This is because the TypeScript compiler isn't smart enough yet to infer this.

6. We can now iterate through the rules, invoking the validator and collecting any errors in a `fieldErrors` array:

```
const rules = Array.isArray(validationRules[fieldName])
  ? (validationRules[fieldName] as Validation[])
  : ([validationRules[fieldName]] as Validation[]);
const fieldErrors: string[] = [];
rules.forEach(rule => {
```

```
    const error = rule.validator(values[fieldName], rule.arg);
    if (error) {
      fieldErrors.push(error);
    }
  });
```

7. Our final task in this function is to update the `errors` state with new errors:

```
rules.forEach(rule => {
  const error = rule.validator(values[fieldName], rule.arg);
  if (error) {
    fieldErrors.push(error);
  }
});
const newErrors = { ...errors, [fieldName]: fieldErrors };
setErrors(newErrors);
return fieldErrors;
```

That completes the invoking of the validation rules.

Rendering validation errors

Let's render the validation errors in `Field.tsx` by going through the following steps:

1. In the `Field` component JSX, destructure the `errors` object from the form context:

```
<FormContext.Consumer>
  {({ values, errors }) => (
    ...
  )}
</FormContext.Consumer>
```

2. At the end of the `div` element, let's render the validation errors:

```
<div css={ ... } >
  ...
  {errors[name] &&
    errors[name].length > 0 &&
    errors[name].map(error => (
      <div
        key={error}
        css={css`
          font-size: 12px;
          color: red;
        `}
```

```
      >
        {error}
      </div>
    ))}
  </div>
```

We use the `map` function to iterate through all of the errors and render each one in a `div` element.

This completes the rendering of any validation error messages.

Implementing validation on the ask and answer forms

We are going to implement validation in both the ask and answer forms now in the following steps:

1. In `AskPage.tsx`, we are going to make sure that the title and content fields are populated by the user with a minimum number of characters. First, let's import the `required` and `minLength` validators:

   ```
   import { Form, required, minLength } from './Form';
   ```

2. Now, we can add the validation rules to the `Form` component in the `AskPage` component JSX:

   ```
   <Form
     submitCaption="Submit Your Question"
     validationRules={{
       title: [
         { validator: required },
         { validator: minLength, arg: 10 },
       ],
       content: [
         { validator: required },
         { validator: minLength, arg: 50 },
       ],
     }}

     >
       ...
   </Form>
   ```

3. Let's give this a try. In the running app, let's go to the ask page by clicking on the **Ask a question** button on the home screen.

4. If we tab through the title without filling it in and then enter content that is less than 50 characters, we'll see the validation errors rendered:

We can still press the submit button because we haven't implemented any logic to disable the submit button if there are any validation errors.

5. Let's move onto the answer form now in `QuestionPage.tsx`. We are going to validate that the content is filled in with at least 50 characters. Let's import the `required` and `minLength` validators:

```
import { Form, required, minLength } from './Form';
```

6. In the `QuestionPage` component JSX, let's add the validation rules to the `Form` component:

```
<Form
  submitCaption='Submit Your Answer'
  validationRules={{
  content: [
  { validator: required },
  { validator: minLength, arg: 50 }
```

```
    ]
  }}
>
    <Field name="content" label="Your Answer" type="TextArea" />
</Form>
```

7. In the running app, we can check that this is working as we expect by clicking on a question on the home page and entering an answer:

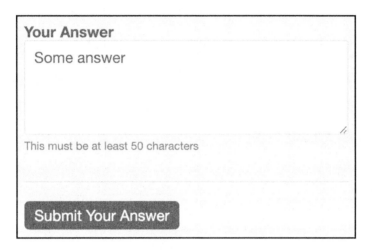

That completes the implementation of validation on our forms. Our final task is to submit the form, which we'll do in the next section.

Submitting forms

Submitting the form is the final part of the form implementation that we'll do in this section. The consumer of the Form component will handle the actual submission. Our Form component will revalidate the form and call a function in the consumer code when the form is submitted.

Handling form submission

We already have a submit button in the `Form` component that submits the form. We aren't handling the form submission yet though. Let's handle form submission, which includes a call to a function passed in by the consumer:

1. In `Form.tsx`, let's import the `FormEvent` type from React:

   ```
   import { FC, useState, createContext, FormEvent } from 'react';
   ```

2. Let's add an event listener for the `submit` event in the `Form` component JSX:

   ```
   <form noValidate={true} onSubmit={handleSubmit}>
     ...
   </form>
   ```

   When the submit button is clicked on the form, the submit event will be triggered and a function called `handleSubmit` will be invoked.

3. Let's start to implement the `handleSubmit` function just beneath the `validate` function:

   ```
   const handleSubmit = async (e: FormEvent<HTMLFormElement>) => {
     e.preventDefault();
     if (validateForm()) {
       // TODO - set state to indicate submission is in progress
       // TODO - call the consumer submit function
       // TODO - set any errors in state
       // TODO - set state to indicate submission has finished
     }
   };
   ```

   So, we prevent the default form submission from happening using the `preventDefault` method in the event parameter. We do this to prevent a full page postback to the server that we don't want. We also call a function, `validateForm`, to validate the whole form, which we still need to implement.

   Notice that we have included the `async` keyword before the function parameters to indicate that the function is asynchronous. This is because the consumers submit a handler function that is likely to call a web service, which is asynchronous.

4. Let's implement the `validateForm` function beneath the `handleSubmit` function:

```
const validateForm = () => {
  const newErrors: Errors = {};
  let haveError: boolean = false;
  if (validationRules) {
    Object.keys(validationRules).forEach(fieldName => {
      newErrors[fieldName] = validate(fieldName);
      if (newErrors[fieldName].length > 0) {
        haveError = true;
      }
    });
  }
  setErrors(newErrors);
  return !haveError;
};
```

So, we iterate through the validation rules for each field, invoking each rule and updating the `errors` state. We also return whether any errors were found.

5. Let's create some additional state for the submission process:

```
const [values, setValues] = useState<Values>({});
const [errors, setErrors] = useState<Errors>({});
const [touched, setTouched] = useState<Touched>({});
const [submitting, setSubmitting] = useState(false);
const [submitted, setSubmitted] = useState(false);
const [submitError, setSubmitError] = useState(false);
```

The `submitting` state indicates whether the submission is in progress, the `submitted` state indicates whether the form has been submitted, and the `submitError` state indicates whether the submission failed.

6. Moving back to the `handleSubmit` function, let's set these state values:

```
const handleSubmit = async (e: FormEvent<HTMLFormElement>) => {
  e.preventDefault();
  if (validateForm()) {
    setSubmitting(true);
    setSubmitError(false);
    // TODO - call the consumer submit function
    // TODO - set any errors in state
    setSubmitting(false);
    setSubmitted(true);
  }
};
```

7. We now need to call a function from the consumer that will do the actual form submission. So, let's create a function prop called onSubmit for this purpose:

```
export interface SubmitResult {
  success: boolean;
  errors?: Errors;
}

interface Props {
  submitCaption?: string;
  validationRules?: ValidationProp;
  onSubmit: (values: Values) => Promise<SubmitResult>;
}
```

The function will be passed the field values from the form and will return an object containing whether the submission was successful and any errors that occurred.

8. Let's destructure the onSubmit prop in the Form component:

```
export const Form: FC<Props> = ({
  submitCaption,
  children,
  validationRules,
  onSubmit
}) => { ... }
```

9. Moving back to the handleSubmit function again, let's call the onSubmit function that has been passed in:

```
const handleSubmit = async (e: FormEvent<HTMLFormElement>) => {
  e.preventDefault();
  if (validateForm()) {
    setSubmitting(true);
    setSubmitError(false);
    const result = await onSubmit(values);
    setErrors(result.errors || {});
    setSubmitError(!result.success);
    setSubmitting(false);
    setSubmitted(true);
  }
};
```

So, we asynchronously call the onSubmit function, update the errors state from the submission result, and set the submitError state accordingly.

10. In the `Form` components JSX, let's disable the form when submission is in progress or the form has been successfully submitted:

```
<form noValidate={true} onSubmit={handleSubmit}>
  <fieldset
    disabled={submitting || (submitted && !submitError)}
    css={ ... }
  >
    ...
  </fieldset>
</form>
```

11. We want to inform the user of whether the submission has been successful or not. We also want the consumer to be able to pass in the success and failure messages. Let's add these to the props interface:

```
interface Props {
  submitCaption?: string;
  validationRules?: ValidationProp;
  onSubmit: (values: Values) => Promise<SubmitResult>;
  successMessage?: string;
  failureMessage?: string;
}
```

12. Destructure these in the `Form` component parameter with some sensible defaults:

```
export const Form: FC<Props> = ({
  submitCaption,
  children,
  validationRules,
  onSubmit,
  successMessage = 'Success!',
  failureMessage = 'Something went wrong'
}) => { ... }
```

13. We can now add these messages to the JSX with the appropriate conditions under the submit button:

```
<fieldset ... >
  {children}
  <div ... >
    <PrimaryButton type="submit">{submitCaption}</PrimaryButton>
  </div>
  {submitted && submitError && (
    <p css={css`color: red;`}>
      {failureMessage}
    </p>
  )}
```

```
{submitted && !submitError && (
  <p css={css`color: green;`}>
    {successMessage}
  </p>
)}
</fieldset>
```

That completes the submission logic in the `Form` component.

Implementing form submission in the search, ask, and answer forms

We are going to implement form submission in our three forms starting with the search form.

Implementing form submission in the search form

In `Header.tsx`, carry out the following steps to implement submission on the search form:

1. Import the `FormEvent` type from React:

   ```
   import { ChangeEvent, FC, useState, FormEvent } from 'react';
   ```

2. Create a submit handler just beneath the `handleSearchInputChange` function:

   ```
   const handleSearchSubmit = (e: FormEvent<HTMLFormElement>) => {
     e.preventDefault();
     history.push(`/search?criteria=${search}`);
   };
   ```

   So, this sets the browser location path to `search` with the appropriate `criteria` query parameter.

3. Let's wire this handler up to the search form:

   ```
   <form onSubmit={handleSearchSubmit}>
     <input ... />
   </form>
   ```

Our project isn't compiling yet because we need to pass the `onSubmit` function prop into the `Form` component from the ask and answer forms. So, we'll try the search form out later.

Implementing form submission in the ask form

Let's carry out the following steps to implement submission on the ask form:

1. In `QuestionsData.ts`, let's create a function to simulate posting a question:

```
export interface PostQuestionData {
  title: string;
  content: string;
  userName: string;
  created: Date;
}

export const postQuestion = async (
  question: PostQuestionData,
): Promise<QuestionData | undefined> => {
  await wait(500);
  const questionId =
    Math.max(...questions.map(q => q.questionId)) + 1;
  const newQuestion: QuestionData = {
    ...question,
    questionId,
    answers: [],
  };
  questions.push(newQuestion);
  return newQuestion;
};
```

The function adds the question to the `questions` array using the `Math.max` method to set `questionId` to the next number.

2. In `AskPage.tsx`, let's import the function we just created along with the values interface from `Form.tsx`:

```
import { Form, required, minLength, Values } from './Form';
import { postQuestion } from './QuestionsData';
```

3. We can now implement the submit handler in the `AskPage` component:

```
export const AskPage = () => {
  const handleSubmit = async (values: Values) => {
    const question = await postQuestion({
      title: values.title,
      content: values.content,
      userName: 'Fred',
      created: new Date()
    });
```

```
        return { success: question ? true : false };
    };
    return (
        . . .
    );
};
```

So, this calls the `postQuestion` function asynchronously, passing in the title and content from the field values with a hardcoded user name and created date.

4. Let's pass this handler in the `onSubmit` prop as well as our required success and failure messages to the `Form` component in the JSX:

```
<Form
  submitCaption="Submit Your Question"
  validationRules={{
    title: [{ validator: required }, { validator: minLength, arg:
10 }],
    content: [{ validator: required }, { validator: minLength, arg:
50 }]
  }}
  onSubmit={handleSubmit}
  failureMessage="There was a problem with your question"
  successMessage="Your question was successfully submitted"
>
    . . .
</Form>
```

That completes the implementation of the ask form. We'll try it out after we've implemented the answer form.

Implementing form submission in the answer form

Let's carry out the following steps to implement a submission on the answer form:

1. In `QuestionsData.ts`, let's create a function to simulate posting an answer:

```
export interface PostAnswerData {
  questionId: number;
  content: string;
  userName: string;
  created: Date;
}

export const postAnswer = async (
  answer: PostAnswerData,
```

```
): Promise<AnswerData | undefined> => {
  await wait(500);
  const question = questions.filter(
    q => q.questionId === answer.questionId,
  )[0];
  const answerInQuestion: AnswerData = {
    answerId: 99,
    ...answer,
  };
  question.answers.push(answerInQuestion);
  return answerInQuestion;
};
```

The function finds the question in the `questions` array and adds the answer to it. The remainder of the preceding code contains straightforward types for the answer to post and the function result.

2. In `QuestionPage.tsx`, let's import the function we just created along with the values interface from `Form.tsx`:

```
import {
  QuestionData,
  getQuestion,
  postAnswer
} from './QuestionsData';
import { Form, required, minLength, Values } from './Form';
```

3. We can now implement the submit handler in the `QuestionPage` component just above the `return` statement:

```
const handleSubmit = async (values: Values) => {
  const result = await postAnswer({
    questionId: question!.questionId,
    content: values.content,
    userName: 'Fred',
    created: new Date()
  });

  return { success: result ? true : false };
};

return ( ... )
```

So, this calls the `postAnswer` function, asynchronously passing in the content from the field values with a hardcoded user name and created date.

Notice `!` after the reference to the `question` state variable. This is a **non-null assertion operator**.

 A non-null assertion operator (`!`) tells the TypeScript compiler that the variable before it cannot be `null` or `undefined`. This is useful in situations when the TypeScript compiler isn't smart enough to figure this fact out itself.

So, `!` in `question!.questionId` stops the TypeScript complaining that `question` could be `null`.

4. Let's pass this handler in the `onSubmit` prop as well as our required success and failure messages to the `Form` component in the JSX:

```
<Form
  submitCaption="Submit Your Answer"
  validationRules={{
    content: [
      { validator: required },
      { validator: minLength, arg: 50 }
    ]
  }}
  onSubmit={handleSubmit}
  failureMessage="There was a problem with your answer"
  successMessage="Your answer was successfully submitted"
>
  ...
</Form>
```

That's all of our forms complete now. We'll try them all out next.

Trying out our forms

Now that the hard work has been done, let's try out our forms in the running app:

1. In the search box, enter the word `typescript` and press *Enter*, like so:

The browser location query parameter is set as expected with the correct result rendering in the search form.

2. Let's go back to the home page and click the **Ask a question** button and fill out the question form and click the submit button:

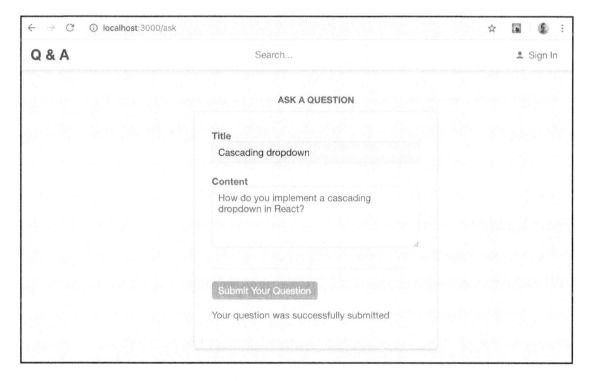

The form is disabled during and after submission and we receive the expected success message.

3. Let's go back to the home page and click on a question and submit an answer:

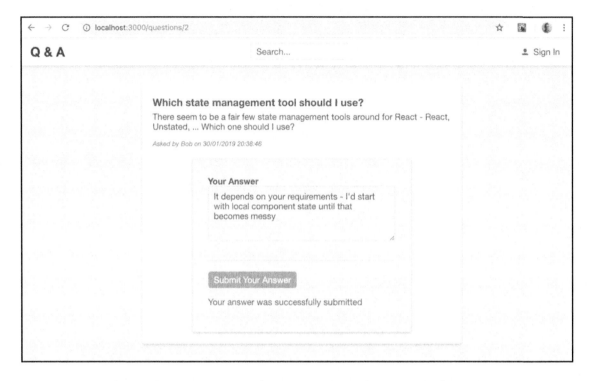

Like the ask form, the answer form is disabled during and after submission and we receive the expected success message.

So, that's our three forms complete and working nicely.

Summary

Controlled components are React's recommended method for handling form data entry. With controlled components, React controls the field component values via the component state.

Implementing many forms that contain lots of fields involves writing lots of repetitive boilerplate code for the field value state and change event handlers. Implementing generic form and field components that do the state management can significantly reduce the amount of code needed to implement a form. The generic form and field components can encapsulate validation and form submission as well.

Our generic components only deal with very simple forms. For example, what if our next form required a drop-down menu or a date picker? What if a validator function needed to call a web service and therefore needed to be asynchronous? We can, of course, enhance our generic component but not surprisingly, there are a fair number of well-established form libraries already out in the wild. A popular choice is Formik, which is similar in some ways to what we have just built but much more powerful.

In the next chapter, we are going to focus heavily on state management in our app and leverage Redux.

Questions

Check whether all of that information about forms has stuck by answering the following questions:

1. In our generic `Form` implementation, why did we make the `onSubmit` function prop asynchronous?
2. When we implemented the generic `Form` and `Field` components, what was the purpose of the `touched` state?
3. When we implement a form field as follows, why do we tie `label` to `input` using the `htmlFor` attribute?

   ```
   <label htmlFor={name}>{label}</label>
   <input
     type="text"
     id={name}
     value={values[name] === undefined ? '' : values[name]}
     onChange={handleChange}
     onBlur={handleBlur}
   />
   ```

4. Why did we use the React context in our generic `Form` and `Field` implementations?
5. Extend our generic `Field` component to include a number editor, using the native number `input`.
6. Implement a validator in `Form.tsx` that will check that the field value is between two numbers.

Further reading

Here are some useful links to learn more about the topics covered in this chapter:

- React forms: `https://reactjs.org/docs/forms.html`
- React context: `https://reactjs.org/docs/context.html`
- Spread syntax: `https://developer.mozilla.org/en-US/docs/Web/JavaScript/Reference/Operators/Spread_syntax`
- TypeScript type aliases: `https://www.typescriptlang.org/docs/handbook/advanced-types.html`
- Formik: `https://github.com/jaredpalmer/formik`

6
Managing State with Redux

So far, in our app, we have managed the state locally within our React components. We've also used the React context when the state needs to be shared between different components. This approach works well for many applications. React Redux helps us handle complex state scenarios robustly. It shines when user interactions result in several changes to state, perhaps some that are conditional, and mainly when the interaction results in web service calls. It's also great when there's lots of shared state across the application.

We'll start this chapter by understanding the Redux pattern and the different terms, such as *actions* and *reducers*. We'll follow the principles of Redux and the benefits it brings.

We are going to change the implementation of our app and use Redux to manage unanswered questions. We'll implement a Redux store with a state containing the unanswered questions and interact with the store in the home and ask pages. These implementations will give us a good grasp of how to use Redux in a React app.

In this chapter, we'll cover the following topics:

- Understanding the Redux pattern
- Installing Redux and Redux Thunk
- Creating the state
- Creating actions
- Creating action creators
- Creating a reducer
- Creating the store
- Connecting components to the store

Technical requirements

We'll use the following tools in this chapter:

- **Visual Studio Code**: We'll use this to edit our React code. This can be downloaded and installed from `https://code.visualstudio.com/`
- **Node.js and npm**: These can be downloaded from `https://nodejs.org/`. If you already have these installed, make sure that Node.js is at least version 8.2 and that npm is at least version 5.2
- **Q and A**: We'll start with the Q&A frontend project we finished in `Chapter 5`, *Working with Forms*. This is available on GitHub at `https://github.com/PacktPublishing/ASP.NET-Core-3-and-React-17`.

All the code snippets in this chapter can be found online at `https://github.com/PacktPublishing/ASP.NET-Core-3-and-React-17`. In order to restore the code from a chapter, the source code repository can be downloaded and the relevant folder opened in the relevant editor. If the code is frontend code, then `npm install` can be entered in the Terminal to restore the dependencies.

Check out the following video to see the code in action:

`http://bit.ly/2PYYOOs`

Understanding the Redux pattern

In this section, we'll start by going through the three principles in Redux before understanding the benefits of Redux and the situations it works well in. Then, we will dive into the core concepts so that we understand the terminology and the steps that happen as the `state` is updated. By doing this, we will be well equipped to implement Redux in our app.

Principles

Let's take a look at the three principles of Redux:

- **Single source of truth**: This means that the whole application state is stored in a single object. In a real app, this object is likely to contain a complex tree of nested objects.

- **The state is read-only**: This means that the `state` can't be directly changed. In Redux, the only way to change the `state` is to dispatch what's called the action.
- **Changes are made with pure functions**: The functions that are responsible for changing the state are called reducers.

Redux shines when many components need access to the same data because the `state` and its interactions are stored in a single place. Having the `state` read-only and only updatable with a function makes the interactions easier to understand and debug. It is particularly useful when many components are interacting with the state and some of the interactions are asynchronous.

In the following sections, we'll dive into actions and reducers a little more, along with the thing that manages them, which is called a store.

Key concepts

The whole state of the application lives inside what is called a **store**. The state is stored in a JavaScript object like the following one:

```
{
  questions: {
    loading: false,
    unanswered: [{
      questionId: 1, title: ...
    }, {
      questionId: 2, title: ...
    }]
  }
}
```

In this example, the single object contains an array of unanswered questions, along with whether the questions are being fetched from a web API.

The `state` won't contain any functions or setters or any getters. It's a simple JavaScript object. The store also orchestrates all the moving parts in Redux. This includes pushing actions through reducers to update the state.

So, the first thing that needs to happen in order to update the `state` in a store is to dispatch an **action**. An action is another simple JavaScript object like the one in the following code snippet:

```
{ type: 'GettingUnansweredQuestions' }
```

The `type` property determines the kind of action that needs to be performed. The `type` property is an important part of the action because the reducer won't know how to change the state without it. In the previous example, the action doesn't contain anything else other than the `type` property. This is because the reducer doesn't need any more information in order to make changes to the `state` for this action. The following example is another action:

```
{
  type: 'GotUnansweredQuestions',
  questions: [{
    questionId: 1, title: ...
  }, {
    questionId: 2, title: ...
  }]
}
```

This time, an additional bit of information is included in the action in a `questions` property. This additional information is needed by the reducer to make the change to the state for this kind of action.

Action creators, which are types of functions, are often used to create the action objects. This is beneficial when a user interaction results in a number of store actions or the interaction is asynchronous, such as fetching data from a server.

Reducers are pure functions that make the actual state changes.

 A **pure function** always returns the same result for a given set of parameters. So, these functions don't depend on any state outside the scope of the function that isn't passed into the function. Pure functions also don't change any state outside the scope of the function.

The following is an example of a reducer:

```
const questionsReducer = (state, action) => {
  switch (action.type) {
    case 'GettingUnansweredQuestions': {
      return {
        ...state,
        loading: true
      };
    }
    case 'GotUnansweredQuestions': {
      return {
        ...state,
        unanswered: action.questions,
        loading: false
```

```
      };
    }
  }
};
```

Here are some key points about reducers:

- Reducers take in two parameters for the current state and the action that is being performed.
- A `switch` statement is used on the action type and creates a new state object appropriately for each action type in each of its branches.
- To create the new state, we spread the current state into a new object and then overwrite it with properties that have changed.
- The new state is returned from the reducer.

You'll notice that the actions and reducer we have just seen didn't have TypeScript types. Obviously, we'll include the necessary types when we implement these in the following sections.

So, now that we have started to get an understanding of what Redux is, it's time to put this into practice in our app.

Installing Redux and Redux Thunk

Before we can use Redux, we need to install it, along with the TypeScript types. We will also install an additional library called Redux Thunk, which we need in order to implement asynchronous actions. Let's look at the steps to install Redux:

1. If we haven't already, let's open our project in Visual Studio Code from where we left off in the previous chapter. We can install the core Redux library via the Terminal with the following command:

   ```
   > npm install redux
   ```

   Note that the core Redux library contains TypeScript types within it, so there is no need for an additional install for these.

2. Now, let's install the React-specific bits for Redux in the Terminal with the following command:

   ```
   > npm install react-redux
   ```

These bits allow us to connect our React components to the Redux store.

3. Let's also install the TypeScript types for React Redux:

   > `npm install @types/react-redux --save-dev`

4. Let's install Redux Thunk as well:

   > `npm install redux-thunk`

Redux Thunk contains its own TypeScript types, so there is no need for an additional install for these.

With all the Redux bits now installed, we can start to build our Redux store.

Creating the state

In this section, we are going to implement the type for the state object in our store, along with the initial value for the state. Follow these steps to do so:

1. Create a new file called `Store.ts` in the `src` folder with the following import statement:

   ```
   import { QuestionData } from './QuestionsData';
   ```

2. Let's create the TypeScript types for the state of our store:

   ```
   interface QuestionsState {
     readonly loading: boolean;
     readonly unanswered: QuestionData[] | null;
     readonly postedResult?: QuestionData;
   }

   export interface AppState {
     readonly questions: QuestionsState;
   }
   ```

   So, our store is going to have a `questions` property that, in turn, contains an array of unanswered questions or `null` in an `unanswered` property. The `questions` property includes whether the unanswered questions are being loaded from the server in a `loading` property. The `questions` property also includes the result of posting a new question in a `postedResult` property.

3. Let's define the initial state for the store so that it has an empty array of unanswered questions and doesn't load questions from the server:

```
const initialQuestionState: QuestionsState = {
  loading: false,
  unanswered: null
};
```

So, defining the state is pretty straightforward. Let's move on and define our actions.

Creating actions

In this section, we are going to create actions that will initiate changes to our store state. Let's get started:

1. We are going to create the actions in `Store.ts`. So, let's add the following import statement at the top of this file:

```
import { Action } from 'redux';
```

The `Action` type is a base type from the core Redux library that contains a `type` property that we can use to type in our actions.

2. Let's create an action interface that will indicate that unanswered questions are being fetched from the server:

```
interface GettingUnansweredQuestionsAction
  extends Action<'GettingUnansweredQuestions'> {}
```

Notice that the interface uses the `extends` keyword.

 Interfaces can inherit properties and methods from another interface using the `extends` keyword. The interface that's being inherited from is specified after the `extends` keyword.

We have extended the generic `Action` type by passing in the type for the `type` property, which is the `'GettingUnansweredQuestions'` string literal.

The action has no other properties, so the object will always be as follows:

```
{
  type: 'GettingUnansweredQuestions'
}
```

The `type` property can only be `'GettingUnansweredQuestions'` and no other string value because we have typed it to that specific string literal.

3. Let's create an action for when the unanswered questions have been retrieved from the server:

```
export interface GotUnansweredQuestionsAction
  extends Action<'GotUnansweredQuestions'> {
  questions: QuestionData[];
}
```

This time, the action contains a property called `questions` to hold the unanswered questions, as well as the fixed `type` property.

4. Our last action is for when a question has been posted to the server and we have the response:

```
export interface PostedQuestionAction extends
Action<'PostedQuestion'> {
  result: QuestionData | undefined;
}
```

The `result` property will hold the result of the question submission.

5. Now, we are going to combine all the action types in a union type:

```
type QuestionsActions =
  | GettingUnansweredQuestionsAction
  | GotUnansweredQuestionsAction
  | PostedQuestionAction;
```

We'll use this union type later in this chapter when we implement the reducer.

That's our actions defined. In the next section, we'll create functions that will dispatch these actions.

Creating action creators

Action creators are functions that create actions. When the process of creating the action is synchronous, the action creator will return the action object. However, when the process of creating the action is asynchronous, the action creator will return a function that dispatches the action. Asynchronous actions can also dispatch more than one action.

In this section, we will create two asynchronous action creators for getting unanswered questions and posting a question. We will also create an asynchronous action creator for clearing the posted question result.

Implementing an action creator for getting unanswered questions

The first action creator we will implement will be for getting unanswered questions. So, let's get started by carrying out the following steps:

1. Let's start by importing the following additional types from the Redux core library:

    ```
    import { Action, ActionCreator, Dispatch } from 'redux';
    ```

2. Next, let's implement the action creator, which will gather unanswered questions:

    ```
    export const getUnansweredQuestionsActionCreator = () => {
      return async (dispatch: Dispatch) => {
        // TODO - dispatch the GettingUnansweredQuestions action
        // TODO - get the questions from server
        // TODO - dispatch the GotUnansweredQuestions action
      };
    };
    ```

    This is an asynchronous action creator and returns a function that will dispatch two actions. So, the returned function has a dispatch parameter, which is used to dispatch the actions.

3. Let's dispatch the GettingUnansweredQuestions action:

    ```
    export const getUnansweredQuestionsActionCreator = () => {
      return async (dispatch: Dispatch) => {
        const gettingUnansweredQuestionsAction:
        GettingUnansweredQuestionsAction = {
          type: 'GettingUnansweredQuestions'
        };
        dispatch(gettingUnansweredQuestionsAction);
        // TODO - get the questions from server
        // TODO - dispatch the GotUnansweredQuestions action
      };
    };
    ```

Using the `GettingUnansweredQuestionsAction` type annotation helps us ensure the action is defined correctly. We simply use the `dispatch` parameter to dispatch the action.

4. Now, let's get the unanswered questions from the server by importing the function that does this:

```
import { QuestionData, getUnansweredQuestions } from
'./QuestionsData';
```

5. Now, we can use this function to get the unanswered questions from the server in our action creator:

```
export const getUnansweredQuestionsActionCreator = () => {
  return async (dispatch: Dispatch) => {
    const gettingUnansweredQuestionsAction:
    GettingUnansweredQuestionsAction = {
      type: 'GettingUnansweredQuestions'
    };
    dispatch(gettingUnansweredQuestionsAction);
    const questions = await getUnansweredQuestions();
    // TODO - dispatch the GotUnansweredQuestions action
  };
};
```

6. Let's dispatch the `GotUnansweredQuestions` action containing the unanswered questions and return this action:

```
export const getUnansweredQuestionsActionCreator = () => {
  return async (dispatch: Dispatch) => {
    const gettingUnansweredQuestionsAction:
    GettingUnansweredQuestionsAction = {
      type: 'GettingUnansweredQuestions'
    };
    dispatch(gettingUnansweredQuestionsAction);
    const questions = await getUnansweredQuestions();
    const gotUnansweredQuestionAction: GotUnansweredQuestionsAction
    = {
      questions,
      type: 'GotUnansweredQuestions'
    };
    dispatch(gotUnansweredQuestionAction);
  };
};
```

7. Our final task for this action creator is to add type annotation. First, we need to import ThunkAction from the Redux Thunk core library:

```
import { ThunkAction } from 'redux-thunk';
```

8. We can use this type in our type annotation:

```
export const getUnansweredQuestionsActionCreator: ActionCreator<
  ThunkAction<
    Promise<void>,
    QuestionData[],
    null,
    GotUnansweredQuestionsAction
  >
> = () => {
  ...
};
```

ActionCreator is a generic type from the core Redux library that takes in a parameter for the type of action that is created.

The type of action that's created isn't straightforward because the action creator is asynchronous, so we use the ThunkAction type from the Redux Thunk library, which is another generic type that has four parameters:

- The first parameter is the return type for the inner function, which is Promise<void> in this case.
- The second parameter is the type of data within the last action, which is QuestionData[] in this case.
- The third parameter is the type for the parameter that is passed into the nested function. In this case, this is null because there is no parameter.
- The last parameter is the type of the last action to be dispatched, which is GotUnansweredQuestionsAction in this case.

That completes the implementation of our first action creator.

Implementing an action creator for posting a question

Our second action creator will be for posting a question. Let's carry out the following steps to implement this:

1. Let's implement the action creator for posting a question by importing the function that posts the question to the server and the type for the posted question:

```
import {
  QuestionData,
  getUnansweredQuestions,
  postQuestion,
  PostQuestionData
} from './QuestionsData';
```

2. Now, we can implement the action creator using the same pattern as the one we have just implemented:

```
export const postQuestionActionCreator: ActionCreator<
  ThunkAction<
    Promise<void>,
    QuestionData,
    PostQuestionData,
    PostedQuestionAction
  >
> = (question: PostQuestionData) => {
  return async (dispatch: Dispatch) => {
    const result = await postQuestion(question);
    const postedQuestionAction: PostedQuestionAction = {
      type: 'PostedQuestion',
      result
    };
    dispatch(postedQuestionAction);
  };
};
```

This is very similar to the first action creator, except we are only dispatching a single action after the response of the posted question has been received. The nested function also takes in a parameter for the question to be posted, so this appears in the ThunkAction generic type as the third parameter.

Implementing an action creator for clearing the posted question

Our final action creator is for clearing the posted question result. Let's implement this in one step:

```
export const clearPostedQuestionActionCreator: ActionCreator<
  PostedQuestionAction
> = () => {
  const postedQuestionAction: PostedQuestionAction = {
    type: 'PostedQuestion',
    result: undefined,
  };
  return postedQuestionAction;
};
```

This action creator is much simpler because it is synchronous – we simply return a `PostedQuestion` action with an `undefined result` property.

So, action creators are straightforward to implement but the type annotations are a little tricky, particularly when they are asynchronous.

Our Redux store is shaping up nicely now. Let's move on and create a reducer.

Creating a reducer

In this section, we are going to implement a reducer, which is responsible for changing the state in the store for a given action. Let's carry out the following steps:

1. We'll start by importing the `Reducer` type from Redux, along with the `combineReducers` function:

```
import {
  Action,
  ActionCreator,
  Dispatch,
  Reducer,
  combineReducers
} from 'redux';
```

2. Let's create the skeleton reducer function:

```
const questionsReducer: Reducer<QuestionsState, QuestionsActions> =
(
  state = initialQuestionState,
  action
) => {
  // TODO - Handle the different actions and return new state
  return state;
};
```

The reducer takes in two parameters: one for the current state and another for the action that is being processed. The state will be `undefined` the first time the reducer is called, so we default this to the initial state we created earlier.

The reducer needs to return the new state object for the given action. We're simply returning the initial state at the moment.

We've used the `Reducer` generic type for the reducer, which takes in parameters for the state type and actions type. Notice that we use the `QuestionsActions` union type for the actions type.

3. Let's add a `switch` statement to handle the different actions:

```
const questionsReducer: Reducer<QuestionsState, QuestionsActions> =
(
  state = initialQuestionState,
  action
) => {
  switch (action.type) {
    case 'GettingUnansweredQuestions': {
      // TODO - return new state
    }
    case 'GotUnansweredQuestions': {
      // TODO - return new state
    }
    case 'PostedQuestion': {
      // TODO - return new state
    }
  }
  return state;
};
```

Notice that the `type` property in the `action` parameter is strongly-typed and that we can only handle the three actions we defined earlier.

4. Let's handle the `GettingUnansweredQuestions` question first:

```
switch (action.type) {
  case 'GettingUnansweredQuestions': {
    return {
      ...state,
      unanswered: null,
      loading: true
    };
  }
  case 'GotUnansweredQuestions': {
    // TODO - return new state
  }
  case 'PostedQuestion': {
    // TODO - return new state
  }
}
```

We use the spread syntax to copy the previous state into a new object, initialize the `unanswered` state to `null`, and set the `loading` state to `true`.

5. Let's move on to the `GotUnansweredQuestions` action:

```
switch (action.type) {
  case 'GettingUnansweredQuestions': { ... };
  case 'GotUnansweredQuestions': {
    return {
      ...state,
      unanswered: action.questions,
      loading: false
    };
  }
  case 'PostedQuestion': {
    // TODO - return new state
  }
}
```

Again, we use the spread syntax to copy the previous state into a new object and set the unanswered and loading properties. Notice how we get IntelliSense only for the properties in the GotUnansweredQuestions action:

```
case "GotUnansweredQuestions": {
  return {
    ...state,
    unanswered: action.,
    loading: false        questions  (property)  GotUnansweredQuestionsAction...
  };                      type
}
```

TypeScript has smartly narrowed down the type in the switch branch from the union type that was passed into the reducer for the action parameter.

6. Let's handle the last action:

```
switch (action.type) {
  case 'GettingUnansweredQuestions': { ... };
  case 'GotUnansweredQuestions': { ... };
  case 'PostedQuestion': {
    return {
      ...state,
      unanswered: action.result
        ? (state.unanswered || []).concat(action.result)
        : state.unanswered,
      postedResult: action.result
    };
  }
}
```

We create a new state from the old state using the spread syntax. If the question has been successfully submitted, the result property in the action will contain a question property, which is added to the unanswered array using the array's concat function. We store the result of the question submission in the postedResult property.

7. We've handled all the different actions now but are going to do a little more work that will help us remember to handle new actions in the reducer as our app grows. To do this, we are going to add a `default` branch in the `switch` statement:

```
switch (action.type) {
  case 'GettingUnansweredQuestions': { ... };
  case 'GotUnansweredQuestions': { ... };
  case 'PostedQuestion': { ... };
  default:
      neverReached(action);
}
```

This will inform the TypeScript compiler that the `default` branch should never be reached. So, if we add a new action and it isn't handled in the reducer, the `default` branch will be reached and a compiler error will be raised.

8. Let's implement the `neverReached` function we just referenced below the reducer:

```
const neverReached = (never: never) => {};
```

The function takes in a parameter that is of the `never` type and returns an empty object.

 The `never` type is a TypeScript type that represents something that would never occur and is typically used to specify unreachable areas of code.

So, if TypeScript can reach this function and the `never` parameter, it will throw an error.

9. Now, we are going to use the `combineReducers` function in Redux to combine all our reducers into a single reducer that returns `AppState`:

```
const rootReducer = combineReducers<AppState>({
  questions: questionsReducer
});
```

An object literal is passed into `combineReducers` that contains the properties in our app state, along with the reducer that is responsible for that state. We only have a single property in our app state called `questions` and a single reducer managing changes to that state called `questionsReducer`.

We will use the `rootReducer` in the next section when we create the store object.

That's the reducers complete. Now, we have all the different pieces implemented for our Redux store, so we are going to create a function to create the store in the next section.

Creating the store

The final task in `Store.ts` is to create a function that creates the store. Let's do this by carrying out the following steps:

1. First, let's import the `Store` type and `createStore` and `applyMiddleware` functions from Redux, along with the `thunk` object from Redux Thunk:

```
import {
  Action,
  ActionCreator,
  Dispatch,
  Reducer,
  combineReducers,
  Store,
  createStore,
  applyMiddleware
} from 'redux';
import thunk, { ThunkAction } from 'redux-thunk';
```

2. Let's create a function to create the store:

```
export function configureStore(): Store<AppState> {
  const store = createStore(
    rootReducer,
    undefined,
    applyMiddleware(thunk)
  );
  return store;
}
```

This function uses the `createStore` function from Redux by passing in the combined reducers, `undefined` as the initial state, and the Thunk middleware using the `applyMiddleware` function. Remember that Thunk is used to enable asynchronous actions because, by default, Redux actions can't be asynchronous.

We use the generic `Store` type as the return type for the function passing in the interface for our app state, which is `AppState`.

That's all we need to do to create the store.

 We have created all the bits and pieces in our store in a single file called `Store.ts`. For larger stores, it may help maintainability to structure the store across different files. Structuring the store by feature where you have all the actions and the reducer for each feature in a file works well because we generally read and write our code by feature.

In the next section, we will connect our store to the components we implemented in the previous chapters.

Connecting components to the store

In this section, we are going to connect the existing components in our app to our store. We will start by adding what is called a store *provider* to the root of our component tree, which allows components lower in the tree to consume the store.

Adding a store provider

Let's provide the store to the root of our component tree:

1. In `App.tsx`, import the `Provider` component from React Redux and the `configureStore` function we created in the previous section. Add these import statements just after the React import statement:

   ```
   import React, { lazy, Suspense } from 'react';
   import { Provider } from 'react-redux';
   import { configureStore } from './Store';
   ```

   This is the first time we have referenced anything from React-Redux. Remember that this library helps React components interact with a Redux store.

2. Just before the `App` component is defined, create an instance of our store using our `configureStore` function:

   ```
   const store = configureStore();
   ```

3. In the `App` component's JSX, wrap a `Provider` component around the `BrowserRouter` component by passing in our store instance:

```
return (
  <Provider store={store}>
    <BrowserRouter>
      ...
    </BrowserRouter>
  </Provider>
);
```

Components lower in the component tree can now connect to the store.

Connecting the home page

Let's connect the home page to the store:

1. In `HomePage.tsx`, let's add the following import statements:

```
import { connect } from 'react-redux';
import { ThunkDispatch } from 'redux-thunk';
import { AnyAction } from 'redux';
```

We've imported a function called `connect` from React Redux that will allow us to connect the `HomePage` component to the store. We've also imported some useful TypeScript types from Redux and Redux Thunk.

2. We are going to use the Redux store for the unanswered questions, so let's import the action creator that will get these, along with the type for the store's state:

```
import {
  getUnansweredQuestionsActionCreator,
  AppState
} from './Store';
```

3. Let's remove the `getUnansweredQuestions` function from the import statement from `QuestionsData.ts`. We will eventually get this data from the Redux store. This should leave this import statement as follows:

```
import { QuestionData } from './QuestionsData';
```

4. The state in the Redux store, as well as the dispatched action creator, is going to be accessible from the `HomePage` component via props. So, let's create a props interface for what we expect:

```
interface Props extends RouteComponentProps {
  getUnansweredQuestions: () => Promise<void>;
  questions: QuestionData[] | null;
  questionsLoading: boolean;
}
```

The interface extends the `RouteComponentProps` type because this is the current props type. We have added three props for getting and storing the unanswered questions, as well as for whether they are in the process of being loaded.

5. Now, we can use this interface in the `HomePage` component and destructure the props:

```
export const HomePage: FC<Props> = ({
  history,
  questions,
  questionsLoading,
  getUnansweredQuestions
}) => { ... }
```

6. We no longer need the `questions` and `questionsLoading` states, so let's remove the `useState` statement inside the component. We need to remember to remove `useState` from the React import statement as well. In addition, the `doGetUnansweredQuestions` function is also redundant, so let's remove this as well.

7. The first statement in the component is now the `useEffect` statement, which gets the unanswered questions when the component is mounted. We need to change this to call the action creator in our Redux store to get the questions:

```
useEffect(() => {
  if (questions === null) {
    getUnansweredQuestions();
  }
}, [questions, getUnansweredQuestions]);
```

So, if the `questions` state in the Redux store is `null`, we start the process of getting the unanswered questions.

Notice that we include the `questions` and `getUnansweredQuestions` functions as dependencies for the `useEffect` function so that it is executed if these ever change.

8. We still need to connect the component to the store. We do this using the `connect` function we imported earlier into a default export statement at the bottom of `HomePage.tsx`:

```
export default connect(
  mapStateToProps,
  mapDispatchToProps
)(HomePage);
```

This connects the component to our store, which is provided to us by the `Provider` component, which is higher up in the component tree. The `connect` function also invokes two mapper functions, `mapStateToProps` and `mapDispatchToProps`, which map the state and action creators from the store into the component props that we'll implement later.

9. Now that we have a default export for the `HomePage` component, let's remove its named export. So, the `HomePage` component should now be defined as follows, without the `export` keyword:

```
const HomePage: FC<Props> = ...
```

10. Let's define the `mapStateToProps` function above the default export statement:

```
const mapStateToProps = (store: AppState) => {
  return {
    questions: store.questions.unanswered,
    questionsLoading: store.questions.loading
  };
};
```

This function takes in the store state and returns the `questions` and `questionLoaded` props that are required by our component. So, it maps state from the store into the component props, as the name suggests.

11. Let's define the `mapDispatchToProps` function just beneath the `mapStateToProps` function:

```
const mapDispatchToProps = (
  dispatch: ThunkDispatch<any, any, AnyAction>,
) => {
  return {
    getUnansweredQuestions: () =>
      dispatch(getUnansweredQuestionsActionCreator()),
  };
};
```

This dispatches and maps the action creator to get unanswered questions into the component props.

Notice that the TypeScript type for the `dispatch` parameter is `ThunkDispatch`. This is a type from the Redux Thunk library that takes in three parameters for the asynchronous function result type, asynchronous function parameter type, and the last action created type, respectively. Although we are dispatching only one action creator in this case, we could be dispatching different action creators, which is why we pass in the `any` type and the `AnyAction` type in the generic parameters.

12. Let's move on to the `App.tsx` file and change the import statement for `HomePage`, so that it uses the default export:

    ```
    import HomePage from './HomePage';
    ```

13. If the app isn't running, type `npm start` in the Terminal to start it. The app will run fine and the unanswered questions will be rendered on the home page, just as they were before we added the Redux store.

Congratulations—we have just connected our first component to a Redux store!

Connecting the ask page

We are going to follow a similar pattern to connect the ask page to our Redux store. Let's get started:

1. In `AskPage.tsx`, let's change the import statements from React, that is, `Form.tsx` and `QuestionsData.tsx`, so that they look as follows:

    ```
    import React, { FC, useEffect } from 'react';
    import {
      Form,
      required,
      minLength,
      Values,
      SubmitResult
    } from './Form';
    import { PostQuestionData, QuestionData } from './QuestionsData';
    ```

2. Let's add the following import statements:

```
import { connect } from 'react-redux';
import { ThunkDispatch } from 'redux-thunk';
import {
  postQuestionActionCreator,
  AppState,
  clearPostedQuestionActionCreator
} from './Store';
import { AnyAction } from 'redux';
```

3. Add a props interface for the data and function coming from the store and use this in the `AskPage` component. Also, remove the named export from the function component:

```
interface Props {
  postQuestion: (
    question: PostQuestionData,
  ) => Promise<void>;
  postedQuestionResult?: QuestionData;
  clearPostedQuestion: () => void;
}

const AskPage: FC<Props> = ({
  postQuestion,
  postedQuestionResult,
  clearPostedQuestion,
}) => ...
```

4. We want to clear the question posted state when the `AskPage` component is unmounted, so let's call the `clearPostedQuestion` action creator in a `useEffect` cleanup function:

```
useEffect(() => {
  return function cleanUp() {
    clearPostedQuestion();
  };
}, [clearPostedQuestion]);

const handleSubmit = ...
```

5. Now, the `handleSubmit` function in the `AskPage` component is going to call the `postQuestion` dispatched action creator from the store. So, let's change this to the following:

```
const handleSubmit = (values: Values) => {
  postQuestion({
    title: values.title,
    content: values.content,
    userName: "Fred",
    created: new Date()
  });
};
```

The function is no longer asynchronous, so the `async` keyword has been removed from it.

6. The `Form` component expects `handleSubmit` to be asynchronous though, so let's go to `Form.tsx` and change the interface so that no results can be returned from the `onSubmit` function prop:

```
interface Props {
  ...
  onSubmit: (values: Values) => Promise<SubmitResult> | void;
  ...
}
```

7. Still in the `Form` component, we need to return from the `handleSubmit` function if a result hasn't been received from `onSubmit`:

```
const handleSubmit = async (e: FormEvent<HTMLFormElement>) => {
  e.preventDefault();
  if (validateForm()) {
    setSubmitting(true);
    setSubmitError(false);
    const result = await onSubmit(values);

    // The result may be passed through as a prop
    if (result === undefined) {
      return;
    }

    setErrors(result.errors || {});
    setSubmitError(!result.success);
    setSubmitting(false);
    setSubmitted(true);
  }
};
```

8. The submission result will be passed through the props if the submission is handled via a Redux store, so let's add a `submitResult` prop:

```
interface Props {
  ...
  onSubmit: (values: Values) => Promise<SubmitResult> | void;
  submitResult?: SubmitResult;
  ...
}

export const Form: FC<Props> = ({
  ...
  onSubmit,
  submitResult,
  ...
}) =>
```

9. We are going to combine the data from `submitResult` with the submission state so that our JSX can deal with the Redux store submission. Add the following highlighted lines just before the `return` statement:

```
const handleSubmit = ...

const validateForm = ...

const disabled = submitResult
  ? submitResult.success
  : submitting || (submitted && !submitError);

const showError = submitResult
  ? !submitResult.success
  : submitted && submitError;

const showSuccess = submitResult
  ? submitResult.success
  : submitted && !submitError;

return ( ... )
```

10. The `Form` component's JSX can now be changed to the following:

```
<form noValidate={true} onSubmit={handleSubmit}>
  <fieldset disabled={disabled} css={ ... }>
    {children}
    <div css={ ... }>
      <PrimaryButton type="submit">{submitCaption}</PrimaryButton>
    </div>
```

```
{showError && <p css={ ... }>{failureMessage}</p>}
{showSuccess && <p css={ ... }>{successMessage}</p>}
</fieldset>
</form>
```

This allows the `Form` component to be used with a Redux store.

11. Back in `AskPage.tsx`, we can now pass the submission result to the `Form` component:

```
<Form
  ...
  onSubmit={handleSubmit}
  submitResult={submitResult}
  ...
>
  ...
</Form>
```

12. We need to construct the `submitResult` variable we have just referenced from the properties in `postedQuestionResult`, which comes from the store:

```
const handleSubmit = (values: Values) => {
  ...
};

let submitResult: SubmitResult | undefined;
if (postedQuestionResult) {
  submitResult = { success: postedQuestionResult !== undefined };
}
return ( ... )
```

13. Now, we can connect the component to the store and replace the previous export statement with the following:

```
const mapStateToProps = (store: AppState) => {
  return {
    postedQuestionResult: store.questions.postedResult,
  };
};
const mapDispatchToProps = (
  dispatch: ThunkDispatch<any, any, AnyAction>,
) => {
  return {
    postQuestion: (question: PostQuestionData) =>
      dispatch(postQuestionActionCreator(question)),
    clearPostedQuestion: () =>
      dispatch(clearPostedQuestionActionCreator()),
```

```
      };
  };

  export default connect(
    mapStateToProps,
    mapDispatchToProps,
  )(AskPage);
```

This is a similar pattern to how we connected the `HomePage` component to the store. A slight difference here is that we pass a parameter into the action creator for the question being submitted.

14. If we go to the ask form in the app and submit a question, it will behave just as it did previously, but via our Redux store.

That completes connecting the ask page to our Redux store.

Summary

In this chapter, we learned that the state in a Redux store is stored in a single place, is read-only, and is changed with a pure function called a reducer. Our components don't talk directly to the reducer; instead, they dispatch functions called action creators, which create objects called actions that describe the change to the reducer.

Redux Thunk was used to allow the store to work with asynchronous actions, which are crucial for an app that uses web services. We told Redux to use Redux Thunk in the Redux `createStore` function. React components are connected to the store with a `connect` function from React Redux, as well as a `Provider` component at the root of the component tree.

There are lots of bits and pieces to get our heads around when implementing Redux within a React app. It does shine in scenarios where the state management is complex because Redux forces us to break the logic up into separate pieces that are easy to understand and maintain. It is also very useful for managing global state such as user information because it is easily accessible below the `Provider` component.

In this chapter, we put the state from the home and ask pages into Redux. Putting the state from the question and search pages into Redux follows a very similar pattern. The code for this can be found at https://github.com/PacktPublishing/ASP.NET-Core-3-and-React-17/tree/master/Chapter06/frontend.

Now, we have built the majority of the frontend in our app, which means it's time to turn our attention to the backend. In the next chapter, we'll focus on how we can interact with the database in ASP.NET Core.

Questions

Before we end this chapter, let's test our knowledge with some questions:

1. When implementing an action object, how many properties can it contain?
2. Why did we need Redux Thunk in our Redux store?
3. How did we make the state in our store read-only?
4. In the `questionsReducer` function we implemented, why didn't we use the array `push` method to add the new question to the state?

```
case 'PostedQuestion': {
  return {
    ...state,
    unanswered: action.result
      ? (state.unanswered || []).push(action.result.question)
      : state.unanswered,
    postedResult: action.result,
  };
}
```

5. Does the `Provider` component from React Redux need to be placed at the top of the component tree?
6. As well as the `Provider` component, what is the other item from React Redux that allows a component to consume data from the Redux store?
7. Is a component that consumes the Redux store allowed to have local state?

Further reading

Here are some useful links so that you can learn more about the topics that were covered in this chapter:

- **Getting Started with Redux:** https://redux.js.org/introduction/getting-started
- **React Redux:** https://react-redux.js.org/
- **Redux Thunk:** https://github.com/reduxjs/redux-thunk
- **Never type:** https://www.typescriptlang.org/docs/handbook/basic-types.html

3
Section 3: Building an ASP.NET Core Backend

In this section, we will build the backend of our Q & A app by creating a REST API for interacting with questions and answers as well as a SignalR server that gives real-time updates on answers. We'll use Dapper and Entity Framework Core behind the web API to interact with the SQL Server database.

This section comprises the following chapters:

7
Interacting with the Database with Dapper

It's time to start work on the backend of our Q and A app. In this chapter, we are going to build the database for the app and interact with it from ASP.NET Core with a library called Dapper.

We'll start by understanding what Dapper is and the benefits it brings over Entity Framework. We'll create the data access layer in our app by learning how to read data from the database into model classes using Dapper. We'll then move on to writing to the database from model classes.

Deploying database changes during releases of our app is an important and non-trivial task. So, we'll set up the management of database migrations using a library called DbUp toward the end of this chapter.

In this chapter, we'll cover the following topics:

- Implementing the database
- Understanding what Dapper is and its benefits
- Installing and configuring Dapper
- Reading data using Dapper
- Writing data using Dapper
- Managing migrations with DbUp

Technical requirements

We'll use the following tools in this chapter:

- **Visual Studio 2019**: We'll use this to edit our ASP.NET Core code. This can be downloaded and installed from `https://visualstudio.microsoft.com/vs/`.
- **.NET Core 3.0**: This can be downloaded and installed from `https://dotnet.microsoft.com/download/dotnet-core`.
- **SQL Server 2017 Express Edition**: We'll use this for our database. This can be downloaded and installed from `https://www.microsoft.com/en-gb/sql-server/sql-server-editions-express`.
- **SQL Server Management Studio**: We'll use this to create our database. This can be downloaded and installed from `https://docs.microsoft.com/en-us/sql/ssms/download-sql-server-management-studio-ssms?view=sql-server-2017`.
- **Q and A**: We'll start with the Q and A backend project we created and finished in `Chapter 2`, *Creating Decoupled React and ASP.NET Core Apps*. This is available on GitHub at `https://github.com/PacktPublishing/ASP.NET-Core-3-and-React-17`.

All of the code snippets in this chapter can be found online at `https://github.com/PacktPublishing/ASP.NET-Core-3-and-React-17`. To restore code from a chapter, the source code repository can be downloaded and the relevant folder opened in the relevant editor. If the code is frontend code, then `npm install` can be entered in the Terminal to restore the dependencies.

Check out the following video to see the code in action:

`http://bit.ly/2EVDsv6`

Implementing the database

In this section, we are going to create the database for our app containing the tables we need along with stored procedures to interact with those tables.

Creating the database

We are going to create the database using **SQL Server Management Studio (SSMS)** by carrying out the following steps:

1. Open SSMS and connect to the SQL Server instance:

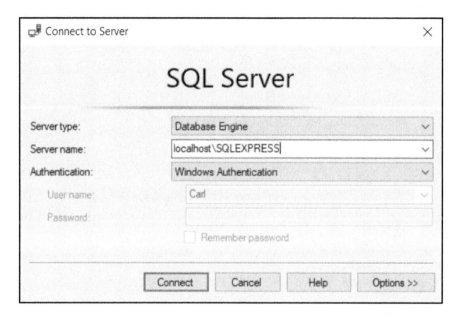

2. In **Object Explorer**, right-click on **Databases** and click on the **New Database...** option.

3. Enter QandA for the name for the database and click **OK**:

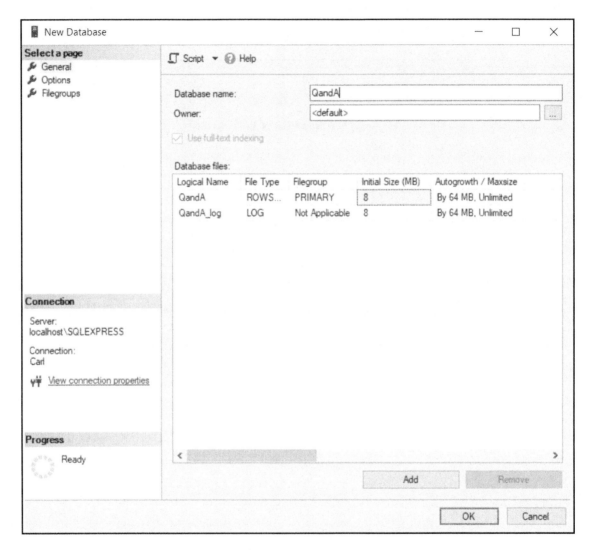

4. After the database is created, we'll see it listed in **Object Explorer**:

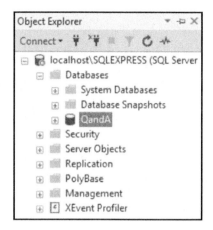

Nice and easy!

Creating database tables

Let's create some tables for the users, questions, and answers in our new database in SSMS:

1. Copy the contents of the SQL Script at `https://github.com/PacktPublishing/ ASP.NET-Core-3-and-React-17/blob/master/Chapter07/backend/SQLScripts/ 01-Tables.sql`

2. In SSMS, with the **QandA** database highlighted, click **New Query** on the toolbar to create a new SQL query and paste in the contents from the copied script.

3. Click the **Execute** option on the toolbar or press *F5* to execute the query.

4. If we look under **Tables** in **Object Explorer**, we should see that several tables have been created:

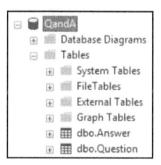

The following have been created:

- The `Question` table contains the questions that have been asked and contains the following fields:
  - An integer-based field called `QuestionId`, which is the primary key Unicode-based `Title` and `Content` fields
  - `UserId` and `UserName` fields, which reference the user who asked the question
  - A field called `Created`, which will hold the date and time the question was asked
- The `Answer` table contains answers to the questions and contains the following fields:
  - An integer-based `AnswerId` field, which is the primary key
  - An integer-based `QuestionId` field, which references the question being answered
  - A Unicode-based `Content` field
  - `UserId` and `UserName` fields, which reference the user who answered the question
  - A field called `Created`, which will hold the date and time the answer was submitted

5. The SQL Script has added some example data. If we right-click on the **Question** table in **Object Explorer** and choose the **Edit Top 200 rows** option, we'll see the data in our table:

QuestionId	Title	Content	UserId	UserName	Created
1	Why should I le...	TypeScript see...	1	bob.test@test.com	2019-05-18 1...
2	Which state ma...	There seem to ...	2	jane.test@test.com	2019-05-18 1...
NULL	NULL	NULL	NULL	NULL	NULL

So, we now have a database that contains our tables with some nice data to work with.

Creating stored procedures

Let's create some stored procedures that our app will use to interact with the database tables:

1. Copy the contents of the SQL Script at `https://github.com/PacktPublishing/ASP.NET-Core-3-and-React-17/blob/master/Chapter07/backend/SQLScripts/02-Sprocs.sql`.

2. Click **New Query** to create a new SQL query and paste in the contents from the copied script.

3. Click the **Execute** option on the toolbar.

4. If we look under **Stored Procedures** under **Programmability** in **Object Explorer**, we should see that several stored procedures have been created:

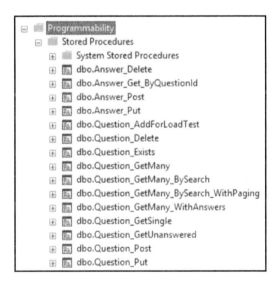

We'll be using these stored procedures to interact with the database from the ASP.NET Core app.

5. Before we finish this section, let's try to run one of the stored procedures. Click **New Query** to create a new SQL query and enter the following:

```
EXEC dbo.Question_GetMany_BySearch @Search = 'type'
```

So, this SQL command will execute the `Question_GetMany_BySearch` stored procedure passing in the `@Search` parameter with a value of `type`. This stored procedure returns questions that have the value of the `@Search` parameter in the title or its content.

6. Click the **Execute** option on the toolbar and we should get the following results:

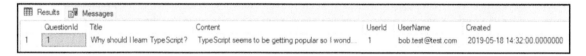

With our SQL Server database in place, we can now turn our attention to Dapper.

Understanding what Dapper is and its benefits

Dapper is a performance-focused simple object mapper for .NET that helps to map SQL query output to instances of a C# class. It is built and maintained by the StackOverflow team and is released as open source and is a popular alternative to Microsoft's Entity Framework.

So, why use Dapper rather than Entity Framework? The goal of Entity Framework is to abstract away the database and so it trades learning SQL for Entity Framework-specific objects such as `DBSet` and `DataContext`. We generally don't write SQL with Entity Framework—instead, we write LINQ queries, which are translated into SQL by Entity Framework.

If we are implementing a large database that serves a large number of users, Entity Framework can be a challenge because the queries it generates can be inefficient. We need to understand Entity Framework well to make it scale, which can be a significant investment. When we find Entity Framework queries that are slow, we need to understand SQL to properly understand the root cause. So, why wouldn't we just spend our time learning SQL and use this directly rather than an abstraction? Also, if we have a team with SQL skills, why would we want to abstract away the database and SQL?

Dapper is really simple. We'll see later in this chapter that we can read and write data from a SQL database with just a few lines of C# code. It allows us to interact with stored procedures in the database, automatically mapping C# class instances to SQL parameters along with the results of the query. In the next section, we will install and start to use Dapper to access our data.

Installing and configuring Dapper

In this section, we are going to install and configure Dapper. We will also install a `System.Data.SqlClient` package that Dapper uses. Let's carry out the following steps:

1. Let's open the backend project in Visual Studio and go to the **Tools** menu and then the **NuGet Package Manager** and choose **Manage NuGet Packages for Solution....**

> NuGet is a tool that downloads third-party and Microsoft libraries and manages the references to them so that the libraries can easily be updated.

2. On the **Browse** tab, enter `Dapper` into the search box.
3. Select the **Dapper** package by **Sam Saffron**, **Marc Gravell**, and **Nick Craver**. Tick our project and click the **Install** button with the latest stable version selected. Refer to the following screenshot:

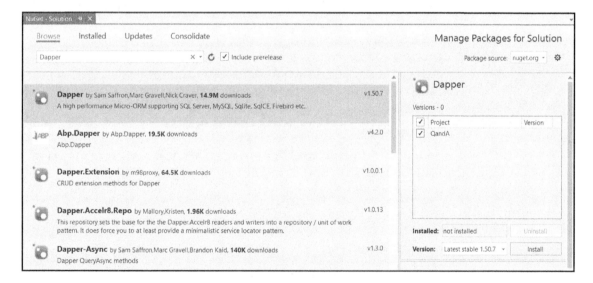

We may be asked to accept a licensing agreement before Dapper is downloaded and installed into our project.

4. Still in the NuGet package manager, search for the `System.Data.SqlClient` package and install the latest stable version. Refer to the following screenshot:

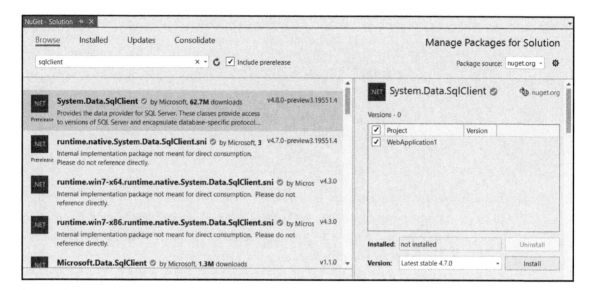

Note that Microsoft is developing a new SQL client library called `Microsoft.Data.SqlClient`, which will eventually replace `System.Data.SqlClient`. When this is released, and when Dapper supports this new library, we'll need to install the `Microsoft.Data.SqlClient` package instead of `System.Data.SqlClient` in the preceding step.

5. Next, we are going to define a connection string in our ASP.NET Core project to our database. In the Solution Explorer, open up a file called `appsettings.json` to add a `ConnectionStrings` field that contains our connection string:

```
{
  "ConnectionStrings": {
    "DefaultConnection":
"Server=localhost\\SQLEXPRESS;Database=QandA;Trusted_Connection=Tru
e;"
  },
  ...
}
```

The `appsettings.json` file is a JSON-formatted file that contains various configuration settings for an ASP.NET Core app.

Obviously, change the connection string so that it references your SQL Server and database.

So, that's Dapper installed along with a connection string to our database in place. Next up is to read data from the database using Dapper.

Reading data using Dapper

We are going to write some C# code in this section to read data from the database.

We are going to use the popular repository design pattern to structure our data access code. This will allow us to provide a nice centralized abstraction of the data layer.

We are going to start by creating a data repository class to hold all of the queries we are going to make to the data. We are going to create C# classes to hold the data we get from the database called models.

Creating the repository class

Let's create a class to hold all of the methods for interacting with the database:

1. In the **Solution Explorer**, right-click on the project, select the **Add** menu, and then choose the **New Folder** option.
2. A new folder will be created in the solution tree. Name the folder `Data`.
3. Right-click on the `Data` folder and select the **Add** menu and then choose the **Class...** option.
4. In the dialog box that appears, enter `DataRepository` for the name of the file to create and click the **Add** button.

5. A skeleton `DataRepository` class will be created:

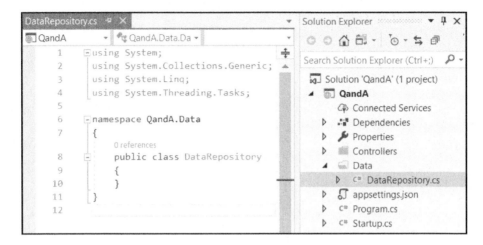

6. We are going to create an interface for the data repository so that it can be mocked when writing unit tests. Right-click on the `Data` folder and select the **Add** menu and then choose the **Class...** option.

7. This time, choose the **Interface** option in the dialog box that appears and name it `IDataRepository` before pressing the **Add** button.

8. Change the modifier for the interface to be `public` and add the following methods:

```
public interface IDataRepository
{
    IEnumerable<QuestionGetManyResponse> GetQuestions();

    IEnumerable<QuestionGetManyResponse>
      GetQuestionsBySearch(string search);

    IEnumerable<QuestionGetManyResponse>
      GetUnansweredQuestions();

    QuestionGetSingleResponse
      GetQuestion(int questionId);

    bool QuestionExists(int questionId);

    AnswerGetResponse GetAnswer(int answerId);
}
```

So, we are going to have six methods in the data repository to read different bits of data from our database. Note that this won't compile yet because we are referencing classes that don't exist.

9. Moving back to `DataRepository.cs`, specify that the class must implement the interface we just created:

```
public class DataRepository: IDataRepository
{
}
```

10. If we click on the class name, a light bulb icon will appear. Click on the light bulb menu and choose **Implement interface**:

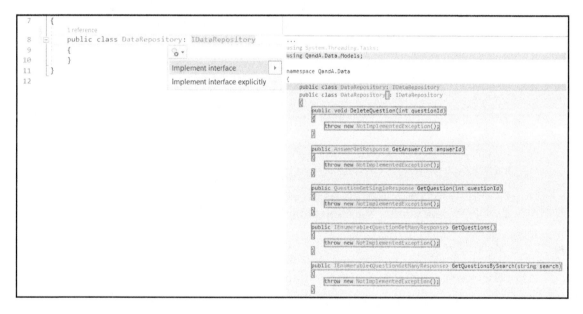

Skeleton methods will be added to the repository class that satisfies the interface.

11. Create a class-level private variable called `_connectionString` to store the database connection string:

```
public class DataRepository : IDataRepository
{
   private readonly string _connectionString;
   ...
}
```

The `readonly` keyword prevents the variable from being changed outside of the class constructor, which is what we want in this case.

12. Let's create a constructor for the repository class that will set the value of the connection string from the `appsettings.json` file:

```
public class DataRepository : IDataRepository
{
    private readonly string _connectionString;

    public DataRepository(IConfiguration configuration)
    {
    _connectionString =
    configuration["ConnectionStrings:DefaultConnection"];
    }

    ...
}
```

The `configuration` parameter in the constructor gives us access to items within the `appsettings.json` file. The key we use when accessing the `configuration` object is the path to the item we want from the `appsettings.json` file with colons being used to navigate fields in the JSON.

How does the configuration parameter get passed into the constructor? The answer is dependency injection, which we'll cover in the next chapter.

13. Our class doesn't recognize `IConfiguration` yet, so, let's click on it, click on the light bulb menu that appears, and choose **using Microsoft.Extensions.Configuration**:

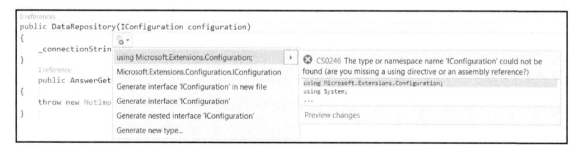

We've made a good start on the repository class. We do have compile errors, but these will disappear as we fully implement the methods.

Creating a repository method to get questions

Let's implement the GetQuestions method first:

1. Let's add a couple of using statements at the top of the file for the ADO.NET SQL client library as well as Dapper:

   ```
   using System.Data.SqlClient;
   using Dapper;
   ```

2. Let's declare a new database connection:

   ```
   public IEnumerable<QuestionGetManyResponse> GetQuestions()
   {
     using (var connection = new SqlConnection(_connectionString))
       {

       }
   }
   ```

   Notice that we've used a using block to declare the database connection.

    A using block automatically disposes of the object defined in the block when the program exits the scope of the block. This includes whether a return statement is invoked within the block as well as errors occurring within the block.

   So, the using statement is a convenient way of ensuring the connection is disposed of. Notice that we are using an ADO.NET connection because this is what the Dapper library extends.

3. Next, let's open the connection:

   ```
   public IEnumerable<QuestionGetManyResponse> GetQuestions()
   {
     using (var connection = new SqlConnection(_connectionString))
     {
       connection.Open();
     }
   }
   ```

4. Now, we can execute the query:

```
public IEnumerable<QuestionGetManyResponse> GetQuestions()
{
  using (var connection = new SqlConnection(_connectionString))
  {
    connection.Open();
    return connection.Query<QuestionGetManyResponse>(
      @"EXEC dbo.Question_GetMany"
    );
  }
}
```

We've used a `Query` extension method from Dapper on the `connection` object to execute the `Question_GetMany` stored procedure. We then simply return the results of this query from our method. Nice and simple!

Notice how we pass in a class, `QuestionGetManyResponse`, into the generic parameter of the `Query` method. This defines the model class the query results should be stored in. We'll define `QuestionGetManyResponse` in the next step.

5. In the **Solution Explorer**, right-click on the `Data` folder, choose **Add**, and then choose the **New Folder** option. Enter `Models` as the name of the new folder. We are going to place all of our models here.
6. In the **Solution Explorer**, right-click on the **Models** folder and select **Add** and then choose the **Class...** option.
7. In the dialog that appears, enter `QuestionGetManyResponse` for the name of the file to create and click the **Add** button. A skeleton class will be created for us.
8. Add the following properties to the class:

```
public class QuestionGetManyResponse
{
  public int QuestionId { get; set; }
  public string Title { get; set; }
  public string Content { get; set; }
  public string UserName { get; set; }
  public DateTime Created { get; set; }
}
```

The property names match the fields outputted from the `Question_GetMany` stored procedure. This allows Dapper to automatically map the data from the database to this class. The property types have also been carefully chosen so this Dapper mapping process works.

> Note that the class doesn't need to contain properties for all of the fields output from the stored procedure. Dapper will ignore fields that don't have corresponding properties in the class.

9. Moving back to `DataRepository.cs`, add a `using` statement so that the class can get access to the models:

   ```
   using QandA.Data.Models;
   ```

10. Let's also add this `using` statement in `IDataRepository.cs`:

    ```
    using QandA.Data.Models;
    ```

Congratulations, we have implemented our first repository method! This consisted of just a few lines of code that opened a database connection and executed a query. So, writing data access code in Dapper is super simple.

Creating a repository method to get questions by a search

Let's implement the `GetQuestionsBySearch` method, which is similar to the `GetQuestions` method, but this time, the method and stored procedure have a parameter. Let's carry out the following steps:

1. Start by creating and opening the connection in the same way as we did when we implemented the last method:

   ```
   public IEnumerable<QuestionGetManyResponse>
   GetQuestionsBySearch(string search)
   {
     using (var connection = new SqlConnection(_connectionString))
     {
       connection.Open();
       // TODO - execute Question_GetMany_BySearch stored procedure
     }
   }
   ```

2. Now, we can execute the `Question_GetMany_BySearch` stored procedure:

```
public IEnumerable<QuestionGetManyResponse>
GetQuestionsBySearch(string search)
{
  using (var connection = new SqlConnection(_connectionString))
  {
    connection.Open();
    return connection.Query<QuestionGetManyResponse>(
      @"EXEC dbo.Question_GetMany_BySearch @Search = @Search",
      new { Search = search }
    );
  }
}
```

Notice how we pass in the stored procedure parameter value.

Parameter values are passed into a Dapper query using an object with its property names matching the parameter names. Dapper will then create and execute a parameterized query.

In this case, we've used an anonymous object for the parameters to save us defining a class for the object.

Why do we have to pass a parameter to Dapper? Why can't we just do the following:

```
return connection.Query<QuestionGetManyResponse>($"EXEC
dbo.Question_GetMany_BySearch '{search}'");
```

Well, there are several reasons, but the main one is that the preceding code is vulnerable to a SQL injection attack. So, it's always best to pass parameters into Dapper rather than trying to construct the SQL ourselves.

That's our second repository method complete. Nice and simple!

Creating a repository method to get unanswered questions

Let's implement the `GetUnansweredQuestions` method, which is very similar to the `GetQuestions` method:

```
public IEnumerable<QuestionGetManyResponse> GetUnansweredQuestions()
{
```

```
  using (var connection = new SqlConnection(_connectionString))
  {
    connection.Open();
    return connection.Query<QuestionGetManyResponse>(
      "EXEC dbo.Question_GetUnanswered"
    );
  }
}
```

So, we open the connection, execute the `Question_GetUnanswered` stored procedure, and return the results in the `QuestionGetManyResponse` class we have already created.

Creating a repository method to get a single question

Let's implement the `GetQuestion` method now:

1. Start by opening the connection and executing the `Question_GetSingle` stored procedure:

```
public QuestionGetSingleResponse GetQuestion(int questionId)
{
  using (var connection = new SqlConnection(_connectionString))
  {
    connection.Open();
    var question =
      connection.QueryFirstOrDefault<QuestionGetSingleResponse>(
        @"EXEC dbo.Question_GetSingle @QuestionId = @QuestionId",
        new { QuestionId = questionId }
      );

    // TODO - Get the answers for the question

    return question;
  }
}
```

This method is a little different from the previous methods because we use the `QueryFirstOrDefault` Dapper method to return a single record (or `null` if the record isn't found) rather than a collection of records.

2. We need to execute a second stored procedure to get the answers for the question, so let's do this:

```
public QuestionGetSingleResponse GetQuestion(int questionId)
{
  using (var connection = new SqlConnection(_connectionString))
  {
    connection.Open();
    var question =
      connection.QueryFirstOrDefault<QuestionGetSingleResponse>(
        @"EXEC dbo.Question_GetSingle @QuestionId = @QuestionId",
        new { QuestionId = questionId }
      );
    question.Answers =
      connection.Query<AnswerGetResponse>(
        @"EXEC dbo.Answer_Get_ByQuestionId
          @QuestionId = @QuestionId",
        new { QuestionId = questionId }
      );

    return question;
  }
}
```

3. The question may not be found and return `null`, so let's handle this case and only add the answers if the question is found:

```
public QuestionGetSingleResponse GetQuestion(int questionId)
{
  using (var connection = new SqlConnection(_connectionString))
  {
    connection.Open();
    var question =
      connection.QueryFirstOrDefault<QuestionGetSingleResponse>(
        @"EXEC dbo.Question_GetSingle @QuestionId = @QuestionId",
        new { QuestionId = questionId }
      );
    if (question != null)
    {
      question.Answers =
        connection.Query<AnswerGetResponse>(
          @"EXEC dbo.Answer_Get_ByQuestionId
            @QuestionId = @QuestionId",
```

```
                  new { QuestionId = questionId }
            );
        }
      return question;
    }
  }
```

4. Let's create the `QuestionGetSingleResponse` class we referenced in the method in a file called `QuestionGetSingleResponse.cs` in the `Models` folder:

```
public class QuestionGetSingleResponse
{
  public int QuestionId { get; set; }
  public string Title { get; set; }
  public string Content { get; set; }
  public string UserName { get; set; }
  public string UserId { get; set; }
  public DateTime Created { get; set; }
  public IEnumerable<AnswerGetResponse> Answers { get; set; }
}
```

These properties match up with the data returned from the `Question_GetSingle` stored procedure.

5. Let's also create the `AnswerGetResponse` class we referenced in the method in a file called `AnswerGetResponse.cs` in the `Models` folder:

```
public class AnswerGetResponse
{
  public int AnswerId { get; set; }
  public string Content { get; set; }
  public string UserName { get; set; }
  public DateTime Created { get; set; }
}
```

These properties match up with the data returned from the `Answer_Get_ByQuestionId` stored procedure.

The `GetQuestion` method should compile fine now.

Creating a repository method to check whether a question exists

Let's implement the `QuestionExists` method now, following the same approach as the previous methods:

```
public bool QuestionExists(int questionId)
{
  using (var connection = new SqlConnection(_connectionString))
  {
    connection.Open();
    return connection.QueryFirst<bool>(
      @"EXEC dbo.Question_Exists @QuestionId = @QuestionId",
      new { QuestionId = questionId }
    );
  }
}
```

We are using the Dapper `QueryFirst` method rather than `QueryFirstOrDefault` because the stored procedure will always return a single record.

Creating a repository method to get an answer

The last method to implement in this section is `GetAnswer`:

```
public AnswerGetResponse GetAnswer(int answerId)
{
  using (var connection = new SqlConnection(_connectionString))
  {
    connection.Open();
    return connection.QueryFirstOrDefault<AnswerGetResponse>(
      @"EXEC dbo.Answer_Get_ByAnswerId @AnswerId = @AnswerId",
      new { AnswerId = answerId }
    );
  }
}
```

There is nothing new here—the implementation follows the same pattern as the previous methods.

We have now implemented all of the methods in the data repository for reading data. In the next section, we'll turn our attention to writing data.

Writing data using Dapper

In this section, we are going to implement methods in our data repository to write to the database. We will start by extending the interface for the repository and then do the actual implementation.

The stored procedures that perform the write operations are already in the database. We will be interacting with these stored procedures using Dapper.

Adding methods to write data to the repository interface

We'll start by adding the methods to the repository interface:

```
public interface IDataRepository
{
    ...
    QuestionGetSingleResponse
      PostQuestion(QuestionPostRequest question);

    QuestionGetSingleResponse
      PutQuestion(int questionId, QuestionPutRequest question);

    void DeleteQuestion(int questionId);

    AnswerGetResponse PostAnswer(AnswerPostRequest answer);
}
```

So, we are required to implement methods to add, change, and delete questions as well as adding an answer.

Creating a repository method to add a new question

Let's create the PostQuestion method in DataRepository.cs to add a new question:

```
public QuestionGetSingleResponse PostQuestion(QuestionPostRequest question)
{
    using (var connection = new SqlConnection(_connectionString))
    {
        connection.Open();
        var questionId = connection.QueryFirst<int>(
```

```
    @"EXEC dbo.Question_Post
      @Title = @Title, @Content = @Content,
      @UserId = @UserId, @UserName = @UserName,
      @Created = @Created",
    question
  );

  return GetQuestion(questionId);
    }
  }
```

This is a very similar implementation to the methods that read data. We use the QueryFirst Dapper method because the stored procedure returns the ID of the new question after inserting it into the database table. Our method returns the saved question by calling the GetQuestion method with questionId that was returned from the Question_Post stored procedure.

We've used a model class called QuestionPostRequest for Dapper to map to the SQL parameters. Let's create this class in the models folder:

```
public class QuestionPostRequest
{
  public string Title { get; set; }
  public string Content { get; set; }
  public string UserId { get; set; }
  public string UserName { get; set; }
  public DateTime Created { get; set; }
}
```

Great stuff! That's our first write method created.

Creating a repository method to change a question

Let's create the PutQuestion method in DataRepository.cs to change a question. This is very similar to the PostQuestion method we have just implemented:

```
public QuestionGetSingleResponse PutQuestion(int questionId,
QuestionPutRequest question)
{
  using (var connection = new SqlConnection(_connectionString))
  {
    connection.Open();
    connection.Execute(
```

```
@"EXEC dbo.Question_Put
   @QuestionId = @QuestionId, @Title = @Title, @Content = @Content",
 new { QuestionId = questionId, question.Title, question.Content }
);
return GetQuestion(questionId);
}
}
```

Notice that we use the Dapper Execute method because we are simply executing a stored procedure and not returning anything.

We've created the SQL parameters from a model class called QuestionPutRequest and the questionId parameters that were passed into the method. Let's create the QuestionPutRequest class in the models folder:

```
public class QuestionPutRequest
{
  public string Title { get; set; }
  public string Content { get; set; }
}
```

That's another method implemented.

Creating a repository method to delete a question

Moving on, let's implement a method for deleting a question now:

```
public void DeleteQuestion(int questionId)
{
  using (var connection = new SqlConnection(_connectionString))
  {
    connection.Open();
    connection.Execute(
      @"EXEC dbo.Question_Delete
         @QuestionId = @QuestionId",
      new { QuestionId = questionId }
    );
  }
}
```

We again use the Dapper Execute method because nothing is returned from the stored procedure.

Creating a repository method to add an answer

The last method we are going to implement is for adding an answer to a question:

```
public AnswerGetResponse PostAnswer(AnswerPostRequest answer)
{
  using (var connection = new SqlConnection(_connectionString))
  {
    connection.Open();
    return connection.QueryFirst<AnswerGetResponse>(
      @"EXEC dbo.Answer_Post
        @QuestionId = @QuestionId, @Content = @Content,
        @UserId = @UserId, @UserName = @UserName,
        @Created = @Created",
      answer
    );
  }
}
```

As well as inserting the answer into the database table, the stored procedure returns the saved answer. So, we use the Dapper `QueryFirst` method to execute the stored procedure and return the saved answer.

We also need to create the `AnswerPostRequest` model class in the `models` folder:

```
public class AnswerPostRequest
{
  public int QuestionId { get; set; }
  public string Content { get; set; }
  public string UserId { get; set; }
  public string UserName { get; set; }
  public DateTime Created { get; set; }
}
```

That completes our data repository. We've chosen to have a single method containing all of the methods to read and write data. We can, of course, create multiple repositories for different areas of the database, which would be a good idea if the app was larger.

As we add features to our app that involve database changes we'll need a mechanism of deploying the database changes. We'll look at this in the next section.

Managing migrations using DbUp

DbUp is an open source library that helps us to deploy changes to SQL Server databases. It keeps track of SQL Scripts embedded with an ASP.NET Core project along with which ones have been executed on the database. It has methods that we can use to execute the SQL Scripts that haven't been executed yet on the database.

In this section, we are going to add DbUp to our project and configure it to do our database migrations when our app starts up.

Installing DbUp into our project

Let's start by installing DbUp by carrying out the following steps in our backend project, in Visual Studio:

1. Go to the **Tools** menu and then the **NuGet Package Manager** and then choose **Manage NuGet Packages for Solution...**.
2. On the **Browse** tab, enter DbUp into the search box.
3. Select the **dbup** package by Paul Stovell, Jim Burger, Jake Ginnivan, and Damian Maclennan. Tick our project and click the **Install** button with the latest stable version selected:

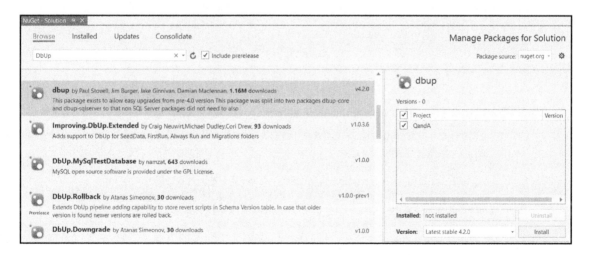

We may be asked to accept a licensing agreement before DbUp is downloaded and installed into our project.

Configuring DbUp to do migrations on app startup

Now that we have DbUp installed into our project, let's get it to do database migrations when the app starts up:

1. Open up `Startup.cs`. We know from `Chapter 1`, *Understanding the ASP.NET Core React Template,* that code in this file executes when an ASP.NET Core app runs up. We'll start by adding a `using` statement so that we can reference the DbUp library:

   ```
   using DbUp;
   ```

2. In the `ConfigureServices` method, add the following two lines:

   ```
   public void ConfigureServices(IServiceCollection services)
   {
     var connectionString =
       Configuration.GetConnectionString("DefaultConnection");
     EnsureDatabase.For.SqlDatabase(connectionString);

     // TODO - Create and configure an instance of the DbUp upgrader
     // TODO - Do a database migration if there are any pending SQL
     //Scripts

     services.AddControllers();
   }
   ```

   This gets the database connection from the `appsettings.json` file and creates the database if it doesn't exist.

3. Let's create and configure an instance of the DbUp upgrader:

   ```
   public void ConfigureServices(IServiceCollection services)
   {
     var connectionString =
       Configuration.GetConnectionString("DefaultConnection");
     EnsureDatabase.For.SqlDatabase(connectionString);

     var upgrader = DeployChanges.To
       .SqlDatabase(connectionString, null)
   ```

```
          .WithScriptsEmbeddedInAssembly(
            System.Reflection.Assembly.GetExecutingAssembly()
          )
          .WithTransaction()
          .Build();

      // TODO - Do a database migration if there are any pending SQL
      //Scripts

      services.AddControllers();
  }
```

We've told DbUp where the database is and to look for SQL Scripts that have been embedded in our project. We've also told DbUp to do the database migrations in a transaction.

4. The final step is to get DbUp to do a database migration if there are any pending SQL Scripts:

```
      public void ConfigureServices(IServiceCollection services)
      {
        var connectionString =
          Configuration.GetConnectionString("DefaultConnection");

        EnsureDatabase.For.SqlDatabase(connectionString);

        var upgrader = DeployChanges.To
          .SqlDatabase(connectionString, null)
          .WithScriptsEmbeddedInAssembly(
            System.Reflection.Assembly.GetExecutingAssembly()
          )
          .WithTransaction()
          .LogToConsole()
          .Build();

        if (upgrader.IsUpgradeRequired())
        {
          upgrader.PerformUpgrade();
        }
        services.AddControllers();
      }
```

We use the IsUpgradeRequired method in the DbUp upgrade to check whether there are any pending SQL Scripts and the PerformUpgrade method to do the actual migration.

Embedding SQL Scripts in our project

In the last subsection, we told DbUp to look for SQL Scripts that have been embedded in our project. So, we are now going to embed SQL Scripts for the tables and stored procedures in our project so that DbUp will execute them if they haven't already been executed when our app loads:

1. In **Solution Explorer**, right-click on the project, and choose **Add | New Folder**. Enter `SQLScripts` as the folder name.
2. Right-click on the **SQLScripts** folder and choose **Add | New Item...**.
3. In the dialog box that appears, select the **General** tab and then **Text File** and enter `01-Tables.sql` as the filename:

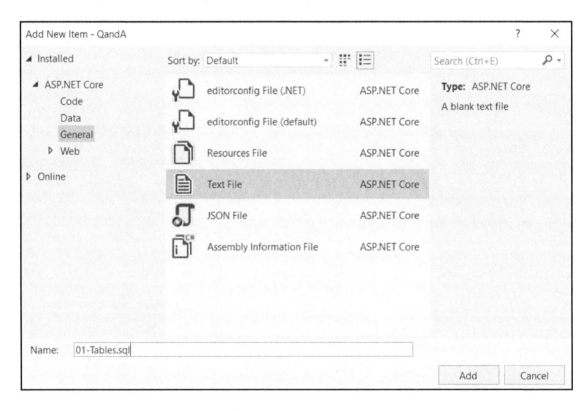

4. Copy the contents of the script from `https://github.com/PacktPublishing/ASP.NET-Core-3-and-React-17/blob/master/Chapter07/backend/SQLScripts/01-Tables.sql` and paste it into the file we just created.

5. Right-click on **01-Tables.sql** in **Solution Explorer** and choose **Properties** to view the properties of this file.

6. Change the **Build Action** property to `Embedded resource`:

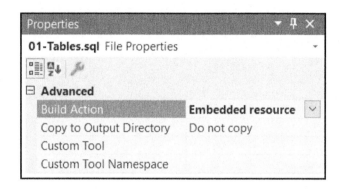

This embeds the SQL Script in our project so that DbUp can find it.

7. Let's repeat this process for the stored procedures by first creating a file called `02-Sprocs.sql` in the `SQLScripts` folder with the content from `https://github.com/PacktPublishing/ASP.NET-Core-3-and-React-17/blob/master/Chapter07/backend/SQLScripts/02-Sprocs.sql`. Let's not forget to embed this file as a project resource.

DbUp will run SQL Scripts in name order, so it's important to have a script naming convention that caters to this. In our example, we are prefixing the script name with a two-digit number.

So, those are the SQL Scripts that make up our database saved within our project.

Performing a database migration

Let's now try a database migration by carrying out the following steps:

1. The database that we are working with already contains the tables and stored procedures in our scripts, so we are going to be brave and delete our database. In SSMS, in **Object Explorer**, right-click the database and choose **Delete**:

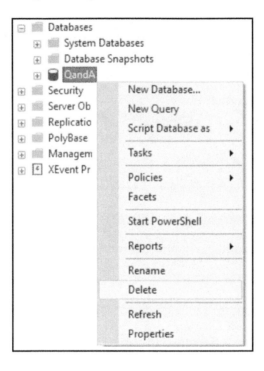

2. We are going to create the database again with the same name. So, in **Object Explorer**, right-click on **Databases** and click on the **New Database...** option. Enter QandA for the name of the database and click **OK**:

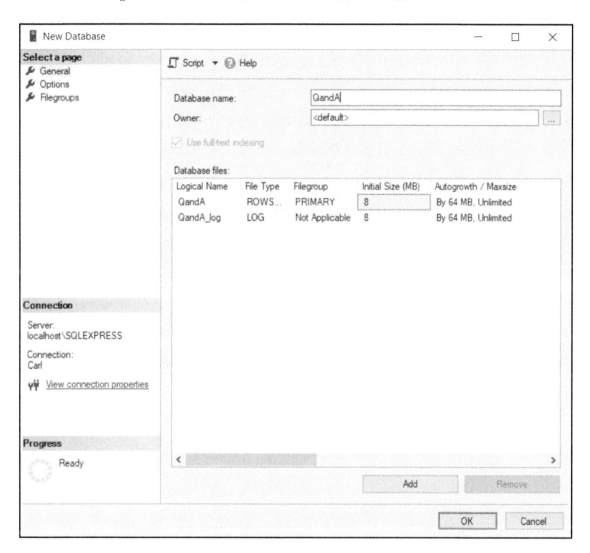

3. Back in Visual Studio, press *F5* to run the app.

4. After the app has run up, go to SSMS, and in **Object Explorer**, we'll see that the tables and stored procedures have been created. We'll also see a table called `SchemaVersions`:

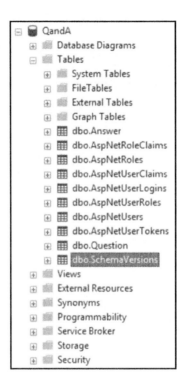

5. Right-click on **dbo.SchemaVersions** and choose **Edit Top 200 Rows:**

Id	ScriptName	Applied
1	QandA.SQLScripts.01-Tables.sql	2019-02-1...
2	QandA.SQLScripts.02-Sprocs.sql	2019-02-1...
NULL	*NULL*	*NULL*

This is a table that DbUp uses to manage what scripts have been executed. So, we'll see our two scripts listed in this table.

6. Back in Visual Studio, stop the app by pressing *Shift + F5*.
7. Run the app again. The app will run up just fine.
8. Inspect the database objects in **Object Explorer** in SSMS. The objects will be unchanged.
9. Examine the contents of the `SchemaVersions` table. We'll find that no new scripts have been added.
10. We can now stop the app again in Visual Studio.

So, our project is now set up to handle database migrations. All we need to do is to add the necessary SQL Script files in the `SQLScripts` folder remembering to embed them as a resource. DbUp will then do the migration when the app next runs.

Summary

We now understand that Dapper is a simple way of interacting with a database in a performant manner. It's a great choice when our team already has SQL Server skills because it doesn't abstract the database away from us.

We learned that Dapper adds various extension methods on the ADO.NET `SqlConnection` object for reading and writing to the database. Dapper maps the results of a query to instances of a C# class automatically by matching field names in the query result to the class properties. Query parameters can be passed in using a C# class with Dapper automatically mapping properties in the C# class to the SQL parameters.

We discovered that DbUp is a simple open source tool that can be used to manage database migrations. We embed SQL Scripts within our project and write code that is executed when our app loads to instruct DbUp to check and perform any necessary migrations.

In the next chapter, we are going to create the RESTful API for our app leveraging the data access code we have written in this chapter.

Questions

Answer the following questions to test the knowledge we have gained in this chapter:

1. What Dapper method can be used to execute a stored procedure that returns no results?
2. What Dapper method can be used to read a single record of data where the record is guaranteed to exist?
3. What Dapper method can be used to read a collection of records?
4. What is wrong with the following statement that calls the Dapper Query method?

    ```
    return connection.Query<BuildingGetManyResponse>(
      @"EXEC dbo.Building_GetMany_BySearch
        @Search = @Search",
      new { Criteria = "Fred"}
    );
    ```

5. We have the following stored procedure:

    ```
    CREATE PROC dbo.Building_GetMany
    AS
    BEGIN
      SET NOCOUNT ON

      SELECT BuildingId, Name
      FROM dbo.Building
    END
    ```

    We have the following statement that calls the Dapper Query method:

    ```
    return connection.Query<BuildingGetManyResponse>(
      "EXEC dbo.Building_GetMany"
    );
    ```

    We also have the following model that is referenced in the preceding statement:

    ```
    public class BuildingGetManyResponse
    {
      public int Id{ get; set; }
      public string Name { get; set; }
    }
    ```

When our app is run, we find that the Id property within the BuildingGetManyResponse class instances is not populated. Can you spot the problem?

6. Can DbUp be used to deploy new reference data within a table?

Further reading

Here are some useful links to learn more about the topics covered in this chapter:

- Creating a SQL Server database: `https://docs.microsoft.com/en-us/sql/relational-databases/databases/create-a-database?view=sql-server-2017`.
- Creating SQL Server tables: `https://docs.microsoft.com/en-us/sql/t-sql/statements/create-table-transact-sql?view=sql-server-2017`.
- Creating SQL Server stored procedures: `https://docs.microsoft.com/en-us/sql/relational-databases/stored-procedures/create-a-stored-procedure?view=sql-server-2017`.
- The C# `using` statement: `https://docs.microsoft.com/en-us/dotnet/csharp/language-reference/keywords/using-statement`.
- Dapper: `https://github.com/StackExchange/Dapper`.
- DbUp: `https://dbup.readthedocs.io/en/latest/`.

Creating REST API Endpoints

8

In Chapter 1, *Understanding the ASP.NET Core React Template*, we learned that a RESTful endpoint is implemented using an API controller in ASP.NET Core. In this chapter, we'll implement an API controller for our Q & A app that will eventually allow the frontend to read and write questions and answers. We'll implement a range of controller action methods that handle different HTTP request methods returning appropriate responses.

We'll learn about dependency injection and use this to inject the data repository we created in the previous chapter into the API controller. We'll validate requests so that we can be sure the data is valid before it reaches the data repository.

At the end of the chapter, we'll ensure we aren't asking for unnecessary information in the API requests. This will prevent potential security issues as well as improving the experience for API consumers.

In this chapter, we'll cover the following topics:

- Creating an API controller
- Creating controller action methods
- Adding model validation
- Removing unnecessary request fields

Technical requirements

We'll use the following tools in this chapter:

- **Visual Studio 2019**: We'll use this to edit our ASP.NET Core code. This can be downloaded from https://visualstudio.microsoft.com/vs/.
- **.NET Core 3.0**: This can be downloaded from https://dotnet.microsoft.com/download/dotnet-core.

- **Postman**: We'll use this to try out the REST API endpoint we'll implement in this chapter. This can be downloaded from `https://www.getpostman.com/downloads/`.
- **Q & A**: We'll start with the Q & A backend project we finished in the previous chapter. This is available on GitHub at `https://github.com/carlrip/ASP.NET-Core-and-React-Book`.

All the code snippets in this chapter can be found online at `https://github.com/carlrip/ASP.NET-Core-and-React-Book`. In order to restore code from a chapter, the source code repository can be downloaded and the relevant folder opened in the relevant editor. If the code is frontend code then `npm install` can be entered in the Terminal to restore the dependencies.

Check out the following video to see the code in action:

`http://bit.ly/2PUriJg`

Creating an API controller

In this section, we are going to create an API controller to handle requests to an `api/questions` endpoint. The controller will call into the data repository we created in the previous chapter. We'll also create an instance of the data repository in the API controller using dependency injection.

Creating an API controller for questions

Let's create a controller for the `api/questions` endpoint. If we don't have our backend project open in Visual Studio, let's do so and carry out the following steps:

1. In **Solution Explorer**, right-click on the **Controllers** folder, choose **Add**, and then Class....
2. In the left-hand panel, find and select **ASP.NET Core** and then **API Controller Class** in the middle panel. Enter `QuestionsController.cs` for the name of the file and click **Add**:

3. If the generated class doesn't inherit from `ControllerBase`, let's add this and remove the example action methods:

```
public class QuestionsController : ControllerBase
{
}
```

`ControllerBase` will give us access to more API-specific methods in our controller.

4. If the generated class isn't decorated with the `Route` and `ApiController` attributes, let's add them:

```
[Route("api/[controller]")]
[ApiController]
```

```
public class QuestionsController : ControllerBase
{
}
```

The Route attribute defines the path that our controller will handle. In our case, the path will be api/questions because [controller] is substituted with the name of the controller minus the word controller.

The ApiController attribute includes behavior such as automatic model validation, which we'll take advantage of later in this chapter.

Injecting the data repository into the API controller

We want to interact with an instance of the data repository we created in the previous chapter into our API controller. Let's carry out the following steps to do this:

1. We'll start by adding using statements to the QuestionsController.cs file so that the data repository and its models can be referenced:

```
using QandA.Data;
using QandA.Data.Models;
```

2. Create a private class-level variable to hold a reference to our repository:

```
[Route("api/[controller]")]
[ApiController]
public class QuestionsController : ControllerBase
{
    private readonly IDataRepository _dataRepository;
}
```

We've used the readonly keyword to make sure the variable's reference doesn't change outside the constructor.

3. Let's create the constructor as follows:

```
private readonly IDataRepository _dataRepository;

public QuestionsController()
{
    // TODO - set reference to _dataRepository
}
```

We need to set up the reference to `_dataRepository` in the constructor. We could try the following:

```
public QuestionsController()
{
    _dataRepository = new DataRepository();
}
```

However, the `DataRepository` constructor requires the connection string to be passed in. Recall that we used something called **dependency injection** in the previous chapter to inject the `configuration` object into the data repository constructor to give us access to the connection string. Maybe we could use dependency injection to inject the data repository into our API controller? Yes, this is exactly what we are going to do.

Dependency injection is the process of injecting an instance of a class into another object. The goal of dependency injection is to decouple a class from its dependencies so that the dependencies can be changed without changing the class. ASP.NET Core has its own dependency injection facility that allows class dependencies to be defined when the app starts up. These dependencies are then available to be injected into other class constructors.

4. Change the constructor to the following:

```
public QuestionsController(IDataRepository dataRepository)
{
 _dataRepository = dataRepository;
}
```

So, our constructor now expects the data repository to be passed into the constructor as a parameter. We then simply set our private class-level variable to the data repository passed in.

Unlike the `configuration` object that was injected into the data repository, the data repository isn't automatically available for dependency injection. ASP.NET Core already sets up the `configuration` object for dependency injection for us because it is responsible for this class. However, the `DataRepository` is our class, so we must register this for dependency injection.

5. Let's go to `startup.cs` and add a `using` statement so that we can reference our data repository:

```
using QandA.Data;
```

6. Enter the following at the bottom of the `ConfigureServices` class to make the data repository available for dependency injection:

```
public void ConfigureServices(IServiceCollection services)
{
    ...
    services.AddScoped<IDataRepository, DataRepository>();
}
```

This tells ASP.NET Core that whenever `IDataRepository` is referenced in a constructor, substitute an instance of the `DataRepository` class.

The `AddScoped` method means that only one instance of the `DataRepository` class is created in a given HTTP request. This means the lifetime of the class that is created lasts for the whole HTTP request.

So, if ASP.NET Core encounters a second constructor that references `IDataRepository` in the same HTTP request, it will use the instance of the `DataRepository` class it created previously.

As well as `AddScoped`, there are other methods for registering dependencies that result in different lifetimes for the generated class. `AddTransient` will generate a new instance of the class each time it is requested. `AddSingleton` will generate only one class instance for the lifetime of the whole app.

So, we now have access to our data repository in our API controller with the help of dependency injection. Next, we are going to implement methods that are going to handle specific HTTP requests.

Creating controller action methods

Action methods are where we can write code to handle requests to a resource. In this section, we are going to implement action methods that will handle requests to the questions resource. We will cover the `GET`, `POST`, `PUT`, and `DELETE` HTTP methods.

Creating an action method for getting questions

Let's implement our first action method, which is going to return an array of all the questions:

1. Let's create a method called `GetQuestions` in our API controller class:

   ```
   [HttpGet]
   public IEnumerable<QuestionGetManyResponse> GetQuestions()
   {
       // TODO - get questions from data repository
       // TODO - return questions in the response
   }
   ```

   We decorate the method with the `HttpGet` attribute to tell ASP.NET Core that this will handle HTTP GET requests to this resource.

   We use the specific `IEnumerable<QuestionGetManyResponse>` type as the return type.

2. Let's get the questions from the repository using the `_dataRepository` class variable:

   ```
   [HttpGet]
   public IEnumerable<QuestionGetManyResponse> GetQuestions()
   {
       var questions = _dataRepository.GetQuestions();
       // TODO - return questions in the response
   }
   ```

3. Let's return the questions in the response:

   ```
   [HttpGet]
   public IEnumerable<QuestionGetManyResponse> GetQuestions()
   {
       var questions = _dataRepository.GetQuestions();
       return questions;
   }
   ```

   ASP.NET Core will automatically convert the `questions` object to JSON format and put this in the response body. It will also automatically return 200 as the HTTP status code. Nice!

4. Let's try this by first pressing *F5* in Visual Studio to start our app.

5. In the browser that opens, change the path to end with `api/questions` rather than `weatherforecast`:

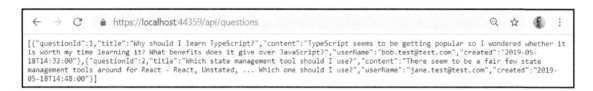

We'll see the questions from our database output in JSON format. Great, that's our first action method implemented!

6. We are going to change the default path that invokes when the app is run to the `api/questions` path. Open up the `launchSettings.json` file in the `Properties` folder in **Solution Explorer** and change the paths referenced to `api/questions`:

```
...
"profiles": {
  "IIS Express": {
    "commandName": "IISExpress",
    "launchBrowser": true,
    "launchUrl": "api/questions",
    "environmentVariables": {
      "ASPNETCORE_ENVIRONMENT": "Development"
    }
  },
  "QandA": {
    "commandName": "Project",
    "launchBrowser": true,
    "launchUrl": "api/questions",
    "applicationUrl":
"https://localhost:5001;http://localhost:5000",
    "environmentVariables": {
      "ASPNETCORE_ENVIRONMENT": "Development"
    }
  }
}
...
```

7. If the `Properties` folder isn't visible in **Solution Explorer**, then switch **Show All Files** on in the toolbar:

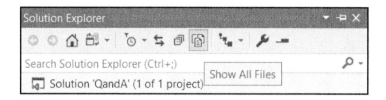

8. Press *Shift* + *F5* to stop the app, and then *F5* to start it again. Our `api/questions` path will now be invoked by default in the browser.

9. Press *Shift* + *F5* again to stop the app. Now, we are ready for implementing more code in our next task.

That completes the action method that will handle GET requests to `api/questions`. We will continue implementing more action methods in the following sub-sections.

Extending the GetQuestions action method for searching

We don't always want all of the questions though. Recall that our frontend had a search feature that returned questions that matched the search criteria. Let's extend our `GetQuestions` method to handle a search request:

1. Add a `search` parameter to the `GetQuestions` method:

```
[HttpGet]
public IEnumerable<QuestionGetManyResponse>
  GetQuestions(string search)
{
    var questions = _dataRepository.GetQuestions();
    return questions;
}
```

2. Put a breakpoint on the statement that gets the questions from the repository and press *F5* to run the app:

```
public IEnumerable<QuestionGetManyResponse> GetQuestions(string search)
{                                                         ● search null ⊢
    var questions = _dataRepository.GetQuestions();
    return questions;
}
```

We'll see that the search parameter is `null`. Press *F5* to let the app continue.

3. With the breakpoint still in place, change the URL in the browser to end with `questions?search=type`:

```
public IEnumerable<QuestionGetManyResponse> GetQuestions(string search)
{                                                      ● search 🔍 ▾ "type" ▣
    var questions = _dataRepository.GetQuestions();  ≤6,711ms elapsed
    return questions;
}
```

This time the `search` parameter is set to the value of the `search` query parameter we put in the browser URL. This process is called **model binding**.

Model binding is a process in ASP.NET Core that maps data from HTTP requests to action method parameters. Data from query parameters is automatically mapped to action method parameters that have the same name. We'll see later in this section that model binding can also map data from the HTTP request body. So, a `[FromQuery]` attribute could be placed in front of the action method parameter to instruct ASP.NET Core to map only from the query parameter.

4. Let's stop the app running by pressing *Shift + F5*.
5. Let's branch our code on whether the `search` parameter contains a value and get and return all the questions if it doesn't:

```
[HttpGet]
public IEnumerable<QuestionGetManyResponse>
  GetQuestions(string search)
{
    if (string.IsNullOrEmpty(search))
    {
        return _dataRepository.GetQuestions();
    }
    else
    {
        // TODO - call data repository question search
    }
}
```

If there is no search value, we get and return all the questions as we did before, but this time in a single statement.

6. Let's add a call to the data repository question search method if we have a `search` value:

```
[HttpGet]
public IEnumerable<QuestionGetManyResponse>
  GetQuestions(string search)
{
    if (string.IsNullOrEmpty(search))
    {
        return _dataRepository.GetQuestions();
    }
    else
    {
        return _dataRepository.GetQuestionsBySearch(search);
    }
}
```

7. Let's run the app and give this a try. All the questions will be returned in the browser when it opens up. Let's add a `search` query parameter with a value of `type`:

We'll see that the TypeScript question is returned as we would expect.

8. Stop our app running by pressing *Shift + F5* so that we can write more code for our next task.

We have started to take advantage of model binding in ASP.NET Core. We'll continue to use it throughout this chapter.

Creating an action method for getting unanswered questions

Recall that the home screen of our app, as implemented in Chapter 3, *Getting Started with React and TypeScript*, shows the unanswered questions.

So, let's implement an action method that provides this functionality:

1. Let's fully implement the method:

```
[HttpGet("unanswered")]
public IEnumerable<QuestionGetManyResponse>
  GetUnansweredQuestions()
{
    return _dataRepository.GetUnansweredQuestions();
}
```

The implementation simply calls into the data repository
`GetUnansweredQuestions` method and returns the results.

Notice that the `HttpGet` attribute contains the string `"unanswered"`. This is an additional path to concatenate to the controller's root path. So, this action method will handle GET requests to the `api/questions/unanswered` path.

2. Let's give this a try by running the app in a browser by entering the `api/questions/unanswered` path:

We get the unanswered question about state management as expected.

3. Stop our app running by pressing *Shift + F5* so that we can write another action method.

That completes the implementation of the action method that handles GET requests to `api/questions/unanswered`.

Creating an action method for getting a single question

Let's move on to implementing the action method for getting a single question:

1. Add the following skeleton method:

```
[HttpGet("{questionId}")]
public ActionResult<QuestionGetSingleResponse>
```

```
GetQuestion(int questionId)
{
    // TODO - call the data repository to get the question
    // TODO - return HTTP status code 404 if the question isn't
       found
    // TODO - return question in response with status code 200
}
```

Note the `HttpGet` attribute parameter.

 The curly brackets tell ASP.NET Core to put the path after the controller root path in a variable that can be referenced as a method parameter.

In this method, the `questionId` parameter will be set to whatever comes after the controller root path. So, for the `api/questions/3` path, `questionId` would be set to `3`.

Notice that the return type is `ActionResult<QuestionGetSingleResponse>` rather than just `QuestionGetSingleResponse`. This is because our action method won't return `QuestionGetSingleResponse` in all the return paths—there will be a path that will return `NotFoundResult` when the question can't be found. `ActionResult` gives us the flexibility to return these different types.

2. Let's call into the repository to get the question:

```
[HttpGet("{questionId}")]
public ActionResult<QuestionGetSingleResponse>
  GetQuestion(int questionId)
{
    var question = _dataRepository.GetQuestion(questionId);
    // TODO - return HTTP status code 404 if the question isn't
       found
    // TODO - return question in response with status code 200
}
```

3. Next, we can check whether the question has been found and return HTTP status code 404 if it hasn't been found:

```
[HttpGet("{questionId}")]
public ActionResult<QuestionGetSingleResponse> GetQuestion(int
questionId)
{
    var question = _dataRepository.GetQuestion(questionId);
    if (question == null)
    {
        return NotFound();
    }
    // TODO - return question in response with status code 200
}
```

If the question isn't found, the result from the repository call will be `null`. So, we check for `null` and return a call to the `NotFound` method in `ControllerBase`, which returns HTTP status code `404`.

4. The last implementation step is to `return` the question that has been found:

```
[HttpGet("{questionId}")]
public ActionResult<QuestionGetSingleResponse> GetQuestion(int
questionId)
{
    var question = _dataRepository.GetQuestion(questionId);
    if (question == null)
    {
        return NotFound();
    }
    return question;
}
```

5. Let's give this a try by running the app and requesting question 1:

https://localhost:44359/api/questions/1

{"questionId":1,"title":"Why should I learn TypeScript?","content":"TypeScript seems to be getting popular so I wondered whether it is worth my time learning it? What benefits does it give over JavaScript?","userId":"1","userName":"bob.test@test.com","created":"2019-05-18T14:32:00","answers": [{"answerId":1,"content":"To catch problems earlier speeding up your developments","userName":"jane.test@test.com","created":"2019-05-18T14:40:00"},{"answerId":2,"content":"So, that you can use the JavaScript features of tomorrow, today","userName":"fred.test@test.com","created":"2019-05-18T16:18:00"}]}

The question is returned as expected.

6. Let's try requesting a question that doesn't exist:

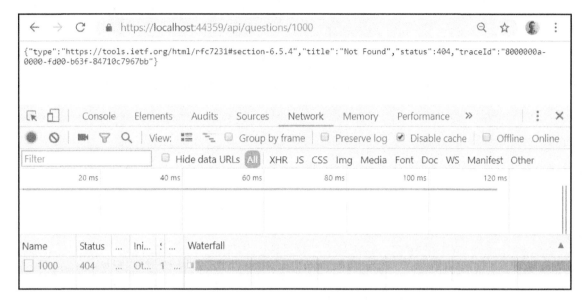

We can get confirmation that a `404` status code is returned by opening the Dev Tools by pressing *F12* and looking at the **Network** panel to see when the request was made.

7. Stop our app running so that we are ready to implement another action method.

We've implemented a range of action methods that handle `GET` requests. It's time to implement action methods for the other HTTP methods next.

Creating an action method for posting a question

Let's implement an action method for posting a question:

1. We'll start with the skeleton method:

```
[HttpPost]
public ActionResult<QuestionGetSingleResponse>
  PostQuestion(QuestionPostRequest questionPostRequest)
{
    // TODO - call the data repository to save the question
    // TODO - return HTTP status code 201
}
```

Note that we use an `HttpPost` attribute to tell ASP.NET Core that this method handles HTTP POST requests.

Note that the method parameter type is a class. Earlier, in the *Extending the GetQuestions action method for searching* section, we introduced ourselves to model binding and explained how it maps data from an HTTP request to method parameters. Well, model binding can map data from the HTTP body as well as the query string. Model binding can also map to properties in parameters. This means that the data in the HTTP request body will be mapped to properties in the instance of the `QuestionPostRequest` class.

2. Let's call into the data repository to post the question:

```
[HttpPost]
public ActionResult<QuestionGetSingleResponse>
  PostQuestion(QuestionPostRequest questionPostRequest)
{
    var savedQuestion =
     _dataRepository.PostQuestion(questionPostRequest);
    // TODO - return HTTP status code 201
}
```

3. The last step in the implementation is to return status code 201 to signify that the resource has been created:

```
[HttpPost]
public ActionResult<QuestionGetSingleResponse>
  PostQuestion(QuestionPostRequest questionPostRequest)
{
    var savedQuestion =
     _dataRepository.PostQuestion(questionPostRequest);
    return CreatedAtAction(nameof(GetQuestion),
      new { questionId = savedQuestion.QuestionId },
      savedQuestion);
}
```

We return a call to the `CreatedAtAction` from `ControllerBase`, which will return status code 201 with the question in the response. In addition, it also includes a `Location` HTTP header that contains the path to get the question.

4. Let's try this out by running the app. This time we'll use Postman, which is a great tool for testing REST APIs. Open Postman, set the HTTP method to POST, enter the path to the questions resource, and add an HTTP header called `Content-Type` with a value of `application/json`:

5. Enter a request body and click the **Send** button to send the request:

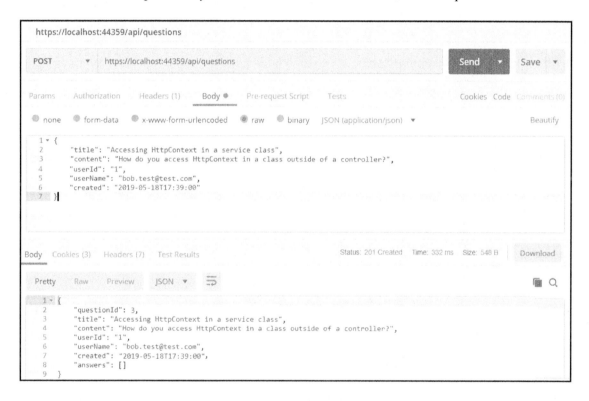

The expected `201` HTTP status code is returned with the saved question in the response.

Note how the question in the response has the generated `questionId`, which will be useful for the consumer when interacting with the question.

6. If we look at the response headers, we can see that ASP.NET Core has also included a `Location` HTTP header that contains the path to get the question:

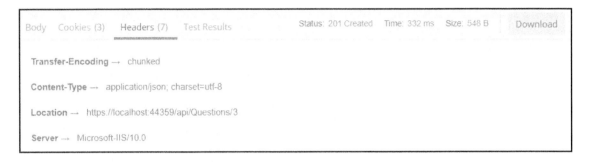

That's a nice touch.

7. Stop our app running so that we are ready to implement another action method.

That completes the implementation of the action method that will handle POST requests to `api/questions`.

Creating an action method for updating a question

Let's move on to updating a question:

1. We'll start with the skeleton action method:

```
[HttpPut("{questionId}")]
public ActionResult<QuestionGetSingleResponse>
  PutQuestion(int questionId,
    QuestionPutRequest questionPutRequest)
{
    // TODO - get the question from the data repository
    // TODO - return HTTP status code 404 if the question isn't
found
    // TODO - update the question model
    // TODO - call the data repository with the updated question
model to update the question in the database
    // TODO - return the saved question
}
```

We use the `HttpPut` attribute to tell ASP.NET Core that this method handles HTTP PUT requests. We are also putting the route parameter for the question ID in the `questionId` method parameter.

ASP.NET Core model binding will populate the `QuestionPutRequest` class instance from the HTTP request body.

2. Let's get the question from the data repository and return HTTP status code 404 if the question isn't found:

```
[HttpPut("{questionId}")]
public ActionResult<QuestionGetSingleResponse>
  PutQuestion(int questionId,
    QuestionPutRequest questionPutRequest)
{
    var question =
      _dataRepository.GetQuestion(questionId);
    if (question == null)
    {
        return NotFound();
    }
    // TODO - update the question model
    // TODO - call the data repository with the updated question
    //model to update the question in the database
    // TODO - return the saved question
}
```

3. Now let's update the `question` model:

```
[HttpPut("{questionId}")]
public ActionResult<QuestionGetSingleResponse>
  PutQuestion(int questionId,
    QuestionPutRequest questionPutRequest)
{
    var question =
      _dataRepository.GetQuestion(questionId);
    if (question == null)
    {
        return NotFound();
    }
    questionPutRequest.Title =
      string.IsNullOrEmpty(questionPutRequest.Title) ?
        question.Title :
        questionPutRequest.Title;
    questionPutRequest.Content =
      string.IsNullOrEmpty(questionPutRequest.Content) ?
        question.Content :
```

```
questionPutRequest.Content;
// TODO - call the data repository with the updated question
//model to update the question in the database
// TODO - return the saved question
}
```

We use ternary expressions to update the request model with data from the existing question if it hasn't been supplied in the request.

Not requiring the consumer to submit the full record, rather just the information that needs to be updated, is a nice touch in making our API easy to consume.

4. The final steps in the implementation are to call the data repository to update the question and then return the saved question in the response:

```
[HttpPut("{questionId}")]
public ActionResult<QuestionGetSingleResponse>
  PutQuestion(int questionId,
    QuestionPutRequest questionPutRequest)
{
    var question =
      _dataRepository.GetQuestion(questionId);
    if (question == null)
    {
        return NotFound();
    }
    questionPutRequest.Title =
      string.IsNullOrEmpty(questionPutRequest.Title) ?
        question.Title :
        questionPutRequest.Title;
    questionPutRequest.Content =
      string.IsNullOrEmpty(questionPutRequest.Content) ?
        question.Content :
        questionPutRequest.Content;
    var savedQuestion =
      _dataRepository.PutQuestion(questionId,
        questionPutRequest);
    return savedQuestion;
}
```

5. Let's try this out by running the app and using Postman. Set the HTTP method to PUT and enter the path to the questions resource. Add a Content-Type HTTP header and enter an updated content field in the request body with the relevant questionId. Click the **Send** button to send the request:

The question is updated just as we expect.

6. Stop our app running so that we are ready to implement another action method.

That completes the implementation of the action method that will handle PUT requests to api/questions.

Creating an action method for deleting a question

Let's implement deleting a question. This follows a similar pattern to the previous methods:

1. We'll add the action method in a single step as it's similar to what we've done before:

```
[HttpDelete("{questionId}")]
public ActionResult DeleteQuestion(int questionId)
{
  var question = _dataRepository.GetQuestion(questionId);
  if (question == null)
  {
```

```
    return NotFound();
    }
    _dataRepository.DeleteQuestion(questionId);
    return NoContent();
}
```

We use the `HttpDelete` attribute to tell ASP.NET Core that this method handles HTTP `DELETE` requests. The method expects the question ID to be included at the end of the path.

The method checks the question that exists before deleting it and returns an HTTP `404` status code if it doesn't exist.

The method returns HTTP status code `204` if the deletion is successful.

2. Let's try this out by running the app and using Postman. Set the HTTP method to `DELETE` and enter the path to a question resource. Add the `Content-Type` HTTP header set to `application/json` and click the **Send** button to send the request:

A response with HTTP status code 204 is returned as expected.

3. Stop our app running so that we are ready to implement our final action method.

That completes the implementation of the action method that will handle DELETE requests to api/questions.

Creating an action method for posting an answer

The final action method we are going to implement is a method for posting an answer to a question:

1. This method will handle an HTTP POST to the api/question/answer path:

```
[HttpPost("answer")]
public ActionResult<AnswerGetResponse>
  PostAnswer(AnswerPostRequest answerPostRequest)
{
    var questionExists =
      _dataRepository.QuestionExists(answerPostRequest.QuestionId);
    if (!questionExists)
    {
        return NotFound();
    }
    var savedAnswer = _dataRepository.PostAnswer(answerPostRequest);
    return savedAnswer;
}
```

The method checks whether the question exists and returns a 404 HTTP status code if it doesn't. The answer is then passed to the data repository to insert into the database. The saved answer is returned from the data repository, which is returned in the response.

2. Let's try this out by running the app and using Postman. Set the HTTP method to `POST` and enter the `api/questions/answer` path. Add the `Content-Type` HTTP header set to `application/json` and a request body containing the answer and then click the **Send** button to send the request:

The answer will be saved and returned in the response as expected.

3. Let's try this again, but don't include the answer content:

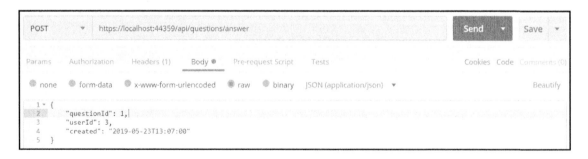

An error occurs in the data repository when the request is sent:

```
104                    connection.Open();
105                    connection.Execute(@"EXEC dbo.Question_Delete @QuestionId    Exception User-Unhandled                                          ↗ X
106            }
107        }                                                                        System.Data.SqlClient.SqlException: 'Cannot insert the value NULL into
108                                                                                  column 'Content', table 'QandA.dbo.Answer'; column does not allow
           2 references                                                             nulls. INSERT fails.
109        public AnswerGetResponse PostAnswer(AnswerPostRequest answer)            The statement has been terminated.'
110        {
111            using (var connection = new SqlConnection(_connectionString))        View Details | Copy Details
112            {                                                                    ▷ Exception Settings
113                connection.Open();
114                return connection.QueryFirst<AnswerGetResponse>("EXEC dbo.Answer_Post @QuestionId = @QuestionId, @Content = @C⊗t
115            }
116        }
117    }
118 }
119
```

This is because the stored procedures expect the content parameter to be passed into it and protest if it is not.

4. Let's stop the app so that we're ready to resolve this issue in the next section.

An answer without any content is an invalid answer. Ideally, we should stop invalid requests being passed to the data repository and return HTTP status code 400 to the client with details about what is wrong with the request. How do we do this in ASP.NET Core? Let's find out in the next section.

Adding model validation

In this section, we are going to add some validation checks on the request models. ASP.NET Core will then automatically send HTTP status code 400 (bad request) with details of the problem.

Validation is critical to preventing bad data from getting in the database or unexpected database errors happening, as we experienced in the previous section. Giving the client detailed information for bad requests also ensures the development experience is good because this will help to correct mistakes.

Adding validation to posting a question

We can add validation to a model by adding validation attributes to properties in the model that specify rules that should be adhered to. Let's add validation to the request for posting a question:

1. Open `QuestionPostRequest.cs` and add the following `using` statement:

   ```
   using System.ComponentModel.DataAnnotations;
   ```

   This namespace gives us access to the validation attributes.

2. Add a `Required` attribute just above the `Title` property:

   ```
   [Required]
   public string Title { get; set; }
   ```

   The `Required` attribute will check that the `Title` property is not an empty string or `null`.

3. Before we try this out, put a breakpoint on the first statement within the `PostQuestion` action method in `QuestionsController.cs`.

4. Let's run the app and try to post a question without a title in Postman:

We get a response with HTTP status code `400` as expected with great information about the problem in the response.

Notice also that the breakpoint wasn't reached. This is because ASP.NET Core checked the model, determined that it was invalid, and returned a bad request response before the action method was invoked.

5. Let's stop the app from running and implement another validation check on the title:

```
[Required]
[StringLength(100)]
public string Title { get; set; }
```

This check will ensure the title doesn't have more than `100` characters. A title containing more than 100 characters would cause a database error, so this is a valuable check.

6. A question must also have some content, so let's add a `Required` attribute to this:

```
[Required]
public string Content { get; set; }
```

7. We can add a custom message to a validation attribute. Let's add a custom message to the validation on the `Content` property:

```
[Required(ErrorMessage =
   "Please include some content for the question")]
public string Content { get; set; }
```

8. Let's run the app and try posting a new question without any content:

We get our custom message in the response as expected.

9. Let's stop the running app.

The `UserId`, `UserName`, and `Created` properties should really be required properties as well. However, we aren't going to add validation attributes on them because we are going to work on them later in this chapter.

Adding validation to updating a question

Let's add validation to the request for updating a question:

1. Open `QuestionPutRequest.cs` and add the following `using` statement:

```
using System.ComponentModel.DataAnnotations;
```

2. Add the following validation attributes:

```
public class QuestionPutRequest
{
    [StringLength(100)]
    public string Title { get; set; }
    public string Content { get; set; }
}
```

We are making sure that a new title doesn't exceed 100 characters.

3. Let's run the app and give this a try by updating a question to have a very long title:

A validation error is returned as expected.

4. Stop the app running so that we're ready to add the next piece of validation.

That completes the implementation of model validation for PUT requests to api/questions.

Adding validation to posting an answer

Let's add validation to the request for posting an answer:

1. Open `AnswerPostRequest.cs` and add the following `using` statement:

   ```
   using System.ComponentModel.DataAnnotations;
   ```

2. Add the following validation attributes and make `QuestionId` nullable:

   ```
   public class AnswerPostRequest
   {
       [Required]
       public int? QuestionId { get; set; }
       [Required]
       public string Content { get; set; }
       ...
   }
   ```

So, we require the `QuestionId` to be supplied along with the answer content.

Notice the `?` after the `int` type on the `QuestionId` property.

 The `?` allows the property to have a `null` value as well as the declared type. `T?` is shortcut syntax for `Nullable<T>`.

So, why does `QuestionId` need to be able to hold a `null` value? This is because an `int` type defaults to `0` and so if there is no `QuestionId` in the request body, `AnswerPostRequest` will come out of the model binding process with `QuestionId` set to `0`, which will pass the required validation check. This means the `Required` attribute won't catch a request body with no `QuestionId`. If the `QuestionId` type is nullable, then it will come out of the model binding processing with a `null` value if it's not in the request body and fail the required validation check, which is what we want.

3. We need to change the `PostAnswer` method in `QuestionsController.cs` to now reference the `Value` property in `QuestionId`:

   ```
   [HttpPost("answer")]
   public ActionResult<AnswerGetResponse>
     PostAnswer(AnswerPostRequest answerPostRequest)
   {
       var questionExists =
   ```

```
_dataRepository.QuestionExists(answerPostRequest.QuestionId.Value);
    if (!questionExists)
    {
        return NotFound();
    }
    var savedAnswer =
      _dataRepository.PostAnswer(answerPostRequest);
    return savedAnswer;

}
```

So, model validation is super easy to implement in our request models. The following are some more validation attributes that are available in ASP.NET Core:

- [Range]: Checks that the property value falls within the given range
- [RegularExpression]: Checks that the data matches the specified regular expression
- [Compare]: Checks that two properties in a model match
- [CreditCard]: Checks that the property has a credit card format
- [EmailAddress]: Checks that the property has an email format
- [Phone]: Checks that the property has a telephone format
- [Url]: Checks that the property has a URL format

We haven't added any validation to the UserId, UserName, or Created properties in our request models. In the next section, we are going to find out why and properly handle these properties.

Removing unnecessary request fields

At the moment, we are allowing the consumer to submit all the properties that our data repository requires, including userId, userName, and created. However, these properties can be set on the server. In fact, the client doesn't need to know or care about the userId.

Exposing the client to more properties than it needs impacts the usability of the API and can also cause security issues. For example, a client can pretend to be any user submitting questions and answers with our current API.

In this section, we are going to tighten up the posting of new questions and answers.

Removing unnecessary request fields from posting a question

Our QuestionPostRequest model is used both in the data repository to pass the data to the stored procedure as well as in the API controller to capture the information in the request body. This single model can't properly cater to both these cases, so we are going to create and use separate models:

1. In the models folder, create a new model called QuestionPostFullRequest as follows:

```
public class QuestionPostFullRequest
{
    public string Title { get; set; }
    public string Content { get; set; }
    public string UserId { get; set; }
    public string UserName { get; set; }
    public DateTime Created { get; set; }
}
```

This contains all the properties that are needed by the data repository to save a question.

2. We can then remove the UserId, UserName, and Created properties from the QuestionPostRequest class:

```
public class QuestionPostRequest
{
    [Required]
    [StringLength(100)]
    public string Title { get; set; }

    [Required(ErrorMessage =
      "Please include some content for the question")]
    public string Content { get; set; }
}
```

3. In the data repository interface, change the PostQuestion method to use the QuestionPostFullRequest model:

```
QuestionGetSingleResponse
  PostQuestion(QuestionPostFullRequest question);
```

4. In the data repository, change the `PostQuestion` method to use the `QuestionPostFullRequest` model:

```
public QuestionGetSingleResponse
  PostQuestion(QuestionPostFullRequest question)
{
    ...
}
```

5. We now need to map the `QuestionPostRequest` received in the API controller to the `QuestionFullPostRequest` that our data repository expects:

```
[HttpPost]
public ActionResult<QuestionGetSingleResponse>
  PostQuestion(QuestionPostRequest questionPostRequest)
{
    var savedQuestion =
      _dataRepository.PostQuestion(new QuestionPostFullRequest
    {
        Title = questionPostRequest.Title,
        Content = questionPostRequest.Content,
        UserId = "1",
        UserName = "bob.test@test.com",
        Created = DateTime.UtcNow
    });
    return CreatedAtAction(nameof(GetQuestion),
      new { questionId = savedQuestion.QuestionId },
      savedQuestion);
}
```

We've hardcoded the `UserId` and `UserName` for now. In Chapter 11, *Securing the Backend*, we'll get them from our identity provider.

We've also set the `Created` property to the current date and time.

6. Let's run our app and give it a try:

The user and created date are set and returned in the response as expected.

7. Let's stop the running app.

That completes the separation of the models for the HTTP request and data repository for adding questions. This means we are only requesting the information that is necessary for `POST` requests to `api/questions`.

Removing unnecessary request fields from posting an answer

Let's tighten up posting an answer:

1. In the `models` folder, create a new model called `AnswerPostFullRequest` as follows:

```
public class AnswerPostFullRequest
{
```

```
        public int QuestionId { get; set; }
        public string Content { get; set; }
        public string UserId { get; set; }
        public string UserName { get; set; }
        public DateTime Created { get; set; }
    }
```

This contains all the properties that are needed by the data repository to save an answer.

2. We can then remove the `UserId` and `Created` properties from the `AnswerPostRequest` class:

```
public class AnswerPostRequest
{
    [Required]
    public int? QuestionId { get; set; }
    [Required]
    public string Content { get; set; }
}
```

3. In the data repository interface, change the `PostAnswer` method to use the `AnswerPostFullRequest` model:

```
AnswerGetResponse PostAnswer(AnswerPostFullRequest answer);
```

4. In the data repository, change the `PostAnswer` method to use the `AnswerPostFullRequest` model:

```
public AnswerGetResponse
  PostAnswer(AnswerPostFullRequest answer)
{
    ...
}
```

5. We now need to map the `AnswerPostRequest` received in the API controller to the `AnswerPostFullRequest` that our data repository expects:

```
[HttpPost("answer")]
public ActionResult<AnswerGetResponse>
  PostAnswer(AnswerPostRequest answerPostRequest)
{
    var questionExists =
_dataRepository.QuestionExists(answerPostRequest.QuestionId.Value);
    if (!questionExists)
    {
        return NotFound();
```

```
    }
    var savedAnswer =
     _dataRepository.PostAnswer(new AnswerPostFullRequest
       {
           QuestionId = answerPostRequest.QuestionId.Value,
           Content = answerPostRequest.Content,
           UserId = "1",
           UserName = "bob.test@test.com",
           Created = DateTime.UtcNow
       }
    );
    return savedAnswer;
}
```

6. Let's run our app and give it a try:

The user and created date are set and returned in the response as expected.

So, that's our REST API tightened up a bit.

In this section, we manually mapped the request model to the model used in the data repository. For large models, it may be beneficial to use a mapping library such as AutoMapper to help us copy data from one object to another. More information on AutoMapper can be found at `https://automapper.org/`.

Summary

In this chapter, we learned how to implement an API controller to create REST API endpoints. We discovered that inheriting from `ControllerBase` and decorating the controller class with the `ApiController` attribute gives us nice features such as automatic model validation handling and a nice set of methods for returning HTTP status codes.

We used `AddScoped` to register the data repository dependency so that ASP.NET Core uses a single instance of it in a request/response cycle. We were then able to inject a reference to the data repository in the API controller class in its constructor.

We learned about the powerful model binding process in ASP.NET and how it maps data from an HTTP request into action method parameters. We discovered that in some cases it is desirable to use separate models for the HTTP request and the data repository because some of the data can be set on the server, and requiring less data in the request helps usability and, sometimes, security.

We used ASP.NET Core validation attributes to validate models. This is a super simple way of ensuring that the database doesn't get infected with bad data.

In the next chapter, we are going to create a real-time API with SignalR.

Questions

Answer the following questions to test the knowledge we have gained in this chapter:

1. We have a class that we want to register for dependency injection and want a new instance of it to be created when injected into a class. What method in `IServiceCollection` should we use to register the dependency?
2. In a controller action method, if a resource can't be found, what method can we use in `ControllerBase` to return status code `404`?
3. In a controller action method to post a new building, we implement some validation that requires a database call to check whether the building already exists. If the building does already exist, we want to return HTTP status code `400`:

```
[HttpPost]
public ActionResult<BuildingResponse>
PostBuilding(BuildingPostRequest buildingPostRequest)
{
    var buildingExists =
    _dataRepository.BuildingExists(buildingPostRequest.Code);
```

```
                if (buildingExists)
                {
                    // TODO - return status code 400
                }
                ...
        }
```

What method from `ControllerBase` can we use to return status code `400`?

4. The model for the preceding action method is as follows:

```
public class BuildingPostRequest
{
    public string Code { get; set; }
    public string Name { get; set; }
    public string Description { get; set; }
}
```

We send an HTTP `POST` request to the resource with the following body:

```
{
    "code": "BTOW",
    "name": "Blackpool Tower",
    "buildingDescription": "Blackpool Tower is a tourist attraction
     in Blackpool"
}
```

The `Description` property in the model isn't getting populated during the request. What is the problem?

5. In the preceding request model, we want to validate that the `code` and `name` fields are populated. How can we do this with validation attributes?

6. What validation attribute could we use to validate that a number property is between 1 and 10?

7. What `Http` attribute could we use to tell ASP.NET Core that an action method handles HTTP `PATCH` requests?

Further reading

Here are some useful links for learning more about the topics covered in this chapter:

- **Create web APIs with ASP.NET Core:** `https://docs.microsoft.com/en-us/aspnet/core/web-api`
- **Dependency injection:** `https://docs.microsoft.com/en-us/aspnet/core/fundamentals/dependency-injection`
- **Model binding:** `https://docs.microsoft.com/en-us/aspnet/core/mvc/models/model-binding`
- **Model validation:** `https://docs.microsoft.com/en-us/aspnet/core/mvc/models/validation`
- **Postman:** `https://learning.getpostman.com/docs/postman/launching_postman/installation_and_updates/`

Creating a Real-Time API with SignalR

9

12In this chapter, we are going to continue to develop our Q&A app. Wouldn't it be great if, when a user was on the question page, any new answers were automatically added to the page without the user having to manually refresh the page? Well, this is exactly what we are going to do in this chapter.

We are going to use a technology called SignalR to implement this feature by creating a real-time API. We'll start this chapter by understanding what SignalR is, how it differs from a REST API, and the benefit it brings. Then, we'll add a real-time API to our ASP.NET backend, thereby creating a SignalR hub. Toward the end of this chapter, we'll interact with the SignalR real-time API from our frontend React app.

In this chapter, we'll cover the following topics:

- Understanding the benefits of SignalR
- Creating a SignalR hub
- Pushing data to SignalR clients from an API controller
- Creating the SignalR real-time API endpoint
- Interacting with the SignalR real-time API from React

Technical requirements

We'll use the following tools in this chapter:

- **Visual Studio 2019:** We'll use this to edit our ASP.NET Core code. This can be downloaded and installed from `https://visualstudio.microsoft.com/vs/`.
- **.NET Core 3.0**: This can be downloaded and installed from `https://dotnet.microsoft.com/download/dotnet-core`.
- **Postman**. We'll use this to test our SignalR code in this chapter. This can be downloaded from `https://www.getpostman.com/downloads/`.
- **Q and A**: We'll start with the backend Q&A project we finished in the previous chapter and the frontend Q&A project we finished in `Chapter 5`, *Working with Forms*. This is available on GitHub at `https://github.com/PacktPublishing/ASP.NET-Core-3-and-React-17`.

All the code snippets in this chapter can be found online at `https://github.com/PacktPublishing/ASP.NET-Core-3-and-React-17`. In order to restore code from a chapter, the source code repository can be downloaded and the relevant folder opened in the relevant editor. If the code is frontend code, then `npm install` can be entered in the Terminal to restore the dependencies.

Check out the following video to see the code in action:

`http://bit.ly/35YrOf2`

Understanding the benefits of SignalR

SignalR is a feature in ASP.NET Core that we can use to create a real-time API. A real-time API is where data is pushed to connected clients when the data arrives at the server.

An example use case of a real-time API is on Twitter, where new tweets automatically appear in our feed as they are tweeted. Chat apps are another common example where we can get messages from other users immediately after they send messages.

Real-time APIs are different from REST APIs. With a REST API, the client needs to make a request to get new data that's available on the server. When there is no updated data, the response data in this type of request isn't needed by the client because it already has a copy of that data. So, this is an inefficient and slow approach to updating the client with new data. SignalR solves this efficiency problem because new data can be pushed from the server to clients.

So, the key feature that SignalR has that a REST API hasn't got is the ability to push data from the server to the client. It uses web sockets as the transport mechanism, if available in the browser and web server, and falls back on other mechanisms if not.

 The Web sockets technology allows an open two-way interactive communication session between the user's browser and a server using a TCP socket. A TCP socket is a lower-level and faster mechanism than HTTP. This technology is available in the latest versions of all modern browsers, including IE.

It sounds like web sockets do everything that a REST API can do, as well as being faster. Why wouldn't we use a real-time API for all communication with the server and not use a REST API at all? Well, a few reasons are as follows:

- There is nothing like an HTTP status code in a web socket message. So, how does the client know that a form that has been submitted has invalid data? Or maybe that the user isn't authorized to submit the form? In the web socket world, we'd need to implement something such as an HTTP status code ourselves.
- HTTP has other features such as caching and compression that aren't available as standard for web sockets.
- Web sockets are stateful and there is no standard way to scale them horizontally. A REST API is stateless and therefore can be easily scaled across multiple web servers.

So, in our app, we are going to use SignalR to create a real-time API where we need to push data from the server to the client. We'll start this implementation in the next section.

Creating a SignalR hub

In this section, we are going to implement what is called a SignalR hub in our ASP.NET core backend. A hub is a class on the server where we can interact with clients. We can choose to interact with a single client, all connected clients, or just a subset of them.

Let's open our backend project in Visual Studio and carry out the following steps:

1. In Solution Explorer, create a new folder called Hubs at the root level.
2. In the Hubs folder, create a new class file called QuestionsHub.cs that contains the following content:

```
using Microsoft.AspNetCore.SignalR;
using System;
using System.Threading.Tasks;
```

```
namespace QandA.Hubs
{
    public class QuestionsHub: Hub
    {
    }
}
```

Our class is called `QuestionsHub` and we inherit from the base `Hub` class in SignalR. The base `Hub` class gives us the features we need to interact with clients.

3. Let's override a method in the base class that gets invoked when a client connects:

```
public class QuestionsHub: Hub
{
    public override async Task OnConnectedAsync()
    {
        await base.OnConnectedAsync();
    }
}
```

So, when a client connects to this hub, this `OnConnectedAsync` method will be called, which calls the base implementation of this method in the first statement.

Notice the `async` keyword in front of the method name and the `await` keyword before the statement in the function. This denotes that the method is asynchronous. We'll cover asynchronous methods later in this book in `Chapter 10`, *Improving Performance and Scalability*.

4. Let's push a message to the client to inform it that a connection has been successfully made:

```
public override async Task OnConnectedAsync()
{
    await base.OnConnectedAsync();
    await Clients.Caller.SendAsync("Message",
      "Successfully connected");
}
```

We use the `Clients` object from the base client to interact with the client that has just been connected using the `Caller` property. We use the `SendAsync` method in the `Caller` object to push some data to the client. The first parameter in `SendAsync` is the handler name in the JavaScript client we need to call, while the second parameter is the data to pass in as a parameter to that handler. So, we are invoking a handler called `Message` in our React client while passing a string parameter with the `"Successfully connected"` value.

In reality, we don't need to inform the client that a connection has been successfully made because SignalR does that for us already. We are purely using this as an example of pushing data from the server to the client.

5. There is also an `OnDisconnectedAsync` method we can override that is invoked when a client disconnects. Let's implement this method by sending a message to the client:

```
public class QuestionsHub: Hub
{
  public override async Task OnConnectedAsync()
  {
    ...
  }

  public override async Task
    OnDisconnectedAsync(Exception exception)
  {
      await Clients.Caller.SendAsync("Message",
        "Successfully disconnected");
      await base.OnDisconnectedAsync(exception);
  }
}
```

So, a handler called `Message` with a parameter value of `"Successfully disconnected"` will be called in our React client when it disconnects from the SignalR API.

6. Now, we are going to expose a method that the client can call to subscribe to updates for a particular question:

```
public class QuestionsHub: Hub
{
  public override async Task OnConnectedAsync()
  {
    ...
  }
```

```
public override async Task
  OnDisconnectedAsync(Exception exception)
{
  ...
}

public async Task SubscribeQuestion(int questionId)
{
    // TODO - add the client to a group of clients interested in
getting updates on the question
    // TODO - send a message to the client to indicate that the
subscription was successful
}
}
```

Our method is called SubscribeQuestion and has a parameter that contains the question ID of the question to subscribe to. We will use this exact name when invoking this function from our React frontend later in this chapter.

Notice that the method is declared as asynchronous with the async keyword. This is because the SignalR methods that we are going to invoke next are asynchronous.

7. We are going to store all the subscribers to the question in a group. So, let's add the client to a group:

```
public async Task SubscribeQuestion(int questionId)
{
    await Groups.AddToGroupAsync(Context.ConnectionId,
      $"Question-{questionId}");
    // TODO - send a message to the client to indicate that the
subscription was successful
}
```

So, SignalR has a groups feature that we use to store all the subscribers to the question in. These groups can be accessed via a Groups property in the base Hub class. We use the AddToGroupAsync method in the Groups property to add the client to the group while passing in the client connection ID, which we can get from the Context property on the Hub base class. The second parameter that's passed to the AddToGroupAsync method is the name of the group, which we set to the word "Question", followed by a hyphen and then the question ID. If the group doesn't exist, SignalR will automatically create the group, which will be the case for the first client that subscribes to a question.

8. Let's finish the `SubscribeQuestion` method's implementation by sending a message to the client to indicate that the subscription was successful:

```
public async Task SubscribeQuestion(int questionId)
{
   await Groups.AddToGroupAsync(Context.ConnectionId,
     $"Question-{questionId}");
   await Clients.Caller.SendAsync("Message",
     "Successfully subscribed");
}
```

9. The last method we are going to implement in the hub is a method to unsubscribe from getting updates about a question:

```
public class QuestionsHub: Hub
{
   public override async Task OnConnectedAsync()
   {
      ...
   }

   public override async Task
     OnDisconnectedAsync(Exception exception)
   {
      ...
   }

   public async Task SubscribeQuestion(int questionId)
   {
      ...
   }

   public async Task UnsubscribeQuestion(int questionId)
   {
      await Groups.RemoveFromGroupAsync(Context.ConnectionId,
        $"Question-{questionId}");
      await Clients.Caller.SendAsync("Message",
        "Successfully unsubscribed");
   }
}
```

This implementation is very similar to the `SubscribeQuestion` method, except that we call the `RemoveFromGroupAsync` method on the `Groups` property in the base `Hub` class to remove the client from the group. When all the clients have been removed from the group, SignalR will automatically remove the group.

That completes the implementation of our SignalR hub. Before finishing this section, let's take some time to explore the different properties that we can use in the `Clients` property in the base `Hub` class. In any method, we can type the property name, that is, `Clients`, followed by a dot, to see all the methods that are available:

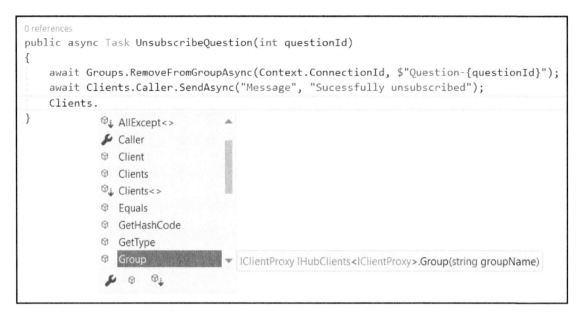

The following are descriptions of some useful methods:

- `AllExcept`: This allows us to interact with clients, except for a list of clients we supply by their connection ID.
- `Client`: This allows us to interact with a specific client by passing their connection ID.
- `Clients`: This allows us to interact with a list of clients by passing a list of their connection IDs.
- `Group`: This allows us to interact with a group of clients by passing the group name.
- `Groups`: This allows us to interact with a list of groups by passing a list of group names.

Don't forget to remove the `Clients` property we just explored before moving on.

We've made a great start on our real-time API, but we aren't pushing new answers to subscribed clients yet. We'll implement this in the next section.

Pushing data to SignalR clients from an API controller

Arguably the most valuable piece of our real-time API is pushing new answers to subscribed clients. In this section, we are going to learn how to do this. If we think about it, the ideal place to do this is in the questions API controller, which is where an answer is posted. So, when an answer is posted, we want SignalR to push the updated question with the saved answer to all the clients that are subscribed to the question. Let's implement this by carrying out the following steps in `QuestionsController.cs`:

1. We'll start by referencing SignalR and our SignalR hub with `using` statements:

   ```
   using Microsoft.AspNetCore.SignalR;
   using QandA.Hubs;
   ```

2. We are going to inject the context of the hub into the API controller using dependency injection:

   ```
   [Route("api/[controller]")]
   [ApiController]
   public class QuestionsController : ControllerBase
   {
     private readonly IDataRepository _dataRepository;
     private readonly IHubContext<QuestionsHub>
       _questionHubContext;

     public QuestionsController(
       IDataRepository dataRepository,
       IHubContext<QuestionsHub> questionHubContext)
     {
       _dataRepository = dataRepository;
       _questionHubContext = questionHubContext;
     }

     ...
   }
   ```

   We have a class-level variable that is set as a reference to the hub context in the constructor. The `IHubContext` interface allows us to interact with SignalR clients.

3. Let's enhance the `PostAnswer` method so that it pushes the question with the new answer to clients that have subscribed to the question:

```
[HttpPost("answer")]
public ActionResult<AnswerGetResponse>
  PostAnswer(AnswerPostRequest answerPostRequest)
{
  var questionExists =
    _dataRepository.QuestionExists(
      answerPostRequest.QuestionId.Value);
  if (!questionExists)
  {
    return NotFound();
  }
  var savedAnswer =
    _dataRepository.PostAnswer(new AnswerPostFullRequest
    {
      QuestionId = answerPostRequest.QuestionId.Value,
      Content = answerPostRequest.Content,
      UserId = "1",
      UserName = "bob.test@test.com",
      Created = DateTime.UtcNow
    });
  _questionHubContext.Clients.Group(
    $"Question-{answerPostRequest.QuestionId.Value}")
      .SendAsync(
        "ReceiveQuestion",
        _dataRepository.GetQuestion(
          answerPostRequest.QuestionId.Value));

  return savedAnswer;
}
```

We get access to the SignalR group through the `Group` method in the `Clients` property in the hub context by passing in the group name. Remember that the group name is the word `"Question"`, followed by a hyphen and then the question ID.

Then, we use the `SendAsync` method to push the question with the new answer to all the clients in the group. A handler called `ReceiveQuestion` will be invoked in the client, with the question being passed in as the parameter after we have got it from the data repository.

That's all the changes we need to make to our API controller in order to push updated questions to subscribed clients.

In the next section, we are going to define our real-time API endpoint.

Creating the SignalR real-time API endpoint

Before we can use our SignalR real-time API, we need to enable SignalR and define the path for the endpoint. Let's carry out the following steps in `Startup.cs`:

1. We'll start by referencing our SignalR hub with the following `using` statement:

   ```
   using QandA.Hubs;
   ```

2. Add SignalR to our ASP.NET app by using the `AddSignalR` method in the `services` parameter in the `ConfigureServices` method:

   ```
   public void ConfigureServices(IServiceCollection services)
   {
     ...

     services.AddSignalR();
   }
   ```

3. The next step is to configure the request pipeline so that we can pass SignalR requests to our SignalR hub:

   ```
   public void Configure(IApplicationBuilder app, IHostingEnvironment env)
   {
     ...
     app.UseEndpoints(endpoints =>
     {
       endpoints.MapControllers();
       endpoints.MapHub<QuestionsHub>("/questionshub");
     });
   }
   ```

   So, SignalR requests to the `/questionshub` path will be handled by our `QuestionHub` class.

That's it—nice and simple! We are ready to interact with our SignalR real-time API from our frontend React app, which we'll do in the next section.

Interacting with the SignalR real-time API from React

In this section, we will work on our React frontend so that we can interact with the SignalR real-time API we have just built. We will make changes to the question page so that we can subscribe to new answers for the question on the page. We will use Postman to post an answer to the question and hopefully receive the updated question in our React frontend.

Installing the SignalR client

Let's open our React frontend project in Visual Studio Code and install the SignalR client. Enter the following command in the Terminal:

```
> npm install @aspnet/signalr
```

Check the version of the `@aspnet/signalr` package in `package.json`. If it is before version 3, then run the following command in the Terminal to get a more up-to-date version of this package:

```
> npm install @aspnet/signalr@next
```

Note that TypeScript types are included in this package, so there is no separate installation process for these. After a few seconds, the SignalR client will be installed in our project.

Setting up the client connection

Let's carry out the following steps to create a function that sets up the SignalR client connection object:

1. Open `QuestionPage.tsx` and import the following from the SignalR client:

```
import {
  HubConnectionBuilder,
  HubConnectionState,
  HubConnection,
} from '@aspnet/signalr';
```

2. We're going to create a function to set up the SignalR connection in the `QuestionPage` component, just below where the `question` state is declared:

```
const [question, setQuestion] = useState<QuestionData |
null>(null);

const setUpSignalRConnection = async (questionId: number) => {
  // TODO - setup connection to real-time SignalR API
  // TODO - handle Message function being called
  // TODO - handle ReceiveQuestion function being called
  // TODO - start the connection
  // TODO - subscribe to question
  // TODO - return the connection
};
```

This asynchronous function simply takes in a question ID, which will eventually be used to subscribe to changes to that question.

3. Let's set up the connection by using the `HubConnectionBuilder` we imported earlier:

```
const setUpSignalRConnection = async (questionId: number) => {
  const connection = new HubConnectionBuilder()
    .withUrl('http://localhost:17525/questionshub')
    .withAutomaticReconnect()
    .build();
  // TODO - handle Message function being called
  // TODO - handle ReceiveQuestion function being called
  // TODO - start the connection
  // TODO - subscribe to question
  return connection
};
```

We need to specify the URL to our questions hub, so change the hostname and port, if required, in the path.

Notice that we've also configured the client so that it reconnects if the connection becomes disconnected using the `withAutomaticReconnect` method. The client will wait for 0, 2, 10, and 30 seconds, respectively, before trying each reconnect attempt, stopping after four failed attempts.

4. With the `connection` object in place, we can now implement handlers for functions that can be called. As you may recall, the first handler that our SignalR server called was a function called `Message` when the client connects and disconnects. Let's implement this:

```
const setUpSignalRConnection = async (questionId: number) => {
  const connection = new HubConnectionBuilder()
    .withUrl('http://localhost:17525/questionshub')
    .withAutomaticReconnect()
    .build();

  connection.on('Message', (message: string) => {
    console.log('Message', message);
  });

  // TODO - handle ReceiveQuestion function being called
  // TODO - start the connection
  // TODO - subscribe to question
  return connection
};
```

We use the `on` method in the `connection` object by passing the function name as the first parameter and an arrow function that will handle the call. The `message` parameter in the arrow function will contain the data that has been sent from the server.

We simply log the message in the console in this case. Remember that, in practice, we don't need this message function for what we are trying to do in our app. This is purely to help us understand how SignalR can push data to clients.

5. The important handler is the one that receives the question with new answers. Let's implement this:

```
const setUpSignalRConnection = async (questionId: number) => {
  const connection = new HubConnectionBuilder()
    .withUrl('http://localhost:17525/questionshub')
    .withAutomaticReconnect()
    .build();

  connection.on('Message', (message: string) => {
    console.log('Message', message);
  });
  connection.on('ReceiveQuestion', (question: QuestionData) => {
    console.log('ReceiveQuestion', question);
    setQuestion(question);
  });
```

```
  // TODO - start the connection
  // TODO - subscribe to question
  return connection
};
```

This follows the same pattern as the previous handler by using the on method on the connection object. We log the question with the new answer to the console, which will be useful when we test that this works later in this chapter. We also update the question state so that the new answer is rendered on the page.

6. Next, let's start the connection:

```
const setUpSignalRConnection = async (questionId: number) => {
  const connection = new HubConnectionBuilder()
    .withUrl('http://localhost:17525/questionshub')
    .withAutomaticReconnect()
    .build();

  connection.on('Message', (message: string) => {
    console.log('Message', message);
  });
  connection.on('ReceiveQuestion', (question: QuestionData) => {
    console.log('ReceiveQuestion', question);
    setQuestion(question);
  });

  try {
    await connection.start();
  } catch (err) {
    console.log(err);
  }

  // TODO - subscribe to question
  return connection
};
```

We use the asynchronous connection start method to start the connection. If this process errors out, we log the error in the console.

7. Now, let's subscribe to the question:

```
const setUpSignalRConnection = async (questionId: number) => {
  const connection = new HubConnectionBuilder()
    .withUrl('http://localhost:17525/questionshub')
    .withAutomaticReconnect()
    .build();
```

```
connection.on('Message', (message: string) => {
  console.log('Message', message);
});
connection.on('ReceiveQuestion', (question: QuestionData) => {
  console.log('ReceiveQuestion', question);
  setQuestion(question);
});

try {
  await connection.start();
} catch (err) {
  console.log(err);
}

if (connection.state === HubConnectionState.Connected) {
  connection
    .invoke('SubscribeQuestion', questionId)
    .catch((err: Error) => {
      return console.error(err.toString());
    });
}

return connection
};
```

First, we check that the connection is in the `Connected` state because it won't be if the connection failed to start properly. Then, we use the `invoke` method on the `connection` object to call the `SubscribeQuestion` method in the SignalR hub on the server, which will subscribe the client to the question.

8. We can call this function in the `QuestionPage` component, as follows:

```
useEffect(() => {
  const doGetQuestion = ...
  let connection: HubConnection;
  if (match.params.questionId) {
    const questionId = Number(match.params.questionId);
    doGetQuestion(questionId);
    setUpSignalRConnection(questionId).then(con => {
      connection = con;
    });
  }
}, [match.params.questionId]);
```

We invoke the `setupSignalRConnection` function when the component has mounted. We also store a reference to the `connection` object, which we'll use when the user navigates away from the page to stop the connection.

Stopping the client connection

When the user navigates away from the question page, we want to unsubscribe the client from the question and stop the connection. Let's look at the steps to do just that:

1. Let's start to implement a function that does this just below the `setUpSignalRConnection` function:

```
const cleanUpSignalRConnection = async (
  questionId: number,
  connection: HubConnection,
) => {
  // TODO - unsubscribe from the question
  // TODO - stop the connection
};
```

So, our function is asynchronous and takes in the question ID and connection as parameters.

2. Let's unsubscribe the client:

```
const cleanUpSignalRConnection = async (
  questionId: number,
  connection: HubConnection,
) => {
  if (connection.state === HubConnectionState.Connected) {
    try {
      await connection.invoke('UnsubscribeQuestion', questionId);
    } catch (err) {
      return console.error(err.toString());
    }
  } else {
  }
  // TODO - stop the connection
};
```

First, we check to see if the connection is connected and then invoke the `UnsubscribeQuestion` function on the SignalR server hub. The `invoke` method is asynchronous, so we use the `await` keyword at the start of the statement. We also catch any errors and output them to the console.

3. Then, we can stop the connection:

```
const cleanUpSignalRConnection = async (
  questionId: number,
  connection: HubConnection
) => {
  if (connection.state === HubConnectionState.Connected) {
    connection
      try {
        await connection.invoke('UnsubscribeQuestion', questionId);
      } catch (err) {
        return console.error(err.toString());
      }
    connection.off('Message');
    connection.off('ReceiveQuestion');
    connection.stop();
  } else {
    connection.off('Message');
    connection.off('ReceiveQuestion');
    connection.stop();
  }
};
```

As well as stopping the connection, we need to remove the handlers for the `Message` and `ReceiveQuestion` functions.

4. Now, we can use the `cleanUpSignalRConnection` function when the component unmounts:

```
useEffect(() => {
  const doGetQuestion = ...
  let connection: HubConnection;
  if (match.params.questionId) {
    const questionId = Number(match.params.questionId);
    doGetQuestion(questionId);
    setUpSignalRConnection(questionId, setQuestion).then(con => {
      connection = con;
    });
  }

  return function cleanUp() {
    if (match.params.questionId) {
      const questionId = Number(match.params.questionId);
      cleanUpSignalRConnection(questionId, connection);
    }
  };
}, [match.params.questionId]);
```

We execute logic when a React component unmounts from the DOM in a function that is returned from the `useEffect` hook. In this function, we get the question ID from the URL and pass it to the `cleanUpSignalRConnection` function, along with the `connection` object.

Now, we have our real-time API in place with our frontend interacting with it. In the next section, we'll try this out.

Adding CORS to our backend

We are going to try our real-time API now and discover a problem with it because the frontend is hosted in a different origin from the backend. Let's carry out the following steps to expose this problem and then correct it:

1. Run the backend project by pressing *F5* in Visual Studio.
2. Run the frontend project by entering `npm start` in the Terminal in Visual Studio Code.
3. When the frontend app runs, press *F12* to open the browser DevTools and select the **Console** panel.
4. Click on a question to open the question page. This is where the SignalR connection should be started and the client can subscribe to the question. We get an error, though:

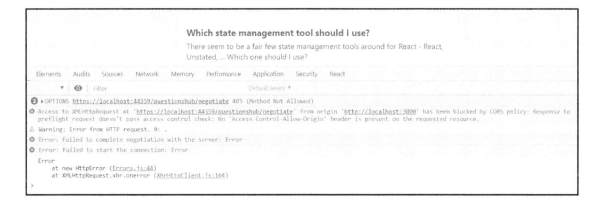

The request to start the SignalR connection has been blocked by a CORS policy.

 CORS stands for Cross-Origin Resource Sharing and is a mechanism that uses HTTP headers to tell a browser to let a web application run at certain origins (domains) so that it has permission to access certain resources on a server at a different origin.

So, we need to configure our ASP.NET backend to allow requests from our React frontend because they are hosted in different origins.

5. Stop the backend from running by pressing *SHIFT+F5* in Visual Studio Code and enter the following statement inside the `ConfigureServices` method in `Startup.cs`:

```
public void ConfigureServices(IServiceCollection services)
{
  ...
  services.AddCors(options =>
    options.AddPolicy("CorsPolicy", builder =>
      builder.AllowAnyMethod()
       .AllowAnyHeader()
       .WithOrigins("http://localhost:3000")
       .AllowCredentials()));

  services.AddSignalR();
}
```

This has defined a CORS policy that allows our frontend app hosted in the `localhost:3000` origin to access the backend. If the origin of your frontend app is different, then simply change the origin in this statement as required.

6. Now, we can enable the use of this policy in the `Configure` method. Let's add the following statement as the first statement in the `Configure` method:

```
public void Configure(IApplicationBuilder app, IHostingEnvironment
env)
{
    app.UseCors("CorsPolicy");

    . . .
}
```

7. Run the backend project again by pressing *F5*.
8. If we hit *F5* to refresh the frontend app, we'll see that it now connects to the SignalR server and subscribes to the question:

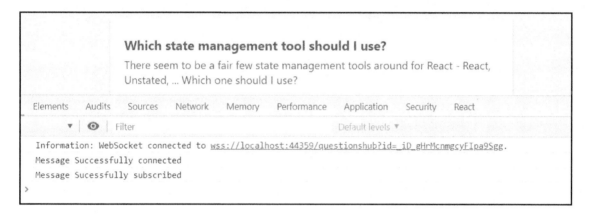

That's great!

Mapping a question from the real-time API to React state

In this section, we are going to use Postman to submit an answer to a question that our React frontend is subscribed to. Hopefully, we should see a new answer automatically appear in our React frontend. Let's carry out the following steps to do so:

1. Make sure the React frontend is on the question page with DevTools open and the **Console** panel selected.
2. Open Postman and send the following request, making sure we submit an answer to the question that is open in the frontend:

3. Let's look at the React app:

```
TypeError: question.created.toLocaleDateString is not a function

QuestionPage
C:/Users/carl.rippon/OneDrive/Documents/books/ASP.NET Core and TypeScript/repo-refactor/Chapter09/frontend-test/src/QuestionPage.tsx:138

  135 | >
  136 |    {question.content}
  137 | </p>
> 138 | <div
  139 | ^ css={css`
  140 |     font-size: 12px;
  141 |     font-style: italic;
```

We can see that the frontend received the question but, unfortunately, there was a problem rendering it. The problem is that the created property in the answer has been serialized as a string rather than a Date object.

4. Let's resolve this problem by creating interfaces for the question that comes from the server in QuestionsData.ts, just beneath the QuestionData and AnswerData interfaces:

```typescript
export interface QuestionData {
  ...
}

export interface AnswerData {
  ...
}

export interface QuestionDataFromServer {
  questionId: number;
  title: string;
  content: string;
  userName: string;
  created: string;
  answers: AnswerDataFromServer[];
}

export interface AnswerDataFromServer {
  answerId: number;
  content: string;
  userName: string;
  created: string;
}
```

These interfaces have string-based dates, which means they properly model the data that is received from the web server.

5. Let's create a function just beneath these interfaces to map a question that comes from the server into the format our frontend expects to work with:

```
export const mapQuestionFromServer = (
  question: QuestionDataFromServer,
): QuestionData => ({
  ...question,
  created: new Date(question.created.substr(0, 19)),
  answers: question.answers.map(answer => ({
    ...answer,
    created: new Date(answer.created.substr(0, 19)),
  })),
});
```

We create a copy of the question and answer using the spread syntax and set the `created` dates to `Date` objects from the string-based date using the `Date` constructor.

6. Back in `QuestionPage.tsx`, let's import this mapping function and interface:

```
import {
  QuestionData,
  getQuestion,
  postAnswer,
  mapQuestionFromServer,
  QuestionDataFromServer
} from './QuestionsData';
```

7. Now, we can use this function and interface in the `ReceiveQuestion` handler and overwrite the previous code:

```
connection.on(
  'ReceiveQuestion',
  (question: QuestionDataFromServer) => {
    console.log('ReceiveQuestion', question);
    setQuestion(mapQuestionFromServer(question));
  },
);
```

The frontend app will automatically refresh in the browser when we save these changes.

8. Send the request in Postman once more and look at the frontend app in the browser:

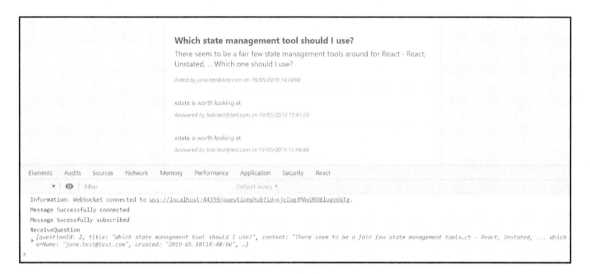

This time, the question with the new answer has been successfully received and shown in the app. Note that we'll see both the answers we submitted to the server because both were successfully saved into the database—the problem was that initially the frontend couldn't show the first submitted answer.

That completes our real-time API, along with a React frontend that interacts with it. Well done!

Summary

In this chapter, we learned that the key difference between a REST API and a SignalR real-time API is that the latter has a two-way connection with the client and can, therefore, push data to the client, as well as receive data from the client. We also learned that a SignalR real-time API uses web sockets under the hood if the server and browser support it. Web sockets are lower-level than HTTP and don't support features such as status codes and caching like HTTP does. Web sockets also don't scale across multiple servers as easily as a REST API, so REST APIs are still preferable over a real-time API for one-way communication between the client and server.

Then, we learned that the `Hub` base class in ASP.NET Core makes it super-easy to interact with clients. It allows us to create and interact with groups of clients, which we found very useful in our scenario. We also discovered that we can reference the hub from an API controller so that we can interact with clients when REST API requests are received. We define the endpoint for the hub in the `Startup` class in the `Configure` method in the `UseEndpoints` method, which is where we define the REST API controllers.

SignalR provides many client libraries for interacting with a SignalR server, including a JavaScript client that we used in our React app. After using `HubConnectionBuilder` to create a `HubConnection` object, we used this to send and receive data from the SignalR server.

In the next chapter, we are going to turn our attention back to our REST API. This time, we will focus on performance and scalability.

Questions

Answer the following questions to check what you've learned in this chapter:

1. In a SignalR hub class, what method can we use to push data to a group of connected clients?
2. In a SignalR hub class, what method can we use to push data to all clients except for the client that has made the request?
3. Why did we need a CORS policy for our React app to be able to interact with our SignalR real-time API?
4. In our React frontend, why did we check whether the connection was in a connected state before subscribing to the question?
5. Why do we stop the connection when the user navigates away from the question page?

Further reading

The following are some useful links if you want to learn more about the topics that were covered in this chapter:

- ASP.NET Core SignalR: https://docs.microsoft.com/en-us/aspnet/core/signalr/introduction
- ASP.NET Core CORS: https://docs.microsoft.com/en-us/aspnet/core/security/cors

10
Improving Performance and Scalability

In this chapter, we are going to improve the performance and scalability of our REST API. When we make each improvement, we'll use load testing and performance tools to verify that there has been an improvement.

We'll start by focusing on database calls and how we can reduce the number of calls to improve performance. We'll then move on to requesting less data with data paging. We'll also look at the impact that caching data in memory has on performance.

Then, we'll learn how to make our API controllers and data repository asynchronous. We'll eventually understand whether this makes our REST API more performant or perhaps more scalable.

We'll also learn how the garbage collection process can harm performance and why it's best to let ASP.NET Core handle binding requests to models.

In this chapter, we'll cover the following topics:

- Reducing database round trips
- Paging data
- Making API controllers asynchronous
- Caching data
- Reducing garbage collection

Technical requirements

We'll use the following tools in this chapter:

- **Visual Studio 2019:** We'll use this to edit our ASP.NET Core code. This can be downloaded and installed from `https://visualstudio.microsoft.com/vs/`.
- **.NET Core 3.0**: This can be downloaded and installed from `https://dotnet.microsoft.com/download/dotnet-core`.
- **SQL Server Management Studio**: We'll use this to execute a stored procedure in our database. This can be downloaded and installed from `https://docs.microsoft.com/en-us/sql/ssms/download-sql-server-management-studio-ssms?view=sql-server-2017`.
- **Postman**. We'll use this to try out changes we make to our REST API endpoints. This can be downloaded from `https://www.getpostman.com/downloads/`.
- **WebSurge**: This is a load testing tool that we can download from `https://websurge.west-wind.com/`.
- **PerfView**: We are going to use this to monitor garbage collection. This can be downloaded from `https://www.microsoft.com/en-us/download/details.aspx?id=28567`.
- **Q and A**: We'll start with the Q and A backend project we finished in the previous chapter. This is available on GitHub at `https://github.com/PacktPublishing/ASP.NET-Core-3-and-React-17`

All of the code snippets in this chapter can be found online at `https://github.com/PacktPublishing/ASP.NET-Core-3-and-React-17`. To restore code from a chapter, the source code repository can be downloaded and the relevant folder opened in the relevant editor. If the code is frontend code, then `npm install` can be entered in the Terminal to restore the dependencies.

Check out the following video to see the code in action:

`http://bit.ly/37awJtm`

Reducing database round trips

Database round trips are expensive. The greater the distance between the web API and the database, the more expensive the round trip is. So, we want to keep the trips from the web API to the database to a minimum in order to gain maximum performance.

N+1 problem

The N+1 problem is a classic query problem where there is a parent-child data model relationship that results in separate database queries for each child record, as well as the query for the parent record.

We are going to add the ability to return answers as well as questions in a GET request to the questions REST API endpoint. We are going to fall into the N+1 trap with our first implementation. Let's open our backend project in Visual Studio and carry out the following steps:

1. First, let's add an Answers property to the QuestionGetManyResponse model:

```
public class QuestionGetManyResponse
{
  public int QuestionId { get; set; }
  public string Title { get; set; }
  public string Content { get; set; }
  public string UserName { get; set; }
  public DateTime Created { get; set; }
  public List<AnswerGetResponse> Answers { get; set; }
}
```

2. Let's add a new method to our data repository interface:

```
public interface IDataRepository
{
    IEnumerable<QuestionGetManyResponse> GetQuestions();
    IEnumerable<QuestionGetManyResponse> GetQuestionsWithAnswers();
    ...
}
```

This method will get all of the questions in the database, including the answers for each question.

3. Now, we can add the implementation for the GetQuestionsWithAnswers method in the data repository:

```
public IEnumerable<QuestionGetManyResponse>
GetQuestionsWithAnswers()
{
  using (var connection = new SqlConnection(_connectionString))
  {
    connection.Open();

    var questions =
      connection.Query<QuestionGetManyResponse>(
```

```
      "EXEC dbo.Question_GetMany");
  foreach (var question in questions)
  {
    question.Answers =
      connection.Query<AnswerGetResponse>(
        @"EXEC dbo.Answer_Get_ByQuestionId
          @QuestionId = @QuestionId",
        new { QuestionId = question.QuestionId })
      .ToList();
  }
  return questions;
  }
}
```

So, this makes a database call to get all of the questions and then additional calls to get the answer for each question. We have fallen into the classic N+1 trap!

4. Let's move on to the `QuestionsController` now and add the ability to include answers with the questions:

```
[HttpGet]
public IEnumerable<QuestionGetManyResponse>
  GetQuestions(string search, bool includeAnswers)
{
  if (string.IsNullOrEmpty(search))
  {
    if (includeAnswers)
    {
      return _dataRepository.GetQuestionsWithAnswers();
    } else
    {
      return _dataRepository.GetQuestions();
    }
  }
  else
  {
    return _dataRepository.GetQuestionsBySearch(search);
  }
}
```

We've added the ability to have an `includeAnswers` query parameter that, if set, will call the `GetQuestionsWithAnswers` data repository method we just added. A fuller implementation would allow answers to be included if a `search` query parameter is defined, but this implementation will be enough for us to see the N+1 problem and how we can resolve it.

5. Let's run the REST API by pressing *F5*.

6. In Postman, let's try requesting questions with answers:

The answers are returned with each question, as we expected.

This doesn't seem like much of a problem though. The request took only **225 ms** to complete. Well, we only have a couple of answers in our database at the moment. If we had more questions, the request would slow down a fair bit. Also, the test we have just done is for a single user. What happens when multiple users make this request? We'll find out next.

Using WebSurge to load test our endpoint

We must load test our API endpoints to verify that they perform appropriately under load. It is far better to find a performance issue in the development process before our users do. WebSurge is a simple load testing tool that we are going to use to test our `questions` endpoint with the N+1 problem. We are going to perform the load test in our development environment, which is fine for us to see the impact the N+1 problem has. Obviously, the load testing results we are going to see would be a lot faster in a production environment:

1. Run the REST API by pressing *F5* if it's not already running.

2. Open WebSurge and click the **New** option on the **Session** tab. Fill in the request details on the **Request** tab in the right-hand pane for a GET request to `api/questions/includeanswers=true`:

3. To check that the request is correct, press the **Test** button at the bottom of the right-hand pane. We'll see the response we expect:

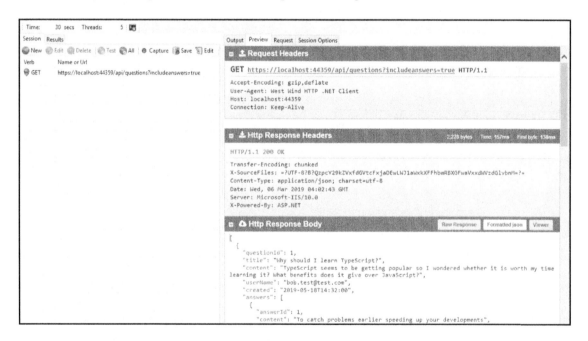

4. We are nearly ready to do the load test now. Let's specify that the test will run for 30 seconds with 5 threads by filling in the relevant boxes under the toolbar:

5. Let's run the load test by clicking the **Start** button. We'll immediately see requests being made in the **Output** tab in the right-hand pane:

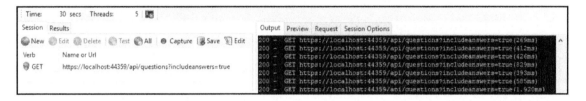

6. When the test has finished, we'll see the test results in the **Output** tab in the right-hand pane:

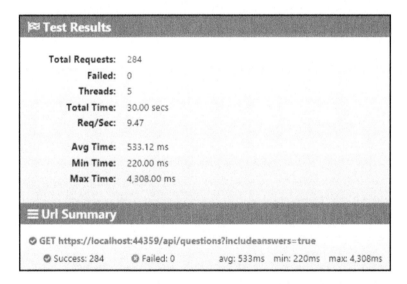

So, we managed to get **9.47** requests per second with this implementation of getting questions with answers. Obviously, the result you get will be different.

7. Stop the ASP.NET Core app from running by pressing *Shift* + *F5* so that you're ready to make the implementation more efficient.

Keep a note of the results—we'll use these in a comparison with an implementation that resolves the N+1 problem next.

Using Dapper multi-mapping to resolve the N+1 problem

Wouldn't it be great if we could get the questions and answers in a single database query and then map this data to the hierarchical structure we require in our data repository? Well, this is exactly what we can do with a feature called **multi-mapping** in Dapper. Let's look at how we can use this:

1. In the data repository, let's change the implementation of the `GetQuestionsWithAnswers` method to the following:

```
public IEnumerable<QuestionGetManyResponse>
  GetQuestionsWithAnswers()
{
  using (var connection = new SqlConnection(_connectionString))
  {
    connection.Open();

    return connection.Query<QuestionGetManyResponse>(
      "EXEC dbo.Question_GetMany_WithAnswers");
  }
}
```

This is a good start but the `Question_GetMany_WithAnswers` stored procedure returns tabular data and we require this to be mapped to the questions and answers hierarchical structure we have in our `QuestionGetManyResponse` model:

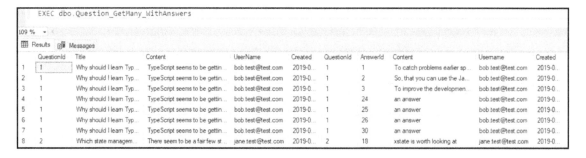

This is where Dapper's multi-mapping feature comes in handy.

2. Change the implementation to the following:

```csharp
public IEnumerable<QuestionGetManyResponse>
GetQuestionsWithAnswers()
{
  using (var connection = new SqlConnection(_connectionString))
  {
    connection.Open();

    var questionDictionary =
      new Dictionary<int, QuestionGetManyResponse>();
    return connection
      .Query<
        QuestionGetManyResponse,
        AnswerGetResponse,
        QuestionGetManyResponse>(
          "EXEC dbo.Question_GetMany_WithAnswers",
          map: (q, a) =>
          {
            QuestionGetManyResponse question;

            if (!questionDictionary.TryGetValue(q.QuestionId, out
question))
            {
              question = q;
              question.Answers =
                new List<AnswerGetResponse>();
              questionDictionary.Add(question.QuestionId,
question);
            }
            question.Answers.Add(a);
            return question;
          },
          splitOn: "QuestionId"
        )
      .Distinct()
      .ToList();
  }
}
```

In the Dapper `Query` method, we provide a lambda function that helps Dapper map each question. The function takes in the question and answers that Dapper has mapped from the stored procedure result and we map it to the structure we require. We use a `Dictionary` called `questionDictionary` to keep track of the questions we've already created so that we can create an instance of `new List<AnswerGetResponse>` for the answers for new questions.

We tell Dapper what models to map to with the first two generic parameters in the `Query` method, which are `QuestionGetManyResponse` and `AnswerGetResponse`, but how does Dapper know which fields that have been returned from the stored procedure map to which properties in the models? The answer is that we tell Dapper using the `splitOn` parameter by saying everything before `QuestionId` goes into the `QuestionGetManyResponse` model and everything after and including `QuestionId` goes into the `AnswerGetResponse` model.

We tell Dapper what model the end result should map to with the last generic parameter in the `Query` method, which is `QuestionGetManyResponse` in this case.

We use the `Distinct` method on the results we get from Dapper to remove duplicate questions and then the `ToList` method to turn the results into a list.

3. With our revised implementation complete, let's run the app by pressing *F5*.
4. In WebSurge, let's run the same load test as we did before by clicking the **Start** button. After 30 seconds, we'll see the results:

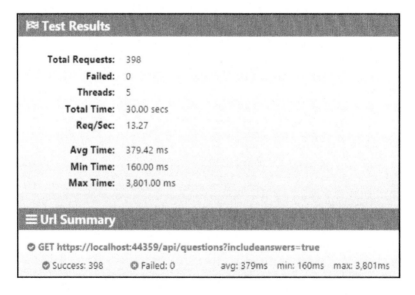

This time, our REST API managed to take **13.27** requests per second, which is much better than before.

So, Dapper's multi-mapping feature can be used to resolve the N+1 problem and generally achieve better performance. We do need to be careful with this approach, though, as we are requesting a lot of data from the database because of the duplicate parent records. Processing large amounts of data in the web server can be inefficient and lead to garbage collection issues, as we'll see later in this chapter.

Using Dapper multi results

There is another feature in Dapper that helps us reduce the amount of database round trips called **multi results**. We are going to use this feature to improve the performance of the endpoint that gets a single question, which, at the moment, is making two database calls:

1. First, let's load test the current implementation using WebSurge. We can use the **Edit** option on the **Session** tab to change the request so that it gets a single question:

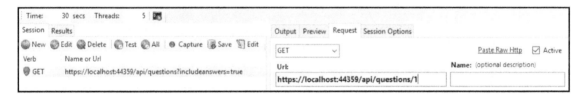

2. We'll leave the duration of the test at **30** seconds with **5** threads. Press the **Start** option to run the load test. When the test has finished, we'll get our results:

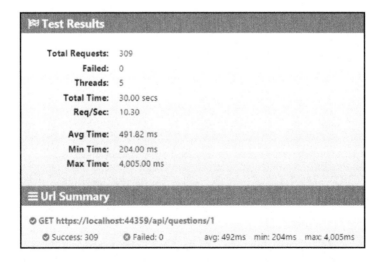

So, the current implementation can take **10.30** requests per second.

3. Now, stop the app from running and start to revise the implementation by adding the following reference to the data repository:

```
using static Dapper.SqlMapper;
```

4. Now, we can change the implementation of QuestionGetSingleResponse to the following:

```
public QuestionGetSingleResponse GetQuestion(int questionId)
{
  using (var connection = new SqlConnection(_connectionString))
  {
    connection.Open();
    using (GridReader results =
      connection.QueryMultiple(
        @"EXEC dbo.Question_GetSingle
          @QuestionId = @QuestionId;
        EXEC dbo.Answer_Get_ByQuestionId
          @QuestionId = @QuestionId",
        new { QuestionId = questionId }
      )
    )
    {
      var question =
        results.Read<QuestionGetSingleResponse>().FirstOrDefault();
      if (question != null)
      {
        question.Answers =
          results.Read<AnswerGetResponse>().ToList();
      }
      return question;
    }
  }
}
```

We use the QueryMultiple method in Dapper to execute our two stored procedures in a single database round trip. The results are added into a results variable and can be retrieved using the Read method by passing the appropriate type in the generic parameter.

5. Let's start the app again in Visual Studio and carry out the same load test:

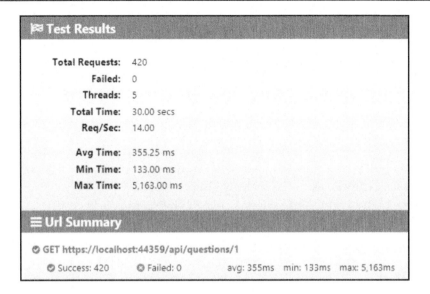

Our improved API can now take **14** requests per second.

Multi-mapping and multi results are two features in Dapper that we can use to reduce database round trips. However, as we mentioned in the multi-mapping example, processing large amounts of data can be problematic. How can we reduce the amount of data we read from the database and process on the web server? We'll find out in the next section.

Paging data

In this section, we are going to force the consumers of our questions endpoint to specify the *page* of data when executing the request with the search query parameter. So, we'll only be returning a portion of the data rather than all of it.

Paging helps with performance and scalability in the following ways:

- The number of the page read I/Os is reduced when SQL Server grabs the data.
- The amount of data that's transferred from the database server to the web server is reduced.
- The amount of memory that's used to store the data on the web server in our model is reduced.
- The amount of data that's transferred from the web server to the client is reduced.

This all adds up to a potentially significant positive impact—particularly for large collections of data.

Adding test questions for the load test

Let's carry out the following steps to add lots of questions to our database. This will allow us to see the impact of data paging:

1. Let's open SQL Server Management Studio, right-click on the **QandA** database in **Object Explorer**, and choose **New Query**.
2. In the query window that opens, add the following command:

```
EXEC Question_AddForLoadTest
```

   This will execute a stored procedure that will add 10,000 questions to our database.

3. Press *F5* to run the stored procedure, which will take a few seconds to complete.

Now that we have our questions in place, let's test out the current implementation.

Load testing the current implementation

Before we implement data paging, let's see how the current implementation performs under load:

1. Let's start our REST API by pressing *F5* in Visual Studio, if it's not already running.
2. Now, we can load test the current implementation using WebSurge. Let's set the request URL path to `/api/questions?search=question` and stick to a duration of 30 seconds with 5 threads.
3. Before running the load test, check that the request works okay by clicking the **Test** option. We may get an error in the response body like the following one:

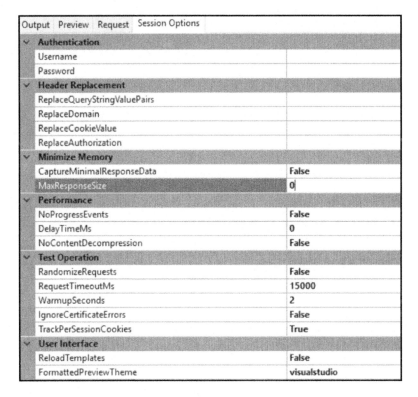

This error can be resolved by changing the **MaxResponseSize** setting to 0:

4. Start the test. When the test has finished, we'll get our results:

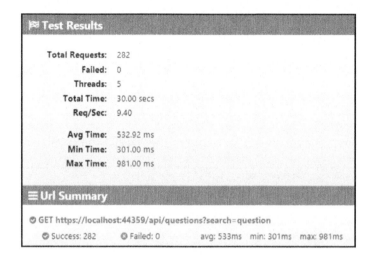

So, the requests per second to beat is **9.40**.

Let's stop the REST API from running so that we can revise the implementation of the `questions` endpoint.

Implementing data paging

Now, let's revise the implementation of the `questions` endpoint with the **search** query parameter so that we can use data paging:

1. Let's start by adding a new method that will search with paging to our data repository interface:

```
public interface IDataRepository
{
  ...
  IEnumerable<QuestionGetManyResponse>
    GetQuestionsBySearch(string search);
  IEnumerable<QuestionGetManyResponse>
    GetQuestionsBySearchWithPaging(
      string search,
      int pageNumber,
      int pageSize);
  ...
}
```

So, the method will take in the page number and size as parameters.

2. Now, we can add the method implementation in the data repository:

```
public IEnumerable<QuestionGetManyResponse>
  GetQuestionsBySearchWithPaging(
    string search,
    int pageNumber,
    int pageSize
  )
{
  using (var connection = new SqlConnection(_connectionString))
  {
    connection.Open();
    var parameters = new
      {
        Search = search,
        PageNumber = pageNumber,
        PageSize = pageSize
      };
    return connection.Query<QuestionGetManyResponse>(
      @"EXEC dbo.Question_GetMany_BySearch_WithPaging
        @Search = @Search,
        @PageNumber = @PageNumber,
        @PageSize = @PageSize", parameters
    );
  }
}
```

So, we are calling a stored procedure called
`Question_GetMany_BySearch_WithPaging` to get the page of data passing in
the search criteria, page number, and page size as parameters.

3. Let's change the implementation of the `GetQuestions` action method in our API
controller so that we can call this repository method:

```
[HttpGet]
public IEnumerable<QuestionGetManyResponse>
  GetQuestions(
    string search,
    bool includeAnswers,
    int page = 1,
    int pageSize = 20
  )
{
  if (string.IsNullOrEmpty(search))
  {
```

```
    if (includeAnswers)
    {
      return _dataRepository.GetQuestionsWithAnswers();
    }
    else
    {
      return _dataRepository.GetQuestions();
    }
  }
  else
  {
    return _dataRepository.GetQuestionsBySearchWithPaging(
      search,
      page,
      pageSize
    );
  }
}
```

Notice that we also accept query parameters for the page number and page size, which are defaulted to 1 and 20, respectively.

4. Let's start our REST API by pressing *F5* in Visual Studio.

5. Now, we can load test the current implementation using WebSurge. Let's change the request URL path to `/api/questions?search=question&page=1&pagesize=20` and stick to a duration of **30** seconds with **5** threads.

6. Start the test. When the test has finished, we'll get our results:

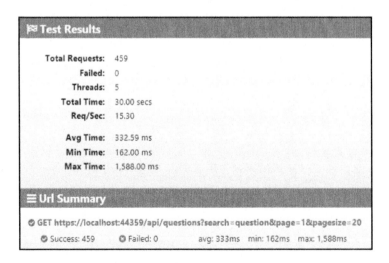

Test Results	
Total Requests:	459
Failed:	0
Threads:	5
Total Time:	30.00 secs
Req/Sec:	15.30
Avg Time:	332.59 ms
Min Time:	162.00 ms
Max Time:	1,588.00 ms

Url Summary

GET https://localhost:44359/api/questions?search=question&page=1&pagesize=20
Success: 459   Failed: 0   avg: 333ms   min: 162ms   max: 1,588ms

We get the performance improvement we hoped for, with the endpoint now able to take **15.30** requests per second.

Data paging is well worth considering for APIs that return collections of data, particularly if the collection is large.

In the next section, we are going to tackle the subject of asynchronous code and how this can help with scalability.

Making API controllers asynchronous

In this section, we are going to make the unanswered questions endpoint asynchronous to make it more scalable.

At the moment, all of our API code has been synchronous. For synchronous API code, when a request is made to the API, a thread from the thread pool will handle the request. If the code makes an I/O call (such as a database call) synchronously, the thread will block until the I/O call has finished. The blocked thread can't be used for any other work—it simply does nothing and waits for the I/O task to finish. If other requests are made to our API while the other thread is blocked, different threads in the thread pool will be used for the other requests. The following diagram is a visualization of synchronous requests in ASP.NET Core:

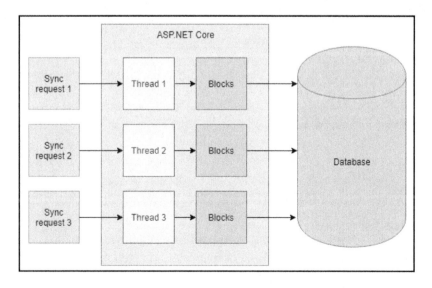

There is some overhead in using a thread—a thread consumes memory and it takes time to spin a new thread up. So, really, we want our API to use as few threads as possible.

If the API was to work in an asynchronous manner, when a request is made to our API, a thread from the thread pool handles the request (as in the synchronous case). If the code makes an asynchronous I/O call, the thread will be returned to the thread pool at the start of the I/O call and can be used for other requests. The following diagram is a visualization of asynchronous requests in ASP.NET Core:

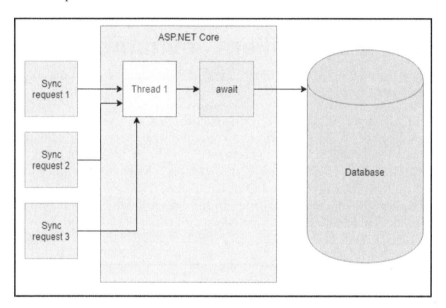

So, if we make our API asynchronous, it will be able to handle requests more efficiently and increase scalability. It is important to note that making an API asynchronous won't make it more performant because a single request will take roughly the same amount of time. The improvement we are about to make is so that our API can use the server's resources more efficiently.

Testing the current implementation

Before we change the unanswered questions endpoint, let's do a load test on the current implementation. We are interested in the number of threads that are being used. Therefore, we are going to do a load test where the API struggles and look at the number of threads being used. Follow these steps to do just that:

1. Let's start our REST API by pressing *F5* in Visual Studio.

2. Now, we can load test the current implementation using WebSurge. Let's set the request URL path to `/api/questions/unanswered` and change the duration to `60` seconds, which will allow us to see requests timing out when the API is struggling to cope with the load.

3. We'll need to experiment with the number of the threads, but let's start with `20` threads and then start the load test.

4. We need to watch for the API struggling by looking at the status bar in the bottom-right corner of WebSurge. The status will turn red when the API is struggling with requests that are starting to fail:

> 248 requests, 1 failed | 43 of 62 secs | 5 request/sec

5. If the load test completes without any failed requests, then increase the thread count and try again until we get a test that overloads the API.

6. When you see the API struggle, switch to Visual Studio and pause the REST API by pressing *Ctrl + Alt + Break* and then look at the **Threads** window by pressing *Ctrl + Alt + H*. We'll see that a lot of threads are being used:

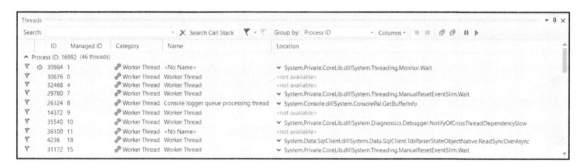

7. Now that we've seen that the current implementation uses a high number of threads when struggling, stop the REST API from running by pressing *Shift + F5*.

Our goal is for our API to use fewer threads, so make a note of the number of threads the current implementation uses.

Implementing an asynchronous controller action method

Now, we are going to change the implementation of the unanswered questions endpoint so that it's asynchronous:

1. We are going to start by creating an asynchronous version of the data repository method that gets unanswered questions. So, let's create a new method in the data repository interface:

   ```
   public interface IDataRepository
   {
     ...
     IEnumerable<QuestionGetManyResponse>
       GetUnansweredQuestions();
     Task<IEnumerable<QuestionGetManyResponse>>
       GetUnansweredQuestionsAsync();
     ...
   }
   ```

   A key difference of an asynchronous method is that it returns a `Task` of the type that will eventually be returned.

2. Let's create the data repository method implementation:

   ```
   public async Task<IEnumerable<QuestionGetManyResponse>>
     GetUnansweredQuestionsAsync()
   {
     using (var connection = new SqlConnection(_connectionString))
     {
       await connection.OpenAsync();
       return await
         connection.QueryAsync<QuestionGetManyResponse>(
           "EXEC dbo.Question_GetUnanswered");
     }
   }
   ```

   The `async` keyword before the return type signifies that the method is asynchronous. The implementation is very similar to the synchronous version, except that we use the asynchronous Dapper version of opening the connection and executing the query with the `await` keyword.

TIP

When making code asynchronous, all the I/O calls in the calling stack must be asynchronous. If any I/O call is synchronous, then the thread will be blocked rather than returning to the thread pool and so threads won't be managed efficiently.

3. Let's change the API controller action method:

```
[HttpGet("unanswered")]
public async Task<IEnumerable<QuestionGetManyResponse>>
  GetUnansweredQuestions()
{
  return await _dataRepository.GetUnansweredQuestionsAsync();
}
```

We mark the method as asynchronous with the `async` keyword and return a `Task` of the type we eventually want to return. We also call the asynchronous version of the data repository method with the `await` keyword.

Our unanswered questions endpoint is now asynchronous.

4. Start the REST API running by pressing *F5* in Visual Studio.
5. Let's load test this in WebSurge with the same configuration we used to test the synchronous implementation. Start the load test.
6. When the REST API is struggling or we are toward the end of the duration, switch to Visual Studio and pause the REST API by pressing *Ctrl + Alt + Break* and then look at the **Threads** window by pressing *Ctrl + Alt + H*. We'll see that only a few threads are being used:

This shows that asynchronous code uses the web server's resources more efficiently under load. When writing asynchronous code, it is really important that all the I/O calls are asynchronous; otherwise, the code will behave as synchronous code, thus using the thread pool inefficiently.

Mixing asynchronous and synchronous code

An easy mistake to make is to mix asynchronous code with synchronous code. In fact, we have made this mistake in our `PostAnswer` action method because the method is synchronous but the call to the `SignalR` hub is asynchronous:

```
[HttpPost("answer")]
public ActionResult<AnswerGetResponse>
  PostAnswer(AnswerPostRequest answerPostRequest)
{
  ...
  _questionHubContext.Clients.Group(
      $"Question-{answerPostRequest.QuestionId.Value}")
    .SendAsync(
      "ReceiveQuestion",
      _dataRepository.GetQuestion(answerPostRequest.QuestionId.Value)
  );

  return savedAnswer;
}
```

The code functions correctly but is suboptimal because not only is the thread that handles the request blocked from handling other requests, but we also have all of the overhead of handling asynchronous code.

The resolution is to make all of the code asynchronous, which includes following the same pattern that we have just followed. The code for this can be found in this book's GitHub repository at `https://github.com/PacktPublishing/ASP.NET-Core-3-and-React-17` in the `Chapter10` folder. In fact, all of the code has been made asynchronous in this repository.

In the next section, we are going to look at how we can optimize requests for data by caching data.

Caching data

In this section, we are going to cache requests for getting a question. At the moment, the database is queried for each request to get a question. If we cache a question and can get subsequent requests for the question from the cache, this should be faster and reduce the load on the database. We will prove this with load tests.

Load testing the current implementation

Before we implement caching, we are going to load test the current implementation of getting a single question using the following steps:

1. Let's start our REST API by pressing *F5* in Visual Studio.
2. Now, we can load test the current implementation using WebSurge. Let's set the request URL path to `/api/questions/1` and change the duration to **30** seconds with **5** threads.
3. Start the test. When the test has finished, we'll get our results:

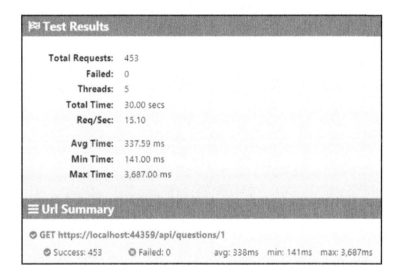

So, we are getting **15.1** requests per second without caching.

Stop the REST API from running so that we can implement and use a data cache.

Implementing a data cache

We are going to implement a cache for the questions using the memory cache in ASP.NET Core:

1. First, let's create an interface in the `Data` folder called `IQuestionCache`:

```
using QandA.Data.Models;

namespace QandA.Data
```

```
{
  public interface IQuestionCache
  {
    QuestionGetSingleResponse Get(int questionId);
    void Remove(int questionId);
    void Set(QuestionGetSingleResponse question);
  }
}
```

So, we need the cache implementation to have methods for getting, removing, and updating an item in the cache.

2. Now, we can create a class in the Data folder called QuestionCache:

```
using Microsoft.Extensions.Caching.Memory;
using QandA.Data.Models;

namespace QandA.Data
{
  public class QuestionCache: IQuestionCache
  {
    // TODO - create a memory cache
    // TODO - method to get a cached question
    // TODO - method to add a cached question
    // TODO - method to remove a cached question
  }
}
```

Notice that we have referenced Microsoft.Extensions.Caching.Memory so that we can use the standard ASP.NET Core memory cache.

3. Let's create a constructor that creates an instance of the memory cache:

```
public class QuestionCache: IQuestionCache
{
  private MemoryCache _cache { get; set; }
  public QuestionCache()
  {
    _cache = new MemoryCache(new MemoryCacheOptions
    {
        SizeLimit = 100
    });
  }

  // TODO - method to get a cached question
  // TODO - method to add a cached question
  // TODO - method to remove a cached question
}
```

Notice that we have set the cache limit to be `100` items. This is to limit the amount of memory the cache takes up on our web server.

4. Let's implement a method to get a question from the cache:

```
public class QuestionCache: IQuestionCache
{
    ...

    private string GetCacheKey(int questionId) =>
        $"Question-{questionId}";

    public QuestionGetSingleResponse Get(int questionId)
    {
        QuestionGetSingleResponse question;
        _cache.TryGetValue(
            GetCacheKey(questionId),
            out question);
        return question;
    }

    // TODO - method to add a cached question
    // TODO - method to remove a cached question
}
```

We have created an expression to give us a key for a cache item, which is the word `Question` with a hyphen, followed by the question ID.

We use the `TryGetValue` method within the memory cache to retrieve the cached question. So, `null` will be returned from our method if the question doesn't exist in the cache.

5. Now, we can implement a method to add a question to the cache. We can add an item to the cache using the `Set` method in the ASP.NET Core memory cache:

```
public class QuestionCache: IQuestionCache
{
    ...

    public void Set(QuestionGetSingleResponse question)
    {
        var cacheEntryOptions =
            new MemoryCacheEntryOptions().SetSize(1);
        _cache.Set(
            GetCacheKey(question.QuestionId),
            question,
            cacheEntryOptions);
```

```
    }

    // TODO - method to remove a cached question
}
```

Notice that we specify the size of the question in the options when setting the cache value. This ties in with the size limit we set on the cache so that the cache will start to remove questions from the cache when there are 100 questions in it.

6. The last method we need to implement is a method to remove questions from the cache:

```
public class QuestionCache: IQuestionCache
{
    ...

    public void Remove(int questionId)
    {
        _cache.Remove(GetCacheKey(questionId));
    }
}
```

Note that if the question doesn't exist in the cache, nothing will happen and no exception will be thrown.

That completes the implementation of our question cache.

Using the data cache in an API controller action method

Now, we are going to make use of the questions cache in the GetQuestion method in our API controller:

1. First, we need to make the cache available for dependency injection so that we can inject it into the API controller. So, let's register this in the Startup class:

```
public void ConfigureServices(IServiceCollection services)
{
    ...

    services.AddMemoryCache();
    services.AddSingleton<IQuestionCache, QuestionCache>();
}
```

We enable the ASP.NET Core memory cache and then register our cache as a singleton in the dependency injection system. This means that a single instance of our class will be created for the lifetime of the app. So, separate HTTP requests will access the same class instance and, therefore, the same cached data. This is exactly what we want for a cache.

2. In QuestionsController, let's inject the cache:

```
. . .
private readonly IQuestionCache _cache;

public QuestionsController(..., IQuestionCache questionCache)
{
    . . .
  _cache = questionCache;
}
```

3. Let's change the implementation of GetQuestion to the following:

```
[HttpGet("{questionId}")]
public ActionResult<QuestionGetSingleResponse>
  GetQuestion(int questionId)
{
  var question = _cache.Get(questionId);
  if (question == null)
  {
    question = _dataRepository.GetQuestion(questionId);
    if (question == null)
    {
        return NotFound();
    }
    _cache.Set(question);
  }
  return question;
}
```

4. When a question changes, we need to remove the item from the cache if it exists in the cache. This is so that subsequent requests for the question get the updated question from the database:

```
[HttpPut("{questionId}")]
public ActionResult<QuestionGetSingleResponse>
  PutQuestion(int questionId, QuestionPutRequest
questionPutRequest)
{
    . . .
```

```
_cache.Remove(savedQuestion.QuestionId);

    return savedQuestion;
}
```

5. Similarly, when a question is deleted, we need to remove it from the cache if it exists in the cache:

```
HttpDelete("{questionId}")]
public ActionResult DeleteQuestion(int questionId)
{
    ...

    _cache.Remove(questionId);

    return NoContent();
}
```

6. We also need to remove the question from the cache when an answer is being posted:

```
[HttpPost("answer")]
public ActionResult<AnswerGetResponse>
    PostAnswer(AnswerPostRequest answerPostRequest)
{
    ...

    _cache.Remove(answerPostRequest.QuestionId.Value);

    _questionHubContext.Clients.Group(
        $"Question-{answerPostRequest.QuestionId.Value}")
      .SendAsync(
        "ReceiveQuestion",
    _dataRepository.GetQuestion(answerPostRequest.QuestionId.Value));

    return savedAnswer;
}
```

7. Let's start our REST API by pressing *F5* in Visual Studio.

8. Let's load test the /api/questions/1 endpoint again with our improved implementation, keeping the duration and number of threads in the test the same.

9. When the test has finished, we'll get our results, confirming the improvement:

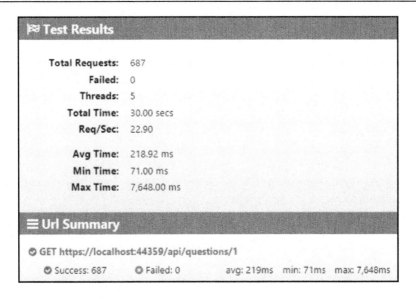

10. Stop the REST API in Visual Studio by pressing *Shift + F5.*

This completes our implementation of the question endpoint with data caching.

It is important to remember to invalidate the cache when the data changes. In our example, this was straightforward, but it can be more complex, particularly if there are other processes outside of the REST API that change the data. So, if we don't have full control of the data changes in the REST API, a cache may not be worth implementing.

Another consideration for whether to use a cache is if the data changes very frequently. In this case, the caching process can actually negatively impact performance because lots of the requests will result in database calls anyway and we have all of the overhead of managing the cache.

However, if the data behind an endpoint changes infrequently and we have control over these changes, then caching is a great way to positively impact performance.

What if the REST API is distributed across several servers? Well, because the memory cache is local to each web server, this could result in database calls where the data is cached on a different server. A solution to this is to implement a distributed cache with `IDistributedCache` in ASP.NET Core, which would have a very similar implementation to our memory cache. The complexity is that this needs to connect to a third-party cache such as Redis, which adds financial costs and complexity to the solution. For high-traffic REST APIs, a distributed cache is well worth considering, though.

The last topic we are going to look at is garbage collection and how this can negatively impact performance.

Reducing garbage collection

Each time we create a new object in .NET, it allocates memory for the object from what is called the managed heap. Eventually, a process called **garbage collection** kicks in, which is responsible for freeing memory. When the garbage collector performs a collection, it checks for objects in the managed heap that are no longer being used by the app and performs the necessary operations to reclaim their memory.

Memory allocation is very cheap but unfortunately, collecting the memory isn't. Allocating objects over 85 KB in size in a single allocation will result in the object ending up on the large object heap, which is expensive to collect.

So, creating large objects in our .NET code can hurt performance and an area where we can fall into this trap in REST APIs is when dealing with large requests. In this section, we are going to look at the post question endpoint as an example that doesn't have a garbage collection issue with our current implementation. We are going to revise the implementation, introduce a garbage collection issue, and observe the problem using the PerfView tool.

Load testing the current implementation

Let's load test the post question endpoint and measure the garbage collection using PerfView. In this load test, we are going to have different requests hitting the endpoint that will challenge the garbage collection process more than the same request being repeated. Let's look at the steps:

1. Start the REST API in Visual Studio.
2. Let's run the PerfView tool and choose the **Collect** option from the **Collect** menu.
3. Tick the **GC Collect Only** and **GC Only** options in the **Advanced Options** section:

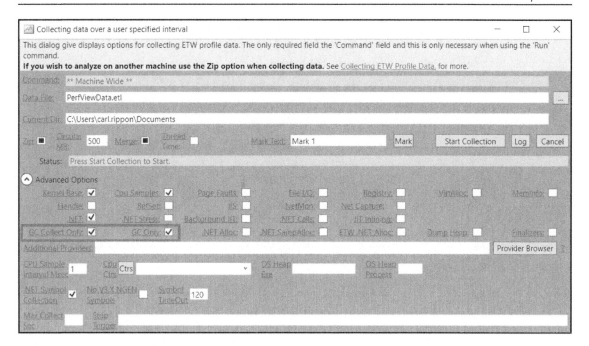

4. Unfortunately, we can't create a large request directly in WebSurge because the **Content** text box has a character limit. However, we can create a large request in Postman and then capture this in WebSurge. So, create a large request to post a question in Postman that includes at least 50,000 characters in the content:

5. In WebSurge, on the **Session** tab, click the **Capture** option and then click on the **Capture** option in the window that appears.

6. Go back to Postman and send the request.

7. Still in Postman, change the question content and send the request again. Repeat this so that we have at least 20 different requests.

8. Flip back to WebSurge to see the request in the **Capture** window:

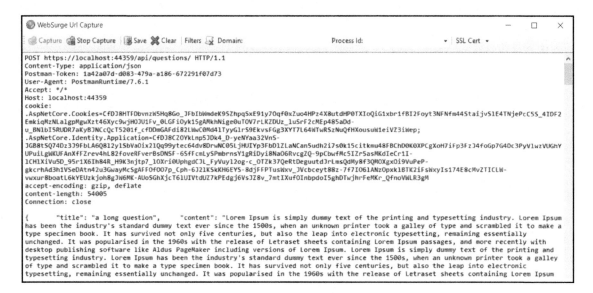

9. Click **Stop Capture** in the **Capture** window. Then, click **Save** and choose a file location for the file.

10. Close the **Capture** window. Now, we'll see our large request in the session tab, ready to be load tested:

11. Set the load test duration to **60** seconds with **5** threads and start the load test.

12. Quickly move to PerfView and click the **Start Collection** button so that it starts to collect data about garbage collection as the load test runs.

13. When the load test finishes, click the **Stop Collection** button in PerfView. PerfView will take a few more seconds to finish collecting the data.

14. In the left-hand pane in **PerfView,** double-click on **GCStats**, which is under **Memory Group** in **PerfViewData.etl.zip**:

We need to find the process for our Q and A app in the list that appears, which is the first one in the following screenshot:

GCStats

- Process 41532: iisexpress applicationhost.config /site:QandA /apppool:QandA_AppPool
- Process 16356: devenv
- Process 5532: StackifyTracerService
- Process 14852: WebSurge

15. Clicking on this process will give us the data that was collected in that process:

				GC Rollup By Generation						
				All times are in msec.						
Gen	Count	Max Pause	Max Peak MB	Max Alloc MB/sec	Total Pause	Total Alloc MB	Alloc MB/ MSec GC	Survived MB/ MSec GC	Mean Pause	Induced
ALL	1	39.8	462.9	0.000	39.8	0.0	0.0	∞	39.8	0
0	0	0.0	0.0	0.000	0.0	0.0	NaN	NaN	NaN	0
1	0	0.0	0.0	0.000	0.0	0.0	NaN	NaN	NaN	0
2	1	39.8	462.9	0.000	39.8	0.0	∞	∞	39.8	0

We are interested in the last row in the preceding table, which is what happened in the generation **2** garbage collection heap. There was just a single pause due to garbage collection, which lasted **39.8** milliseconds.

So, the current implementation didn't really suffer any significant impact with garbage collection. Make sure the REST API has been stopped before we rework this implementation.

Implementing custom model binding

Now, we are going to rework the implementation of the post question endpoint so that we have a naive implementation of custom model binding:

1. First, let's install `Newtonsoft.Json` via NuGet. We are going to use this library to deserialize the request body.

2. Now, add the following `using` statements in `QuestionsController.cs`:

```
using System.IO;
using Newtonsoft.Json;
```

3. In the `PostQuestion` action method, remove the parameters and manually create the `questionPostRequest` model using JSON.NET:

```
[HttpPost]
public async Task<ActionResult<QuestionGetSingleResponse>>
PostQuestion()
{
  var json =
    await new StreamReader(Request.Body).ReadToEndAsync();
  var questionPostRequest =
    JsonConvert.DeserializeObject<QuestionPostRequest>(json);
```

```
        var savedQuestion = _dataRepository.PostQuestion(...);
    ...
}
```

We also need to flag the method as asynchronous with the `async` keyword and return `Task` because reading the response body is asynchronous. We should, of course, make the call to the data repository asynchronous as well, but the change we have made will be fine to demonstrate the garbage collection problem.

This implementation is inefficient for large requests. This is because it will be processing large string objects that could be placed on the large object heap, which will be expensive to collect.

4. Start the REST API in Visual Studio.
5. Set up a PerfView collection to collect garbage collection data, exactly like we did before.
6. Start the same load test again in WebSurge and start the collection in PerfView.
7. When the load test has finished, stop the collection and look at the data that was collected:

GC Rollup By Generation										
All times are in msec.										
Gen	Count	Max Pause	Max Peak MB	Max Alloc MB/sec	Total Pause	Total Alloc MB	Alloc MB/ MSec GC	Survived MB/ MSec GC	Mean Pause	Induced
ALL	68	85.3	239.9	176.847	1,102.3	1,621.6	1.5	∞	16.2	0
0	2	6.3	86.8	56.876	11.4	60.5	0.0	∞	5.7	0
1	1	3.9	106.8	124.772	3.9	61.4	0.0	∞	3.9	0
2	65	85.3	239.9	176.847	1,087.0	1,499.7	0.7	∞	16.7	0

There were **65** objects added to generation **2** in this test, resulting in a total pause of **1,087** milliseconds. So, there was just over 1 second of a delay due to the garbage collection process.

8. Before we finish this section, let's clean a few things up. First, let's revert the `PostQuestion` action method implementation to the previous version:

```
[HttpPost]
public ActionResult<QuestionGetSingleResponse>
    PostQuestion(QuestionPostRequest questionPostRequest)
{
    var savedQuestion =
        _dataRepository.PostQuestion(new QuestionPostFullRequest
        {
```

```
            Title = questionPostRequest.Title,
            Content = questionPostRequest.Content,
            UserId = "1",
            UserName = "bob.test@test.com",
            Created = DateTime.UtcNow
        });
        return CreatedAtAction(nameof(GetQuestion), new
        {
            questionId = savedQuestion.QuestionId
        }, savedQuestion);
    }
```

9. Let's remove the `System.IO` and `Newtonsoft.Json` using statements, as well as the `Newtonsoft.Json` NuGet dependency.

10. Let's also remove the questions that were generated by the load tests. Open SQL Server Management Studio, right-click on the **QandA** database in Object Explorer, and choose **New Query**. In the query window that opens, add the following command:

```
DELETE FROM dbo.Question WHERE QuestionId > 2
```

11. Press *F5* to run the command, which will take a few seconds to complete.

There are two morals to this story. The first is to avoid processing large strings to keep the garbage collection process nice and efficient. The second is to try to stick to the standard model binding process because it is very efficient!

Summary

In this chapter, we learned that we can use Dapper's multi-mapping and multi result features to reduce database round trips to positively impact performance and allow our REST API to accept more requests per second. We learned also that forcing the client to page through the data they need to consume helps with performance as well.

We learned how to make controller action methods asynchronous and how it positively impacts the scalability of a REST API built in ASP.NET Core. We also understood that all of the I/O calls in a method and child methods need to be asynchronous to achieve scalability benefits.

We also learned how to cache data in memory to reduce the number of expensive database calls. We understand that data that is read often and rarely changed is a great case for using a cache.

Toward the end of this chapter, we learned how large objects can negatively impact performance in the garbage collection process. In terms of a web API, it is best to let ASP.NET Core handle model binding because it is very efficient.

We will continue to focus on the backend in the next chapter and turn our attention to the topic of security.

Questions

Try to answer the following questions to check the knowledge that you have gained in this chapter:

1. We have the following code in a data repository that uses Dapper's multi result feature to return a single order with the many related detail lines in a single database call:

```
using (var connection = new SqlConnection(_connectionString))
{
  connection.Open();
  using (GridReader results = connection.QueryMultiple(
    @"EXEC dbo.Order_GetHeader @OrderId = @OrderId;
    EXEC dbo.OrderDetails_Get_ByOrderId @OrderId = @OrderId",
    new { OrderId = orderId }))
  {

    // TODO - Read the order and details from the query result

    return order;
  }
}
```

What are the missing statements that will read the order and its details from the results putting the details in the order model? The order model is of the `OrderGetSingleResponse` type and contains a `Details` property of the `IEnumerable<OrderDetailGetResponse>` type.

2. What is the downside of using Dapper's multi-mapping feature when reading data from a many to one-related table in a single database call?

3. How does data paging help performance?

4. Does making code asynchronous make it faster?

5. What is the problem with the following asynchronous method?

```
public async AnswerGetResponse GetAnswer(int answerId)
{
  using (var connection = new SqlConnection(_connectionString))
  {
    connection.Open();
    return await connection
      .QueryFirstOrDefaultAsync<AnswerGetResponse>(
        "EXEC dbo.Answer_Get_ByAnswerId @AnswerId = @AnswerId",
        new { AnswerId = answerId });
  }
}
```

6. Why it is a good idea to have a size limit on a memory cache?
7. In our `QuestionCache` implementation, when adding a question to the cache, how can we invalidate that item in the cache after 30 minutes?
8. When we registered our `QuestionCache` class for dependency injection, why did we use the `AddSingleton` method and not the `AddScoped` method like in the following code?

```
services.AddScoped<QuestionCache>();
```

Further reading

Here are some useful links if you want to learn more about the topics that were covered in this chapter:

- Dapper multi-mapping: https://dapper-tutorial.net/result-multi-mapping
- Dapper multi results: https://dapper-tutorial.net/result-multi-result
- Asynchronous programming with `async` and `await`: https://docs.microsoft.com/en-us/dotnet/csharp/programming-guide/concepts/async/
- ASP.NET Core memory cache: https://docs.microsoft.com/en-us/aspnet/core/performance/caching/memory
- ASP.NET Core distributed cache: https://docs.microsoft.com/en-us/aspnet/core/performance/caching/distributed
- .NET garbage collection: https://docs.microsoft.com/en-us/dotnet/standard/garbage-collection/
- David Fowler's ASP.NET Core diagnostic scenarios: https://github.com/davidfowl/AspNetCoreDiagnosticScenarios/blob/master/AsyncGuidance.md

11
Securing the Backend

In this chapter, we'll implement authentication and authorization in our Q and A app. We will use a popular service called Auth0, which implements **OpenID Connect (OIDC)**, to help us to do this. We will start by understanding what OIDC is and why it is a good choice before getting our app to interact with Auth0.

At the moment, our web API is accessible by unauthenticated users, which is a security vulnerability. We will resolve the vulnerability by protecting the necessary endpoints with simple authorization. This will mean that only authenticated users can access protected resources.

Authenticated users shouldn't have access to everything though. We will learn how to ensure authenticated users only get access to what they are allowed to by using custom authorization policies.

We'll also learn how to get details about the authenticated user so that we can include these when questions and answers are saved to the database.

In this chapter, we'll cover the following topics:

- Understanding OpenID Connect
- Setting up Auth0 with our ASP.NET Core backend
- Protecting endpoints
- Using the authenticated user when posting questions and answers

Technical requirements

We'll use the following tools and services in this chapter:

- **Visual Studio 2019**: We'll use this to edit our ASP.NET Core code.
- **.NET Core 3.0**: This can be downloaded and installed from `https://dotnet.microsoft.com/download/dotnet-core`.
- **Auth0**: We will use this to authenticate and manage users. The service is free to try and do some testing with, and an account can be created at `https://auth0.com/signup`.
- **Postman**: We'll use this to try out the changes to our REST API in this chapter. This can be downloaded from `https://www.getpostman.com/downloads/`.
- **Q and A**: We'll start with the Q and A backend in the `Chapter10` folder in the GitHub repository at `https://github.com/PacktPublishing/ASP.NET-Core-3-and-React-17`. This is the project we finished in the last chapter in addition to all our asynchronous action methods. You must start from this project rather than the one you completed in the last chapter.

All of the code snippets in this chapter can be found online at `https://github.com/PacktPublishing/ASP.NET-Core-3-and-React-17`. To restore code from a chapter, the source code repository can be downloaded and the relevant folder opened in the relevant editor. If the code is frontend code, then `npm install` can be entered in the Terminal to restore the dependencies.

Check out the following video to see the code in action:

`http://bit.ly/2EPQ8DY`

Understanding OIDC

Before we understand OIDC, let's make sure we understand authentication and authorization. Authentication verifies that the user is who they say they are. In our app, the user will enter their email and password to prove who they are. Authorization decides whether a user has permission to access a resource. In our app, some of the REST API endpoints, such as posting a question, will eventually be protected by authorization checks.

OIDC is an industry-standard way of handling both authentication and authorization as well as other user-related operations. This works well for a wide variety of architectures including **single-page applications (SPAs)** such as ours where there is a JavaScript client and a server-side REST API that need to be secured.

The following diagram shows the high-level flow of a user of our app being authenticated and then gaining access to protected resources in the REST API:

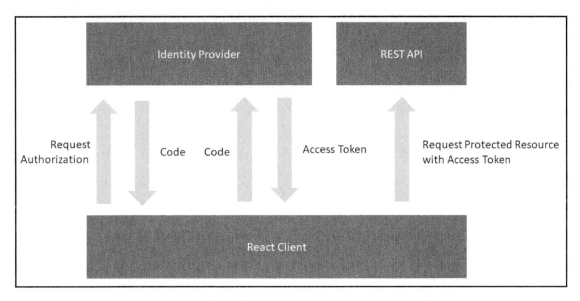

Here are some more details of the steps that take place:

1. The client makes an authorization request to an identity provider because it wants to get access to a protected resource in the REST API.
2. The client is redirected to the identity provider so that the user can enter their credentials to prove who they are.
3. The identity provider then generates a code and redirects back to the client with the code.
4. The client then makes a web API request containing the generated code to get an access code. The identity provider validates the code and responds with an access token.
5. The client can then access protected resources in the REST API by including the access token in the requests.

Notice that our app never handles user credentials. When user authentication is required, the user will be redirected to the identity provider to carry out this process. Our app only ever deals with a secure token, which is referred to as an **access token**, which is a long encoded string. This token is in **JSON Web Token (JWT)** format, which again is industry standard. The content of a JWT can be inspected using the following website: `https://jwt.io/`:

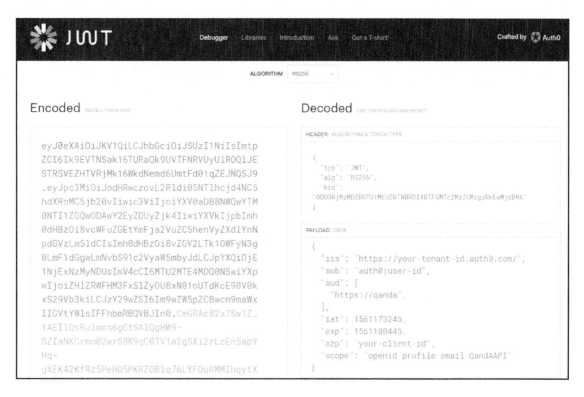

There are three parts to a JWT separated by dots and they appear as different colors in `jwt.io`:

- **HEADER**
- **PAYLOAD**
- **SIGNATURE**

The header usually contains the type of the token in a `typ` field and the signing algorithm being used in an `alg` field. So, the preceding token is a JWT that uses an RSA signature with the SHA-256 asymmetric algorithm. There also is a `kid` field in the header, which is an opaque identifier that can be used to identify the key that was used to sign the JWT.

The payload of JWTs vary but the following fields are often included:

- `iss`: This is the identity provider that issued the token.
- `sub`: This is short for `subject` and is the user's identifier. This will be `UserId` for our app.
- `aud`: This is the intended audience. For our app, this will contain the name of our REST API.
- `iat`: This is when the JWT was issued. This is in Unix epoch time format, which is the seconds that have passed since January 1, 1970.
- `exp`: This is when the token expires and again is in Unix epoch time format.
- `azp`: This is the party to which the token was issued, which is a unique identifier for the client using the JWT. This will be the client ID of our React app in our case.
- `scope`: This is what the client can get access to. For our app, this is the REST API as well as user profile information and their email address.
- The `openid` scope allows the client to verify a user's identity.

OIDC deals with securely storing passwords, authenticating users, generating access tokens, and much more. Being able to leverage an industry-standard technology such as OIDC not only saves us lots of time but also gives us the peace of mind that the implementation is very secure and will receive updates as attackers get smarter.

What we have just learned is implemented by Auth0. We'll start to use Auth0 in the next section.

Setting up Auth0 with our ASP.NET Core backend

Auth0 is a service that implements OpenID Connect. In this section, we are going to set up Auth0 and integrate it into our ASP.NET Core backend.

Setting up Auth0

Let's carry out the following steps to set up Auth0 as our identity provider:

1. If you haven't already got an Auth0 account, sign up at `https://auth0.com/signup`.

2. Once we have an Auth0 account and have logged in, we need to change the default audience in our tenant settings. To get to our tenant settings, click on the user avatar and choose **Settings**:

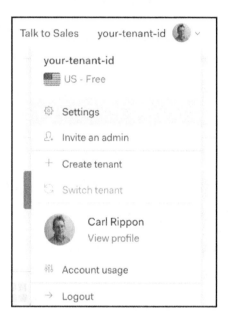

3. The **Default Audience** option is in the **API Authorization Settings** section. Change this to `https://qanda`:

This tells Auth0 to add `https://qanda` to the `aud` payload field in the JWT it generates. This setting triggers Auth0 to generate access tokens in JWT format. Our ASP.NET Core backend will also check that access tokens contain this data before granting access to protected resources.

4. Next, we are going to tell Auth0 about our React frontend. On the left-hand navigation menu, click **Applications** and then click the **Create Application** button.

5. Select the **Single Page Web Applications** application type and click the **CREATE** button:

Our SPA client configuration will then be created.

6. We need to change a few settings in the SPA client configuration, so select the **Settings** tab and set the following settings:
    - The **Name** will appear on the login screen, so change it to `QandA`.
    - We need to specify the origin of the frontend in the **Allowed Web Origins** setting. So, let's set this to `http://localhost:3000`.

- We need to specify the page Auth0 will redirect back to after a successful login in the **Allowed Callback URLs** setting. So, set this to `http://localhost:3000/signin-callback`. We will implement the `signin-callback` page in our frontend in `Chapter 12`, *Interacting with RESTful APIs*.

- Similarly, we need to specify the page Auth0 will redirect back to after a successful logout in the **Allowed Logout URLs** setting. So, set this to `http://localhost:3000/signout-callback`. We will implement the `signout-callback` page in our frontend in `Chapter 12`, *Interacting with RESTful APIs*.

- Don't forget to scroll to the bottom of the page and click the **Save Changes** button after entering these settings.

7. We now need to tell Auth0 about our ASP.NET Core backend. On the left-hand navigation menu, click **APIs** and then click the **Create API** button:

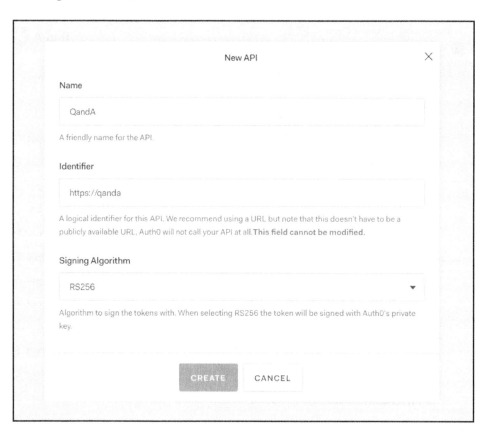

The **Name** can be anything we choose, but the **Identifier** setting must match the default audience we set on the tenant. Make sure the **Signing Algorithm** is **RS256** and then click the **CREATE** button.

That completes the setup of Auth0.

Configuring our ASP.NET Core backend to authenticate with Auth0

We can now change our ASP.NET Core backend to authenticate with Auth0. Let's open the backend project in Visual Studio and carry out the following steps:

1. Install the following NuGet package:

    ```
    Microsoft.AspNetCore.Authentication.JwtBearer
    ```

2. Add the following using statement to the Startup class:

    ```
    using Microsoft.AspNetCore.Authentication.JwtBearer;
    ```

Make sure the version of the package you select is supported by the version of .NET Core you are using. So, for example, if you are targeting .NET Core 3.0, then select the package version 3.0.0.

3. Add the following lines to the ConfigureServices method in the Startup class:

    ```
    public void ConfigureServices(IServiceCollection services)
    {
      ...
      services.AddAuthentication(options =>
      {
        options.DefaultAuthenticateScheme =
          JwtBearerDefaults.AuthenticationScheme;
        options.DefaultChallengeScheme =
          JwtBearerDefaults.AuthenticationScheme;
      }).AddJwtBearer(options =>
      {
        options.Authority = Configuration["Auth0:Authority"];
        options.Audience = Configuration["Auth0:Audience"];
      });
    }
    ```

This adds JWT-based authentication specifying the authority and expected audience as the `appsettings.json` settings.

4. Let's add the authentication middleware in the `Configure` method. It needs to be placed between the routing and authorization middleware:

```
public void Configure(IApplicationBuilder app, IWebHostEnvironment env)
{
  ...
  app.UseRouting();
  app.UseAuthentication();
  app.UseAuthorization();
  ...
}
```

This will validate the access token in each request if one exists. If the check succeeds, the user on the request context will be set.

5. The final step is to add the settings in `appsettings.json`, which we have referenced:

```
{
  ...,
  "Auth0": {
    "Authority": "https://your-tenant-id.auth0.com/",
    "Audience": "https://qanda"
  }
}
```

We will need to substitute our Auth0 tenant ID into the `Authority` field. The tenant ID can be found in Auth0 to the left of the user avatar:

So, `Authority` for the preceding tenant is `https://your-tenant-id.auth0.com/`. The `Audience` field needs to match the audience we specified in Auth0.

Now that our web API is validating access tokens in the requests, we are going to start protecting some endpoints in the next section.

Protecting endpoints

We are going to start this section by protecting the `questions` endpoint for adding, updating, and deleting questions as well as posting answers so that only authenticated users can do these operations. We will then move on to implement and use a custom authorization policy so that only the author of the question can update or delete it.

Protecting endpoints with simple authorization

Let's protect the `questions` endpoint for the `POST`, `PUT`, and `DELETE` HTTP methods by carrying out these steps:

1. Open `QuestionsController` and add the following `using` statements:

   ```
   using Microsoft.AspNetCore.Authorization;
   ```

2. To secure the actions, we decorate them with an `Authorize` attribute:

   ```
   [Authorize]
   [HttpPost]
   public async ... PostQuestion(QuestionPostRequest
   questionPostRequest)
   ...


   [Authorize]
   [HttpPut("{questionId}")]
   public async ... PutQuestion(int questionId, QuestionPutRequest
   questionPutRequest)
   ...


   [Authorize]
   [HttpDelete("{questionId}")]
   public async ... DeleteQuestion(int questionId)
   ...


   [Authorize]
   [HttpPost("answer")]
   public async ... PostAnswer(AnswerPostRequest answerPostRequest)
   ...
   ```

3. Run the Visual Studio project by pressing *F5*. We'll notice, as the browser opens with the `api/questions` path, that the data is successfully returned. This means that the `GetQuestions` action method is unprotected, as we expected.

4. Open Postman now and try to post a question:

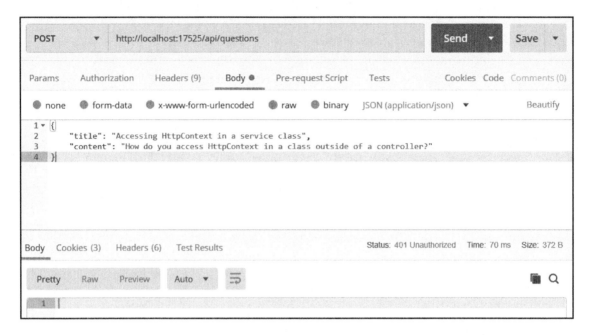

We receive a response with status code **401 Unauthorized**. This shows that this action method is now protected.

5. We can obtain a test access token from Auth0 to check that we can post a question with a valid token. In Auth0, click on **APIs** in the left-hand navigation menu and then our **QandA** API.
6. Click on the **Test** tab and we will see a token that we can use for testing purposes.
7. Click the **COPY TOKEN** option to copy the access token to the clipboard:

8. Back in Postman, we need to add this token in an `Authorization` HTTP header after the word `bearer` and the space:

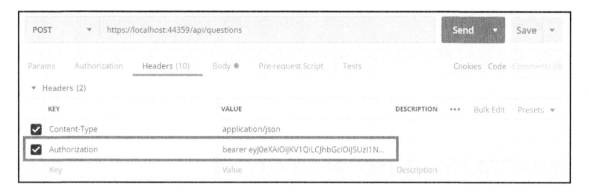

9. If we send the request, it will now be successful:

10. Press *Shift + F5* to stop the Visual Studio project from running so that we can add more code.

So, once the authentication middleware is in place, the `Authorize` attribute protects action methods. If a whole controller needs to be protected, the `Authorize` attribute can decorate the `controller` class:

```
[Authorize]
[Route("api/[controller]")]
[ApiController]
public class QuestionsController : ControllerBase
```

All of the action methods in the controller will then be protected without having to specify the `Authorize` attribute. We can also unprotect action methods in a protected controller by using the `AllowAnonymous` attribute:

```
[AllowAnonymous]
[HttpGet]
public IEnumerable<QuestionGetManyResponse> GetQuestions(string search,
bool includeAnswers, int page = 1, int pageSize = 20)
```

So, in our example, we could have protected the whole controller using the `Authorize` attribute and unprotected the `GetQuestions`, `GetUnansweredQuestions`, and `GetQuestion` action methods with the `AllowAnonymous` attribute to achieve the behavior we want.

Protecting endpoints with a custom authorization policy

At the moment, any authenticated user can update or delete questions. We are going to implement and use a custom authorization policy and use it to enforce that only the author of the question can do these operations. Let's carry out the following steps:

1. In the `Startup` class, let's add the following `using` statements:

    ```
    using Microsoft.AspNetCore.Http;
    using Microsoft.AspNetCore.Authorization;
    using QandA.Authorization;
    ```

    Note that the reference to the `QandA.Authorization` namespace doesn't exist yet. We'll implement this in a later step.

2. We'll need to eventually call an Auth0 web service, so let's make the HTTP client available in the `ConfigureServices` method. Let's also add an authorization policy called `MustBeQuestionAuthor`:

```
public void ConfigureServices(IServiceCollection services)
{
  ...
  services.AddHttpClient();
  services.AddAuthorization(options =>
    options.AddPolicy("MustBeQuestionAuthor", policy =>
      policy.Requirements
        .Add(new MustBeQuestionAuthorRequirement())));
}
```

The authorization policy has its requirements defined in a class called `MustBeQuestionAuthorRequirement`, which we'll implement in a later step.

3. We also need to have a handler for the requirement, so let's register this for dependency injection:

```
public void ConfigureServices(IServiceCollection services)
{
  ...
  services.AddHttpClient();
  services.AddAuthorization(...);
  services.AddScoped<
    IAuthorizationHandler,
    MustBeQuestionAuthorHandler>();
}
```

So, the handler for `MustBeQuestionAuthorRequirement` will be implemented in a class called `MustBeQuestionAuthorHandler`.

4. Our `MustBeQuestionAuthorHandler` class will need access to the HTTP requests to find out the question that is being requested. We need to register `HttpContextAccessor` for dependency injection to get access to the HTTP request information in a class. Let's do this now:

```
public void ConfigureServices(IServiceCollection services)
{
  ...
  services.AddHttpClient();
  services.AddAuthorization(...);
  services.AddScoped<
    IAuthorizationHandler,
```

```
        MustBeQuestionAuthorHandler>();
    services.AddSingleton<
      IHttpContextAccessor,
      HttpContextAccessor>();
}
```

5. We are going to create the `MustBeQuestionAuthorRequirement` class now.
   Let's create a folder called `Authorization` in the root of the project and then
   create a class called `MustBeQuestionAuthorRequirement` containing the
   following:

```
using Microsoft.AspNetCore.Authorization;

namespace QandA.Authorization
{
  public class MustBeQuestionAuthorRequirement :
    IAuthorizationRequirement
  {
    public MustBeQuestionAuthorRequirement()
    {
    }
  }
}
```

6. Next, we'll create the handler class for this requirement. Create a class called
   `MustBeQuestionAuthorHandler` with the following content:

```
using System;
using System.Security.Claims;
using System.Threading.Tasks;
using Microsoft.AspNetCore.Authorization;
using Microsoft.AspNetCore.Http;
using QandA.Data;

namespace QandA.Authorization
{
  public class MustBeQuestionAuthorHandler :
    AuthorizationHandler<MustBeQuestionAuthorRequirement>
  {
    private readonly IDataRepository _dataRepository;
    private readonly IHttpContextAccessor _httpContextAccessor;

    public MustBeQuestionAuthorHandler(
      IDataRepository dataRepository,
      IHttpContextAccessor httpContextAccessor)
    {
      _dataRepository = dataRepository;
```

```
        _httpContextAccessor = httpContextAccessor;
    }

    protected async override Task
      HandleRequirementAsync(
        AuthorizationHandlerContext context,
        MustBeQuestionAuthorRequirement requirement)
    {
      // TODO - check that the user is authenticated
      // TODO - get the question id from the request
      // TODO - get the user id from the name identifier claim
      // TODO - get the question from the data repository
      // TODO - if the question can't be found go to the next piece
of middleware
      // TODO - return failure if the user id in the question from
the data repository is different to the user id in the request
      // TODO - return success if we manage to get here
    }
  }
}
```

This inherits from the `AuthorizationHandler` class, which takes in the requirement it is handling as a generic parameter. We have injected the data repository and the HTTP context into the class.

7. We now need to implement the `HandleRequirementAsync` method. The first task is to check that the user is authenticated:

```
protected async override Task
  HandleRequirementAsync(
    AuthorizationHandlerContext context,
    MustBeQuestionAuthorRequirement requirement)
{
  if (!context.User.Identity.IsAuthenticated)
  {
    context.Fail();
    return;
  }
  // TODO - get the question id from the request
  // TODO - get the user id from the name identifier claim
  // TODO - get the question from the data repository
  // TODO - if the question can't be found go to the next piece of
middleware
  // TODO - return failure if the user id in the question from the
data repository is different to the user id in the request
  // TODO - return success if we manage to get here
}
```

The context parameter in the method contains information about the user's identity in an Identity property. We use the IsAuthenticated property with the Identity object to determine whether the user is authenticated or not. We call the Fail method on the context argument to tell it that the requirement failed.

8. Next, we need to get questionId from the request path:

```
protected async override Task
  HandleRequirementAsync(
    AuthorizationHandlerContext context,
    MustBeQuestionAuthorRequirement requirement)
{
  if (!context.User.Identity.IsAuthenticated)
  {
    context.Fail();
    return;
  }

  var questionId =
    _httpContextAccessor.HttpContext.Request
      .RouteValues["questionId"];
  int questionIdAsInt = Convert.ToInt32(questionId);
  // TODO - get the user id from the name identifier claim
  // TODO - get the question from the data repository
  // TODO - if the question can't be found go to the next piece of
middleware
  // TODO - return failure if the user id in the question from the
data repository is different to the user id in the request
  // TODO - return success if we manage to get here
}
```

We use the RouteValues dictionary within the HTTP context request to get access to this.

9. Next, we need to get userId from the user's identity claims:

```
protected async override Task
  HandleRequirementAsync(
    AuthorizationHandlerContext context,
    MustBeQuestionAuthorRequirement requirement)
{
  ...
  var questionId =
    _httpContextAccessor.HttpContext.Request
      .RouteValues["questionId"];
  int questionIdAsInt = Convert.ToInt32(questionId);
```

```
var userId =
  context.User.FindFirst(ClaimTypes.NameIdentifier).Value;
// TODO - get the question from the data repository
// TODO - if the question can't be found go to the next piece of
middleware
// TODO - return failure if the user id in the question from the
data repository is different to the user id in the request
// TODO - return success if we manage to get here
}
```

`userId` is stored in the name identifier claim.

 A claim is information about a user from a trusted source. A claim represents what the subject is, not what the subject can do. The ASP.NET Core authentication middleware automatically puts `userId` in a name identifier claim for us.

We have used the `FindFirst` method on the `User` object from the `context` parameter to get the value of the name identifier claim. The `User` object is populated with the claims by the authentication middleware earlier in the request pipeline after it has read the access token.

10. We can now get the question from the data repository. If the question isn't found, we want to pass the requirement because we want to return HTTP status code 404 (not found) rather than 401 (unauthorized). The action method in the controller will then be able to execute and return the 404 HTTP status code:

```
protected async override Task
  HandleRequirementAsync(
    AuthorizationHandlerContext context,
    MustBeQuestionAuthorRequirement requirement)
{
  ...
  var userId =
    context.User.FindFirst(ClaimTypes.NameIdentifier).Value;

  var question =
    await _dataRepository.GetQuestion(questionIdAsInt);
  if (question == null)
  {
    // let it through so the controller can return a 404
    context.Succeed(requirement);
    return;
  }
  // TODO - return failure if the user id in the question from the
data repository is different to the user id in the request
```

```
    // TODO - return success if we manage to get here
}
```

11. We can then check that `userId` in the request matches the question in the database and return `Fail` if not:

```
protected async override Task
  HandleRequirementAsync(
    AuthorizationHandlerContext context,
    MustBeQuestionAuthorRequirement requirement)
{
  ...

  var question =
    await _dataRepository.GetQuestion(questionIdAsInt);
  if (question == null)
  {
    // let it through so the controller can return a 404
    context.Succeed(requirement);
    return;
  }

  if (question.UserId != userId)
  {
    context.Fail();
    return;
  }

  context.Succeed(requirement);
}
```

12. The final task is to add the policy we have just created to the `Authorize` attribute on the relevant action methods in the question controller:

```
[Authorize(Policy = "MustBeQuestionAuthor")]
[HttpPut("{questionId}")]
public ... PutQuestion(int questionId, QuestionPutRequest
questionPutRequest)
  ...

[Authorize(Policy = "MustBeQuestionAuthor")]
[HttpDelete("{questionId}")]
public ... DeleteQuestion(int questionId)
  ...
```

We have now applied our authorization policy to updating and deleting a question.

Unfortunately, we can't use the test access token that Auth0 gives us to try this out but we will circle back to this and confirm that it works in Chapter 12, *Interacting with RESTful APIs*.

Custom authorization policies give us lots of flexibility and power to implement complex authorization rules. As we have just experienced in our example, a single policy can be implemented centrally and used on different action methods.

Using the authenticated user when posting questions and answers

Now that our REST API knows about the user interacting with it, we can use this to post the correct user against questions and answers. Let's carry out the following steps:

1. We'll start by adding the following using statements in QuestionsController.cs:

   ```
   using System.Security.Claims;
   using Microsoft.Extensions.Configuration;
   using System.Net.Http;
   using System.Text.Json;
   ```

2. Let's focus on posting a question first and by posting it with the authenticated user's ID:

   ```
   public async ...
     PostQuestion(QuestionPostRequest questionPostRequest)
   {
     var savedQuestion =
       await _dataRepository.PostQuestion(new QuestionPostFullRequest
       {
         Title = questionPostRequest.Title,
         Content = questionPostRequest.Content,
         UserId = User.FindFirst(ClaimTypes.NameIdentifier).Value,
         UserName = "bob.test@test.com",
         Created = DateTime.UtcNow
       });
     ...
   }
   ```

   ControllerBase contains a User property that gives us information about the authenticated user including the claims. So, we use the FindFirst method to get the value of the name identifier claim.

3. Unfortunately, the username isn't in the JWT, so we are going to need to get this from Auth0. Let's create a model that will represent an Auth0 user. Create a new class called `User` in the `Models` folder with the following content:

```
namespace QandA.Data.Models
{
    public class User
    {
        public string Name { get; set; }
    }
}
```

Note that there is more user information that we can get from Auth0 but we are only interested in the username in our app.

4. Now, inject the HTTP client as well as the path to get information about the user from Auth0 into `QuestionsController`:

```
...
private readonly IHttpClientFactory _clientFactory;
private readonly string _auth0UserInfo;

public QuestionsController(
    ...,
    IHttpClientFactory clientFactory,
    IConfiguration configuration)
{
    ...
    _clientFactory = clientFactory;
    _auth0UserInfo = $"{configuration["Auth0:Authority"]}userinfo";
}
```

5. Let's create a method that will call Auth0 to get the username:

```
private async Task<string> GetUserName()
{
    var request = new HttpRequestMessage(
      HttpMethod.Get,
      _auth0UserInfo);
    request.Headers.Add(
      "Authorization",
      Request.Headers["Authorization"].First());

    var client = _clientFactory.CreateClient();

    var response = await client.SendAsync(request);
```

```
if (response.IsSuccessStatusCode)
{
    var jsonContent =
        await response.Content.ReadAsStringAsync();
    var user =
        JsonSerializer.Deserialize<User>(
            jsonContent,
            new JsonSerializerOptions
            {
                PropertyNameCaseInsensitive = true
            });
    return user.Name;
}
else
{
    return "";
}
}
```

We make a GET HTTP request to the Auth0 user information endpoint with the `Authorization` HTTP header from the current request to the ASP.NET Core backend. This HTTP header will contain the access token that will give us access to the Auth0 endpoint.

If the request is successful, we parse the response body into our `User` model. Notice that we use the new JSON serializer in .NET Core 3.0. Notice also that we specify case-insensitive property mapping so that the camel case fields in the response map correctly to the title case properties in the class.

6. Use the username in the `PostQuestion` method now:

```
public async ... PostQuestion(QuestionPostRequest
questionPostRequest)
{
  var savedQuestion = await _dataRepository.PostQuestion(new
QuestionPostFullRequest
  {
    Title = questionPostRequest.Title,
    Content = questionPostRequest.Content,
    UserId = User.FindFirst(ClaimTypes.NameIdentifier).Value,
    UserName = await GetUserName(),
    Created = DateTime.UtcNow
  });
  ...
}
```

7. Do the same in the `PostAnswer` action method:

```
[Authorize]
[HttpPost("answer")]
public ActionResult<AnswerGetResponse> PostAnswer(AnswerPostRequest
answerPostRequest)
{
  ...
  var savedAnswer = _dataRepository.PostAnswer(new
AnswerPostFullRequest
  {
    QuestionId = answerPostRequest.QuestionId.Value,
    Content = answerPostRequest.Content,
    UserId = User.FindFirst(ClaimTypes.NameIdentifier).Value,
    UserName = await GetUserName(),
    Created = DateTime.UtcNow
  });
  ...
}
```

Unfortunately, we can't use the test access token that Auth0 gives us to try this out because it doesn't have a user associated with it. However, we will circle back to this and confirm that it works in Chapter 12, *Interacting with RESTful APIs*.

Our question controller is interacting with the authenticated user nicely now.

Summary

Auth0 is an OIDC identity provider that we can leverage to authenticate and authorize clients. An access token in JWT format is available from an identity provider when a successful sign in has been made. An access token can be used in requests to access protected resources.

ASP.NET Core can validate JWTs by first using the `AddAuthentication` method in the `ConfigureServices` method in the `Startup` class and then `UseAuthentication` in the `Configure` method.

Once authentication has been added to the request pipeline, REST API resources can be protected by decorating the controller and action methods using the `Authorize` attribute. Protected action methods can then be unprotected by using the `AllowAnonymous` attribute. We can access information about a user, such as their claims, via a controller's `User` property.

Custom policies are a powerful way to allow a certain set of users get access to protected resources. Requirement and handler classes must be implemented that define the policy logic. The policy can be applied to an endpoint using the `Authorize` attribute by passing in the policy name as a parameter.

Our backend is close to completion now. In the next chapter, we'll turn our attention back to the frontend and start to interact with the backend we have built.

Questions

Let's answer the following questions to practice what we have learned in this chapter:

1. In the `Configure` method in the `Startup` class, what is wrong with the following:

```
public void Configure(...)
{
   ...
  app.UseEndpoints(...);
  app.UseAuthentication();
}
```

2. What attribute can be added to a protected action method to allow unauthenticated users to access it?

3. We are building an app with an ASP.NET Core backend and using an identity provider to authenticate users. The default audience has been set to `http://my-app` in the identity provider, and we have configured the authentication service in our ASP.NET Core backend as follows:

```
services.AddAuthentication(options =>
{
    options.DefaultAuthenticateScheme =
      JwtBearerDefaults.AuthenticationScheme;
    options.DefaultChallengeScheme =
      JwtBearerDefaults.AuthenticationScheme;
}).AddJwtBearer(options =>
{
    ...
    options.Audience = "https://myapp";
});
```

When we try to access protected resources in our ASP.NET Core backend, we receive an HTTP status code 401. What is the problem here?

4. A JWT has the following decoded payload data. What date and time does it expire:

```
{
  "nbf": 1559876843,
  "auth_time": 1559876843,
  "exp": 1559900000,
  ...
}
```

5. We have a valid access token from an identity provider and are using it to access a protected resource. We have set the following HTTP header in the request:

```
Authorisation: bearer some-access-token
```

We receive an HTTP status code 401 from the request though. What is the problem?

6. How can we access HTTP request information in a class outside of an API controller?

7. In an API controller, how can we access an authenticated user ID?

Further reading

Here are some useful links to learn more about the topics covered in this chapter:

- Open ID Connect: https://openid.net/connect/
- ASP.NET Core Security and Identity: https://docs.microsoft.com/en-us/aspnet/core/security
- JSON Web Tokens: https://jwt.io/introduction/
- Auth0: https://auth0.com/docs

Interacting with RESTful APIs 12

Having completed the REST API, it's now time to interact with it in our React frontend app. We will start by interacting with the unauthenticated endpoints to get questions by using the browser's `fetch` function. We will deal with the situation when a user navigates away from a page before data is fetched, preventing state errors.

We will leverage the Auth0 tenant we set up in the last chapter to securely sign users in and out of our app. We will then use the access token from Auth0 to access protected endpoints. We will also make sure that only authenticated users are able to see options that they have permission to perform.

At the end of this chapter, our frontend will be fully interacting with the backend securely and robustly.

In this chapter, we'll cover the following topics:

- Using `fetch` to interact with unauthenticated REST API endpoints
- Interacting with Auth0 from the frontend
- Controlling authenticated options
- Using `fetch` to interact with authenticated REST API endpoints
- Stopping a data state being set if the user navigates away from the page

Technical requirements

We'll use the following tools and services in this chapter:

- **Visual Studio Code**: We'll use this to edit our React code. This can be downloaded and installed from https://code.visualstudio.com/.
- **Node.js and npm**: These can be downloaded from https://nodejs.org/. If you already have these installed, make sure that Node.js is at least version 8.2 and that npm is at least version 5.2.

- **Visual Studio 2019**: We'll use this to run our ASP.NET Core code backend. This can be downloaded and installed from `https://visualstudio.microsoft.com/vs/`.
- **.NET Core 3.0**: This can be downloaded and installed from `https://dotnet.microsoft.com/download/dotnet-core`.
- **Auth0**: We will use the tenant we set up in the last chapter to authenticate and manage users.
- **Q and A**: We'll start with the Q and A frontend project that is available at `https://github.com/PacktPublishing/ASP.NET-Core-3-and-React-17`, in the `Start`, folder in the `Chapter12` folder. It is important to start from this project for all of the code to work correctly in this chapter.

All of the code snippets in this chapter can be found online at `https://github.com/PacktPublishing/ASP.NET-Core-3-and-React-17`. To restore code from a chapter, the source code repository can be downloaded and the relevant folder opened in the relevant editor. If the code is frontend code, then `npm install` can be entered in the Terminal to restore the dependencies.

Check out the following video to see the code in action:

`http://bit.ly/35XyLgv`

Using fetch to interact with unauthenticated REST API endpoints

In this section, we are going to use the native `fetch` function to get unanswered questions from our real REST API. We are then going to use a wrapper function over `fetch` to make interacting with our backend a little easier. This approach will also centralize our code that interacts with the REST API, which is beneficial when we want to make improvements to it. We'll then move on to using the real REST API to get a single question and search for questions.

Getting unanswered questions from the REST API

We are going to start interacting with the REST API on the home page when displaying the list of unanswered questions. The `HomePage` component won't actually change, but the `getUnansweredQuestions` function in `QuestionsData.ts` will.

In `getUnansweredQuestions`, we'll leverage the native browser `fetch` function to interact with our REST API. If you haven't already, let's open Visual Studio Code and carry out the following steps:

1. Open `QuestionsData.ts`, find the `getUnansweredQuestions` function, and replace the implementation with the following content:

    ```
    export const getUnansweredQuestions = async ():
    Promise<QuestionData[]> => {
      let unansweredQuestions: QuestionData[] = [];

      // TODO - call api/questions/unanswered
      // TODO - put response body in unansweredQuestions

      return unansweredQuestions;
    };
    ```

    The function takes exactly the same parameters and returns the same type as before, so the components that consume this function shouldn't be impacted by the changes we are about to make.

2. Let's call `fetch` to request unanswered questions from our backend:

    ```
    export const getUnansweredQuestions = async ():
    Promise<QuestionData[]> => {
      let unansweredQuestions: QuestionData[] = [];

      await fetch('http://localhost:17525/api/questions/unanswered')

      // TODO - put response body in unansweredQuestions
      return unansweredQuestions;
    };
    ```

    So, for a `GET` request, we simply put the path we are requesting in the `fetch` argument. If your REST API is running on a different port, then don't forget to change the path so that it calls your REST API.

Notice the `await` keyword before the `fetch` call. This is because it is an asynchronous function and we want to wait for its promises to be resolved before the next statement is executed.

3. `fetch` is promise-based and has a `then` method that is called when the HTTP response arrives. Let's implement this:

```
export const getUnansweredQuestions = async ():
Promise<QuestionData[]> => {
  let unansweredQuestions: QuestionData[] = [];

  await fetch('http://localhost:17525/api/questions/unanswered')
    .then(res => res.json())
  // TODO - put response body in unansweredQuestions
  return unansweredQuestions;
};
```

The `then` method allows us to interact with items in the response body. Here are some useful properties we could interact with:

- `ok`: Whether the response was successful (in other words, whether the HTTP status code is in the range 200-299)
- `status`: The HTTP status code for the response
- `headers`: An object that gives access to the headers in the HTTP response

Notice that we have used a method called `json` to request the parsed JSON body.

4. The `json` method is promised-based, so we need another `then` method to get the parsed JSON:

```
export const getUnansweredQuestions = async ():
Promise<QuestionData[]> => {
  let unansweredQuestions: QuestionData[] = [];

  await fetch('http://localhost:17525/api/questions/unanswered')
    .then(res => res.json())
    .then(body => {
      unansweredQuestions = body;
    })
  return unansweredQuestions;
};
```

5. We can catch any network errors in a `catch` method:

```
export const getUnansweredQuestions = async ():
Promise<QuestionData[]> => {
  let unansweredQuestions: QuestionData[] = [];

  await fetch('http://localhost:17525/api/questions/unanswered')
  .then(res => res.json())
  .then(body => {
  unansweredQuestions = body;
  })
  .catch(err => {
    console.error(err);
  });
  return unansweredQuestions;
};
```

We simply output any errors to the console.

It is important to note that requests that contain HTTP error codes are not handled by the `catch` method. HTTP errors must be handled in the first `then` method by looking at the `ok` or `status` properties on the response parameter.

6. Let's give this a try then. First, let's open the backend project in Visual Studio and run it. We'll leave this running for the whole of this chapter.

7. Back in Visual Studio Code, start our frontend by typing `npm start` in the Terminal. When the app runs, we get the following error:

```
←    →    1 of 2 errors on the page                                          ✕

TypeError: data.created.toLocaleDateString is not a function

Question
C:/code/_temp/proof-read/frontend/src/Question.tsx:48

  45 |        : data.content}
  46 |    </div>
  47 |  )}
> 48 |  <div
  49 |  ^ css={css`
  50 |      font-size: 12px;
  51 |      font-style: italic;
```

The problem here is that the `created` property is deserialized as a string and not a `Date` object like the `Question` component expects.

8. Let's resolve this by mapping the `created` property to a `Date` object:

```
export const getUnansweredQuestions = async ():
Promise<QuestionData[]> => {
  let unansweredQuestions: QuestionData[] = [];

  await fetch('http://localhost:17525/api/questions/unanswered')
    .then(res => res.json())
    .then(body => {
      unansweredQuestions = body;
    })
    .catch(err => {
      console.error(err);
    });
  return unansweredQuestions.map(question => ({
    ...question,
    created: new Date(question.created),
  }));
};
```

We use the array `map` function to iterate through all of the questions returning a copy of the original question (using the spread syntax) and then overwriting the `created` property with a `Date` object from the `string` date.

9. If we save the file and look at the running app, we'll see the unanswered questions rendered correctly.

Great stuff; our React app is now interacting with our REST API!

Extracting out a generic HTTP function

We'll need to use the `fetch` function in every function that needs to interact with the REST API. So, we are going to create a generic `http` function that we'll use to make all of our HTTP requests. This will nicely centralize the code that calls the REST API. Let's carry out the following steps:

1. Create a new file called `http.ts` with the following content:

```
import { webAPIUrl } from './AppSettings';

export interface HttpRequest<REQB> {
  path: string;
```

```
}
export interface HttpResponse<RESB> extends Response {
  parsedBody?: RESB;
}
```

We've started by importing the root path to our REST API from
AppSettings.ts, which was set up in our starter project. The
AppSettings.ts file is where we will build all of the different paths that
will vary between development and production. Make sure webAPIUrl
contains the correct path for your REST API.

We have also defined interfaces for the request and response. Notice that the
interfaces contain a generic parameter for the type of the body in the request
and response.

2. Let's use these interfaces to implement a generic http function that we'll use to
make HTTP requests:

```
export const http = <REQB, RESB>(
  config: HttpRequest<REQB>,
): Promise<HttpResponse<RESB>> => {
  return new Promise((resolve, reject) => {
    // TODO - make the HTTP request
    // TODO - resolve the promise with the parsed body if a
successful request
    // TODO - reject the  promise if the request is unsuccessful
  });
};
```

We've created and returned a new Promise object, which we'll resolve or
reject in the subsequent steps. This will allow us to use async and await
nicely when consuming the http function.

3. Use fetch to invoke the request:

```
export const http = <REQB, RESB>(
  config: HttpRequest<REQB>,
): Promise<HttpResponse<RESB>> => {
  return new Promise((resolve, reject) => {
    const request = new Request(`${webAPIUrl}${config.path}`);
    let response: HttpResponse<RESB>;
    fetch(request);

    // TODO - resolve the promise with the parsed body if a
       successful request
    // TODO - reject the promise if the request is unsuccessful
```

```
        });
    };
```

Notice that we create a new instance of a `Request` object and pass that into `fetch` rather than just passing the request path into `fetch`. This will be useful later in this chapter as we expand this function for different HTTP methods and authentication.

4. We'll finish off our first implementation of the `http` function by adding the parsed body to the response and using this in the resolved `Promise` if the response is successful. We reject the `Promise` if the request is unsuccessful or a network error occurs:

```
export const http = <REQB, RESB>(
  config: HttpRequest<REQB>,
): Promise<HttpResponse<RESB>> => {
  return new Promise((resolve, reject) => {
    const request = new Request(`${webAPIUrl}${config.path}`);
    let response: HttpResponse<RESB>;
    fetch(request)
      .then(res => {
        response = res;
        return res.json();
      })
      .then(body => {
        if (response.ok) {
          response.parsedBody = body;
          resolve(response);
        } else {
          reject(response);
        }
      })
      .catch(err => {
        console.error(err);
        reject(err);
      });
  });
};
```

5. Go back to `QuestionData.ts` and leverage the `http` function we have just implemented in `getUnansweredQuestions`. First, we need to import it:

```
import { http } from './http';
```

6. We can now refactor `getUnansweredQuestions`:

```
export const getUnansweredQuestions = async (): Promise<
  QuestionData[]
> => {
  try {
    const result = await http<
      undefined,
      QuestionDataFromServer[]
    >({
      path: '/questions/unanswered',
    });
    if (result.parsedBody) {
      return result.parsedBody.map(mapQuestionFromServer);
    } else {
      return [];
    }
  } catch (ex) {
    console.error(ex);
    return [];
  }
};
```

We pass `undefined` into the `http` function as the `request body` type because there isn't one and `QuestionDataFromServer[]` as the expected `response body` type. `QuestionDataFromServer` is an interface that was added to our starter project for this chapter that has the `created` date as a string—exactly how it arrives from the REST API.

We use a mapping function to return the parsed response body with the `created` property set as a proper date if there is a response body. Otherwise, we return an empty array. The `mapQuestionFromServer` mapping function was added to our starter project for this chapter.

This renders the unanswered questions when we save these changes, like it did before:

Our revised implementation of `getUnansweredQuestions` is a little better because the root path to our REST API isn't hardcoded within it and we are handling HTTP errors better. We'll continue to use and expand our generic `http` function throughout this chapter.

Getting a question from the REST API

Let's use our `http` function to get a single question from our REST API:

1. We'll start by clearing out the current implementation, like so:

```
export const getQuestion = async (
  questionId: number,
): Promise<QuestionData | null> => {
  // TODO - make the request
  // TODO - return null if the request fails or there is a network
    error
  // TODO - return response body with correctly typed dates if
    request is successful
};
```

2. Let's make the request and then return `null` if the request fails or there is a network error:

```
export const getQuestion = async (
  questionId: number,
): Promise<QuestionData | null> => {
  try {
    const result = await http<undefined, QuestionDataFromServer>({
      path: `/questions/${questionId}`,
    });
    if (result.ok && result.parsedBody) {
      // TODO - return response body with correctly typed dates if
      //    request is successful
    } else {
      return null;
    }
  } catch (ex) {
    console.error(ex);
    return null;
  }
};
```

3. Return the response body with correctly typed dates if the request is successful:

```
export const getQuestion = async (
  questionId: number,
): Promise<QuestionData | null> => {
  try {
    const result = await http<undefined, QuestionDataFromServer>({
      path: `/questions/${questionId}`,
    });
    if (result.ok && result.parsedBody) {
      return mapQuestionFromServer(result.parsedBody);
    } else {
      return null;
    }
  } catch (ex) {
    console.error(ex);
    return null;
  }
};
```

4. When we save the changes and go to the question page in the running app, we will see the question correctly rendered on the screen:

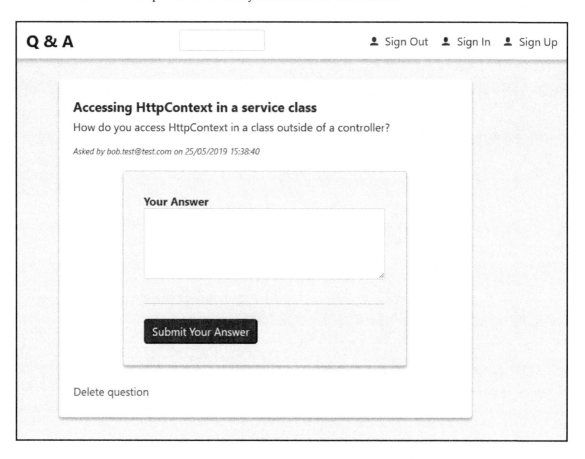

We didn't have to make any changes to any of the frontend components. Nice!

Searching questions with the REST API

Let's interact with the REST API to search for questions using our `http` function. This is very similar to what we have just done, so, we'll do this in one go:

```
export const searchQuestions = async (
  criteria: string,
): Promise<QuestionData[]> => {
  try {
    const result = await http<undefined, QuestionDataFromServer[]>({
```

```
    path: `/questions?search=${criteria}`,
  });
  if (result.ok && result.parsedBody) {
    return result.parsedBody.map(mapQuestionFromServer);
  } else {
    return [];
  }
} catch (ex) {
  console.error(ex);
  return [];
}
};
```

We make a request to the questions endpoint with the `search` query parameter containing the criteria. We return the response body with created `Date` objects if the request is successful or an empty array if the request fails.

The `searchQuestions` parameter and return type haven't changed. So, when we save the changes and search for a question in the running app, the matched questions will render correctly:

In the next section, we will take a break from implementing our generic `http` function and implement code to sign users in to our app via our Auth0.

Interacting with Auth0 from the frontend

In this section, we will fully implement the sign-in and sign-out processes from our React frontend. We are going to interact with Auth0 as a part of these processes.

Installing the Auth0 JavaScript client

There is a standard Auth0 JavaScript library for single-page applications that we can leverage that will interact nicely with Auth0. The npm package for the library is called @auth0/auth0-spa-js. Let's install this by running the following command in the Visual Studio Code Terminal:

```
> npm install @auth0/auth0-spa-js
```

TypeScript types are included in this library, so the Auth0 client library for single-page applications is now installed into our project.

Recapping the sign-in and sign-out flow

Let's quickly recap the sign-in flow between our app and Auth0:

1. Our app redirects to Auth0 to allow the user to enter their credentials.
2. After the user has successfully signed in, Auth0 redirects back to our app with a code.
3. Our app can then request an access token from Auth0 with the code.

The sign-out flow is as follows:

1. Our app redirects to Auth0 to perform the logout.
2. A redirect then occurs back to our app.

So, we will have the following routes in our frontend app:

- /signin: Our app will navigate to this page to start the sign-in process. This page will call a method in the Auth0 client, which will redirect to a page in Auth0.
- /signin-callback: This is the page in our app that Auth0 will redirect back to with the code.
- /signout: Our app will navigate to this page to start the sign-out process. This page will call a method in the Auth0 client, which will redirect to a page in Auth0.
- /signout-callback: This is the page in our app that Auth0 will redirect back to after the logout has completed.

Creating the sign-in and sign-out routes

We now understand that we need four routes in our app to handle the sign-in and sign-out processes. The SignInPage component will handle both of the signin and signin-callback routes. The SignOutPage component will handle both the signout and signout-callback routes.

Our app already knows about the SignInPage component with the route we have declared in App.tsx. However, it is not handling the sign-in callback from the Auth0. Our app also isn't handling signing out. Let's implement all of this in App.tsx by following these steps:

1. We'll start by importing the SignOutPage component into App.tsx:

   ```
   import { SignOutPage } from './SignOutPage';
   ```

2. We will start with the sign-in route. Instead of just referencing the SignInPage component, we need to render it and pass 'signin' in the action prop:

   ```
   <Switch>
     <Redirect from="/home" to="/" />
     <Route exact path="/" component={HomePage} />
     <Route path="/search" component={SearchPage} />
     <Route path="/ask">
       ...
     </Route>
     <Route
       path="/signin"
       render={() => <SignInPage action="signin" />}
     />
     <Route path="/questions/:questionId" component={QuestionPage} />
     <Route component={NotFoundPage} />
   </Switch>
   ```

   The action prop doesn't exist yet on the SignInPage component; hence, our app will not compile at the moment. We'll implement the action prop later.

3. Next, let's implement the sign-in callback route:

   ```
   <Switch>
     ...
     <Route
       path="/signin"
       render={() => <SignInPage action="signin" />}
   ```

```
    />
    <Route
      path="/signin-callback"
      render={() => <SignInPage action="signin-callback" />}
    />
    ...
  </Switch>
```

4. Lastly, we'll implement the routes for the sign-out process:

```
<Switch>
  ...
  <Route
    path="/signin"
    render={() => <SignInPage action="signin" />}
  />
  <Route
    path="/signin-callback"
    render={() => <SignInPage action="signin-callback" />}
  />
  <Route
    path="/signout"
    render={() => <SignOutPage action="signout" />}
  />
  <Route
    path="/signout-callback"
    render={() => <SignOutPage action="signout-callback" />}
  />
  ...
</Switch>
```

All of the routes are in place now for the sign-in, sign-up, and sign-out processes.

Implementing a central authentication context

We are going to implement a context that contains state and functions for authentication that we'll provide to all of the components in our app. Let's carry out the following steps:

1. Create a new file in the src folder called Auth.tsx with the following import statements:

```
import React, {
  useState,
  useEffect,
  useContext,
  createContext,
```

```
    FC,
} from 'react';
import createAuth0Client from '@auth0/auth0-spa-js';
import Auth0Client from '@auth0/auth0-spa-
js/dist/typings/Auth0Client';
import { authSettings } from './AppSettings';
```

2. We'll start the implementation by creating a context that our app components will use to get access to authentication-related information and functions:

```
interface Auth0User {
  name: string;
  email: string;
}
interface IAuth0Context {
  isAuthenticated: boolean;
  user?: Auth0User;
  signIn: () => void;
  signOut: () => void;
  loading: boolean;
}
export const Auth0Context = createContext<IAuth0Context>({
  isAuthenticated: false,
  signIn: () => {},
  signOut: () => {},
  loading: true
});
```

So, our context provides properties for whether the user is authenticated, the user's profile, and whether the context is loading as well as functions for signing in and out.

3. Let's provide a custom Hook that returns the authentication context for components to use:

```
export const useAuth = () => useContext(Auth0Context);
```

4. Next, we'll implement a provider component for the context:

```
export const AuthProvider: FC = ({ children }) => {
  const [isAuthenticated, setIsAuthenticated] = useState<
    boolean
  >(false);
  const [user, setUser] = useState<Auth0User | undefined>(
    undefined,
  );
  const [auth0Client, setAuth0Client] = useState<Auth0Client>();
  const [loading, setLoading] = useState<boolean>(true);
```

```
        return (
          <Auth0Context.Provider
            value={{
              isAuthenticated,
              user,
              signIn: () =>
                getAuth0ClientFromState().loginWithRedirect(),
              signOut: () => getAuth0ClientFromState().logout({
                client_id: authSettings.client_id,
                returnTo: window.location.origin + '/signout-callback'
              }),
              loading,
            }}
          >
            {children}
          </Auth0Context.Provider>
        );
      };
```

This returns the context's `Provider` component from React with the value object wrapped around any child components. The properties for the user profile, whether the user is authenticated, and whether the context is loading are stored in state. We also have a state called `auth0Client` for the instance of the Auth0 client. The functions for signing in and out simply call the relevant functions in the Auth0 client.

5. We have referenced a function called `getAuth0ClientFromState` in the provider, which isn't implemented. Let's implement this:

```
export const AuthProvider: FC = ({ children }) => {
  ...

  const getAuth0ClientFromState = () => {
    if (auth0Client === undefined) {
      throw new Error('Auth0 client not set');
    }
    return auth0Client;
  };

  return (
    <Auth0Context.Provider
      ...
    </Auth0Context.Provider>
  );
};
```

So, this function returns the Auth0 client from the state but throws an error if it is `undefined`.

6. When the provider is loaded, we want to create the instance of the Auth0 client and set the state values. Let's implement this using a `useEffect` Hook:

```
export const AuthProvider: FC = ({ children }) => {
  ...

  useEffect(() => {
    const initAuth0 = async () => {
      setLoading(true);
      const auth0FromHook = await createAuth0Client(authSettings);
      setAuth0Client(auth0FromHook);

      const isAuthenticatedFromHook = await
auth0FromHook.isAuthenticated();
      if (isAuthenticatedFromHook) {
        const user = await auth0FromHook.getUser();
        setUser(user);
      }
      setIsAuthenticated(isAuthenticatedFromHook);
      setLoading(false);
    };
    initAuth0();
  }, []);

  ...

  return (
    <Auth0Context.Provider
      ...
    </Auth0Context.Provider>
  );
};
```

We've put the logic in a nested `initAuth0` function and invoked this because the logic is asynchronous.

We use the `createAuth0Client` from Auth0 to create the Auth0 client instance. We pass in some settings using an `authSettings` variable, which is located in a file called `AppSettings.ts`. We'll change these settings later in this chapter to reference our specific Auth0 instance.

We call the `isAuthenticated` function in the Auth0 client to determine whether the user is authenticated and set our `isAuthenticated` state value. If the user is authenticated, we call the `getUser` function in the Auth0 client to get the user profile and set our `user` state.

7. We want to handle the sign-in callback when the provider loads, so let's add a branch of code to do that:

```
const initAuth0 = async () => {
  setLoading(true);
  const auth0FromHook = await createAuth0Client(authSettings);
  setAuth0Client(auth0FromHook);

  if (
    window.location.pathname === '/signin-callback' &&
    window.location.search.indexOf('code=') > -1
  ) {
    await auth0FromHook.handleRedirectCallback();
    window.location.replace(window.location.origin);
  }

  const isAuthenticatedFromHook = await
auth0FromHook.isAuthenticated();
  if (isAuthenticatedFromHook) {
    const user = await auth0FromHook.getUser();
    setUser(user);
  }
  setIsAuthenticated(isAuthenticatedFromHook);
  setLoading(false);
};
```

We call the Auth0 client `handleRedirectCallback` function, which will parse the URL, extract the code, and store it in a variable internally. We also redirect the user to the home page after this has been completed.

That's our authentication provider component complete.

8. The last item we are going to implement in `Auth.tsx` is a function that gets the access token:

```
export const getAccessToken = async () => {
  const auth0FromHook = await createAuth0Client(authSettings);
  const accessToken = await auth0FromHook.getTokenSilently();
  return accessToken;
};
```

This calls the Auth0 client `getTokenSilently` function, which will, in turn, make a request to the Auth0 `token` endpoint to get the access token securely.

We will use our `getAccessToken` function later in this chapter to make REST API requests to protected resources.

9. Let's move to `App.tsx` and import our authentication provider component:

```
import { AuthProvider } from './Auth';
```

10. Now, we'll provide the authentication context to all of the components in our app:

```
const App: React.FC = () => {
  return (
    <AuthProvider>
      <BrowserRouter>
        ...
      </BrowserRouter>
    </AuthProvider>
  );
};
```

That's our central authentication context complete. We'll use this extensively throughout this chapter.

The `App` component still isn't compiling because of the missing `action` prop on the `SignInPage` and `SignOutPage` components. We'll resolve these issues next.

Implementing the sign-in process

Let's implement the sign-in page in `SignInPage.tsx`:

1. We'll start by adding the following `import` statements:

```
import React, { FC } from 'react';
import { Page } from './Page';
import { StatusText } from './Styles';
import { useAuth } from './Auth';
```

`StatusText` is a shared style we are going to use when we inform the user that we are redirecting to and from Auth0. `useAuth` is the custom Hook we implemented earlier that will give us access to the authentication context.

2. Let's define the `Props` type for the page component:

```
type SigninAction = 'signin' | 'signin-callback';

interface Props {
  action: SigninAction;
}
```

The component takes in an `action` prop that gives the current stage of the sign-in process.

3. We can start to implement the component now:

```
export const SignInPage: FC<Props> = ({ action }) => {

};
```

4. Let's get the `signIn` function from the authentication context:

```
export const SignInPage: FC<Props> = ({ action }) => {
  const { signIn } = useAuth();
};
```

5. We can now call the `signIn` function if we are in the process of signing in:

```
export const SignInPage: FC<Props> = ({ action }) => {
  const { signIn } = useAuth();

  if (action === 'signin') {
    signIn();
  }
};
```

6. Our final task is to render the JSX:

```
export const SignInPage: FC<Props> = ({ action }) => {
  const { signIn } = useAuth();

  if (action === 'signin') {
    signIn();
  }

  return (
    <Page title="Sign In">
      <StatusText>Signing in ...</StatusText>
    </Page>
  );
};
```

We render the page informing the user that the sign-in process is taking place.

Implementing the sign-out process

Let's implement the sign-out page in `SignOutPage.tsx`, which is similar in structure to the `SignInPage` component:

```
import React, { FC } from 'react';
import { Page } from './Page';
import { StatusText } from './Styles';
import { useAuth } from './Auth';

type SignoutAction = 'signout' | 'signout-callback';

interface Props {
  action: SignoutAction;
}

export const SignOutPage: FC<Props> = ({ action }) => {
  let message = 'Signing out ...';

  const { signOut } = useAuth();

  switch (action) {
    case 'signout':
      signOut();
      break;
    case 'signout-callback':
      message = 'You successfully signed out!';
      break;
  }

  return (
    <Page title="Sign out">
      <StatusText>{message}</StatusText>
    </Page>
  );
};
```

A slight difference is that when the component receives the callback, this component will stay in view with a message informing them that they have been successfully signed out.

Configuring Auth0 settings in our frontend

We are nearly ready to give the sign-in and sign-out processes a try. First, we need to configure our frontend to interact with the correct Auth0 tenant. These are configured in `AppSettings.ts`:

```
export const authSettings = {
  domain: 'your-tenantid.auth0.com',
  client_id: 'your-clientid',
  redirect_uri: window.location.origin + '/signin-callback',
  scope: 'openid profile QandAAPI email',
  audience: 'https://qanda',
};
```

We need to substitute our specific `tenantid` and `clientid` in this settings file.

We have already discovered where to find our Auth0 tenant in the last chapter but, as a reminder, it is to the left of our user avatar:

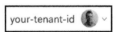

The `domain` setting doesn't include `https://` at the front.

The client ID can be found in the **Applications** section in our Q and A single-page application:

We are now ready to try the sign-in and sign-out processes.

Testing the sign-in and sign-out processes

All of the bits are in place now to give the sign-in and sign-out processes a try. Let's carry out the following steps:

1. First, we need to create an Auth0 user to sign in with. In Auth0, on the left-hand navigation menu, choose **Users & Roles | Users** and then click the **Create User** button. Fill in the form with the user we want to create and click the **CREATE** button:

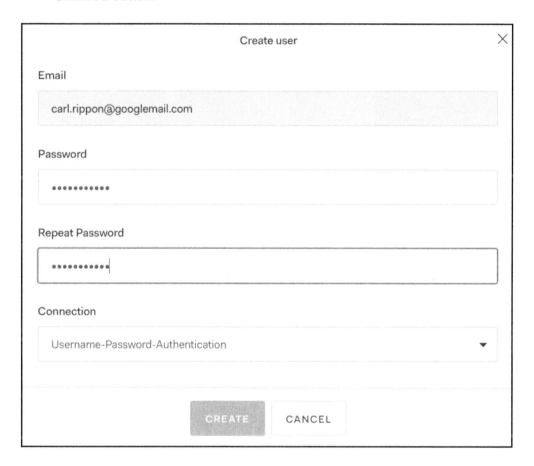

2. Let's make sure both the backend and frontend are running. Then, we can click the **Sign In** button in the header of the frontend. We are redirected to Auth0 to log in:

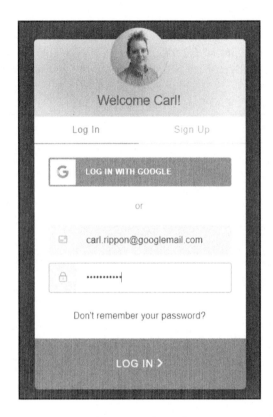

3. After entering the user's credentials, click the **LOG IN** button. We are then asked to authorize the Q and A app to access the profile and email data:

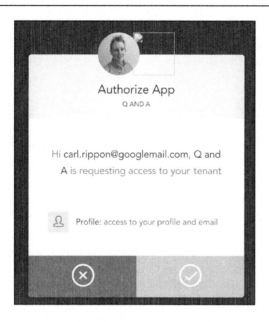

This authorization process happens because this is the first login for this user.

4. After clicking on the tick icon, we will then be successfully logged in and redirected back to our frontend.

5. Now, let's click the **Sign Out** button. The browser briefly navigates to Auth0 to log the user out and then redirects to our sign-out callback page:

That completes the sign-in and sign-out process implementations.

At the moment, all of the options in our app are visible regardless of whether the user is authenticated. However, certain options will only function correctly if the user is signed in. For example, if we try submitting a question while not signed in, it will fail. We'll clean this up in the next section.

Controlling authenticated options

In this section, we are going to only make relevant options visible for authenticated users. We are going to store user authentication information in a context that components can consume and use to show and hide options.

Displaying the relevant options in the header

At the moment, the `Header` component shows the **Sign Up** and **Sign Out** options, but the **Sign In** option is only relevant if the user hasn't signed in. The **Sign Out** option is only relevant if the user is authenticated. Let's clean this up in `Header.tsx` in the following steps:

1. We'll start by importing the authentication context Hook:

   ```
   import { useAuth } from './Auth';
   ```

2. Let's Hook into the authentication context and return the `user` object, whether the user is authenticated, and whether the context has loaded just before the JSX is returned:

   ```
   export const Header: FC<RouteComponentProps> = ( ... ) => {
     ...
     const { isAuthenticated, user, loading } = useAuth();

     return (
       ...
     );
   };
   ```

3. We can use the `loading` and `isAuthenticated` properties to show the relevant options in the JSX:

   ```
   <div ...>
     <Link ...>
       Q & A
     </Link>
   ```

```
<form onSubmit={handleSearchSubmit}>
  ...
</form>
<div>
  {!loading &&
    (isAuthenticated ? (
      <div>
        <span>{user!.name}</span>
        <Link
          to={{ pathname: '/signout', state: { local: true } }}
          css={buttonStyle}
        >
          <UserIcon />
          <span>Sign Out</span>
        </Link>
      </div>
    ) : (
      <Link to="/signin" css={buttonStyle}>
        <UserIcon />
        <span>Sign In</span>
      </Link>
    ))}
</div>
</div>
```

We use a short circuit expression to ensure the **Sign In** and **Sign Out** buttons can't be accessed while the context is loading. We use a ternary expression to show the username and the **Sign Out** button if the user is authenticated and the **Sign In** button if not.

4. Let's give this a try by first making sure the frontend and backend are running. We should see the **Sign In** and **Sign Up** buttons before the user has signed in:

5. Click the **Sign In** button and authenticate as a user. We should see the username and a **Sign Out** button after the user has been authenticated:

That completes the changes needed in the `Header` component.

Only allowing authenticated users to ask a question

Let's move to the HomePage component and only show the **Ask a question** button if the user is authenticated:

1. We'll start by importing the authentication Hook:

   ```
   import { useAuth } from './Auth';
   ```

2. Let's Hook into the authentication context and return whether the user is authenticated just before the JSX is returned:

   ```
   export const HomePage: FC<Props> = ( ... ) => {
     ...

     const { isAuthenticated } = useAuth();

     return (
       ...
     );
   };
   ```

3. We can then use the isAuthenticated property from the auth variable and a short-circuit operator to only render the **Ask a question** button if the user is signed in:

   ```
   <Page>
     <div
       ...
     >
       <PageTitle>Unanswered Questions</PageTitle>
       {isAuthenticated && (
         <PrimaryButton onClick={handleAskQuestionClick}>
           Ask a question
         </PrimaryButton>
       )}
     </div>
     ...
   </Page>
   ```

   That completes the change to the home page. However, the user could still get to the ask page by manually putting the relevant path in the browser.

4. Let's stop unauthenticated users from manually navigating to the ask page and asking a question in `AskPage.tsx`. We are going to create an `AuthorizedPage` component to help us to do this that will only render its child components if the user is authenticated. Let's create a file called `AuthorizedPage.tsx` in the `src` folder with the following content:

```
import React, { FC, Fragment } from 'react';
import { Page } from './Page';
import { useAuth } from './Auth';

export const AuthorizedPage: FC = ({ children }) => {
  const { isAuthenticated } = useAuth();
  if (isAuthenticated) {
    return <Fragment>{children}</Fragment>;
  } else {
    return <Page title="You do not have access to this page" />;
  }
};
```

We use our `useAuth` Hook and render the child components if the user is authenticated. If the user isn't authenticated, we inform them that they don't have access to the page.

5. Let's move to `App.tsx` and import `AuthorizedPage`:

```
import { AuthorizedPage } from './AuthorizedPage';
```

6. We can then wrap the `AuthorizedPage` component around the `AskPage` component in the `App` component JSX:

```
<Route path="/ask">
  <Suspense
    ...
  >
    <AuthorizedPage>
      <AskPage />
    </AuthorizedPage>
  </Suspense>
</Route>
```

7. Let's give this all a try in the running app. Make sure the user is signed out and go to the home page:

We'll see that there is no button to ask a question, as we expected.

8. Let's try to go to the ask page by manually putting the path into the browser:

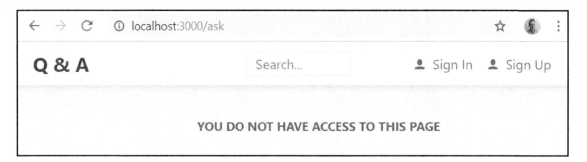

We are informed that we don't have permission to view the page, as we expected.

9. Let's sign in now:

The **Ask a question** button is now available, as we expected.

That concludes the changes we need to make for asking a question.

Only allowing authenticated users to answer a question

Let's focus on the `QuestionPage` component now and only allow an answer to be submitted if the user is authenticated:

1. We'll start by importing the authentication Hook in `QuestionPage.tsx`:

```
import { useAuth } from './Auth';
```

2. Let's Hook into the authentication context and return whether the user is authenticated just before the JSX is returned:

```
export const QuestionPage: ... = ( ... ) => {
  ...

  const { isAuthenticated } = useAuth();

  return (
    ...
  );
};
```

3. We can then use the `isAuthenticated` property and a short-circuit operator to only render the answer form if the user is signed in:

```
<AnswerList data={question.answers} />
{isAuthenticated && (
  <div
    ...
  >
    <Form
      submitCaption="Submit Your Answer"
      ...
    >
    ...
    </Form>
  </div>
)}
```

4. Let's give this all a try in the running app. Make sure the user is signed out and go to the question page:

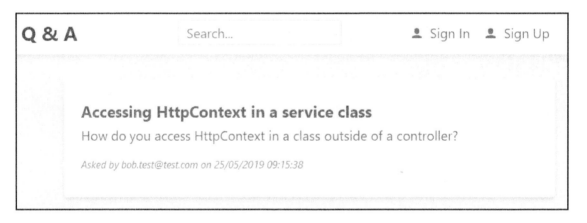

There is no answer form, as we expect.

5. Let's sign in and go to the question page again:

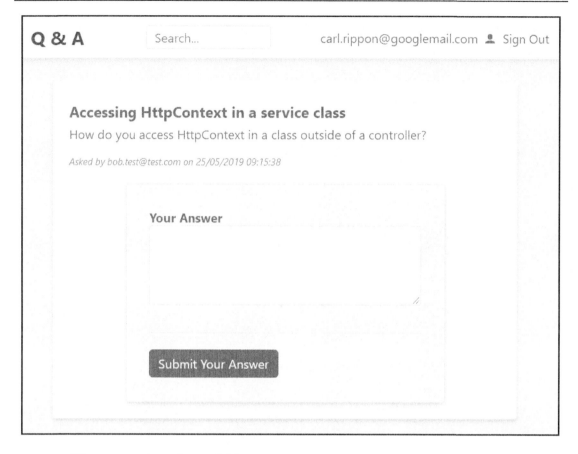

The answer form is available, as we expect.

That completes the changes to the question page.

In the next section, we are going to interact with the REST API endpoints that require an authenticated user to perform tasks such as submitting a question.

Using fetch to interact with authenticated REST API endpoints

In this section, we'll properly wire up posting questions and answers to our REST API. All of our changes will be in `QuestionsData.ts`—our user interface components will be unchanged.

Posting a question to the REST API

We are going to change the implementation for posting a question to use an access token from Auth0:

1. Let's start by importing the function that gets the access token from Auth0 into `QuestionsData.ts`:

```
import { getAccessToken } from './Auth';
```

2. Let's revise the implementation of the `postQuestion` function to the following:

```
export const postQuestion = async (
  question: PostQuestionData,
): Promise<QuestionData | undefined> => {
  const accessToken = await getAccessToken();
  try {
    const result = await http<
      PostQuestionData,
      QuestionDataFromServer
    >({
      path: '/questions',
      method: 'post',
      body: question,
      accessToken,
    });
    if (result.ok && result.parsedBody) {
      return mapQuestionFromServer(result.parsedBody);
    } else {
      return undefined;
    }
  } catch (ex) {
    console.error(ex);
    return undefined;
  }
};
```

We get the access token from Auth0 and pass it into the generic `http` function. If the request was successful, we return the question from the response body with the correct type for the created dates; otherwise, we return `undefined`.

3. The ability to do POST requests in our http function is not supported yet. Access tokens aren't supported as well. So, let's move to http.ts and start to implement these features:

```
export interface HttpRequest<REQB> {
  path: string;
  method?: string;
  body?: REQB;
  accessToken?: string;
}
```

We've started by adding the HTTP method, body, and access token to the request interface.

4. Let's move on to the changes we need to make in the http function:

```
export const http = <REQB, RESB>(
  config: IHttpRequest<REQB>,
): Promise<IHttpResponse<RESB>> => {
  return new Promise((resolve, reject) => {
    const request = new Request(`${webAPIUrl}${config.path}`, {
      method: config.method || 'get',
      headers: {
        'Content-Type': 'application/json',
      },
      body: config.body
        ? JSON.stringify(config.body)
        : undefined,
    });
    ...
  });
};
```

We are providing a second argument to the Request constructor that defines the HTTP request method, headers, and body.

Notice that we convert the request body into a string using JSON.stringify. This is because the fetch function doesn't convert the request body into a string for us.

5. Now, let's add support for the access token:

```
export const http = <REQB, RESB>(
  config: IHttpRequest<REQB>,
): Promise<IHttpResponse<RESB>> => {
  return new Promise((resolve, reject) => {
    const request = new Request(`${rootUrl}${config.path}`, {
```

```
      method: config.method || 'get',
      headers: {
        'Content-Type': 'application/json',
      },
      body: config.body ? JSON.stringify(config.body) : undefined,
    });
    if (config.accessToken) {
      request.headers.set(
        'authorization',
        `bearer ${config.accessToken}`
      );
    }
    ...
  });
};
```

If the access token is provided, we add it to an HTTP request header called
authorization after the word bearer and the space.

authorization is a standard HTTP header that contains credentials to
authenticate a user. The value is set to the type of authentication followed
by a space, followed by the credentials. So, the word bearer in our case
denotes the type of authentication.

6. The final addition to the http function is to handle responses that don't have a
   payload:

```
export const http = <REQB, RESB>(
  config: IHttpRequest<REQB>,
): Promise<IHttpResponse<RESB>> => {
  return new Promise((resolve, reject) => {
    ...
    fetch(request)
      .then(res => {
        response = res;
        if (
          res.headers.get('Content-Type') ||
          ''.indexOf('json') > 0
        ) {
          return res.json();
        } else {
          resolve(response);
        }
      })
      ...
  });
};
```

7. Let's give this a try by first making sure the frontend and backend are running. Let's sign in as a user, open up the browser's DevTools and go to the **Network** panel. Let's submit a new question:

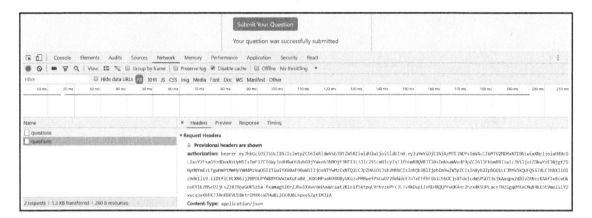

The question is saved successfully, as we expected. We can also see the access token sent in the HTTP `authorization` header with the request.

One of the things we couldn't check in the last chapter was whether the correct user was being saved against the question. If we have a look at the question in the database, we'll see the correct user ID and username stored against the question:

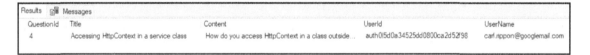

That completes posting a question. No changes are required to the `AskPage` component.

Posting an answer to the REST API

We are going to change the implementation for posting an answer to use the access token and our generic `http` function. Let's revise the implementation of the `postAnswer` function to the following:

```
export const postAnswer = async (
  answer: PostAnswerData,
): Promise<AnswerData | undefined> => {
  const accessToken = await getAccessToken();
```

```
  try {
    const result = await http<PostAnswerData, AnswerData>({
      path: '/questions/answer',
      method: 'post',
      body: answer,
      accessToken,
    });
    if (result.ok) {
      return result.parsedBody;
    } else {
      return undefined;
    }
  } catch (ex) {
    console.error(ex);
    return undefined;
  }
};
```

This follows the same pattern as the `postQuestion` function, getting the access token from Auth0 and making the HTTP `POST` request with the JWT using the `http` function.

That completes the changes needed for posting an answer.

We can now remove the `questions` array mock data from `QuestionsData.ts` as this is no longer used. The `wait` function can also be removed.

Testing protected endpoints with Postman

Before we finish this chapter, we are going to learn how to use the access token from our app to test a protected REST API endpoint. In the last chapter, we never checked the custom authorization policy that protects questions from being deleted by users other than the author of the question. Let's carry out the following steps to do this with both the frontend and backend running:

1. Open DevTools in the browser with our frontend app running. Sign in as a user and go to the **Network** panel in DevTools:

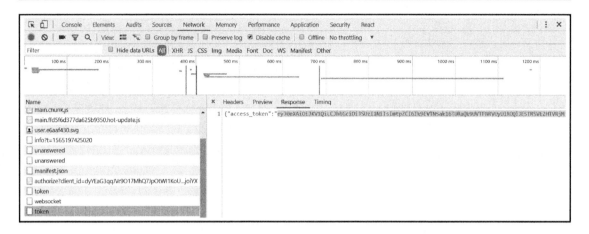

2. Find the request to the Auth0 `token` endpoint and find the access token in the response. Copy the access token to the clipboard.

3. Open Postman and create a `DELETE` request that the user hasn't authored. Create an `Authorization` HTTP header by pasting in the access token from the clipboard in the value:

4. If we send the request, we an get HTTP status code 403 (forbidden), indicating the user isn't authorized to make this request:

5. If we change the request to delete a question that the user did author, the requests succeed as we expect:

Using Postman to check protected REST API endpoints without the frontend is handy when diagnosing problems in the app to help to determine whether the problem is in the frontend or backend code.

This completes this section on interacting with protected REST API endpoints.

Stopping a data state being set if the user navigates away from the page

There is a slight problem in the page components at the moment when they request data and set this in the state. The problem is if the user navigates away from the page while the data is still being fetched, the state will attempt to be set on a component that no longer exists. We are going to resolve this issue on the HomePage, QuestionPage, and SearchPage components by carrying out the following steps:

1. In HomePage.tsx, let's change the useEffect call to the following:

```
useEffect(() => {
let cancelled = false;
const doGetUnansweredQuestions = async () => {
const unansweredQuestions = await getUnansweredQuestions();
if (!cancelled) {
setQuestions(unansweredQuestions);
setQuestionsLoading(false);
}
};
doGetUnansweredQuestions();
return () => {
cancelled = true;
};
}, []);
```

We use a cancelled variable to track whether the user has navigated away from the page and don't set any state if this is true. We know whether the user has navigated away from the page because the return function will be called, which sets the cancelled flag.

2. Let's follow the same pattern for the QuestionPage component:

```
useEffect(() => {
  let cancelled = false;
  const doGetQuestion = async (questionId: number) => {
    const foundQuestion = await getQuestion(questionId);
    if (!cancelled) {
      setQuestion(foundQuestion);
    }
  };
  ...
  return function cleanUp() {
    cancelled = true;
    ...
```

```
    };
  }, [match.params.questionId]);
```

3. Lastly, let's follow the same pattern for the `SearchPage` component:

```
useEffect(() => {
  let cancelled = false;
  const doSearch = async (criteria: string) => {
    const foundResults = await searchQuestions(criteria);
    if (!cancelled) {
      setQuestions(foundResults);
    }
  };
  doSearch(search);
  return () => {
    cancelled = true;
  };
}, [search]);
```

This completes the changes to the page components. The data fetching process within the page components is now a little more robust.

Summary

In this chapter, we learned that the browser has a handy `fetch` function that allows us to interact with REST APIs. This allows us to specify HTTP headers such as `authorization`, which we use to supply the user's access token in order to access the protected endpoints.

Leveraging the standard Auth0 JavaScript library allows single-page applications to interact with the Auth0 identity provider. It makes all of the required requests and redirects to Auth0 in a secure manner.

Using the React context to share information about the user to components allows them to render information and options that are only relevant to the user. The `AuthProvider` and `AuthorizedPage` components we built in this chapter are generic components that could be used in other apps to help to implement frontend authorization logic.

Our app is very nearly complete now. In the next chapter, we are going to put the frontend and backend through its paces with some automated tests.

Questions

The following questions will test our knowledge of what we have just learned:

1. What is wrong with the following HTTP POST request using the `fetch` function?

```
fetch('http://localhost:17525/api/person', {
  method: 'post',
  headers: {
    'Content-Type': 'application/json',
  },
  body: {
    firstName: 'Fred'
    surname: 'Smith'
  }
})
```

2. What is wrong with the following request using the `fetch` function?

```
fetch('http://localhost:17525/api/person/1')
  .then(res => {
    console.log('firstName', res.body.firstName);
  })
```

3. What is wrong with the following request using the `fetch` function?

```
fetch('http://localhost:17525/api/person/21312')
  .then(res => res.json())
  .catch(res => {
    if (res.status === 404) {
      console.log('person not found')
    }
  });
```

4. We have an endpoint for deleting users that only administrators have access to use. We have the user's access token in a variable called `jwt`. What is wrong with the following request?

```
fetch('http://localhost:17525/api/person/1', {
  method: 'delete',
  headers: {
    'Content-Type': 'application/json',
    'authorization': jwt
  });
```

5. In this chapter, we implemented a `AuthorizedPage` component that we could wrap around a page component so that it is only rendered for authenticated users. We could implement a similar component to wrap around components within a page so that they are only rendered for authenticated users. Have a go at implementing this.

Further reading

Here are some useful links to learn more about the topics covered in this chapter:

- The Fetch API: `https://developer.mozilla.org/en-US/docs/Web/API/Fetch_API`
- Auth0: `https://auth0.com/docs`

4
Section 4: Moving into Production

In this last section, we will add automated tests to both the ASP.NET Core and React apps and deploy them to Azure.

This section comprises the following chapters:

- Chapter 13, *Adding Automated Tests*
- Chapter 14, *Configuring and Deploying to Azure*
- Chapter 15, *Implementing CI and CD with Azure DevOps*

13
Adding Automated Tests

Now, it's time to get our *Q and A* app ready for production. In this chapter, we are going to add automated tests to the frontend and backend of our app, which will give us the confidence to take the next step: moving our app into production.

First, we will focus on the backend and use xUnit to implement unit tests on pure functions with no dependencies. Then, we'll move on to test controllers and mock out their dependencies using Moq.

Next, we will turn our attention to testing frontends with the popular Jest tool. We will learn how to implement unit tests on pure functions and integration tests on React components by leveraging the fantastic React Testing Library.

Then, we will learn how to implement end-to-end tests with Cypress. We'll use this to test a key path through the app where the frontend and backend will be working together.

In this chapter, we'll cover the following topics:

- Understanding the different types of automated test
- Implementing .NET tests with xUnit
- Implementing React tests with Jest
- Testing React components
- Implementing end-to-end tests with Cypress

Technical requirements

We'll use the following tools and services in this chapter:

- **Visual Studio 2019**: We'll use this to write tests for our ASP.NET Core code backend. This can be downloaded and installed from `https://visualstudio.microsoft.com/vs/`.
- **.NET Core 3.0**: This can be downloaded and installed from `https://dotnet.microsoft.com/download/dotnet-core`.
- **Visual Studio Code:** We'll use this to implement tests on our React code. This can be downloaded and installed from `https://code.visualstudio.com/`.
- **Node.js and npm:** These can be downloaded from `https://nodejs.org/`. If you already have these installed, make sure that Node.js is at least version 8.2 and that npm is at least version 5.2.
- **Q and A**: We'll start with the Q and A frontend and backend projects we finished in the previous chapter, which are available at `https://github.com/PacktPublishing/ASP.NET-Core-3-and-React-17`.

All the code snippets in this chapter can be found online at `https://github.com/PacktPublishing/ASP.NET-Core-3-and-React-17`. In order to restore code from a chapter, the source code repository can be downloaded and the relevant folder opened in the relevant editor. If the code is frontend code, then `npm install` can be entered in the Terminal to restore the dependencies.

Check out the following video to see the code in action:

`http://bit.ly/37kqqUr`

Understanding the different types of automated test

A robust suite of automated tests helps us deliver software faster without sacrificing its quality. There are various types of test, though, with each type having benefits and challenges. In this section, we are going to understand the different types of test and the benefits they bring to a single-page application.

The following diagram shows the three different types of test:

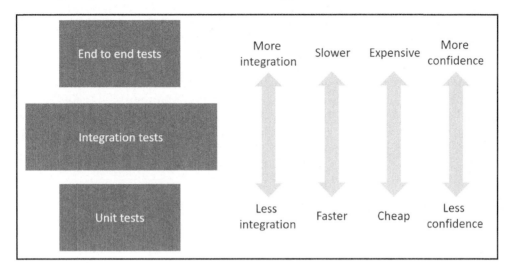

In the following subsections, we will examine each type of test and its pros and cons.

Unit tests

Unit tests verify that individual and isolated parts of an app work as expected. These tests generally execute very fast, thus giving us a very tight feedback loop so that we know the part of the app that we are developing is working correctly.

These tests can be quick to implement but this is not necessarily the case if we need to mock out the dependencies of the unit we are testing. This is often the case when unit-testing a React frontend because a true unit test on a component needs to mock out any child components that are referenced in its JSX.

Perhaps the biggest downside of these tests is that they give us the least amount of confidence that the app as a whole is working correctly. We can have a large unit test suite that covers all the different parts of our app, but this is no guarantee that all the parts work together as expected.

End-to-end tests

End-to-end tests verify that key paths work together as expected. No parts of the app are isolated and mocked away. These tests run a fully functioning app just like a user would and so it gives us the maximum amount of confidence that our app is functioning correctly.

These tests are slow to execute, though, which can delay the feedback loop during development; they're also the most expensive to write and maintain. This is because everything that the tests rely on, such as the data in the database, needs to be consistent each time the tests are executed, which is a challenge when we implement multiple tests that have different data requirements.

Integration tests

Integration tests verify that several parts of an app work together correctly and give us more confidence than unit tests in terms of ensuring that the app as a whole is working as expected. These tests provide the most scope in terms of what is tested because of the many app part combinations that we can choose to test.

These tests are generally quick to execute because slow components such as database and network requests are often mocked out. The time it takes to write and maintain these tests is also short.

For single-page applications, the **return on investment** (**ROI**) of integration tests is arguably greater than the other two testing types if we choose our tests wisely. This is why the relevant box in the preceding diagram is bigger than other testing types.

Now that we understand the different types of test, we are going to start implementing them on our Q and A app. We'll start by unit-testing the .NET backend.

Implementing .NET tests with xUnit

In this section, we are going to implement some backend unit tests on our question controller using a library called **xUnit**. Before we do this, we are going to become familiar with xUnit by implementing some unit tests on a class with no dependencies.

Getting started with xUnit

In this section, we are going to create a new project in our backend Visual Studio solution and start to implement simple unit tests to get comfortable with xUnit, which is the tool we are going to use to run our backend tests. So, let's open our backend ASP.NET Core project and carry out the following steps:

1. Open up the Solution Explorer, right-click on **Solution**, choose **Add**, and then choose **New Project....**
2. Select **xUnit Test Project (.NET Core)** from the dialog box that opens and click on the **Next** button:

3. Enter **BackendTests** as the project name and set **Location** to the folder that the solution is in. Click **Create** to create the project.
4. We are going to create a simple class so that we can write some unit tests for it. This will get you comfortable with xUnit. Create a static class in our unit test project called `Calc` with the following content:

```
using System;

namespace BackendTests
{
```

```
public static class Calc
{
  public static decimal Add(decimal a, decimal b)
  {
    return a + b;
  }
}
}
```

The class contains a method called Add, which simply adds two numbers together that are passed in its parameters. Add is a pure function, which means the return value is always consistent for a given set of parameters and it doesn't give any side-effects. Pure functions are super-easy to test, as we'll see next.

5. We are going to create some unit tests for the Add method in the Calc class. Let's create a new class in the unit test project called CalcTests with the following content:

```
using Xunit;

namespace BackendTests
{
  public class CalcTests
  {
    [Fact]
    public void Add_When2Integers_ShouldReturnCorrectInteger()
    {
      // TODO - call the Calc.Add method with 2 integers
      // TODO - check the result is as expected
    }
  }
}
```

We have named our test method
Add_When2Integers_ShouldReturnCorrectInteger.

It is useful to have a good naming convention for tests so that, when we look at a failed test report, we can start to get an understanding of the problem immediately. In this case, the name starts with the method we are testing, followed by a brief description of the conditions for the test. The last part of the name is what we expect to happen.

Note that the test method is decorated with the Fact attribute.

The `Fact` attribute denotes that the method is a unit test for xUnit. Another attribute that denotes a unit test is called `Theory`. This can be used to feed the method a range of parameter values.

6. Let's implement the unit test:

```
[Fact]
public void Add_When2Integers_ShouldReturnCorrectInteger()
{
    var result = Calc.Add(1, 1);
    Assert.Equal(2, result);
}
```

We call the method we are testing and put the return value in a `result` variable. Then, we use the `Assert` class from xUnit and its `Equal` method to check that the result is equal to `2`.

7. Let's run our test by right-clicking inside the test method and choosing **Debug Tests(s)** from the menu:

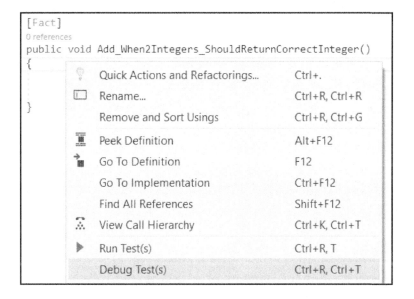

8. After a few seconds, the test will run and the result will appear in the **Test Explorer**:

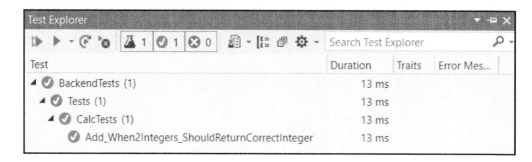

As we expected, the test passes. Congratulations—you have just created our first unit test!

We used the `Equal` method in the `Assert` class in this test. The following are globally some other useful methods in this class:

- `True`: Checks that a value is `true`
- `NotNull`: Checks that a value isn't `null`
- `Contains`: Checks that the value is in a `string`
- `InRange`: Checks that the value is within a range
- `Throws`: Checks that an exception is raised

Now, we are starting to understand how to write unit tests. We haven't written any tests on our Q and A app yet, but we will do so next.

Testing controller action methods

In this section, we are going to create tests for some question controller actions. Let's get started:

1. First, we need to reference the `QandA` project from the `Tests` project. We do this by right-clicking on the **Dependencies** node in the **Solution Explorer** in the `Tests` project and choosing **Add Reference...**:

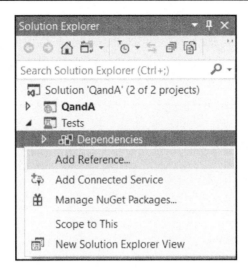

2. Then, we need to tick the **QandA** project and click the **OK** button:

3. Our controller has dependencies for a cache, a data repository, and a SignalR hub. Due to this, we'll need to mock these out in our tests. We are going to use a library called Moq to help us set up mocks in our tests. Let's install **Moq** into our test project using the **NuGet Package Manager**:

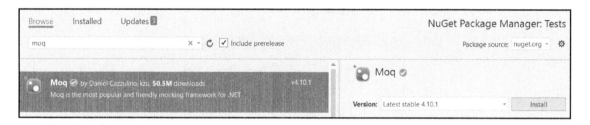

Great stuff—that's the first test on our web API completed!

Testing the action method to implement GetQuestions

Follow these steps to implement a couple of tests on the `GetQuestions` method:

1. We'll start by creating a new class called `QuestionsControllerTests` in the `Tests` project with the following content:

```
using System.Collections.Generic;
using System.Linq;
using System.Threading.Tasks;
using Microsoft.AspNetCore.Mvc;
using Microsoft.Extensions.Configuration;
using Xunit;
using Moq;
using QandA.Controllers;
using QandA.Data;
using QandA.Data.Models;

namespace BackendTests
{
  public class QuestionsControllerTests
  {
  }
}
```

2. We are going to verify that calling `GetQuestions` with no parameters returns all the questions. Let's create the test method for this and 10 mock questions:

```
[Fact]
public async void
    GetQuestions_WhenNoParameters_ReturnsAllQuestions()
{
    var mockQuestions = new List<QuestionGetManyResponse>();
    for (int i = 1; i <= 10; i++)
    {
        mockQuestions.Add(new QuestionGetManyResponse
        {
            QuestionId = 1,
            Title = $"Test title {i}",
            Content = $"Test content {i}",
            UserName = "User1",
            Answers = new List<AnswerGetResponse>()
        });
    }
}
```

Notice that the method is flagged as asynchronous with the `async` keyword because the action method we are testing is asynchronous.

3. Let's create a mock data repository definition using Moq:

```
[Fact]
public async void
    GetQuestions_WhenNoParameters_ReturnsAllQuestions()
{
    ...
    var mockDataRepository = new Mock<IDataRepository>();
    mockDataRepository
        .Setup(repo => repo.GetQuestions())
        .Returns(() => Task.FromResult(mockQuestions.AsEnumerable()));
}
```

We create a mock object from the `IDataRepository` interface using the `Mock` class from Moq. Now, we can use the `Setup` and `Returns` methods on the mock object to define that the `GetQuestions` method should return our mock questions. The method we are testing is asynchronous, so we need to wrap the mock questions with `Task.FromResult` in the mock result.

4. We need to mock the configuration object that reads `appsettings.json`. This is what the controller depends on:

```
[Fact]
public async void
  GetQuestions_WhenNoParameters_ReturnsAllQuestions()
{
  ...
  var mockConfigurationRoot = new Mock<IConfigurationRoot>();
 mockConfigurationRoot.SetupGet(config =>
 config[It.IsAny<string>()]).Returns("some setting");
}
```

The preceding code will return any string when `appsettings.json` is read, which is fine for our test.

5. Next, we need to create an instance of the controller by passing in an instance of the mock data repository and mock configuration settings:

```
[Fact]
public async void
  GetQuestions_WhenNoParameters_ReturnsAllQuestions()
{
  ...
  var questionsController = new QuestionsController(
    mockDataRepository.Object, null,
    null, null, mockConfigurationRoot.Object);
}
```

The `Object` property on the mock data repository definition gives us an instance of the mock data repository to use.

Notice that we can pass in `null` for cache, SignalR hub, HTTP client factory, and configuration dependencies. This is because they are not used in the action method implementation we are testing.

6. Now, we can call the action method we are testing:

```
[Fact]
public void async
  GetQuestions_WhenNoParameters_ReturnsAllQuestions()
{
  ...
  var result = await questionsController.GetQuestions(null, false);
}
```

We pass `null` in as the `search` parameter and `false` as the `includeAnswers` parameter. The other parameters are optional, so we don't pass these in.

7. Now, we can check the result is as expected:

```
[Fact]
public void async
  GetQuestions_WhenNoParameters_ReturnsAllQuestions()
{

  . . .

  Assert.Equal(10, result.Count());
  mockDataRepository.Verify(
    mock => mock.GetQuestions(), Times.Once());
}
```

We have checked that 10 items are returned.

We have also checked that the `GetQuestions` method in the data repository is called once.

8. Let's give this a try by right-clicking the test in **Test Explorer** and selecting **Run Selected Tests**:

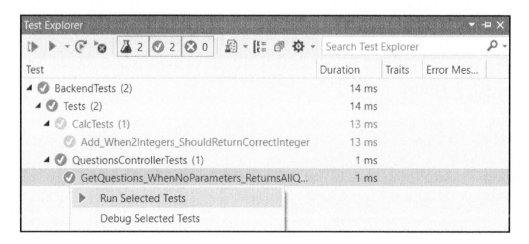

The test passes, as we expected.

9. Now, we are going to create a second test to verify that calling `GetQuestions` with a search parameter calls the `GetQuestionsBySearchWithPaging` method in the data repository:

```
[Fact]
public async void
  GetQuestions_WhenHaveSearchParameter_ReturnsCorrectQuestions()
{
  var mockQuestions = new List<QuestionGetManyResponse>();
  mockQuestions.Add(new QuestionGetManyResponse
  {
    QuestionId = 1,
    Title = "Test",
    Content = "Test content",
    UserName = "User1",
    Answers = new List<AnswerGetResponse>()
  });

  var mockDataRepository = new Mock<IDataRepository>();
  mockDataRepository
    .Setup(repo =>
      repo.GetQuestionsBySearchWithPaging("Test", 1, 20))
    .Returns(() =>
      Task.FromResult(mockQuestions.AsEnumerable()));

  var mockConfigurationRoot = new Mock<IConfigurationRoot>();
  mockConfigurationRoot.SetupGet(config =>
    config[It.IsAny<string>()]).Returns("some setting");

  var questionsController = new QuestionsController(
    mockDataRepository.Object, null,
    null, null, mockConfigurationRoot.Object);

  var result =
    await questionsController.GetQuestions("Test", false);

  Assert.Single(result);
  mockDataRepository.Verify(mock =>
    mock.GetQuestionsBySearchWithPaging("Test", 1, 20),
    Times.Once());
}
```

This follows the same pattern as the previous test, but this time we're mocking the `GetQuestionsBySearchWithPaging` method in the data repository and checking that this is called. If we run the test, it will pass as expected.

That completes the tests on the `GetQuestions` method.

Testing the action method to get a single question

Follow these steps to implement a couple of tests on the `GetQuestion` method:

1. Let's add the following test in the `QuestionsControllerTests` class to verify that we get the correct result when the question isn't found:

```
[Fact]
public async void GetQuestion_WhenQuestionNotFound_Returns404()
{
  var mockDataRepository = new Mock<IDataRepository>();
  mockDataRepository
    .Setup(repo => repo.GetQuestion(1))
    .Returns(() =>
Task.FromResult(default(QuestionGetSingleResponse)));

    var mockQuestionCache = new Mock<IQuestionCache>();
    mockQuestionCache
      .Setup(cache => cache.Get(1))
      .Returns(() => null);

    var mockConfigurationRoot = new Mock<IConfigurationRoot>();
    mockConfigurationRoot.SetupGet(config =>
      config[It.IsAny<string>()]).Returns("some setting");

    var questionsController = new QuestionsController(
      mockDataRepository.Object, null, mockQuestionCache.Object,
      null, mockConfigurationRoot.Object);

    var result = await questionsController.GetQuestion(1);
    var actionResult =
      Assert.IsType<
        ActionResult<QuestionGetSingleResponse>
      >(result);
    Assert.IsType<NotFoundResult>(actionResult.Result);
}
```

We need to mock the cache in this test because this is used in the `GetQuestion` method.

Here, we check that the result is of the `NotFoundResult` type.

2. Let's add another test to verify a question is returned when the one that's requested does exist:

```
[Fact]
public async void GetQuestion_WhenQuestionIsFound_ReturnsQuestion()
```

```
{
  var mockQuestion = new QuestionGetSingleResponse
  {
    QuestionId = 1,
    Title = "test"
  };

  var mockDataRepository = new Mock<IDataRepository>();
  mockDataRepository
    .Setup(repo => repo.GetQuestion(1))
    .Returns(() => Task.FromResult(mockQuestion));

  var mockQuestionCache = new Mock<IQuestionCache>();
  mockQuestionCache
    .Setup(cache => cache.Get(1))
    .Returns(() => mockQuestion);

  var mockConfigurationRoot = new Mock<IConfigurationRoot>();
  mockConfigurationRoot.SetupGet(config =>
    config[It.IsAny<string>()]).Returns("some setting");

  var questionsController = new QuestionsController(
    mockDataRepository.Object, null, mockQuestionCache.Object,
    null, mockConfigurationRoot.Object);

  var result = await questionsController.GetQuestion(1);

  var actionResult =
    Assert.IsType<
      ActionResult<QuestionGetSingleResponse>
    >(result);
  var questionResult =
    Assert.IsType<QuestionGetSingleResponse>(actionResult.Value);
  Assert.Equal(1, questionResult.QuestionId);
}
```

This time, we check that the result is of the `QuestionGetSingleResponse` type and that the correct question is returned by checking the question ID.

That completes the tests we are going to perform on our `GetQuestion` action method.

The same approach and pattern can be used to add tests for controller logic we haven't covered yet. We can do this using Moq, which mocks out any dependencies that the method relies on. In the next section, we'll start to implement tests on the frontend.

Implementing React tests with Jest

In this section, we are going to turn our attention to creating automated tests for the frontend with Jest. We are going to start by testing a simple function so that we can get familiar with Jest before moving on to testing a React component.

Getting started with Jest

Jest is the de-facto testing tool in the React community and is maintained by Facebook. Jest is included in **Create React App (CRA)** projects, which means that it is already installed and configured in our project. We'll start to get familiar with Jest by adding some unit tests on the `required` function in the `Form` component. So, let's open our frontend project in Visual Studio Code and carry out the following steps:

1. Create a new file called `Form.test.ts` in the `src` folder that contains the following content:

   ```
   import { required } from './Form';

   test('When required is called with empty string, an error should be
   returned', () => {
     // TODO - call required passing in an empty string
     // TODO - check that an error is returned
   });
   ```

   Notice that the extension of the file is `test.ts`.

   > The `test.ts` extension is important because Jest automatically looks for files with this extension when searching for tests to execute. Note that if our tests contained JSX, we would need to use the `test.tsx` extension.

   The `test` function in Jest takes in two parameters:

   - The first parameter is a description of the test that will be shown in the test output.
   - The second parameter is an arrow function, which will contain our test.

   So, the test is going to check that the `require` function returns an error when an empty string is passed into it.

2. Let's call the `required` function with an empty string and check the result:

```
test('When required is called with empty string, an error should be
returned', () => {
  const result = required('');
  expect(result).toBe('This must be populated');
});
```

We pass the `result` variable we are checking into the Jest `expect` function. Then, we chain a `toBe` matcher function onto this, which checks that the result from the `expect` function is the same as the parameter that was supplied to the `toBe` function.

`toBe` is one of many Jest matcher functions we can use to check a variable value. The full list of functions can be found at `https://jestjs.io/docs/en/expect`.

3. Let's create another test on the `required` function for when a non-empty string is passed into it:

```
test('When required is called with a value, an empty string should
be returned', () => {
  const result = required('test');
  expect(result).toBe('');
});
```

So, we expect an empty string to be returned when a non-empty string is passed into the `required` function.

4. It's time to check that our tests pass. Enter the following command in the Terminal:

```
> npm test
```

Jest will run the tests that it finds in our project and output the results:

```
PASS  src/Form.test.ts
PASS  src/App.test.tsx

Test Suites: 2 passed, 2 total
Tests:       3 passed, 3 total
Snapshots:   0 total
Time:        3.343s
Ran all test suites.

Watch Usage: Press w to show more.
```

So, Jest finds our two tests, and the example test on the `App` component that came with CRA. All three tests pass—that's great news!

The `require` function is straightforward to test because it has no dependencies. How do we test a React component that has lots of dependencies, such as the browser's DOM and React itself? We'll find out in the next section.

Testing React components

In this section, we are going to implement tests on the `Page`, `Question`, and `HomePage` components. React component tests can be challenging because they have dependencies, such as the browser's DOM and sometimes HTTP requests. Due to this, we are going to leverage the React Testing Library and Jest's mocking functionality to help us implement our tests.

Testing the Page component

Carry out the following steps to test that the `Page` component renders correctly:

1. Create a file for the tests called `Page.test.tsx` with the following content:

```
import React from 'react';
import { render, cleanup } from '@testing-library/react';
import { Page } from './Page';

test('When the Page component is rendered, it should contain the
correct title and content', () => {
});
```

We imported React with our `Page` component, along with some useful functions from the React Testing Library.

The React Testing Library was installed by Create React App when we created the frontend project. This library will help us select elements that we want to check without using internal implementation details such as element IDs or CSS class names.

2. Let's render the `Page` component:

```
test('When the Page component is rendered, it should contain the
correct title and content', () => {
  const { getByText } = render(
```

```
  <Page title="Title test">
    <span>Test content</span>
  </Page>,
 );
});
```

We use the `render` function from the React Testing Library to render the `Page` component by passing in JSX.

The `render` function returns various useful items. One of these items is the `getByText` function, which will help us select elements that we'll use and understand in the next step.

3. Now, we can check that the page title has been rendered:

```
test('When the Page component is rendered, it should contain the
correct title and content', () => {
  const { getByText } = render(
    <Page title="Title test">
      <span>Test content</span>
    </Page>,
  );
  const title = getByText('Title test');
  expect(title).not.toBeNull();
});
```

We use the `getByText` function from the React Testing Library that was returned from the `render` function to find the element that has "`Title test`" in the text's content. Notice how we are using something that the user can see (the element text) to locate the element rather than any implementation details. This means that our test won't break if implementation details such as the DOM structure or DOM IDs change.

Having located the title element, we then use Jest's `expect` function to check that the element was found by asserting that it is not `null`.

4. We can do a similar check on the page content:

```
test('When the Page component is rendered, it should contain the
correct title and content', () => {
  const { getByText } = render(
    <Page title="Title test">
      <span>Test content</span>
    </Page>,
  );
  const title = getByText('Title test');
```

```
    expect(title).not.toBeNull();
    const content = getByText('Test content');
    expect(content).not.toBeNull();
});
```

5. The last thing we need to do is clean up the DOM after the test was executed. We can do this for all the tests in a file by using the `afterEach` function from Jest and the `cleanup` function from the React Testing Library. Let's add this after the import statements:

```
afterEach(cleanup);
```

6. If Jest is still running after we save the file, our new test will run. If we have killed Jest, then we can start it again by executing `npm test` in the Terminal:

```
Test Suites: 3 passed, 3 total
Tests:       4 passed, 4 total
Snapshots:   0 total
Time:        5.38s
Ran all test suites.

Watch Usage: Press w to show more.
```

Our tests pass as expected, which makes four passing tests in total.

Testing the Question component

Carry out the following steps to test that the `Question` component renders correctly:

1. Let's start by creating a new file called `Question.test.tsx` with the following content:

```
import React from 'react';
import { render, cleanup } from '@testing-library/react';
import { QuestionData } from './QuestionsData';
import { Question } from './Question';
import { BrowserRouter } from 'react-router-dom';

afterEach(cleanup);

test('When the Question component is rendered, it should contain
the correct data', () => {
});
```

This imports all the items we need for our test. We have also implemented the cleanup function, which will run after the test.

2. Now, let's try to render the component:

```
test('When the Question component is rendered, it should contain
the correct data', () => {
  const question: QuestionData = {
    questionId: 1,
    title: 'Title test',
    content: 'Content test',
    userName: 'User1',
    created: new Date(2019, 1, 1),
    answers: [],
  };
  const { getByText } = render(
    <Question data={question} />,
  );
});
```

We render the `Question` component using the `render` function by passing in a mocked `data` prop value.

There's a problem, though. If we run the test, we will receive an error message that includes `Invariant failed: You should not use <Link> outside a <Router>`. The problem here is that the `Question` component uses a `Link` component, which expects the `Router` component to be higher up in the component tree. However, it isn't present in our test.

3. The solution is to include `BrowserRouter` in our test:

```
test('When the Question component is rendered, it should contain
the correct data', () => {
  const question: QuestionData = {
    ...
  };
  const { getByText } = render(
    <BrowserRouter>
      <Question data={question} />
    </BrowserRouter>,
  );
});
```

4. Now, we can assert that the correct data is being rendered:

```
test('When the Question component is rendered, it should contain
the correct data', () => {
  const question: QuestionData = {
    ...
  };
  const { getByText } = render(
    <BrowserRouter>
      <Question data={question} />
    </BrowserRouter>,
  );

  const titleText = getByText('Title test');
  expect(titleText).not.toBeNull();

  const contentText = getByText('Content test');
  expect(contentText).not.toBeNull();

  const userText = getByText(/User1/);
  expect(userText).not.toBeNull();

  const dateText = getByText(/2019/);
  expect(dateText).not.toBeNull();
});
```

We use the `getByText` method again to locate rendered elements and check that the element that's been found isn't `null`. Notice that, when finding the element that contains the username and date, we pass in a regular expression to do a partial match.

Testing the HomePage component

The final component we are going to implement tests for is the `HomePage` component. Carry out the following steps to do so:

1. Let's create a file called `HomePage.test.tsx` with the following content:

```
import React from 'react';
import { render, cleanup, waitForElement } from '@testing-
library/react';
import { HomePage } from './HomePage';
import { BrowserRouter } from 'react-router-dom';

afterEach(cleanup);

test('When HomePage first rendered, loading indicator should show',
```

```
() => {
  const { getByText } = render(
    <BrowserRouter>
      <HomePage />
    </BrowserRouter>,
  );

  const loading = getByText('Loading...');
  expect(loading).not.toBeNull();
});
```

The test verifies that a **Loading...** message appears in the HomePage component when it is first rendered.

There is a problem, though, because the HomePage component expects the history, location, and match props to be passed into it:

```
HomePage.test.tsx ▷ ...
import React from 'react';
import { render, cleanup, waitForElement } from '@testing-library/react';
import
import      (alias) const HomePage: FunctionComponent<RouteComponentProps<
            {}, StaticContext, any>>
            import HomePage
afterEa
            Type '{}' is missing the following properties from type
test('W      'RouteComponentProps<{}, StaticContext, any>': history,
  const     location, match ts(2739)
    <Br   Quick Fix...   Peek Problem
      <HomePage />
    </BrowserRouter>,
  );

  const loading = getByText('Loading...');
  expect(loading).not.toBeNull();
});
```

2. We are going to create a mock property and pass this into the history, location, and match props:

```
test('When HomePage first rendered, loading indicator should show',
  () => {
    let mock: any = jest.fn();
    const { getByText } = render(
      <BrowserRouter>
        <HomePage history={mock} location={mock} match={mock} />
      </BrowserRouter>,
```

```
);

    const loading = getByText('Loading...');
    expect(loading).not.toBeNull();
});
```

We create the mock property using `jest.fn()`. Now, the test will execute and pass as expected.

3. Let's implement another test to check that unanswered questions are rendered okay:

```
test('When HomePage data returned, it should render questions',
async () => {
  let mock: any = jest.fn();
  const { getByText } = render(
    <BrowserRouter>
      <HomePage history={mock} location={mock} match={mock} />
    </BrowserRouter>,
  );

  await waitForElement(() => getByText('Title1 test'));

  const question2TitleText = getByText('Title2 test');
  expect(question2TitleText).not.toBeNull();
});
```

This test is similar to our first test on the `HomePage` component except that we wait for the first question to render using the `waitForElement` function from the React Testing Library.

However, the test fails. This is because the `HomePage` component is making an HTTP request to get the data but there is no REST API to handle the request.

4. We are going to mock the `getUnansweredQuestions` function with a Jest mock. Let's add the following code above our test:

```
jest.mock('./QuestionsData', () => ({
  getUnansweredQuestions: jest.fn(() => {
    return Promise.resolve([
      {
        questionId: 1,
        title: 'Title1 test',
        content: 'Content2 test',
        userName: 'User1',
        created: new Date(2019, 1, 1),
        answers: [],
```

```
    },
    {
      questionId: 2,
      title: 'Title2 test',
      content: 'Content2 test',
      userName: 'User2',
      created: new Date(2019, 1, 1),
      answers: [],
    },
  ]);
}),
})));

test('When HomePage first rendered, loading indicator should show',
() => ...
```

The mock function returns two questions that we use in the test assertions.

Now, the test will pass when it runs.

That completes our component tests. It's worth noting that the tests on the Page and Question components are unit tests, whereas those on the HomePage component are integration tests because the test renders the QuestionList and Question components rather than mocking them out.

As we've seen, tests on components are more challenging to write than tests on pure functions, but the React Testing Library and Jest mocks make life fairly straightforward.

In the next section, we are going to complete our test suite by implementing an end-to-end test.

Implementing end-to-end tests with Cypress

Cypress is an end-to-end testing tool that works really well for **single-page applications (SPAs)** like ours. In this section, we are going to implement an end-to-end test for signing in and asking a question.

Getting started with Cypress

Cypress executes in our frontend, so let's carry out the following steps to install and configure Cypress in our frontend project:

1. We'll start by installing cypress from the Terminal:

   ```
   > npm install cypress --save-dev
   ```

2. We are going to add an npm script to open Cypress by adding the following line to package.json:

   ```
   "scripts": {
     ...,
     "cy:open": "cypress open"
   },
   ```

3. Let's open Cypress by executing our npm script in the Terminal:

   ```
   > npm run cy:open
   ```

   After a few seconds, Cypress will open, showing a list of example test files that have just been installed:

   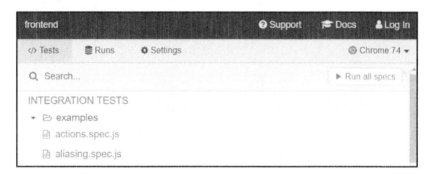

These examples can be found in the cypress/integration/examples folder in our project. If we open one of these test files, we'll see that they're are written in JavaScript. These examples are a great reference source as we learn and get up to speed with Cypress.

4. Click the `actions.spec.js` item. This will open this test and execute it:

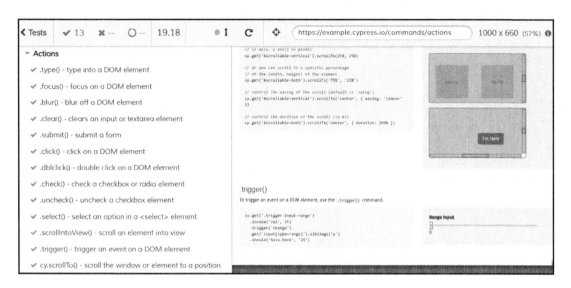

We can see the tests on the left and check whether they have passed or failed with the app that is being tested on the right.

5. If we click the **submit() - submit a form** test, we'll see all the steps in the test. If we click on a step, we'll see the app on the right in the state it was in at that juncture:

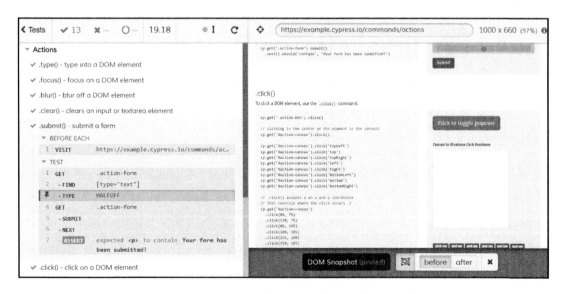

This is really useful when debugging test failures.

6. Let's close Cypress for now and return to the Terminal to install the Cypress Testing Library:

```
> npm install @testing-library/cypress --save-dev
```

The Cypress Testing Library is similar to the React Testing Library in that it helps us select elements to check without using internal implementation details.

7. To add Cypress Testing Library commands, we need to insert the following line at the top of the `commands.js` file, which can be found in the `support` folder of the `cypress` folder:

```
import '@testing-library/cypress/add-commands';
```

8. Let's add some Cypress configuration settings by opening the `cypress.json` file in the root of the project and adding the following settings:

```
{
  "baseUrl": "http://localhost:3000",
  "chromeWebSecurity": false
}
```

The `baseUrl` setting is the root URL of the app we are testing.

Our test will be using Auth0 and our app, so it will be working on two different origins. We need to disable Chrome security using the `chromeWebSecurity` setting to allow the test to work across different origins.

9. Cypress runs our app and Auth0 in an IFrame. To prevent clickjacking attacks, running in an IFrame is disabled by default in Auth0. So, let's disable clickjacking protection in Auth0 by selecting the **Settings** option under our user avatar menu and then selecting the **Advanced** tab. An option called **Disable clickjacking protection for Classic Universal Login** can be found toward the bottom of the **Advanced** tab. We need to turn this option on:

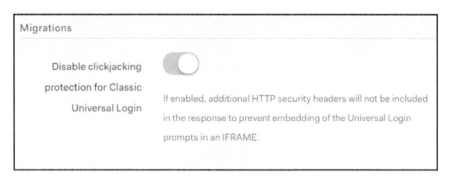

10. When we write our tests, we will be accessing a global `cy` object from Cypress. Let's tell ESLint that `cy` is okay by adding the following to the `.eslintrc.json` file:

```
{
  ...,
  "globals": {
    "cy": true
  }
}
```

Now, Cypress has been installed and configured so that we can implement a test on our Q and A app.

Testing asking a question

We are going to implement a test on our app using Cypress; the test signs in and then asks a question. Carry out the following steps to do so:

1. Let's create a new file called `qanda.js` in the `integration` folder in the `cypress` folder with the following content:

```
describe('Ask question', () => {
  beforeEach(() => {
    cy.visit('/');
```

```
   });
   it('When signed in and ask a valid question, the question should
successfully save', () => {
     });
   });
```

The `describe` function allows us to group a collection of tests on a feature. The first parameter is the title for the group, while the second parameter is a function that contains the tests in the group.

The `it` function allows us to define the actual test. The first parameter is the title for the test and the second parameter is a function that contains the steps in the test.

The `beforeEach` function allows us to define steps to be executed before each test runs. In our case, we are using the `visit` command to navigate to the root of the app. Remember that the root URL for the app is defined in the `baseUrl` setting in the `cypress.json` file.

2. Let's add the following step in our test:

```
   it('When signed in and ask a valid question, the question should
successfully save', () => {
     cy.contains('Q & A');
   });
```

We are checking that the page contains the Q & A text using the `contains` Cypress command. We can access Cypress commands from the global `cy` object.

Cypress commands are built to fail if they don't find what they expect to find. Due to this, we don't need to add an assert statement. Neat!

3. Let's give the test a try. We'll need to run our backend in our Visual Studio project. We'll also need to run our frontend by executing `npm start` in the Terminal. In an additional Terminal window, enter the following to open Cypress:

```
> npm run cy:open
```

4. Cypress will detect our test and list it underneath the example tests:

5. Click on the test to execute it:

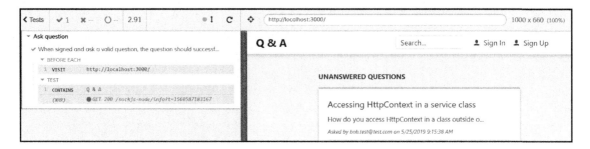

The test successfully executes and passes. We'll leave the test runner open because it will automatically rerun as we implement and save our test.

6. Let's add the following additional step in our test:

```
cy.contains('UNANSWERED QUESTIONS');
```

Here, we are checking that the page contains the correct title. If we save the test and look at the test runner, we'll see that the test has failed:

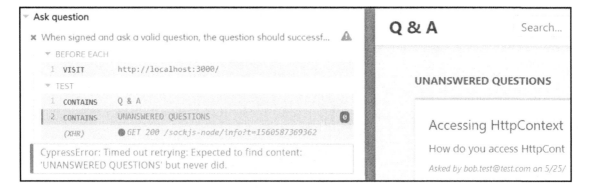

This is because the title's text isn't actually in capitals – a CSS rule transformed the text into capitals.

Notice the message Cypress uses to inform us of the failing test: **Timed out retrying**. Cypress will keep trying commands until they pass or a timeout occurs. This behavior is really convenient for us because it allows us to write synchronous style code, even though the operations we are testing are asynchronous. Cypress abstracts this complexity from us.

7. We'll correct *step 6*:

```
cy.contains('Unanswered Questions');
```

8. Let's add code to go to the sign-in page:

```
cy.contains('Sign In').click();
cy.url().should('include', 'auth0');
```

Here, we use the Cypress `contains` command to locate the **Sign In** button and chain a `click` command on this to click the button.

Then, we use the `url` command to get the browser's URL and chain a `should` command on this statement to verify that it contains the correct path.

If we look at the test runner, we'll see that the test managed to navigate to Auth0 correctly.

Let's think about these steps that Cypress is executing. The navigation to Auth0 is an asynchronous operation but our test code doesn't appear to be asynchronous. We haven't added a special wait function to wait for the page navigation to complete. Cypress makes testing single-page apps that have asynchronous user interfaces a breeze because it deals with this complexity for us!

9. Next, we'll implement some steps so that we can fill in the sign-in form:

```
cy.findByLabelText('Email')
  .type('your username')
  .should('have.value', 'your username');

cy.findByLabelText('Password')
  .type('your password')
  .should('have.value', 'your password');
```

Here, we use the `findByLabelText` command from the Cypress Testing Library to locate the `input`. It does this by finding the label containing the text we specified and then finding the associated `input` (referenced in the label's `for` attribute). This is another neat function that frees the tests from implementation details such as element IDs and class names.

We chain the Cypress `type` command so that we can enter characters into the `input` and then the `should` command to verify that the input's `value` property has been set correctly.

 Substitute your test username and password appropriately.

10. Let's submit the sign-in form and check that we are taken back to the Q and A app:

```
cy.get('form').submit(); .

cy.contains('Unanswered Questions');
```

We use the Cypress `get` command to locate the form and then submit it. Then, we check that the page contains the `Unanswered Questions` text to verify we are back in the Q and A app. Cypress takes care of the asynchronicity of these steps for us.

11. Next, we'll click the **Ask a question** button to go to the ask page:

```
cy.contains('Ask a question').click();
cy.contains('Ask a Question');
```

12. Then, we'll fill in the ask form:

```
var title = 'title test';
var content = 'Lots and lots and lots and lots and lots of content
test';
cy.findByLabelText('Title')
  .type(title)
  .should('have.value', title);
cy.findByLabelText('Content')
  .type(content)
  .should('have.value', content);
```

We fill in the title and content fields by using the same commands that we did on the sign-in form. The title must be at least 10 characters, and the content must be at least 50 characters, to satisfy the validation rules.

13. Next, we'll submit the question and check that the submission is okay:

```
cy.contains('Submit Your Question').click();
cy.contains('Your question was successfully submitted');
```

14. To complete the test, we are going to sign out and check we've been redirected to the correct page:

```
cy.contains('Sign Out').click();
cy.contains('You successfully signed out!');
```

If we look at the test runner, we'll discover that our test runs and passes successfully:

That completes our end-to-end test and all the tests we are going to create in this chapter. Now that we've written the appropriate unit tests, integration tests, and end-to-end tests, we have a feel for the benefits and challenges of each type, and how to implement them.

Summary

End-to-end tests with Cypress allows us to quickly cover areas of our app. However, they require a fully operational frontend and backend, including the database. Cypress abstracts away the complexity of the asynchronous nature of single-page applications, making our tests nice and easy to write.

Unit tests can be written using xUnit in .NET and can be placed in a xUnit project, separate from the main app. xUnit test methods are decorated with the `Fact` attribute and we use the `Assert` class to carry out checks on the item that we are testing.

Unit tests can be written using Jest for React apps and are contained in files with `test.ts` or `test.tsx` extensions. Jest's `expect` function gives us many useful matcher functions, such as `toBe`, that we can use to make test assertions.

Unit tests often require dependencies to be mocked. Moq is a popular mocking tool in the .NET community and has a `Mock` class, which can be used to mock dependencies. On the frontend, Jest has a range of powerful mocking capabilities that we can use to mock out dependencies, such as REST API calls.

A page is often composed of several components and sometimes it is convenient to just write integration tests on the page component without mocking the child components. We can implement these tests using Jest in exactly the same way as we can implement a unit test.

The React Testing Library and the Cypress Testing Library help us write robust tests by allowing us to locate elements in a way that doesn't depend on implementation details. This means that, if the implementation changes while its features and the behavior remain the same, the test is unlikely to break. This approach reduces the maintenance cost of our test suite.

Now that our app has been built and we've covered automated tests, it's time to deploy it to Azure. We'll do this in the next chapter.

Questions

The following questions will test your knowledge of the topics that were covered in this chapter:

1. We have the following xUnit test method, but it isn't being picked up by the test runner. What's wrong?

```
public void Minus_When2Integers_ShouldReturnCorrectInteger()
{
 var result = Calc.Add(2, 1);
 Assert.Equal(1, result);
}
```

2. We have a `string` variable called `successMessage` in a xUnit test and we need to check that it contains the word `"success"`. What method in the `Assert` class could we use?

3. We have created some Jest unit tests on a `List` component in a file called `ListTests.tsx`. However, when the Jest test runner runs, the tests aren't picked up. Why is this happening?

4. We are implementing a test in Jest and we have a variable called `result` that we want to check isn't `null`. Which Jest matcher function can we use?

5. Let's say we have a variable called `person` that is of the `Person` type:

```
interface Person {
   id: number;
   firstName: string;
   surname: string
}
```

We want to check that the person variable is `{ id: 1, firstName: "Tom", surname: "Smith" }`. What Jest matcher function can we use?

6. We are writing an end-to-end test using Cypress for a page. The page has a heading called **Sign In**. What Cypress command can we use to check that this has rendered okay?

7. We are writing an end-to-end test using Cypress for a page that renders some text, **Loading...**, while data is being fetched. How can we assert that this text is being rendered and then disappears when the data has been fetched?

Further reading

The following resources are useful if you want to find out more about testing with xUnit and Jest:

- Unit testing in .NET
  Core: `https://docs.microsoft.com/en-us/dotnet/core/testing/unit-testing-with-dotnet-test`
- xUnit: `https://xunit.net/`
- Moq: `https://github.com/moq/moq`
- Jest: `https://jestjs.io/`
- React Testing Library: `https://github.com/kentcdodds/react-testing-library`
- Cypress: `https://docs.cypress.io`
- Cypress Testing Library: `https://github.com/testing-library/cypress-testing-library`

14
Configuring and Deploying to Azure

In this chapter, we'll deploy our app into production in Microsoft Azure so that all of our users can start to use it. We will focus on the backend to start with, making the necessary changes to our code so that it can work in production and staging environments in Azure. We will then deploy our backend APIs, along with the SQL database, to both staging and production from within Visual Studio. After the first deploy, subsequent deploys will be able to be done with the click of a button in Visual Studio.

We will then turn our attention to the frontend, again making changes to our code to support development, staging, and production environments. We will then deploy our frontend to Azure to both the staging and production environments.

In this chapter, we'll cover the following topics:

- Getting started with Azure
- Configuring the ASP.NET Core backend for staging and production
- Publishing our ASP.NET Core backend to Azure
- Configuring the React frontend for staging and production
- Publishing the React frontend to Azure

Technical requirements

We'll use the following tools and services in this chapter:

- **Visual Studio 2019:** We'll use this to edit our ASP.NET Core code. This can be downloaded and installed from `https://visualstudio.microsoft.com/vs/`.
- **.NET Core 3.0**: This can be downloaded and installed from `https://dotnet.microsoft.com/download/dotnet-core`.
- **Visual Studio Code:** We'll use this to edit our React code. This can be downloaded and installed from `https://code.visualstudio.com/`.
- **Node.js and npm:** These can be downloaded from `https://nodejs.org/`. If you already have these installed, make sure that Node.js is at least version 8.2, and that `npm` is at least version 5.2
- **Microsoft Azure**. We will use several Azure app services and SQL databases for our app. An account can be created at `https://azure.microsoft.com/en-us/free/`.
- **Q and A**: We'll start with the Q and A frontend and backend projects we finished in the last chapter, which are available at `https://github.com/PacktPublishing/ASP.NET-Core-3-and-React-17`.

All of the code snippets in this chapter can be found online at `https://github.com/PacktPublishing/ASP.NET-Core-3-and-React-17`. To restore code from a chapter, the source code repository can be downloaded and the relevant folder opened in the relevant editor. If the code is frontend code, then `npm install` can be entered in the Terminal to restore the dependencies.

Check out the following video to see the code in action:

`http://bit.ly/2MvYu7M`

Getting started with Azure

In this section, we are going to sign up for Azure if we haven't already got an account. We'll then have a quick look around the Azure portal and understand the services we are going to use to run our app.

Signing up to Azure

If you already have an Azure account, there's never been a better time to sign up and give Azure a try. At the time of writing this book, you can sign up to Azure and get 12 months of free services at the following link: `https://azure.microsoft.com/en-us/free/`.

We'll need a Microsoft account to sign up for Azure, which is free to create if you haven't already got one. You are then required to complete a sign-up form that contains the following personal information:

- Country of origin
- Name
- Email address
- Phone number

You then need to go through two different verification processes. The first is verification via a text message or call on your phone. The second is to verify your credit card details.

 Note that your credit card won't be charged unless you upgrade from the free trial.

The last step in the sign-up process is to agree to the terms and conditions.

Understanding the Azure services we are going to use

After we have an Azure account, we can sign in to the Azure portal using our Microsoft account. The URL for the portal is `https://portal.azure.com`.

When we log in to the Azure portal, we'll see that it contains a wide variety of services:

We are going to use just a couple of these fantastic services:

- **App services**: We will use this service to host our ASP.NET Core backend API as well as our React frontend.
- **SQL database**: We will use this service to host our SQL Server database.

 If our frontend React didn't contain multiple client-side pages, we could host it using the static website option in Azure Storage, which is nice and cheap. For multiple client-side page apps, we need a URL rewrite rule so that deep links to the pages work. The URL rewrite rule requires IIS, which is available in an Azure App Service but, unfortunately, not in Azure Storage.

We are going to put all of these resources into what's called a **resource group**. Let's create the resource group now:

1. Click on the **Resource groups** option. A list of resource groups appears, which of course will be empty if we have just signed up to Azure. Click on the **Create resource group** button:

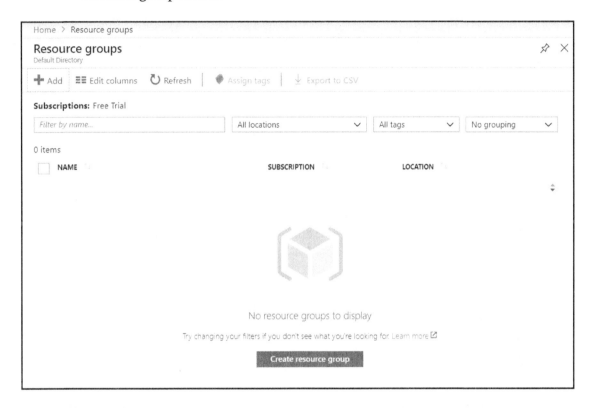

2. Fill in the form that opens. Choose an appropriate name for the resource group. We'll need to use this name later in this chapter, so make sure you remember it. Click the **Review + Create** button:

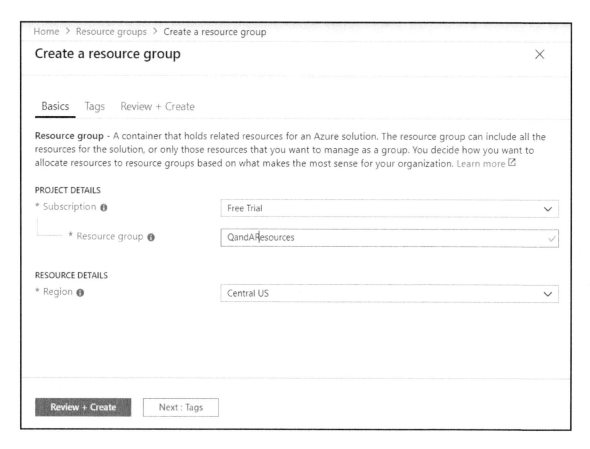

3. Click on the **Create** button on the review screen that opens. Our resource group will eventually be shown in the resource group list:

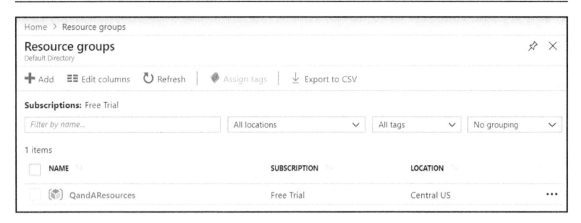

If the resource group doesn't show after a few seconds, click the **Refresh** option to refresh the resource groups.

Our resource group is now ready for the other services to be provisioned. Before we provision any other services, we'll configure our backend for production in the next section.

Configuring the ASP.NET Core backend for staging and production

In this section, we are going to change our CORS configuration to reference `appsettings.json` so that it's not hardcoded. We are then going to create separate `appsettings.json` files for staging and production as well for working locally in development. Let's open our backend project in Visual Studio and carry out the following steps:

1. In the `StartUp` class in the `ConfigureServices` method, let's change our call to the `AddCors` method to the following:

```
services.AddCors(options => options.AddPolicy("CorsPolicy",
    builder => builder
                .AllowAnyMethod()
                .AllowAnyHeader()
                .AllowCredentials()
                .WithOrigins(Configuration["Frontend"])));
```

We have simply changed the origin to reference a `Frontend` configuration setting instead of being hardcoded. We will add this setting in a later step.

2. Let's now go to the **Solution Explorer**:

Notice that two settings files start with the word `appsettings`.

 We can have different settings files for different environments. The `appsettings.json` file is the default settings file and can contain settings common to all environments. `appsettings.Development.json` is used during development when we run the backend in Visual Studio and overrides any duplicate settings that are in the `appsettings.json` file. The middle part of the filename needs to match an environment variable called `ASPNETCORE_ENVIRONMENT`, which is set to `Development` in Visual Studio by default and `Production` by default in Azure. So, `appsettings.Production.json` can be used for settings specific to the production environment in Azure.

3. At the moment, all of our settings are in the default `appsettings.json` file. Let's add our `ConnectionStrings` setting and also a frontend setting to the `appsettings.Development.json` file:

```
{
  "ConnectionStrings": {
    "DefaultConnection":
"Server=localhost\\SQLEXPRESS;Database=QandA;Trusted_Connection=Tru
```

```
    e;"
      },
      "Frontend": "http://localhost:3000"
  }
```

We will leave the Auth0 settings in the default `appsettings.json` file because these will apply to all environments.

4. Let's add an `appsettings.Production.json` file now by right-clicking the **QandA** project in **Solution Explorer**, choosing **Add | New Item...**, selecting the **App Settings File** item, and then clicking the **Add** button:

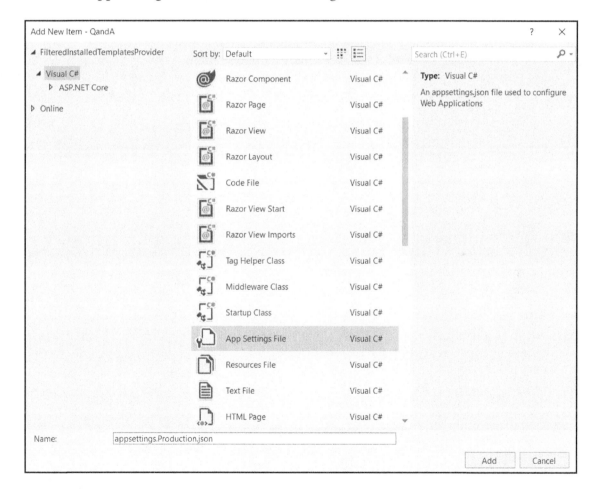

5. Change the content in the `appsettings.Production.json` file to the following:

```
{
  "ConnectionStrings": {
    "DefaultConnection": "Server=tcp:your-
server.database.windows.net,1433;Initial Catalog=your-db;Persist
Security Info=False;User ID=qanda;Password=your-
password;MultipleActiveResultSets=False;Encrypt=True;TrustServerCer
tificate=False;Connection Timeout=30;"
  },
  "Frontend": "https://your-frontend.azurewebsites.net"
}
```

So, this contains references to the production database and app services we are going to create in Azure. Choose your own server name, database name, username, and password. Also, choose a name for your frontend website. Take note of these settings because we will need these when we provision the services in Azure.

6. Similarly, let's add an `appsettings.Staging.json` file with the following content:

```
{
  "ConnectionStrings": {
    "DefaultConnection": "Server=tcp:your-
server.database.windows.net,1433;Initial Catalog=your-db-
staging;Persist Security Info=False;User ID=qanda;Password=your-
password;MultipleActiveResultSets=False;Encrypt=True;TrustServerCer
tificate=False;Connection Timeout=30;"
  },
  "Frontend": "https://your-frontend-staging.azurewebsites.net"
}
```

We are now ready to start to create Azure services and deploy our backend. We'll do this in the next section.

Publishing our ASP.NET Core backend to Azure

In this section, we are going to deploy our database and backend API to Azure using Visual Studio. We are going to deploy to a production environment first and then a staging environment.

Publishing to production

Let's carry out the following steps to deploy our backend to production:

1. In **Solution Explorer**, right-click on the **QandA** project and select **Publish...**.
2. The **Publish** screen opens. Select the **Publish** section and then click the **Start** button:

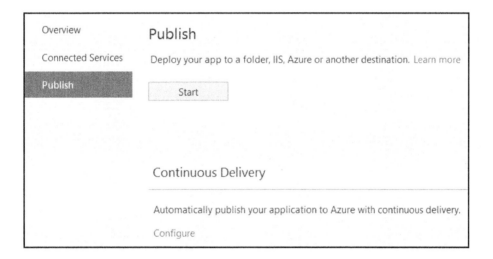

3. We are then prompted to choose a publish target. Choose **Create New** and click the **Create Profile** button:

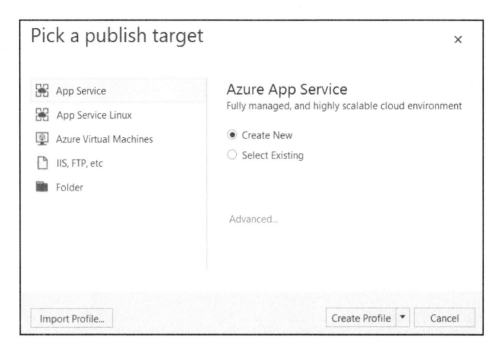

4. The next step is to specify our Microsoft account and name the production app service. Note down the name you choose because we'll eventually reference this in the frontend project:

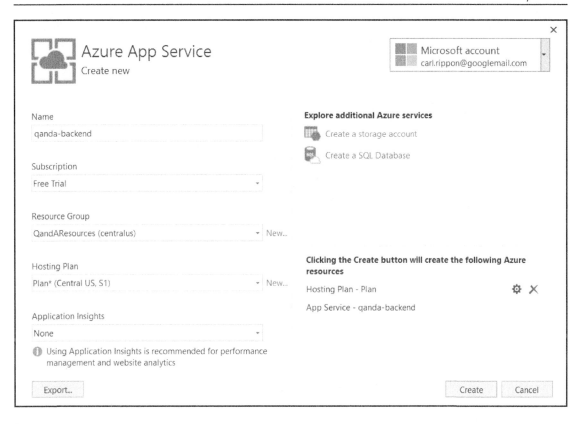

5. We can also create a SQL database on this screen. Let's do this by clicking the **Create a SQL Database** option.

6. In the dialog that opens, enter the database name to match what we have specified in the connection string in the `appsettings.Production.json` file.

7. We need to create a new database server, so click the **New...** option to the right of the **Database server** field.

8. Let's use the server name and credentials we specified in the connection string in the `appsettings.Production.json` file.

9. Click the **OK** button to confirm the server details and then the **OK** button on the database screen beneath it.

10. We are taken back to the **Azure App Service** dialog with the details that we have just specified in the bottom-right corner.

11. Click the **Create** button to create the services in Azure. This will take a few minutes to complete.

Notice the warning at the bottom of the screen:

> Your application is making use of SignalR. For environments that need to scale
> we strongly recommend adding a dependency on Azure SignalR Service.
> More info

This is a reminder that there is a SignalR Service in Azure that we could use for our real-time API. Implementing this is beyond the scope of this chapter, so we'll continue to use the real-time API within our app service.

12. We can then publish our code to the Azure services by clicking the **Publish** button. Again, this will take a few minutes to complete.

13. Just before deployment is complete, the following prompt may appear:

Microsoft Visual Studio

We have detected that your app makes use of SignalR, but we have not detected an instance of Azure SignalR Service. For performance and scale we recommend using Azure SignalR Service. If you decide not to, we recommend enabling Web sockets on your Azure App Service as an alternative. Would you like to turn Web sockets on?

Yes No

Choose **Yes** to turn web sockets on in our app service.

14. Eventually, a browser window will open containing the path to our deployed backend. Add /api/questions to the path in the browser:

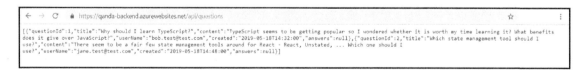

We will see the default questions from our database. Congratulations! We have just deployed our first SQL database and ASP.NET Core app in Azure!

15. Let's go to the Azure portal by navigating to `https://portal.azure.com`. Select the **All resources** option:

As expected, we see the services that we have just provisioned.

Excellent! We have just successfully deployed our backend in Azure!

Publishing to staging

Let's carry out the following steps to deploy our backend to a staging environment:

1. In **Solution Explorer**, right-click on the **QandA** project and select **Publish...**
2. Select the **New** option to create a new publish profile:

3. Select **Create New** on the **App Service** tab and click **Create Profile.**
4. In the dialog that appears, enter the name for the app service. This is going to be the service to host our backend in the staging environment. Note down the name you choose because we'll eventually reference this in the frontend project.

5. Click on the **Create a SQL Database** option. We are going to use the database server we have already provisioned, but create a new database within it for the staging environment. Remember that these settings need to be reflected in the `DefaultConnection` setting in `appsettings.Staging.json`.

6. We then click on the **Create** button to create the new app service and database, which will take a few minutes.

7. We can then publish our code to the Azure services by clicking the **Publish** button. Again, this will take a few minutes to complete.

8. A browser window will eventually open that points to the new app service. However, our app service will be referencing the production database at the moment because this is the default environment if not specified.

9. We need to tell our new app service that it is the staging environment. Let's go to the Azure portal and select the staging app service in the **App Services** area.

10. In the **Settings** area, select **Configuration** and go to the **Application settings** tab.

11. Under **Application settings**, click the **New application setting** option and enter `ASPNETCORE_ENVIRONMENT` as the name and `Staging` as the value, and then click the **OK** button followed by the **Save** button. This creates an environment variable called `ASPNETCORE_ENVIRONMENT` with the `Staging` value. ASP.NET Core will look at this variable and then use the `appsettings.Staging.json` file for its configuration settings:

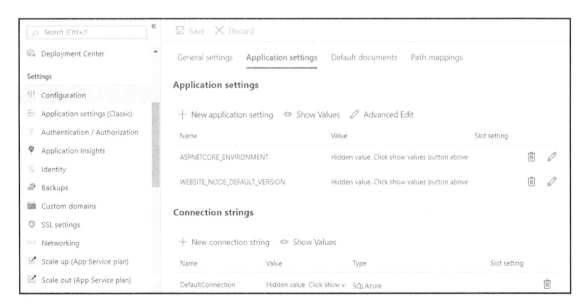

That completes the deployment of our app to a staging environment.

That's great progress! Azure works beautifully with Visual Studio. In the next section, we are going to turn our attention to the frontend and make changes so that it will work in the Azure staging and production environments as well as in development.

Configuring the React frontend for staging and production

In this section, we are going to change our frontend so that it makes requests to the correct backend APIs in staging and production. At the moment, both the REST API and SignalR API have hardcoded paths set to the localhost. We are going to make use of environment variables like we did in our backend to differentiate between the different environments. Let's open our frontend project in Visual Studio Code and carry out the following steps:

1. First, we are going to install a library called `cross-env` that will allow us to set environment variables. Let's execute the following command in the Terminal:

   ```
   > npm install cross-env --save-dev
   ```

2. Let's add the following scripts in `package.json` to execute staging and production builds:

   ```
   "scripts": {
     ...,
     "build": "react-scripts build",
     "build:production": "cross-env REACT_APP_ENV=production npm run build",
     "build:staging": "cross-env REACT_APP_ENV=staging npm run build",
     ...
   },
   ```

   These scripts use the `cross-env` library to set an environment variable called `REACT_APP_ENV` to `staging` and `production` before doing an optimized build.

   So, `npm run build:staging` will execute a staging build and `npm run build:production` will execute a production build.

3. Let's make use of the `REACT_APP_ENV` environment variable when setting the `server` variable in the `AppSettings.ts` file:

```
export const server =
  process.env.REACT_APP_ENV === 'production'
    ? 'https://your-backend.azurewebsites.net'
    : process.env.REACT_APP_ENV === 'staging'
    ? 'https://your-backend-staging.azurewebsites.net'
    : 'http://localhost:17525';
```

We use a ternary expression to set the correct backend location depending on the environment the app is running in. The production server is set to `https://your-backend.azurewebsites.net`, and the staging server is set to `https://your-backend-staging.azurewebsites.net`.

Make sure the staging and production locations you enter match the location of your deployed backends.

4. For deep links to work in Azure, we need to specify a URL rewrite rule to redirect all requests to the frontend to our `index.html` file. We can do this by adding a `web.config` file to the `public` folder with the following content:

```xml
<?xml version="1.0" encoding="utf-8"?>
<configuration>
  <system.webServer>
    <rewrite>
      <rules>
        <rule name="React Routes" stopProcessing="true">
          <match url=".*" />
          <conditions logicalGrouping="MatchAll">
            <add input="{REQUEST_FILENAME}" matchType="IsFile"
negate="true" />
          </conditions>
          <action type="Rewrite" url="/" appendQueryString="true"
/>
        </rule>
      </rules>
    </rewrite>
  </system.webServer>
</configuration>
```

5. Now, let's do one final thing in preparation for deploying our frontend. Let's change the app to render the environment we are in. Let's open `Header.tsx` and add the environment name after the link to the home page:

```
<div css={...}>
  <div>
    <Link to="/" css={...}>Q & A</Link>
    <span
      css={css`
        margin-left: 10px;
        font-size: 16px;
        color: ${gray2};
      `}
    >
      {process.env.REACT_APP_ENV || 'development'}
    </span>
  </div>
  ...
</div>
```

If the environment variable isn't populated, we assume we are in the development environment.

That completes the changes we need to make to our frontend. In the next section, we are going to deploy the frontend to Azure.

Publishing the React frontend to Azure

In this section, we are going to deploy our React frontend to Azure to both staging and production environments.

Publishing to production

Let's carry out the following steps to publish our frontend to a production environment:

1. We'll start by provisioning an Azure App Service. So, let's go to the Azure portal in a browser and go to the **App Services** area and click the **Add** option.

2. Complete the form that opens by choosing the existing resource group, choosing an app name, and selecting `.NET Core 3.0` as the runtime stack and `Windows` as the operating system. Note that the app name we choose needs to be reflected in the `Frontend` setting in the `appsettings.Production.json` file in our backend project. Click the **Review + create** button and then the **Create** button to create the app service.

3. Let's move to Visual Studio Code now and create a production build by running the following command in the Terminal:

   ```
   > npm run build:production
   ```

   After the build has finished, the production build will consist of all of the files in the `build` folder.

4. We are going to use the **Azure App Service** extension to perform the Azure deployment. So, let's install this:

5. Click the Azure icon in the left-hand navigation options and then the **Sign in to Azure...** option:

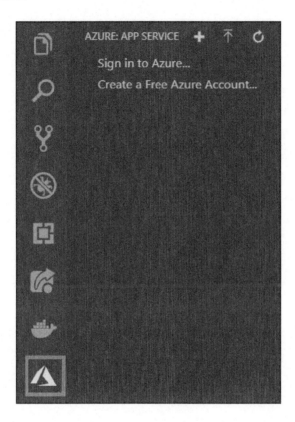

6. We are prompted to enter our Microsoft account credentials, so let's enter these.

7. We should see the frontend app service listed in the tree. Right-click on this and choose the **Deploy to Web App...** option:

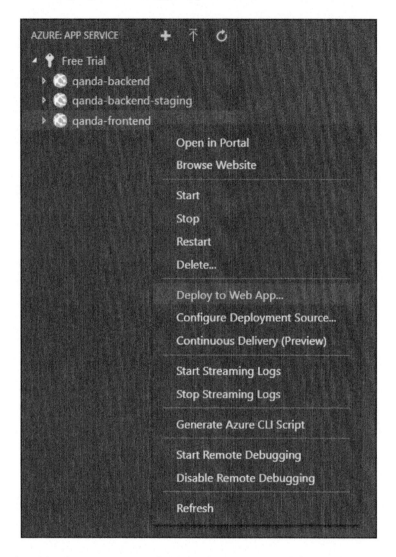

8. We should select our `build` folder when prompted for the folder to deploy.

9. We are then asked to confirm the deployment, which we do by clicking the **Deploy** button:

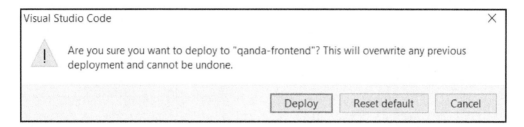

10. Deployment will take a minute or so before we get confirmation that it is complete:

11. If we click on the **Browse Website** option, our frontend in Azure will display in a browser:

Our frontend is now deployed nicely to the production environment. We won't be able to sign in successfully yet—we'll resolve this after we have published our frontend to the staging environment.

Publishing to staging

Let's carry out the following steps to deploy our frontend to a staging environment:

1. We'll start by provisioning another Azure App Service. So, let's go to the Azure portal in a browser and go to the **App Services** area and click the **Add** option.

2. Enter an app name and choose the existing resource group. Remember that the app name we choose needs to be reflected in the `Frontend` setting of the `appsettings.Staging.json` file in our backend project. Remember also that the runtime stack should be `.NET Core 3.0` and `Windows` should be the operating system. Click the **Review + Create** button and then the **Create** button to create the app service.

3. Let's move to Visual Studio Code now and create a staging build by running the following command in the Terminal:

   ```
   > npm run build:staging
   ```

   After the build has finished, the staging build will consist of all of the files in the `build` folder overwriting the production build.

4. In the Azure App Service section in Visual Studio Code, we should see the frontend staging app service listed in the tree. Note that we might need to click the **Refresh** toolbar option for it to appear. Right-click on the frontend staging app service and choose the **Deploy to Web App...** option:

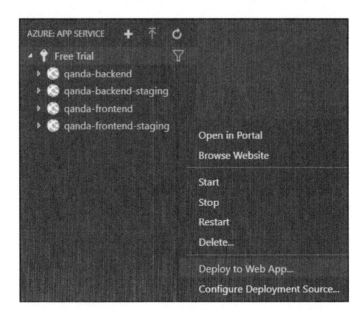

5. We should select our `build` folder when prompted for the folder to deploy and then confirm the deployment when prompted.

6. After a minute or so, we'll get confirmation that the deployment is complete. If we click on the **Browse Website** option, our staging frontend in Azure will show in a browser:

7. Next, let's tell Auth0 about the Azure staging and production URLs it should trust. In Auth0, we need to update the following settings against our Q and A application:

   • **Allowed Callback URLs**: This is shown in the following screenshot:

- **Allowed Web Origins**: This is shown in the following screenshot:

Allowed Web Origins	http://localhost:3000,https://qanda-frontend-staging.azurewebsites.net.https://qanda-frontend.azurewebsites.net/

- **Allowed Logout URLs**: This is shown in the following screenshot:

Allowed Logout URLs	http://localhost:3000/signout-callback,https://qanda-frontend-staging.azurewebsites.net/signout-callback,https://qanda-frontend.azurewebsites.net/signout-callback

We can find these settings by clicking on the **Applications** item in the left-hand navigation menu and then clicking on the **Q and A** application. We add the additional URLs for both the staging and production environments after the development environment URLs. The URLs for the different environments need to be separated by a comma.

8. We should now be able to sign in to our production and staging Q and A apps successfully.

That completes the deployment of our frontend to both production and staging environments.

Summary

Azure works beautifully with both React and ASP.NET Core apps. In ASP.NET Core, we can have different `appsettings.json` files to store the different settings for the different environments, such as database connection strings and the frontend location for CORS. In our React code, we can use an environment variable to make requests to the appropriate backend. We also need to include a `web.config` file in our React app so that deep links are redirected to the `index.html` page and then handled by React Router. The environment variable can be set in specific build `npm` scripts for each environment. We used three environments in this chapter, but both the frontend and backend could easily be configured to support more environments.

Azure has integration from both Visual Studio and Visual Studio Code that makes deploying React and ASP.NET Core apps a breeze. We use the built-in **Publish...** option in Visual Studio to provision the SQL database with App Services and then perform the deployment. We can also provision App Services in the Azure Portal, which we did for our frontend. We can then use the Azure App Services Visual Studio Code extension to deploy the frontend to an App Service.

Although deploying our app to Azure was super easy, we can make it even easier by automating the deployment when we check code into source control. We'll do this in the next chapter.

Questions

The following questions will test what we have learned in this chapter:

1. In ASP.NET Core, what is the name of the file where we store any settings specific to the production environment?
2. What were the reasons for our ASP.NET Core backend needing the `Frontend` setting?
3. Let's pretend we have introduced a QA environment and have created the following `npm` script to execute a build for this environment:

   ```
   "build:qa": "cross-env REACT_APP_ENV=qa npm run build"
   ```

   What `npm` command would we use to produce a QA build?

4. What would be broken if we didn't include the `web.config` file with our React frontend?
5. Why didn't we use Azure Storage to host our frontend instead of Azure App Service?

Further reading

The following resources are useful for finding more information on deploying ASP.NET Core and React apps to Azure:

- Using multiple environments in ASP.NET Core: `https://docs.microsoft.com/en-us/aspnet/core/fundamentals/environments`
- Deploying ASP.NET Core apps to Azure: `https://docs.microsoft.com/en-us/aspnet/core/host-and-deploy/azure-apps`
- Deploy a static website to Azure from VS Code: `https://code.visualstudio.com/tutorials/static-website/getting-started`
- Azure SignalR Service: `https://docs.microsoft.com/en-us/azure/azure-signalr/signalr-concept-scale-aspnet-core`

15
Implementing CI and CD with Azure DevOps

In this chapter, we are going to implement **Continuous Integration (CI)** and **Continuous Delivery (CD)** for our Q and A app using Azure DevOps. We'll start by understanding exactly what CI and CD are before getting into Azure DevOps.

In Azure DevOps, we'll implement CI for the frontend and backend using a build pipeline. The CI process will be triggered when developers push code to our source code repository. Then, we'll implement CD for the frontend and backend using a release pipeline that will be automatically triggered when a CI build completes successfully. The release pipeline will do a deployment to the staging environment automatically, run our backend integration tests, and then promote the staging deployment to production.

By the end of this chapter, we'll have a robust process of delivering features to our users incredibly fast with a great level of reliability, thus making our team very productive.

In this chapter, we'll cover the following topics:

- Getting started with CI and CD
- Implementing CI
- Implement CD

Technical requirements

We'll use the following tools and services in this chapter:

- **GitHub**: This chapter assumes that the source code for our app is hosted on GitHub. An account and repository can be set up for free at `https://github.com`.
- **Azure DevOps**: We will use this to implement and host our CI and CD processes. This can be found at `https://dev.azure.com/`.
- **Microsoft Azure**: We will use the Azure app services and SQL databases that we set up in the previous chapter. The Azure portal can be found at `https://portal.azure.com`.
- **Visual Studio Code**: This can be downloaded and installed from `https://code.visualstudio.com/`.
- **Node.js and npm**: These can be downloaded from `https://nodejs.org/`. If you already have these installed, make sure that Node.js is at least version 8.2 and that npm is at least version 5.2.
- **Q and A**: We'll start with the Q and A frontend and backend projects we finished in the previous chapter, which are available at `https://github.com/PacktPublishing/ASP.NET-Core-3-and-React-17`.

All the code snippets in this chapter can be found online at `https://github.com/PacktPublishing/ASP.NET-Core-3-and-React-17`. In order to restore code from a chapter, the source code repository can be downloaded and the relevant folder opened in the relevant editor. If the code is frontend code, then `npm install` can be entered in the Terminal to restore the dependencies.

Check out the following video to see the code in action:

`http://bit.ly/2rphsFQ`

Getting started with CI and CD

In this section, we'll start by understanding what CI and CD are before making a change in our frontend code to allow the frontend tests to work in CI. Then, we'll create our Azure Devops project, which will host our build and release pipelines.

Understanding CI and CD

CI is when developer working copies are merged to a shared master branch of code in a source code system several times a day, automatically triggering what is called a *build*. A *build* is the process of automatically producing all the artifacts that are required to successfully deploy, test, and run our production software. The benefit of CI is that it automatically gives the team feedback on the quality of the changes that are being made.

CD is the process of getting changes that developers make to the software into production, regularly and safely, in a sustainable way. So, it is the process of taking the build from CI and getting that deployed to the production environment. The CI build may be deployed to a staging environment where the end-to-end tests are executed and passed before deployment is made to the production environment. At its most extreme, the CD is fully automated and triggered when a CI build finishes. Often, a member of the team has to approve the final step of deploying the software to production, which should have already passed a series of automated tests in staging. CD is also not always triggered automatically when a CI build finishes; sometimes, it is automatically triggered at a particular time of day. The benefit of CD is that the development team deliver value to the users of the software faster and more reliably.

The following diagram shows the high-level CI and CD flow that we are going to set up:

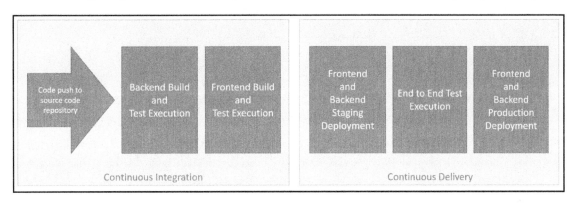

When code is pushed to our source code repository, we are going to build all the backend and frontend artifacts and execute the xUnit and Jest tests. If the builds and tests are successful, this will automatically kick off a staging deployment. The Cypress tests will execute on the staging deployment and, if they pass, a production deployment will be triggered.

Enabling our tests to run in CI and CD

We need to make some changes to the configuration of the frontend tests and end-to-end tests so that they execute correctly in the build and deployment pipelines. Let's open the frontend project in Visual Studio Code and make the following changes:

1. First, we'll add a script named `test:ci` in the `package.json` file, which will run the Jest tests in CI mode:

   ```
   ...
   "scripts": {
     ...
     "test": "react-scripts test",
     "test:ci": "cross-env CI=true react-scripts test",
     ...
   },
   ...
   ```

   This script sets an environment variable called `CI` to `true` before running the Jest tests.

2. Our Cypress tests are going to execute in the deployment pipeline on the staging app after it has been deployed. We need to do a few things to ensure that our Cypress tests run in the deployment pipeline. First, let's create a `cypress.json` file in the `cypress` folder with the following content:

   ```
   {
     "baseUrl": "https://your-frontend-staging.azurewebsites.net",
     "integrationFolder": "integration",
     "pluginsFile": "plugins/index.js",
     "supportFile": "support/index.js"
   }
   ```

   This is going to be the `cypress.json` file that runs the tests on the staging app after it has been deployed. Here's an explanation of the settings we have added:

   - `baseUrl`: This is the root path for the app, which should be the URL of our staging app. Change this appropriately for the staging app that you have deployed.

- `integrationFolder`: This is the folder where our end-to-end tests are located, relative to the `cypress.json` file. In our case, this is a folder called `integration`.
- `pluginsFile`: This is a file that contains any plugins that are relative to the `cypress.json` file. In our case, this is a file called `index.js`, which can be found in the `plugins` folder.
- `supportFile`: This is a file that's relative to the `cypress.json` file that contains code to execute before the tests run. In our case, this is a file called `index.js`, which can be found in the `support` folder.

3. Next, let's create a `package.json` file in the `cypress` folder with the following content:

```
{
  "name": "cypress-app-tests",
  "version": "0.1.0",
  "private": true,
  "scripts": {
    "cy:run": "cypress run"
  },
  "devDependencies": {
    "@testing-library/cypress": "^4.0.4",
    "cypress": "^3.3.1"
  }
}
```

The key items in this file are declaring Cypress and the Cypress Testing Library as development dependencies and the `cy:run` script, which we'll use later to run the Cypress tests.

4. Next, we are going to remove all the example tests that Cypress originally installed for us. So, let's delete the `examples` folder from the `integration` folder, which can be found in the `cypress` folder. Now, the only file in the integration folder should be our `qanda.js` file.

Now, our Jest and Cypress tests will be able to execute during a build and deployment.

Creating an Azure DevOps project

Let's carry out the following steps to create our Azure DevOps project:

1. Azure DevOps can be found at `https://dev.azure.com/`. We can create an account for free if we haven't got one already. To create a new project, click the **New project** button on the home page and enter a name for the project in the panel that appears. We can choose to make our project public or private before clicking the **Create** button:

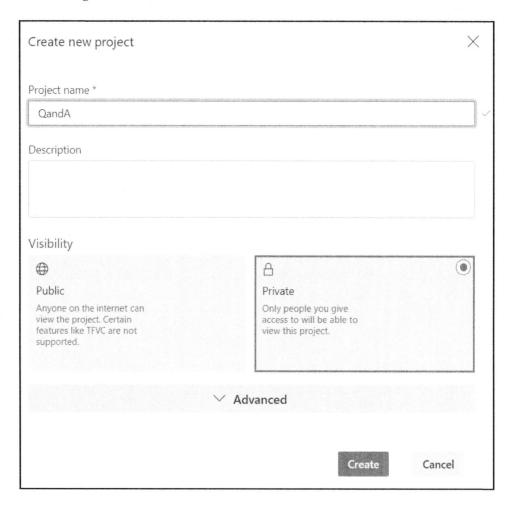

2. Azure DevOps contains several areas, but we are focused on its pipeline feature. So, let's click on **Pipelines** in the left-hand navigation menu and then click on **New pipeline.**

3. We will be asked to specify where our code repository is hosted:

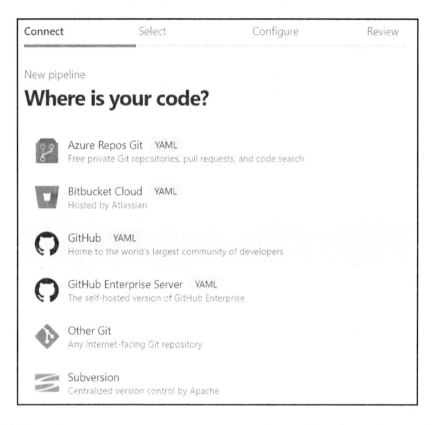

Click on the appropriate option. Azure DevOps will go through an authorization process to allow Azure DevOps to access our repositories.

4. Then, we will be prompted to choose a specific repository for our code and authorize access to it:

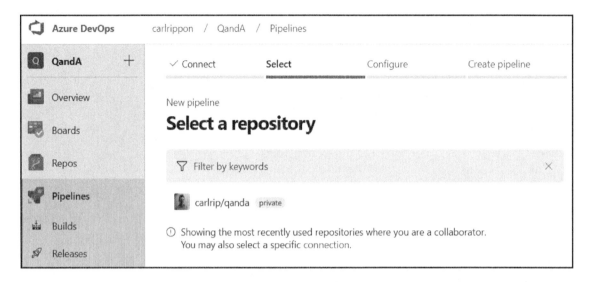

5. Azure DevOps will inspect the code in the repository so that it can suggest an appropriate CI template for the technology in play. Let's select the **ASP.NET Core** template:

Don't choose the **ASP.NET Core (.NET Framework)** template. You may need to click the **Show more** button to find the **ASP.NET Core** template.

6. Then, a build pipeline is created for us from the template. The steps in the pipeline are defined in an `azure-pipelines.yml` file, which will be added to our source code repository. We will make changes to this file in the next section, *Implementing CI*, but, for now, let's click the **Save and run** button:

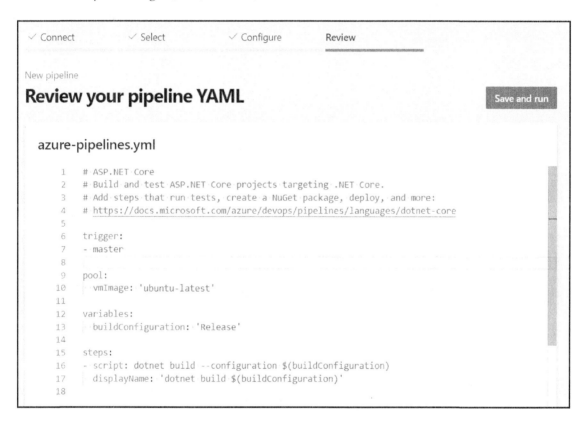

7. Click on the **Save and run** button in the confirmation panel that appears. The pipeline will be saved and a build will be triggered. The build will fail, but don't worry about that—we'll resolve this in the next section, *Implementing CI*.

8. Click on the **Builds** navigation option in the **Pipelines** section. We'll see the build history, along with an **Edit** option, which we can use to change build steps. There is also a **Queue** option, which allows us to manually trigger a build:

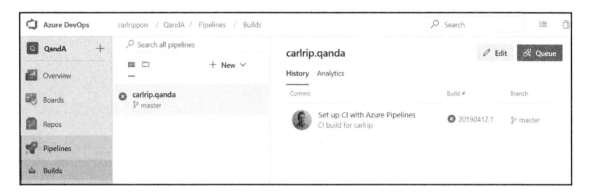

That's our Azure DevOps project created. It contains a build pipeline from the ASP.NET Core template. In the next section, we'll fully implement the build pipeline.

Implementing CI

In this section, we are going to complete the implementation of the CI build. We'll also observe the build trigger when code is pushed to our source code repository. Let's carry out the following steps:

1. In our Azure DevOps project, in the pipeline builds section, click the **Edit** button to edit the build configuration. The build configuration is defined in a YAML file called `azure-pipelines`. Azure DevOps lets us edit this file in its YAML editor.

 YAML Ain't Markup Language (YAML) is commonly used for configuration files because it is a little more compact than JSON and can contain comments.

The following YAML file was generated by the ASP.NET Core build pipeline template:

```
# ASP.NET Core
# Build and test ASP.NET Core projects targeting .NET Core.
# Add steps that run tests, create a NuGet package, deploy, and
more:
#
```

```
https://docs.microsoft.com/azure/devops/pipelines/languages/dotnet-
core

trigger:
- master

pool:
  vmImage: 'Ubuntu-latest'

variables:
  buildConfiguration: 'Release'

steps:
- script: dotnet build --configuration $(buildConfiguration)
  displayName: 'dotnet build $(buildConfiguration)'
```

> The steps in a build are defined after the steps: keyword. Each step is defined after a hyphen (–). The script: keyword allows a command to be executed, while the displayName: keyword is the description of the step that we'll see in the log file. The variables that are used in the steps are declared after the variables: keyword. The trigger: keyword determines when a build should be started.

So, the build contains a single step, which executes the dotnet build command with Release passed into the --configuration parameter.

2. The reason our build failed was that the agent couldn't find a .NET solution to build because it isn't in the root directory in our source code repository – it is in a folder called backend. So, let's change this step to the following:

```
steps:
- script: dotnet build --configuration $(buildConfiguration)
  workingDirectory: backend
  displayName: 'backend build'
```

We have specified that the working directory is the backend folder and changed the step name slightly.

3. Let's click the **Save** button to save the build configuration. A build will automatically be triggered because the `azure-pipelines.yml` file will be changed in our repository. The build should succeed this time:

History	Analytics				⛉
Commit			Build #		Branch
	Update azure-pipelines.yml for Azure Pipelines CI build for carlrip		✅ 20190412.2		⎇ master
	Set up CI with Azure Pipelines CI build for carlrip		❌ 20190412.1		⎇ master

4. We need to do more work in our build configuration before it is complete. So, let's edit the configuration again and run the .NET tests:

```
steps:
- script: dotnet build --configuration $(buildConfiguration)
  workingDirectory: backend
  displayName: 'backend build'

- script: dotnet test
  workingDirectory: backend
  displayName: 'backend tests'
```

Here, we use the `dotnet test` command to run the automated tests.

5. Next, let's add a step so that we can publish the .NET backend:

```
steps:
...

- script: dotnet publish --configuration $(buildConfiguration)
  workingDirectory: backend
  displayName: 'backend publish'
```

Here, we use the `dotnet publish` command in order to publish the code. What's the difference between `dotnet build` and `dotnet publish`? Well, the `dotnet build` command just outputs the artifacts from the code we have written and not any third-party libraries such as Dapper.

6. Now, we need to zip up the published files using the `ArchiveFile@2` task:

```
steps:
  ...

  - task: ArchiveFiles@2
    inputs:
      rootFolderOrFile: 'backend/bin/Release/netcoreapp3.0/publish'
      includeRootFolder: false
      archiveType: zip
      archiveFile:
'$(Build.ArtifactStagingDirectory)/backend/$(Build.BuildId).zip'
      replaceExistingArchive: true
    displayName: 'backend zip files'
```

7. The last step for our backend build is to publish the ZIP file we have just created to the pipeline so that it can be picked up by the release pipeline, which we'll configure in the next section:

```
steps:
  ...

  - task: PublishBuildArtifacts@1
    inputs:
      pathtoPublish: '$(Build.ArtifactStagingDirectory)/backend'
      artifactName: 'backend'
    displayName: 'backend publish to pipeline'
```

Here, we use the `PublishBuildArtifacts@1` task to publish the ZIP to the pipeline. We named it `backend`.

This completes the build configuration for the backend. Let's move on to the frontend now:

1. In the same YML file, add the following command to install the frontend dependencies:

```
steps:
  ...

  - script: npm install
    workingDirectory: frontend
    displayName: 'frontend install dependencies'
```

Here, we use the `npm install` command to install the dependencies. Notice that we have set the working directory to `frontend`, which is where our frontend code is located.

2. The next step is to run the frontend tests:

    ```
    steps:
    ...

    - script: npm run test:ci
      workingDirectory: frontend
      displayName: 'frontend tests'
    ```

    Here, we use the `npm run test:ci` command to run the tests rather than `npm run test`, because the `CI` environment variable is set to `true`, meaning that the tests will run correctly in our build.

3. In the next block of steps, we will produce a frontend build for the staging environment, zip up the files in this build, zip up the Cypress tests, and then publish this to the pipeline:

    ```
    steps:
    ...

    - script: npm run build:staging
      workingDirectory: frontend
      displayName: 'frontend staging build'

    - task: ArchiveFiles@2
      inputs:
        rootFolderOrFile: 'frontend/build'
        includeRootFolder: false
        archiveType: zip
        archiveFile: '$(Build.ArtifactStagingDirectory)/frontend-
    staging/build.zip'
        replaceExistingArchive: true
      displayName: 'frontend staging zip files'

    - task: ArchiveFiles@2
      inputs:
        rootFolderOrFile: 'frontend/cypress'
        includeRootFolder: false
        archiveType: zip
        archiveFile: '$(Build.ArtifactStagingDirectory)/frontend-
    staging/tests.zip'
        replaceExistingArchive: true
      displayName: 'frontend cypress zip files'

    - task: PublishBuildArtifacts@1
      inputs:
        pathtoPublish: '$(Build.ArtifactStagingDirectory)/frontend-
    ```

```
staging'
    artifactName: 'frontend-staging'
  displayName: 'frontend staging publish to pipeline'
```

Here, we use the `npm run build:staging` command to produce the staging build, which sets the REACT_APP_ENV environment variable to `staging`. We use the `ArchiveFiles@2` task we used previously to zip up the frontend build and Cypress tests, and then the `PublishBuildArtifacts@1` task to publish the ZIP to the pipeline.

4. Next, we'll produce a build for the production environment, zip it up, and then publish this to the pipeline:

```
steps:
...

- script: npm run build:production
  workingDirectory: frontend
  displayName: 'frontend production build'

- task: ArchiveFiles@2
  inputs:
  rootFolderOrFile: 'frontend/build'
  includeRootFolder: false
  archiveType: zip
  archiveFile: '$(Build.ArtifactStagingDirectory)/frontend-
production/build.zip'
  replaceExistingArchive: true
  displayName: 'frontend production zip files'

- task: PublishBuildArtifacts@1
  inputs:
  pathtoPublish: '$(Build.ArtifactStagingDirectory)/frontend-
production'
  artifactName: 'frontend-production'
  displayName: 'frontend production publish to pipeline'
```

Here, we use the `npm run build:production` command to produce the build, which sets the REACT_APP_ENV environment variable to `production`. We use the `ArchiveFiles@2` task we used previously to zip up the build and the `PublishBuildArtifacts@1` task to publish the ZIP to the pipeline.

5. That completes the build configuration. So, let's save the configuration by clicking the **Save** button. The build will trigger and succeed:

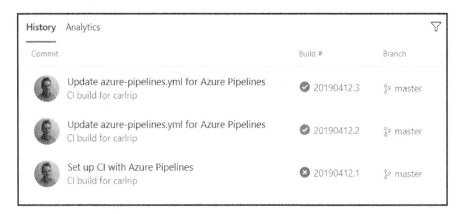

6. Let's click on the most recent build history item to view the details of the build so that we can see how long each step took. We can also see all the artifacts that were published to the pipeline by going to the **Artifacts** menu:

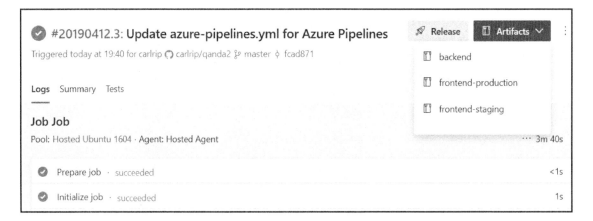

We will use the published build artifacts in the next section when we deploy these to Azure using CD.

Implementing CD

In this section, we are going to implement a release pipeline in Azure DevOps by implementing a continuous delivery process for our app. This process will consist of deploying to the staging environment, followed by the Cypress end-to-end tests being executed before the deployment is promoted to production.

Deploying to staging

Carry out the following steps in the Azure DevOps portal to deploy a build to the staging environment:

1. On the most recent build screen, click the **Release** button:

2. We will be prompted to select a template for the release pipeline. Let's choose the **Azure App Service deployment** template:

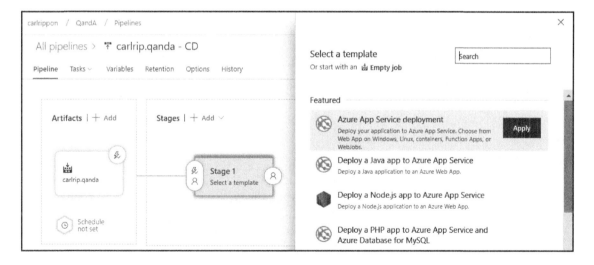

3. A nice visual representation of the release pipeline will appear, along with a panel to the right, where we can set some properties of the first stage. Let's call the stage `Staging` since this is where we will deploy our app to the staging environment and execute the automated integration tests. We can close the right-hand panel by clicking the cross icon at the top right of the panel:

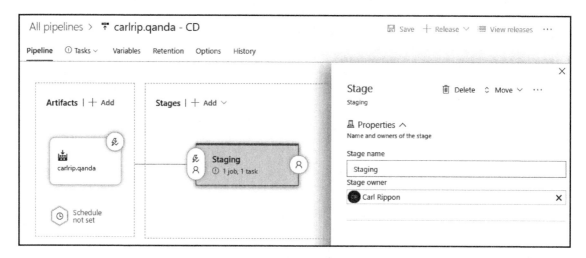

4. Let's click on the **Tasks** tab. We are deploying to two different app services, so we are going to remove the parameters by clicking the **Unlink all** option:

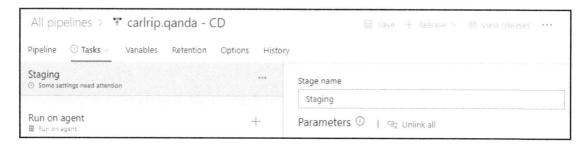

5. We already have a task from the template to deploy to Azure App Service, but we need to specify some additional information.

6. We are going to use this task to deploy the backend, so let's change the display name to `Backend App Service`.

7. We'll need to specify our Azure subscription and then authorize it.

8. We also need to specify the service name, which is `qanda-backend-staging`.

9. Lastly, we need to specify where the build ZIP file is, which is `$(System.DefaultWorkingDirectory)/**/backend/*.zip`:

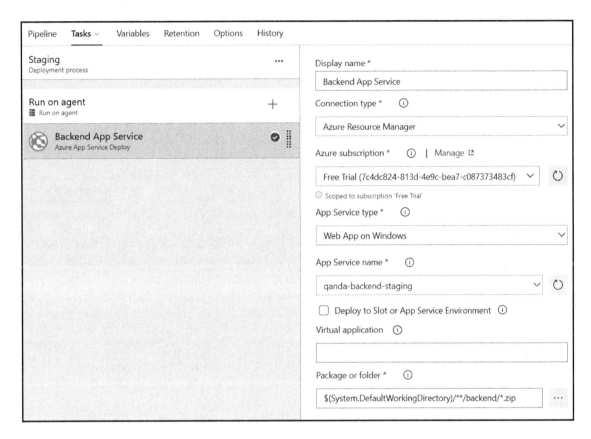

10. Click the **Save** option to save the changes to the task.

11. Click the **+** icon at the top of the task list to add a new task. Select the **Azure App Service Deploy** task and click **Add**:

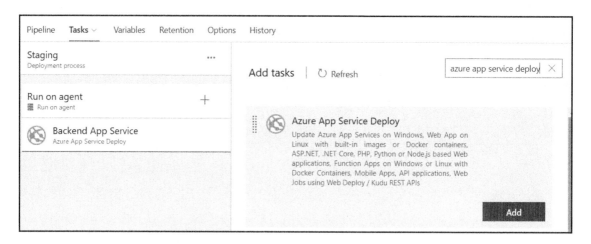

12. Now, we need to set the different properties of the task, just like we did in the backend service. This time, we'll call the task `Frontend App Service` and set the App Service and the build ZIP to the frontend staging ones:

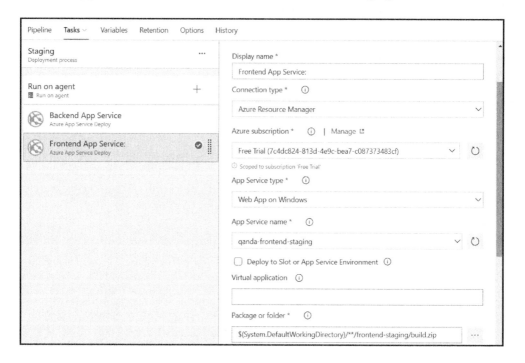

13. Click the **Save** option to save the changes to the task.
14. Click the **+** icon at the top of the task list to add a new task. Select the **Extract Files** task and click **Add.**
15. This task is going to extract the Cypress test files so that they're ready for when the tests are executed in the next task. So, let's call the task `Extract Cypress test files` and set the ZIP file patterns to `$(System.DefaultWorkingDirectory)/**/frontend-staging/tests.zip` and set the destination folder to `$(System.DefaultWorkingDirectory)/cypress`:

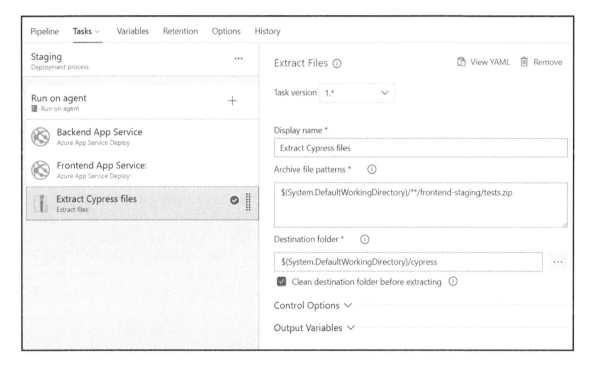

16. Click the **Save** option to save the changes to the task.
17. Click the **+** icon at the top of the task list to add a new task. Select the **Command Line** task and click **Add.**
18. This task is going to execute the Cypress tests, so let's call it `Run Cypress tests`. The script to execute is as follows:

```
> npm install
> npm run cy:run
```

We need to make sure that the working directory
is $(System.DefaultWorkingDirectory)/cypress:

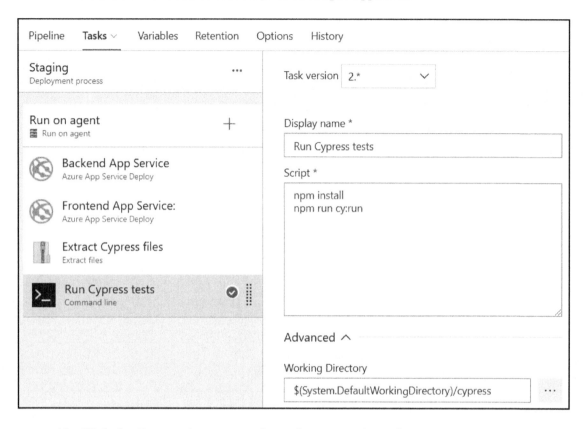

19. Click the **Save** option to save these changes to the task.

That completes the staging deployment configuration.

Deploying to production

Carry out the following steps in the Azure DevOps portal to deploy a build to the
production environment:

1. Here, we are going to add a stage for the production deployment. So, let's go
   back to the visual diagram, hover over the **Staging** card, and click on the **Clone**
   option:

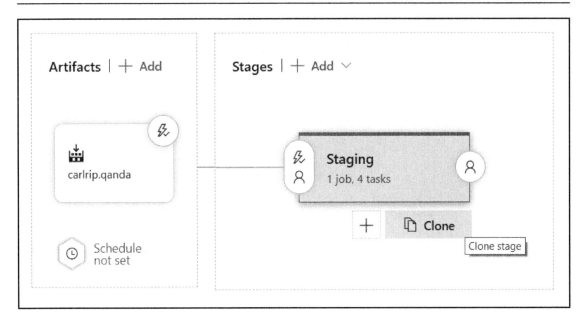

2. Let's click on the stage we have just created and call it Production:

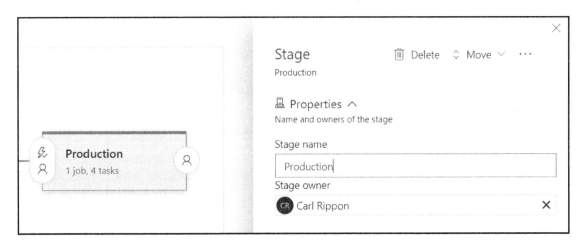

3. Click on the tasks for the **Production** stage. The last two tasks can be removed because we don't need to run any tests. To remove a task, click on it and click the **Remove** option.

4. We need to change the **Backend App Service** task so that we can deploy to the production App Service:

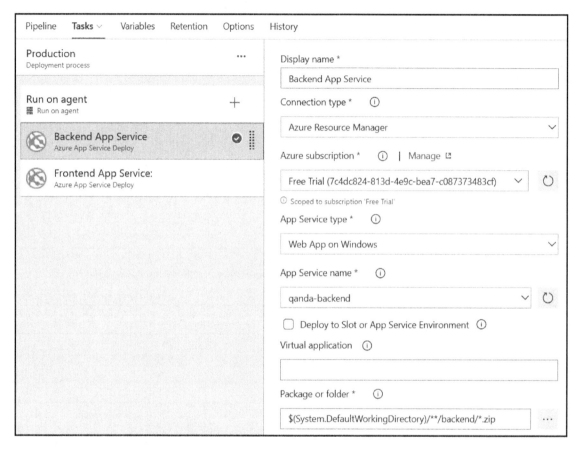

5. We also need to change the **Frontend App Service** task so that we can deploy to the production App Service from the production ZIP:

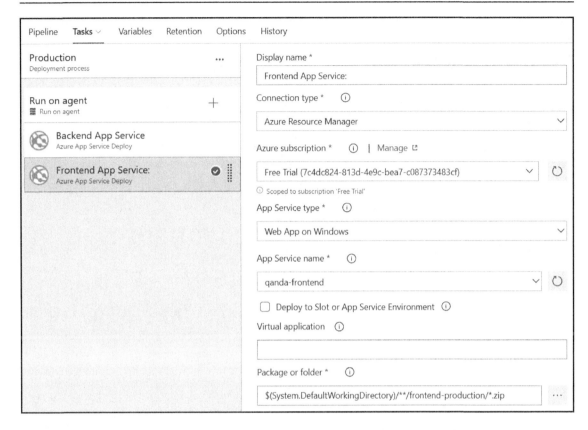

That completes the production deployment configuration.

6. If we make a code change and push it to our source code repository, we'll find that a build is automatically triggered. When the build has finished, a staging deployment will be automatically triggered.

7. Finally, when the staging deployment completes successfully, the production deployment is triggered. The successful release will appear in the release history:

8. Our CD configuration is fully automated at the moment. Often, we'll want to trigger the production deployment manually. We can do this by clicking on the **Pre-deployment conditions** option on the left edge of the Production card and changing the trigger to **Manual only**. Then, some options will appear so that you can choose who can perform the deployment:

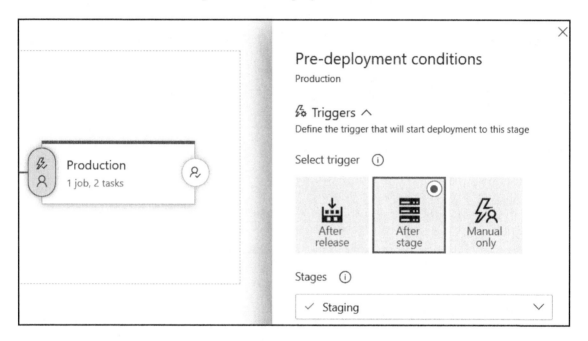

The trusted user will need to approve the production deployments.

That completes our continuous delivery pipeline.

Summary

In this final chapter, we learned that CI and CD are automated processes that get code changes that developers make into production. Implementing these processes improves the quality of our software and helps us deliver value to the users of the software extremely fast.

Implementing CI and CD processes in Azure DevOps is ridiculously easy. CI is implemented using a build pipeline and Azure DevOps has loads of great templates for different technologies to get us started. The CI process is scripted in a YAML file where we execute a series of steps, including command-line commands and other tasks such as zipping up files. The steps in the YAML file must include tasks that publish the build artifacts to the build pipeline so that they can be used in the CD process.

The CD process is implemented using a release pipeline and a visual editor. Again, there are lots of great templates to get us started. We define stages in the pipeline, which execute tasks on the artifacts that are published from the build pipeline. We can have multiple stages deploying to our different environments. We can make each stage automatically execute or execute only when a trusted member of the team approves it. There are many task types that can be executed, including deploying to an Azure service such as an App Service and running .NET tests.

So, we have reached the end of this book. We've created a performant and secure REST API that interacts with a SQL Server database using Dapper. Our backend also has a Real-Time API that we implemented with SignalR. Our React frontend interacts beautifully with both of these APIs and has been structured so that it scales in complexity by using TypeScript throughout.

We've learned how to manage simple as well as complex frontend state requirements and learned how to build reusable components to help speed up the process of building frontends. We completed the development of our app by adding automated tests and deployed it to Azure with CI and CD processes using Azure DevOps.

Questions

The following questions will test your knowledge of the topics that were covered in this chapter:

1. What environment variable needs to be set for Jest tests to work well in a continuous integration environment?
2. When we change the `azure-pipelines.yml` file, why does this trigger a build?
3. What YML step task can be used to execute npm commands?
4. What YML step task can be used to publish artifacts to the pipeline?
5. Why do we have several builds of a React frontend for different environments?
6. What task type in a release pipeline stage can be used to deploy build artifacts to Azure App Service?
7. What task type in a release pipeline stage can be used to run SQL Server scripts?

Further reading

The following resource is useful if you want to find out more about implementing CI and CD with Azure DevOps: `https://docs.microsoft.com/en-us/azure/devops/pipelines/?view=azure-devops`.

Assessments

Answers

Here, we have answered all of the questions asked at the end of each chapter. You can use these questions to review what you have learned throughout this book.

Chapter 1 – Understanding the ASP.NET Core React Template

1. What is the entry point method in an ASP.NET Core app?

    A method called `Main` in the `Program` class

2. What is the single HTML page filename in an ASP.NET Core React app created by the template, and what folder is this located in?

    A file called `index.html`, which is located in the `public` folder with the `ClientApp` folder

3. What file are the React app dependencies defined in?

    A file called `package.json` in the `ClientApp` folder

4. What `npm` command will run the React app in the WebPack development server?

    `npm start`

5. What `npm` command builds the React app ready for production?

    `npm run build`

6. What is the method name in a React component class that renders the component?

    `render`

7. Have a look at the following snippet of code, which configures the request/response pipeline in an ASP.NET Core app:

```
public void Configure(IApplicationBuilder app, IHostingEnvironment
env)
{
  app.UseAuthentication();
  app.UseHttpsRedirection();
  app.UseMvc();
}
```

Which is invoked first in the request/response pipeline, authentication or the MVC controllers?

Authentication

8. Does the class that configures the services and request/response pipeline need to be called `Startup`? Or can we give it a different name?

We can give this class a different name by defining this class in `IWebHostBuilder` that is created, as in the following example:

```
public static IWebHostBuilder CreateWebHostBuilder(string[]
args) =>
  WebHost.CreateDefaultBuilder(args).UseStartup<MyStartup>();
```

9. What browsers are supported by a React app created by CRA?

All modern browsers, including IE

Chapter 2 – Creating Decoupled React and ASP.NET Core Apps

1. What class does an API controller need to inherit from for invalid models to automatically return HTTP status code 400?

```
ControllerBase
```

2. What option on `create-react-app` did we use to create a React with a TypeScript project?

```
--typescript
```

3. What ESLint rule could we use to help to prevent `console.log` statements being added to our code?

   `no-console`

4. What setting in `.prettierrc` could we set to use single quotes in our code?

   `"singleQuote": true`

5. What file can we use to tell Visual Studio Code to validate TypeScript code using ESLint and to automatically format code using Prettier?

   `settings.json` in a `.vscode` folder

Chapter 3 – Getting Started with React and TypeScript

1. Does a component re-render when its props change?

   Yes

2. Does a component re-render when a parent's props change?

   Yes

3. How can we ensure a component re-renders only when its props change?

   Wrap the component in the `memo` function

4. What function prop would we use to add a `keydown` event listener?

   `onKeyDown`

5. A component has the following props interface:

```
interface Props {
  name: string;
  active: boolean;
}
```

How can we destructure the props parameter and default `active` to `true`?

We can do the following:

```
export const myComponent: FC<Props> = ({ name, active = true })
=> ( ... )
```

6. Let's say we have a state called `dateOfBirth`. How can we type this to be `Date`?

We can do the following:

```
const [dateOfBirth, setDateOfBirth] =
useState<Date>(undefined);
```

7. How could we use the `useEffect` hook to call a synchronous function called `getItems` when a piece of state called `category` changes, passing in `category` to `getItems`?

We can do the following:

```
useEffect(() => {
  getItems(category);
}, [category]);
```

Chapter 4 – Routing with React Router

1. We have the following routes defined:

```
<BrowserRouter>
  <Route path="/" component={HomePage} />
  <Route path="/search" component={SearchPage} />
</BrowserRouter>
```

What component(s) will be rendered when the / location is entered in the browser?

```
HomePage
```

What about when the /search location is entered in the browser?

Both `HomePage` **and** `SearchPage`

2. We have the following routes defined:

```
<BrowserRouter>
  <Switch>
    <Route path="/" component={HomePage} />
    <Route path="/search" component={SearchPage} />
  </Switch>
</BrowserRouter>
```

What component(s) will be rendered when the / location is entered into the browser?

```
HomePage
```

What about when the /search location is entered into the browser?

```
HomePage
```

3. We have the following routes defined:

```
<BrowserRouter>
  <Switch>
    <Route path="/search" component={SearchPage} />
    <Route path="/" component={HomePage} />
  </Switch>
</BrowserRouter>
```

What component(s) will be rendered when the / location is entered in the browser?

```
HomePage
```

What about when the /search location is entered in the browser?

```
SearchPage
```

4. In our Q and A app, we want a /login path to navigate to the sign-in page as well as the /signin path. How can we implement this?

We can do the following:

```
<Redirect from="/login" to="/signin" />
```

5. We have the following routes defined:

```
<BrowserRouter>
  <Switch>
    <Route path="/search" component={SearchPage} />
    <Route path="/" component={HomePage} />
    <Route component={NotFoundPage} />
  </Switch>
</BrowserRouter>
```

What component(s) will be rendered when the /signin location is entered in the browser?

```
HomePage
```

6. We have the following routes defined:

```
<BrowserRouter>
  <Switch>
    <Route path="/" component={HomePage} />
    <Route path="/search" component={SearchPage} />
    <Route component={NotFoundPage} />
  </Switch>
</BrowserRouter>
```

With the preceding implementation, when a user navigates to the /search path or an invalid path such as /unknown, the HomePage component is rendered.

How can we change the code to render HomePage when only the / path is entered in the browser?

We can do the following:

```
<Route exact path="/" component={HomePage} />
```

7. We have the following route defined:

```
<Route path="/users/:userId" component={UserPage} />
```

How can we reference the userId route parameter in the UserPage component?

If we make the props type for UserPage RouteComponentProps<{ userId: string }>, then props.match.params.userId will hold the userId route parameter.

Chapter 5 – Working with Forms

1. In our generic `Form` implementation, why did we make the `onSubmit` function prop asynchronous?

    The `onSubmit` function prop is likely to call a web service asynchronously and so needs to be asynchronous.

2. When we implemented the generic `Form` and `Field` components, what was the purpose of the `touched` state?

    The `touched` state allowed us to prevent validation checks when the user first enters the field, which can be annoying for the user. Generally, it is better to do the validation checks when the field loses focus and if the user comes back to the field and changes it.

3. When we implement a form field like the following, why do we tie `label` to `input` using the `htmlFor` attribute?

    ```
    <label htmlFor={name}>{label}</label>
    <input
      type="text"
      id={name}
      value={values[name] === undefined ? '' : values[name]}
      onChange={handleChange}
      onBlur={handleBlur}
    />
    ```

    This makes the field accessible, which means a screen reader will read `label` when `input` gains focus. Clicking on `label` will also set focus to `input`.

4. Why did we use the React context in our generic `Form` and `Field` implementations?

    We used the React context to allow `Field` to access state such as the field value from `Form`. We couldn't pass the state via props because `Form` doesn't directly reference `Field`—it indirectly references it via the `children` prop.

5. Extend our generic `Field` component to include a number editor, using the native number `input`.

    Here, we extend the `type` prop in `Form`:

    ```
    interface Props {
      name: string;
      label?: string;
      type?: "Text" | "TextArea" | "Password" | "Number";
    }
    ```

    In `Form`, JSX allows `FieldInput` to be rendered if `type` is `Number`:

    ```
    {(type === "Text" || type === "Password" || type === "Number")
    && (
      <FieldInput
        type={type.toLowerCase()}
        id={name}
        value={values[name]}
        onChange={handleChange}
        onBlur={handleBlur}
      />
    )}
    ```

6. Implement a validator in `Form.tsx` that will check that the field value is between two numbers:

    ```
    export const between: Validator = (
      value: any,
      bounds: { lower: number; upper: number }
    ): string =>
      value && (value < bounds.lower || value > bounds.upper)
        ? `This must be between ${bounds.lower} and ${bounds.upper}`
        : "";
    ```

Chapter 6 – Managing State with Redux

1. When implementing an action object, how many properties can it contain?

    As many as we like! It needs to include at least one for the `type` property. It can then include as many other properties as we need for the reducer to change the state, but this is generally lumped in one additional property. So, generally, an action will have one or two properties.

2. Why did we need Redux Thunk in our Redux store?

> By default, a Redux store can't manage asynchronous action creators. Middleware needs to be added to the Redux store to facilitate asynchronous action creators. Redux Thunk is the middleware we added to do this.

3. How did we make the state in our store read-only?

> We used the `readonly` keyword in the properties in the interface for the state.

4. In the `questionsReducer` function we implemented, why didn't we use the array `push` method to add the new question to the state?

```
case 'PostedQuestion': {
  return {
    ...state,
    unanswered: action.result
      ? (state.unanswered || []).push(action.result.question)
      : state.unanswered,
    postedResult: action.result,
  };
}
```

> The `push` method would mutate the product's state directly, which would make the function impure. This is because we have changed the state argument, which lives outside the scope of our function.

5. Does the `Provider` component from React Redux need to be placed at the top of the component tree?

> The `Provider` component needs to be placed above the components that need access to the store. So, it doesn't need to be right at the top of the tree.

6. As well as the `Provider` component, what is the other item from React Redux that allows a component to consume data from the Redux store?

> The other key item from React Redux is a function called `connect`, which wraps a component, giving it access to the store.

7. Is a component that consumes the Redux store allowed to have a local state?

> Yes, it is. If the state is not useful outside the component, then it is perfectly acceptable to have this state local within the component.

Chapter 7 – Interacting with the Database with Dapper

1. What Dapper method can be used to execute a stored procedure that returns no results?

   ```
   Execute
   ```

2. What Dapper method can be used to read a single record of data where the record is guaranteed to exist?

   ```
   QueryFirst
   ```

3. What Dapper method can be used to read a collection of records?

   ```
   Query
   ```

4. What is wrong with the following statement that calls the Dapper `Query` method?

   ```
   return connection.Query<BuildingGetManyResponse>(
     @"EXEC dbo.Building_GetMany_BySearch
       @Search = @Search",
     new { Criteria = "Fred"}
   );
   ```

   The query expects a parameter called `Search` but we have passed it a parameter called `Criteria`. So, Dapper won't be able to map the SQL parameter.

5. We have the following stored procedure:

   ```
   CREATE PROC dbo.Building_GetMany
   AS
   BEGIN
     SET NOCOUNT ON

     SELECT BuildingId, Name
     FROM dbo.Building
   END
   ```

We have the following statement that calls the Dapper `Query` method:

```
return connection.Query<BuildingGetManyResponse>(
  "EXEC dbo.Building_GetMany"
);
```

We also have the following data model that is referenced in the preceding statement:

```
public class BuildingGetManyResponse
{
  public int Id{ get; set; }
  public string Name { get; set; }
}
```

When our app is run, we find that the `Id` property within the `BuildingGetManyResponse` class instances is not populated. Can you spot the problem?

The problem is that the stored procedure returns a field called `BuildingId`, which won't automatically get mapped to the `Id` property in the class because the names are different.

6. Can DbUp be used to deploy new reference data within a table?

Yes! DbUp can execute any SQL script.

Chapter 8 – Creating REST API Endpoints

1. We have a class that we want to register for dependency injection and want a new instance of it to be created when injected into a class. What method in `IServiceCollection` should we use to register the dependency?

`AddTransient`

2. In a controller action method, if a resource can't be found, what method can we use in `ControllerBase` to return status code 404?

`NotFound()`

3. In a controller action method to post a new building, we implement some validation that requires a database call to check whether the building already exists. If the building does already exist, we want to return HTTP status code 400:

```
[HttpPost]
public ActionResult<BuildingResponse>
PostBuilding(BuildingPostRequest buildingPostRequest)
{
    var buildingExists =
_dataRepository.BuildingExists(buildingPostRequest.Code);
    if (buildingExists)
    {
        // TODO - return status code 400
    }
    ...
}
```

What method from `ControllerBase` can we use to return status code 400?

```
BadRequest()
```

4. The model for the preceding action method is as follows:

```
public class BuildingPostRequest
{
    public string Code { get; set; }
    public string Name { get; set; }
    public string Description { get; set; }
}
```

We send an HTTP POST request to the resource with the following body:

```
{
    "code": "BTOW",
    "name": "Blackpool Tower",
    "buildingDescription": "Blackpool Tower is a tourist attraction
in Blackpool"
}
```

The `Description` property in the model isn't getting populated during the request. What is the problem?

The `buildingDescription` in the request doesn't match the name of the `Description` property in the model. If the request is changed to have a `description` field, then this will resolve the problem.

5. In the preceding request model, we want to validate that the `code` and `name` fields are populated. How can we do this with validation attributes?

   We can do the following:

   ```
   public class BuildingPostRequest
   {
       [Required]
       public string Code { get; set; }
       [Required]
       public string Name { get; set; }
       public string Description { get; set; }
   }
   ```

6. What validation attribute could we use to validate that a number property is between 1 and 10?

   ```
   [Range(0, 10)]
   ```

7. What `Http` attribute could we use tell ASP.NET Core that an action method handles HTTP PATCH requests?

   ```
   HttpPatch
   ```

Chapter 9 – Creating a Real-Time API with SignalR

1. In a SignalR hub class, what method can we use to push data to a group of connected clients?

   We can use the following:

   ```
   Clients.Group("GroupName").SendAsync()
   ```

2. In a SignalR hub class, what method can we use to push data to all clients except for the client that has made the request?

   We can use the following:

   ```
   Clients.AllExcept(Context.ConnectionId).SendAsync()
   ```

3. Why did we need a CORS policy for our React app to be able to interact with our SignalR real-time API?

   A CORS policy is required because the frontend and backend were hosted in different domains.

4. In our React frontend, why did we check whether the connection was in a connected state before subscribing to the question?

   If starting the connection failed, the connection would be in an unconnected state and not able to make the request for the subscription.

5. Why did we stop the connection when the user navigates away from the question page?

   The user is unsubscribed from question updates when navigating away from the question page and so there is no requirement to interact with the SignalR server anymore. So, we stop the connection to save resources.

Chapter 10 – Improving Performance and Scalability

1. We have the following code in a data repository that uses Dapper's multi recordset feature to return a single order with many related detail lines in a single database call:

```
using (var connection = new SqlConnection(_connectionString))
{
  connection.Open();
  using (GridReader results = connection.QueryMultiple(
    @"EXEC dbo.Order_GetHeader @OrderId = @OrderId;
    EXEC dbo.OrderDetails_Get_ByOrderId @OrderId = @OrderId",
    new { OrderId = orderId }))
  {

    // TODO - Read the order and details from the query result

    return order;
  }
}
```

What are the missing statements that will read the order and its details from the results putting the details in the order model? The order model is of the `OrderGetSingleResponse` type, which contains a `Details` property of the `IEnumerable<OrderDetailGetResponse>` type.

We can use the following:

```
using (var connection = new SqlConnection(_connectionString))
{
  connection.Open();
  using (GridReader results = connection.QueryMultiple(
    @"EXEC dbo.Order_GetHeader @OrderId = @OrderId;
    EXEC dbo.OrderDetails_Get_ByOrderId @OrderId = @OrderId",
    new { OrderId = orderId }))
  {
    var order =
results.Read<OrderGetSingleResponse>().FirstOrDefault();
    if (order != null)
    {
      order.Details =
results.Read<OrderDetailGetResponse>().ToList();
    }
    return order;
  }
}
```

2. What is the downside of using Dapper's multi-mapping feature when reading data from many-to-one related tables in a single database call?

   The trade-off is that more data is transferred between the database and web server and then processed on the web server, which can hurt performance.

3. How does data paging help performance?

   - The number of the page read I/Os is reduced when SQL Server grabs the data.
   - The amount of data transferred from the database server to the web server is reduced.
   - The amount of memory used to store the data on the web server in our model is reduced.
   - The amount of data transferred from the web server to the client is reduced.

4. Does making code asynchronous make it faster?

No, it makes it more scalable by using the thread pool more efficiently.

5. What is the problem with the following asynchronous method:

```
public async AnswerGetResponse GetAnswer(int answerId)
{
  using (var connection = new SqlConnection(_connectionString))
  {
    connection.Open();
    return await connection
      .QueryFirstOrDefaultAsync<AnswerGetResponse>(
        "EXEC dbo.Answer_Get_ByAnswerId @AnswerId = @AnswerId",
        new { AnswerId = answerId });
  }
}
```

Opening the connection is synchronous, which will mean the thread is blocked and not returned to the thread pool until the connection is opened. So, the whole code will have the same thread pool inefficiency as synchronous code but will have the overhead of asynchronous code as well.

Here is the corrected implementation:

```
public async AnswerGetResponse GetAnswer(int answerId)
{
  using (var connection = new SqlConnection(_connectionString))
  {
    await connection.OpenAsync();
    return await connection
      .QueryFirstOrDefaultAsync<AnswerGetResponse>(
        "EXEC dbo.Answer_Get_ByAnswerId @AnswerId = @AnswerId",
        new { AnswerId = answerId });
  }
}
```

6. Why it is a good idea to set a size limit on a memory cache?

This is to prevent the cache from taking up too much memory on the web server.

7. In our `QuestionCache` implementation, when adding a question to the cache, how can we invalidate that item in the cache after 30 minutes?

    We can do the following:

    ```
    public void Set(QuestionGetSingleResponse question)
    {
      var cacheEntryOptions =
        new MemoryCacheEntryOptions()
        .SetSize(1)
        .SetSlidingExpiration(TimeSpan.FromMinutes(30));
      _cache.Set(GetCacheKey(question.QuestionId), question,
    cacheEntryOptions);
    }
    ```

8. When we registered our `QuestionCache` class for dependency injection, why did we use the `AddSingleton` method and not the `AddScoped` method like in the following?

    ```
    services.AddScoped<QuestionCache>();
    ```

    `AddScoped` would create a new instance of the cache for every request, which means the cache would be lost after each request.
    Using `AddSingleton` means that the cache lasts for the lifetime of the app.

Chapter 11 – Securing the Backend

1. In the `Configure` method in the `Startup` class, what is wrong with the following?

    ```
    public void Configure(IApplicationBuilder app, IHostingEnvironment
    env)
    {
      ...
      app.UseEndpoints(...);
      app.UseAuthentication();
    }
    ```

    The problem is that authentication comes after the endpoints are handled in the request pipeline, which means that the user will always be unauthenticated in controller action methods even if the request has a valid access token. This means that protected resources will never be able to be accessed. `UseAuthentication` should come before `UseEndpoints` in the `Configure` method.

2. What attribute can be added to a protected action method to allow unauthenticated users to access it?

```
AllowAnonymous
```

3. We are building an app with an ASP.NET Core backend and using an identity provider to authenticate users. The default audience has been set to `http://my-app` in the identity provider and we have configured the authentication service as follows in our ASP.NET Core backend:

```
services.AddAuthentication(options =>
{
    options.DefaultAuthenticateScheme =
      JwtBearerDefaults.AuthenticationScheme;
    options.DefaultChallengeScheme =
      JwtBearerDefaults.AuthenticationScheme;
}).AddJwtBearer(options =>
{
    . . .
    options.Audience = "https://myapp";
});
```

When we try to access protected resources in our ASP.NET Core backend, we receive HTTP status code 401. What is the problem here?

The problem is that the ASP.NET Core backend validates that the audience in the JWT is `https://myapp`, but the identity provider has been configured to set the audience to `http://my-app`. This results in the request being unauthorized.

4. A JWT has the following decoded payload data. What date and time does it expire?

```
{
  "nbf": 1559876843,
  "auth_time": 1559876843,
  "exp": 1559900000,
  . . .
}
```

The `exp` field gives the expiry date, which is `1559900000` seconds after 1 Jan 1970, which, in turn, is 7 Jun 2019 9:33:20 (GMT).

5. We have a valid access token from an identity provider and are using it to access a protected resource. We have set the following HTTP header in the request:

```
Authorisation: bearer some-access-token
```

We receive HTTP status code 401 from the request though. What is the problem?

The problem is that the HTTP header name needs to be `Authorization`—that is, we have spelled it with an *s* rather than a *z*.

6. How can we access HTTP request information in a class outside of an API controller?

The request can be accessed by injecting `IHttpContextAccessor` into the class as follows:

```
private readonly IHttpContextAccessor _httpContextAccessor;

public MyClass(IHttpContextAccessor httpContextAccessor)
{
    _httpContextAccessor = httpContextAccessor;
}

public SomeMethod()
{
    var request = _httpContextAccessor.HttpContext.Request;
}
```

The `HttpContextAccessor` service must be added in the `ConfigureServices` method in the `Startup` class as follows:

```
services.AddSingleton<IHttpContextAccessor,
HttpContextAccessor>();
```

7. In an API controller, how can we access an authenticated user ID?

We can access the user ID via the sub claim in the controller's `User` property as follows:

```
User.FindFirst(ClaimTypes.NameIdentifier).Value
```

Chapter 12 – Interacting with RESTful APIs

1. What is wrong with the following HTTP POST request using the fetch function?

```
fetch('http://localhost:17525/api/person', {
  method: 'post',
  headers: {
    'Content-Type': 'application/json',
  },
  body: {
    firstName: 'Fred'
    surname: 'Smith'
  }
})
```

The problem is that the fetch function expects the body to be in string format. The corrected call is as follows:

```
fetch('http://localhost:17525/api/person', {
  method: 'post',
  headers: {
    'Content-Type': 'application/json',
  },
  body: JSON.stringify({
    firstName: 'Fred'
    surname: 'Smith'
  })
})
```

2. What is wrong with the following request using the fetch function?

```
fetch('http://localhost:17525/api/person/1')
  .then(res => {
    console.log('firstName', res.body.firstName);
  })
```

The problem is that the response body cannot be accessed directly in the response like this. Instead, the response's json asynchronous method should be used:

```
fetch('http://localhost:17525/api/person/1')
  .then(res => res.json())
  .then(body => {
    console.log('firstName', body.firstName);
  });
```

3. What is wrong with the following request using the `fetch` function?

```
fetch('http://localhost:17525/api/person/21312')
  .then(res => res.json())
  .catch(res => {
    if (res.status === 404) {
      console.log('person not found')
    }
  });
```

The problem is that the `catch` method is for network errors and not HTTP request errors. HTTP request errors can be dealt with in the `then` method:

```
fetch('http://localhost:17525/api/person/21312')
  .then(res => {
    if (res.status === 404) {
      console.log('person not found')
    } else {
      return res.json();
    }
  });
```

4. We have an endpoint for deleting people that only administrators have access to use. We have the users' access token in a variable called `jwt`. What is wrong with the following request?

```
fetch('http://localhost:17525/api/person/1', {
  method: 'delete',
  headers: {
    'Content-Type': 'application/json',
    'authorization': jwt
  });
```

The problem is that the word `bearer` followed by a space is missing from the `authorization` HTTP header. The corrected call is as follows:

```
fetch('http://localhost:17525/api/person/1', {
  method: 'delete',
  headers: {
    'Content-Type': 'application/json',
    'authorization': `bearer ${jwt}`
  });
```

5. In this chapter, we implemented an `AuthorizedPage` component that we could wrap around a page component so that it is only rendered for authenticated users. We could implement a similar component to wrap around components within a page so that they are only rendered for authenticated users. Have a go at implementing this.

   The component implementation is as follows:

   ```
   import React, { FC, Fragment } from 'react';
   import { useAuth } from './Auth';

   export const AuthorizedElement: FC = ({ children }) => {
     const auth = useAuth();
     if (auth.isAuthenticated) {
       return <Fragment>{children}</Fragment>;
     } else {
       return null;
     }
   };
   ```

   The component would be consumed as follows:

   ```
   <AuthorizedElement>
     <PrimaryButton ...>
       Ask a question
     </PrimaryButton>
   </AuthorizedElement>
   ```

Chapter 13 – Adding Automated Tests

1. We have the following xUnit test method but it isn't being picked up by the test runner. What is wrong?

   ```
   public void Minus_When2Integers_ShouldReturnCorrectInteger()
   {
   var result = Calc.Add(2, 1);
   Assert.Equal(1, result);
   }
   ```

   The `Fact` attribute is missing.

2. We have a `string` variable called `successMessage` in an xUnit test and we need to check that it contains the word `"success"`. What method in the `Assert` class could we use?

   `Assert.Contains`

3. We have created some Jest unit tests on a `List` component in a file called `ListTests.tsx`. However, when the Jest test runner runs, the tests aren't picked up. Why is this so?

   The test filename needs to end with `.test.tsx`. So, if we rename the file `List.test.tsx`, then the test will get picked up.

4. We are implementing a test in Jest and we have a variable called `result`, which we want to check isn't `null`. Which Jest matcher function can we use?

   `expect(result).not.toBeNull();`

5. Let's say we have a variable called `person` that is of the, `Person` type:

   ```
   interface Person {
     id: number;
     firstName: string;
     surname: string
   }
   ```

   We want to check that the `person` variable is `{ id: 1, firstName: "Tom", surname: "Smith" }`. What Jest matcher function can we use?

   We can use the `toEqual` function to compare objects:

   ```
   expect(person).toEqual({ id: 1, firstName: "Tom", surname: "Smith" });
   ```

6. We are writing an end to end test using Cypress for a page. The page has a heading: **Sign In**. What Cypress command can we use to check that this is rendered okay?

   We can use the following:

   ```
   cy.contains('Sign In');
   ```

7. We are writing an end-to-end test using Cypress for a page that renders the text **Loading...** while data is being fetched. How can we assert that this text is rendered and then disappears when the data has been fetched?

   We can use the following:

   ```
   cy.contains('Loading...');
   cy.contains('Loading...').should('not.exist');
   ```

   The first command will check that the page renders Loading... on the initial render. The second command will wait until the Loading... disappears—that is, the data has been fetched.

Chapter 14 – Configuring and Deploying to Azure

1. In ASP.NET Core, what is the name of the file where we store any settings specific to the production environment?

   ```
   appsettings.Production.json
   ```

2. What were the reasons for our ASP.NET Core backend needing the Frontend setting?

   Firstly, to set up the allowed origin in a CORS policy and secondly, to build correct links in the sign-up and forgotten password emails

3. Let's pretend we have introduced a QA environment and have created the following npm script to do a build for this environment:

   ```
   "build:qa": "cross-env REACT_APP_ENV=qa npm run build"
   ```

   What npm command would we use to produce a QA build?

   ```
   npm run build:qa
   ```

4. What would be broken if we didn't include the web.config file with our React frontend?

   We wouldn't be able to deep-link into our app. For example, putting the path to a question, such as https://qandafrontend.z19.web.core.windows.net/questions/1, directly in the browser's address bar and pressing *Enter* will result in a **Page not found** error being returned.

5. Why didn't we use Azure Storage to host our frontend rather than Azure App Service?

   Azure Storage has no facility to let the React `index.html` handle deep links into the app.

Chapter 15 – Implementing CI and CD with Azure DevOps

1. What environment variable needs to be set for Jest tests to work well in a continuous integration environment?

   An environment variable called `CI` needs to be set to `true`.

2. When we change the `azure-pipelines.yml` file, why does this trigger a build?

   The `azure-pipelines.yml` file is committed and pushed to our source code repository and the build is triggered when any code is pushed to the repository.

3. What YML step task can be used to execute `npm` commands?

   `-script`

4. What YML step task can be used to publish artifacts to the pipeline?

   `PublishBuildArtifacts@1`

5. Why do we have several builds of a React frontend for the different environments?

   The build sets the environment variable called `REACT_APP_ENV`, which the code uses to determine which environment it is in.

6. What task type in a release pipeline stage can be used to deploy build artifacts to Azure App Service?

   Azure App Service Deploy

7. What task type in a release pipeline stage can be used to run SQL Server scripts?

   Azure App Database Deployment

Other Books You May Enjoy

If you enjoyed this book, you may be interested in these other books by Packt:

React Projects
Roy Derks

ISBN: 978-1-78995-493-7

- Create a wide range of applications using various modern React tools and frameworks
- Discover how React Hooks modernize state management for React apps
- Develop progressive web applications using React components
- Build test-driven React applications using the Jest and Enzyme frameworks
- Understand full stack development using React, Apollo, and GraphQL
- Perform server-side rendering using React and React Router
- Design gestures and animations for a cross-platform game using React Native

Hands-On Mobile Development with .NET Core
Can Bilgin

ISBN: 978-1-78953-851-9

- Implement native applications for multiple mobile and desktop platforms
- Understand and use various Azure Services with .NET Core
- Make use of architectural patterns designed for mobile and web applications
- Understand the basic Cosmos DB concepts
- Understand how different app models can be used to create an app service
- Explore the Xamarin and Xamarin.Forms UI suite with .NET Core for building mobile applications

Leave a review - let other readers know what you think

Please share your thoughts on this book with others by leaving a review on the site that you bought it from. If you purchased the book from Amazon, please leave us an honest review on this book's Amazon page. This is vital so that other potential readers can see and use your unbiased opinion to make purchasing decisions, we can understand what our customers think about our products, and our authors can see your feedback on the title that they have worked with Packt to create. It will only take a few minutes of your time, but is valuable to other potential customers, our authors, and Packt. Thank you!

Index

Printed in Great Britain
by Amazon

49676154R00339